Acknowledgments

This book has been written against a background of unexpected personal happiness. Had my life not changed as it did I would have continued to write, but I could not have written this particular book. To my husband, Maurice Shadbolt, therefore, I owe the greatest debt, and deepest thanks.

I would also like to thank my agent and friend, Diana Tyler. Her loyalty and encouragement play a vital part in my writing life.

Thanks are due too to Gwynnedd Somerville, Jonathan Bailey, and Ken Ward, who provided me with a home in London during the final stages of the novel's preparation: also to Merryl Alley, whose generosity sparked the idea for this novel.

Lastly I wish to acknowledge the assistance of the Literature Committee of the New Zealand Arts Council, and express my thanks for their support.

River
Lines

SCEPTRE

River
Lines

ELSPETH SANDYS

SCEPTRE

First published in 1995 by Hodder and Stoughton
A division of Hodder Headline PLC
A Sceptre Book

British Library Cataloguing in Publication Data

Sandys, Elspeth
  River Lines
  I. Title
  823 [F]

ISBN 0 340 64056 1

Typeset by Palimpsest Book Production Limited,
Polmont, Stirlingshire
Printed and bound in Great Britain by
Mackays of Chatham PLC, Chatham, Kent

Hodder and Stoughton
A division of Hodder Headline PLC
338 Euston Road
London NW1 3BH

For my daughter, Josie,
with love and pride

'Tales of love and death can be mortal to the teller' –
Saul Bellow

'To keep our dead alive within us is to keep connection' –
P.J. Kavanagh

'This is the unresolved question that imaginative people
will always have, in every time of life, in every time of
the world: where do I belong, and what price do I pay for
where I choose to stand?' –
Diana Trilling

Part One

PRELUDE

13 July 1912
  May, my wife, died today.
  Also my son, Sean (3), my daughter, Molly (18 months), and the child born twelve days ago, a son.

So pretty you look, Deidre. Like a picture . . . And Sean, in your best breeches. Aren't you the swell? . . . That's a good girl, Deidre. Take Molly's hand . . . See? The baby's asleep. Pale as sand he looks . . . Come now, my little ones, we're going for a walk . . .

Deidre was four years old when her mother died. It was her father who found her, shivering on the riverbank. What she remembered of that day was the cold – even the act of turning her eyes towards her father hurt – and his hands on her shoulders; fingers like knives as he screamed, 'Where are they? What happened? Jesus'n Mary, do I have to *thrash* you to get you to speak?'

And she remembered the funeral: the way people talked as if she wasn't there.

'What a strange little child she is. Not a single tear.'

'You knew the mother, did you?'

'By sight only.'

'A pretty woman. Too pretty perhaps.'

'What possessed her to go walking in this weather?'

'The child's said nothing. Can't remember, she says.'

Six months after his wife's funeral Pearse Byrne married again. In his diary he wrote:

1 January 1913,
Married today, Jessie Potter.

In Deidre's mind marriage and funeral were one event. At her own wedding, three decades later, she chose to wear black.

The land allotted to Pearse O'Connell Byrne in the ballot of February, 1907, was officially described as 'a five-hundred-acre block comprising considerable flat lands, with a steep gully to the north-west presently covered in scabweed and briar. The river running along the southern boundary provides the inestimable boon of an immediate fresh water supply'.

In February, 1907, Pearse was twenty years old. All he owned were the clothes he stood up in, a battered edition of the Latin missal, a shovel, spade, pick, scythe, whetstone, hammer, and an axe, gift of his former employer, Colonel Lance Rattray. Emerging from the dingy hall where the ballot had been held, Pearse considered himself a wealthy man.

Six weeks later he married May Johnson, recently employed by Mrs Rattray as a music teacher to her three daughters. The ceremony was performed by the visiting Catholic priest in the living room of Willowbank, the Rattrays' home near Springfield in Canterbury. The unseemly haste of the proceedings prompted Mrs Rattray to enquire of the bride whether she were with child. 'He's not even kissed me,' the music teacher answered. 'We talk of nothing but his land.'

On a chill evening at the end of March the silence of the valley once known as *Deadman's Flat* was broken by the shriek of iron wheels on gravel. The day, which had been overcast, was sinking into early darkness, but there was enough light still clinging to the hills to illuminate the scurrying of rabbits disturbed in their search for fodder. It was the only visible movement. The rest, May Byrne registered bleakly, was still as the grave.

With the coming of morning, the enormity of the task

confronting him caused Pearse Byrne to utter his first word of doubt. 'The land's dead,' he confided. 'The life's been beaten out of it.'

'Perhaps that's why they gave it to you.'

'We'll start as we intend to carry on. With a prayer.'

On 10 January, 1908, the following entry was recorded in Pearse's diary: 'My first child, a daughter, born this morning.'

The birth was a difficult one. The midwife, hastily fetched from the town a dozen miles away, warned the distraught husband to expect the worst. 'Your wife is very weak,' she scolded. 'Not to put too fine a point on it, she's undernourished. Her body's got nothing to fight with.'

The world on which Deidre May Byrne opened her eyes was a room fifteen feet by twelve, with an adjoining scullery and washroom. Two small windows, glazed with calico, looked out on a verandah where, on summer evenings, her parents sat in creaking rocking chairs to read aloud the day's Bible lesson. Beyond the verandah the land now called Kilkenny stretched from river to hill. Little had changed in the ten months of Pearse and May's occupation. Pyramids of stone bore witness to the long hours of labour Pearse had worked preparing the land for planting. And the pale patches of green among the stones showed that his labours had not been in vain. Otherwise, to the passer-by, the only signs of habitation were the wire fence marking the borders of Kilkenny, and the smoke gusting from the chimney of the sod cottage on the riverbank. 'You'll start on the house soon, won't you?' May had urged, when the baby's determination to be born could no longer be ignored. 'It won't be safe here once the child's walking.'

'The only safety is discipline. Somethin' ya need to learn fer yerself, Mrs Byrne.'

When, a little over a year later, Sean Patrick announced his arrival with a furious yell, May repeated her words to her husband. 'Deidre's walking now,' she reminded him. 'I can't watch her every minute of the day. Not with a baby to care for.'

The look Pearse gave her was one May knew well. While she

could still pretend she loved him she'd called that look *stubborn*. But this last winter, which had seen the loss of half their flock of sheep when the river burst its banks, had taught her to fear those lines of cold defiance. It made no difference whether it was she who crossed him, or Nature. Pearse Byrne would defy God if he had to.

By the middle of 1910, Kilkenny, for all its inauspicious beginnings, had begun to prosper. The potatoes and cabbages planted in the autumn fed the family through the winter, with surplus to sell at the market. The cows which Pearse had bought for two guineas each at the Eichardt sale ('One man's misfortune is another's opportunity,' he'd observed to his wife) were proving excellent milkers. The imported grasses, nourished by Pearse's pioneering use of lime, and the ingenious irrigation scheme he'd devised, were greening not just the valley, but the surrounding hills. By year's end even the sheep losses had been made good. Each evening, as she rocked on the verandah, May could hear, behind the sound of her husband's voice, the monotonous bleating of sheep. Day and night, indoors and out, the sound followed her, so that she began to imagine it was the voice of God Himself.

With the birth of Molly, in January, 1911, Pearse at last began work on the house. It was to be built on higher ground some two hundred yards back from the river. A fence of galvanised wire would separate house and garden from the paddocks.

May was boiling syrup to make apple jelly when the first load of timber arrived. She heard a shout, looked up from the range, and saw two men standing, as she thought, in the river. She pulled the pot to one side, called for Deidre to watch over the babies, wiped her hands on her apron, and ran outside. It was all she could do not to cry out with excitement. The house, which had existed only in her dream, was suddenly as real to her as her own reddened hands.

'My husband's gone into town,' she told the men who greeted her from the riverbank. Behind them the precious timber swayed on the current that had carried their sheep away. 'He wasn't expecting you till next week.'

'Time and tide wait for no man,' the elder of the two called back to her.

'Would you care for some refreshment? You must be tired after your journey.'

The flush in her mother's cheeks, and the nervous manner of her speech, was a puzzle to three-year-old Deidre. She was used to the company of a silent, sighing woman, who occasionally sang to her babies in a voice of entrancing sweetness. Perhaps it was the presence of the two strangers. The only visitors Kilkenny ever saw were passing tinkers, and Father Driscoll, who came once a month to say Mass. Deidre's mother didn't explain who the two men tucking into hot bread and tea were. But that didn't stop the child listening. The places she'd not heard of before – Wanaka, Trooper's Track, Dead Horse Creek, Chinaman's Flat – assumed mythical proportions in her mind. The men's journey had been perilous. That much she understood. Their cargo of timber for the house was *worth its weight in gold.*

'It's desert country back there, lady,' the one who smelt of wet cabbages complained. 'A whole damn province stripped of trees.'

'All this'll be legend to you one day, wee lass,' the other, younger man remarked. The smile he threw in Deidre's direction was like Sean's smile when she tickled him. 'You'll have a fine house to live in, and a carriage, I daresay, to take you calling.'

When Pearse Byrne returned from town he found the timber stacked up beside the jetty, and his wife asleep in the rocking chair. 'What are ya thinkin' of?' he fumed. 'Why is the lamp not lit?'

Through the window Deidre watched and listened. She had recently learned to count. 1–2–3–4, her father paced. A pause while he turned, then, 1–2–3–4 again. How heavy his boots were, and how silent her mother. 'If yer after thinkin' I can stop everythin' now an' work on the house, ya best think again,' Pearse said, in the voice Deidre most feared to hear him use. 'There's haymakin' to finish, oats to cut, potatoes to get in fer the winter. Plenty o' women'd give their eye-teeth to have what you have, so they would. Look at ya. Ya've food in yer belly, a roof over yer head, a husband who's pledged to touch no spirituous liquors. I tell ya, May, I can't abide that look on yer face, an' that's the God's own truth. It follows me round like a curse . . .'

When her father stopped pacing, and Deidre heard the drone of his Bible-reading voice, her eyes filled with hot tears. 'I *won't* stay here, I won't, I won't,' she resolved. 'I'll run away to the town.' The babies, behind her, stirred in their cots. It was one of those nights when Deidre fancied she could hear the stars breathing. Every household creak, every movement outside, from the cows munching, to the water licking the stones on the riverbank, could be identified. She could hear the dogs tied to the boundary posts to scare away the rabbits. She could even, if she concentrated, feel their desperate straining at the leash. Somewhere, far away, as far as dead Mr Eichardt's land perhaps, a morepork called. Mr Eichardt had cut his throat. Deidre had committed the words to memory. How did a person cut his own throat? She'd asked her mother, but she'd just shaken her head in that way she had which made clear the question should never have been asked. When she spoke of it to her father he made her wash her mouth out with soap and water.

'Everything will be all right when we have our house,' her mother said, to comfort her. Her mother always comforted her when she was punished. 'Your father works hard for us and that makes him tired.'

Deidre scrunched up the hem of her nightdress, and wiped her nose and eyes. When she grew up she was going to have what the nice man said: a proper house to live in, and a carriage to take her calling. She was *never* going to marry; *never* going to have children. Children gave you shadows under your eyes, and made your shoulders slump over the washtub in the yard. Children made your face vanish in the steam, so that Deidre, watching, cried out in fear, and wondered ever after if it was *her* bad magic made her mother disappear forever.

2 ∫

Today, being Dominion Day, I rode with Deidre to the top of Fenian Heights.

'If anyone ever asks ya who you are,' Pearse exhorted his daughter, 'ya must tell them yer a New Zealander. You mark my words now. Never, never must ya call yerself English.'

The view from the Heights was one Pearse carried with him wherever he went. On the miners' maps this peak was called Maori Point. But Pearse's dealings with the Maori were practical – the shearing gangs at Willowbank; the casual acquaintanceships of the town – and posed no threat to his own ruling mythology. Fenian Heights, like Parnell Gully and the Wicklow Hills, were places on the maps *he* had drawn. Soon no one would remember the old names. As no one now remembered what the river (known by a variety of names, but called, by Pearse, the *Boyne*) had once been titled.

In the last week Pearse had arranged to lease a block of Widow Eichardt's land on the other side of the Boyne. So there was added pleasure now in contemplation of Kilkenny's acres. Almost everything he could see was his, from the barge tied up at the jetty to the horse whinnying at his side. Lesser men had come to this valley and been defeated by it. But not him. Not Pearse Byrne. Nothing he'd found here had been wasted. The stones thrown up from the river bed by the alluvial miners of the last century had built a cowshed and dairy. The water race that scarred the hill was an irrigation channel. Even the broken remnants of the miners' dishes, dug up by his plough, had been repaired and put to use.

'Take a good look, girlie,' Pearse instructed. 'Four years ago, when yer mother'n I first pitched our tent, there was nothin' here but stones'n rabbits. Take a long, hard look. Those are Corriedales ya see grazin'. Best crossbreed on the market. I'm gettin' up'ards of fifty bales o'wool per shearin' now. And that mist of green ya see in the paddocks is a fresh crop of oats. I've been lucky this year. The rains came when I needed 'em.'

'Why don't people take their babies to town and sell them?' Deidre asked.

Pearse laughed. 'What sort o' question is that? Babies aren't like lambs.'

'Yes they are. Muvver's got a lamb by the fire and she feeds it just like a baby.'

'Yer a strange wee creature, Deidre. I don't know what to make of ya half the time, an' that's the God's own truth.'

'God lives in those clouds,' the girl announced. 'I seen His face.'

'God is everywhere,' her father replied. 'Not just in the clouds.'

'Can He see us then?'

'He sees everythin' ya do.'

'Even when I . . .' She giggled. 'I don't want Him to see that,' she said. 'It's rude.'

Her father didn't reply. His eye had been caught by the timber frame of the house standing, silently accusing, above the river. 'How are we to live?' his wife had cried, when he'd pulled her into his arms last night. 'If there's another child . . .'

They'd made no noise. He was always most careful of that. But he knew what May was thinking. That the little ones sleeping on the other side of the curtain might wake . . .

On the way down from the Heights Pearse told his daughter a story. 'Once upon a time,' he said, 'there were two very poor people who had no money, an' nothin' to eat. They'd come to this country from another land far away. A land even poorer than this. Their names were Seamus and Kathleen. At first they had dreams, like everyone else. They were young. They dreamed of their own house, their own farm. They saw the children they would have, the children God would send them, playin' on the lawn outside their cottage. They made up names for these children – Patrick, Marie, Declan, Brigid, Teresa, Pearse . . . But they never got their house, or their farm. They worked till they died fer other people. English people . . .'

'Is that the end?' Deidre piped.

'Death is always the end,' her father answered.

'I don't think I like your story.'

'Then ya best write one fer yerself,' Pearse snapped.

Deidre pressed her fist into her eye. Her father's arms were a belt around her chest; his hands, on the reins, looked like hard baked scones. She'd never ridden this far with him before. She mustn't spoil it. 'Tell me another story, Father. A happy one. *Please.*'

'Stop wrigglin', child. Yer upsettin' Eddie.'

Deidre took a deep breath, counted to six, then slowly breathed out. *Playing dead,* she called it. It was a game she could play anywhere. After a minute or two her father's grip slackened, but Deidre kept breathing and counting, only pausing long enough to pat Eddie's mane, and whisper encouragement to him. She knew that would please her father. He liked horses; better than he liked babies, Deidre secretly believed. 'Were they your children, Father?' she asked. 'Your boys'n girls?'

There was a sound like a laugh, only Deidre didn't think it was that. Her father hardly ever laughed. Perhaps he'd breathed in something nasty. Though why that should happen up here in the hills, where the air was as sweet as her mother's breath, puzzled her. If they'd been near the house, with its brew of smells from cowshed, chicken-run, and lavatory, she would have understood.

'Yer a puzzle Deidre, so ya are. A little enigma.'

The words meant nothing, but the tone reassured. Deidre placed her small hand on the speckled brown scone. 'I liked your story, Father. Cross my heart. Please may I have another?'

While she waited for the words, and the pictures they would draw, Deidre wondered if all men were like her father, possessed of the power to make people happy or sad. The only other man, apart from her father, whom she saw regularly, was Father Driscoll, and he talked about God, who most certainly had that power, and about His Son, who made His Holy Mother very sad by dying on the Cross, even though He could have stopped it if He'd wanted.

'When I first saw your mother . . .' Pearse began.

Deidre smiled. Happy or sad, it *was* a story. The best kind, because there was no book.

'. . . she reminded me of a story *my* mother used to tell. It was about the young girls of Leinster who wore white for their first communion, an' looked like poppies bobbin' in the sunlight.'

'What are poppies?'

The question wasn't answered. 'She were sittin' at the piano playin' fer Colonel an' Mrs Rattray. I shouldn'ta bin there. Not in ma boots an' moleskins. But the music drew me in. I could no more 'ave stayed outside than you, Miss Inquisitive, can sit still.'

Deidre took a deep breath, and held it till she felt her chest would burst. Her father's words were like pebbles flying from his mouth into hers.

'She were beautiful,' he said. 'Her fingers caressed the notes . . .'

Some of the words wouldn't go down. Like that word, *caressed*. It was in her throat now, stuck like a chicken-bone.

'I'll say this fer the Colonel,' her father said. 'He were not one to stand on ceremony. "Come in, man," he called. "Not every day we hear music o' such delicacy. Schubert, my wife tells me . . ." I felt awkward in that room. Clumsy. When the music came to an end, an' Mrs Rattray introduced us, me tongue cleaved to the roof o' me mouth. But *she* were no better, your mother. Blushin' an' stammerin' like a girl o' twelve. Her name were Johnson. May Johnson. I didn't care fer that part of it. I'd always seen meself wed to an Irish girl. But she were a white poppy, sure enough. Tall, with hair the colour ya see in rivers round here, in the stones that carry gold.'

The hand on which his daughter's rested pulled sharply on the rein. Deidre looked round fearfully. But her father had only acted to keep Eddie on the path. There was no anger in his face.

'Good horsie, good boy,' Deidre encouraged.

'I'd lived at Willowbank all me life,' the voice at her shoulder went on. 'Born'n bred there. Me brothers an' sisters had moved away. The last, Teresa, left when our mother died. I don't know where they all are now. Brigid became a nun. Patrick wanted to go back to the old country, to fight the English. All I knew was that I must get away too. The serving life, the life my parents had led, that weren't for me. Some days I felt, if I heard the station bell ring one more time, summonin' me like a dog to get up, to work, to eat, it wouldn't be rabbits I killed with the Colonel's rifle, it'd be the Colonel himself, so help me.'

Deidre didn't know what a Colonel was, but she'd already dressed him, in her mind, in Father Driscoll's robes. And given him the priest's breath, that smelled of sour milk. '*Did* you kill the Colonel-man, Father?' she asked.

'Saints preserve us! What kinda question is that? You'd not be here if I had.'

But that was too deep for Deidre to fathom. And as much, she realised, with sudden disappointment, as her father was going to tell her. They'd reached the foothills. Working country. Her father would be looking out for stray lambs, or ewes in difficulty. His eyes would be peeled for signs of the scab; or a dead sheep, fly-blown, and smelling a thousand times nastier than Father Driscoll's breath, which he would heave across the saddle and carry home. Deidre dreaded those days, when the fire was lit under the vat in the yard, and the rancid carcass boiled down for tallow. She'd bury her face in a blanket to escape the smell, and the sound of her mother being sick, but there was never anywhere to hide from the pictures.

'So what are ya, my girl?' Pearse shouted, when the foothills were behind them, and the sight of the smoke curling above the cottage had spurred Eddie on to a gallop. To their left the Boyne, snaking between sharp black rocks, flashed white and gold in the slanting sunlight. Deidre had been warned never to go near the river. The current would carry her away, she'd been told. But her mother went. Deidre had watched her take off her boots, tuck petticoat and skirt into her bloomers, and wade into the shallows till the water lapped her waist. Once she'd heard her crying. But though Deidre, watching, had shed hot tears of her own, she'd said nothing. It was her secret, buried like the stash of treasure she'd hidden behind the chicken-run. No one knew about that either. Not even Sean. The strange-shaped bottles, bluer than the sky, the bucket with the hole in it, the rusted wheel, the pieces of china for making patterns in the dust, were her *holy relics*, rescued from the ground her father turned with his plough. She only had to think of them to feel safe.

'I'm a New Zealander,' Deidre answered her father confidently. 'I'm not English. But isn't Muvver English?' she asked, with no pause for breath.

'Leave yer mother out of it,' Pearse Byrne growled.

It was many years before Pearse Byrne confided in his daughter again. The exchanges between them, after that day, were of a different order: Deidre was wilful, stubborn, disobedient, *a child of the Devil*. She was too clever for her own good. She would learn, her father told her, what it was to be a woman. She would learn, if he had to thrash the knowledge into her.

Deidre bore these blows, physical and mental, in silence, knowing, without knowing that she knew, that her father hated her because he'd told her things. It was a pattern she would come to recognise. People, without warning, would unburden themselves to her. They would confide secrets never spoken of before. But these confidences wouldn't lead to love. On the contrary, they'd lead to resentment. As she, four decades later, would resent, to the point of obsession, the person she chose to trust with her own buried secret.

'Seamus, my little bu-bu,' Deidre whispered in the baby's ear. The baby didn't have a name yet. But Deidre had decided for herself what her newest brother should be called. 'You're Seamus of Kilkenny,' she told the sleeping bundle. 'And you've come from a land far away across the sea.'

'That's enough now!' a voice behind her declared. It was the fat woman who smelled of lard. The woman who always came when Deidre's mother was sick. Mrs Robinson, she'd been told to call her. But Deidre had another name for her: 'Fat Cow'. 'Give the baby to me.'

'It's my baby.'

'That it is not.'

'You're English. You can't have him. He's mine.'

'I'll tell you what's yours, Miss Impertinence,' Fat Cow hissed. 'A clip around the ears.'

Deidre turned her outraged face to her mother. But May Byrne, like her new-born son, was asleep.

3

Jessie Potter's first sight of Kilkenny was from the seat of her father's spring-cart. It was the day of May Byrne's funeral. The Church of the Holy Trinity had been packed. Not many people knew May Byrne. She scarcely ever ventured into town. But everyone knew what had happened. News like that travelled fast.

'Ask me, it was no accident,' Jessie's father commented, as he tethered the horse to the hitching post. 'Don't care what folk say, Mrs Pearse Byrne was lucky to be given Christian burial.'

The funeral tea had been provided by neighbours. Widow Eichardt had been especially generous. Her contribution – three large pound cakes, twice as many batches of scones – made up the bulk of the food spread on the table.

'Thank ya fer comin',' Pearse Byrne greeted, as Jessie and her father reached the door. His eyes, Jessie noticed, were of a penetrating pale blue. They skimmed over her face with no change in expression. 'Thank ya fer comin',' he said, to the next in line, Bill and Violet Cairns.

The cottage was packed. It was mid-winter, but the heat from the range seared the faces of the mourners, obliging the women to mop their brows with their handkerchiefs, and the men to squirm inside their starched collars. Jessie, whose interest in human nature might have led her, in another age, to study psychology, observed first one man, then another, surreptitiously pulling out his watch. Even Archie Drummond, Pearse Byrne's neighbour, a man other men deferred to, had a hunted look on his face.

'Miss Potter.'

Jessie turned. The pale eyes stared down at her. Pearse Byrne was tall; close on six foot, Jessie reckoned, though he didn't seem tall when seen in a crowd. Probably, Jessie decided, because he was so thin. A long thin face; long thin hands; a wispy beard that stretched to the middle button of his waistcoat. Did he look like a man who'd just lost a wife and three children? How *should* such a man look? His suit was pressed; his collar white; the child at his side (Jessie lowered her eyes) neatly dressed in feather-stitched tunic and black-laced boots.

'I'd like it if ya'd say hullo to ma daughter,' Pearse said. 'Her name is Deidre.'

The child stared ferociously. She had eyes exactly like her father's; milky-blue, and cold.

'She's a talkative wee miss normally,' Pearse explained.

'Hullo, Deidre.'

'Deidre, this is Miss Potter.'

Jessie pushed a stray curl under the rim of her straw hat. What sort of mother could May Byrne have been that her daughter should stare so?

'I've bin talkin' to yer father,' Pearse said.

'Mr Byrne, would it inconvenience you if we went outside? I'm feeling rather faint.'

Jessie couldn't explain, then or later, why she'd said those words. True, it was hot in the cottage, but that didn't mean she had to stoop to the level of the time-watchers. Appearances had to be maintained. Duty seen to be done. Those were her rules of conduct. So what possessed her, in full view of her neighbours, to drag Mr Byrne and his disconcerting daughter out of the room? She could only assume it was an aberration: a consequence of the awfulness of the occasion.

She adjusted her hat, placed a gloved hand on her burning cheek, and followed father and child out on to the verandah. How can he be so calm? she wondered. He'd not wept during the service. Nor after, when friends and acquaintances came forward to offer condolences. When her father asked him why the service had been held in the Anglican, and not the Catholic church, he replied, with no hint of emotion, 'My wife never converted. It woulda bin her wish.'

'But *you* would want the comfort of your priest, surely?'

'I want no priest now,' Pearse Byrne said. 'I've done with all that.'

It was mercifully cool on the verandah. The wind from the hills whipped Jessie's face, bringing sudden tears to her eyes.

'Yer father'n I 'ave bin talkin',' Pearse said.

Jessie looked down at his daughter. I should feel sorry for you, she thought, but I don't. I'll wager you know more than you've let on, too. Can't remember indeed! Those eyes forget nothing.

'Yer seventeen, he tells me. He can't keep ya at home forever.'

'He needs me,' Jessie said. 'There's no one else.'

'He also needs money.'

This time the flush Jessie felt in her cheeks had nothing to do with the heat from the range.

'I told 'im I could pay ya three pounds a week. You'd have yer board of course.'

'Mr Byrne . . .'

'Yer father's fallen on hard times, Miss Potter. He can no longer afford to support ya.'

'You have no right . . . Our private affairs are none of your business.'

The slight movement of Pearse Byrne's lips could have been the beginnings of a smile. 'No one regrets more than I do, Miss Potter,' he said, 'the openin' of a rival establishment. Yer father's bin blacksmith in these parts since the turn o' the century. But the facts are plain. Frederick Cashell is young. He can offer better terms than yer father. His success is inevitable. It'd be foolish of ya to imagine otherwise.'

Deidre, who'd listened to this exchange with mouth half open, sifted the words to find the ones responsible for the knot at the back of her throat. She'd taken a dislike to the lady in the black skirt and tight-fitting jacket. She had the face of a ferret, all nose and no eyes. *And* she was stupid. She said stupid things. Like all the other people here. Even her father. Her mother was dead, they were saying. Drowned. Sean and Molly and little Seamus too. What did they know? People ran away. Didn't they know that? When the smell got bad, you had to run to the river or the hills just to *breathe*.

'I'm sorry for you, Mr Byrne,' Jessie Potter said. 'But I must ask you not to speak to my father again on this matter. I know my duty. And I know my rights. And now I really must take my leave.'

Deidre turned the words over suspiciously. Did they mean what she thought they did? That it was all right after all? That the dread she'd felt was nothing? A false alarm? Her mother was coming back, and everything was going to be as before . . .

'I won't, I won't, I won't,' she'd screamed, when her father had taken her to see the bodies laid out on the bed.

'God will punish that tongue o'yours,' her father had snarled, forcing her head down so that her hair fell over her mother's face. 'Look! See what wickedness has been done. Yer only a child, but ya understand many things. Understand this then. The words you refuse to speak, one day, I warn ya, they'll rise up an' choke ya . . .'

'Father?' Deidre said. She had a sudden urge to comfort him; to tell him *she* would look after him till her mother came back.

'Say goodbye to Miss Potter,' her father instructed.

'Goodbye,' Deidre said.

A few minutes later Miss Potter and her father climbed into their cart and drove away from Kilkenny. Deidre watched till the dust had settled. Then she hitched up her skirts, in imitation of her mother, and ran towards the hills.

Jessie Potter waited till the cart was clear of Kilkenny before speaking her mind. 'What right had you, Father, to talk of me to Mr Byrne? Am I to be sold to the highest bidder? We are not so poor, surely, that I must be treated as a slave.'

Her father, a timid man, whipped the horse into a gallop. 'A temporary arrangement only,' he muttered, dodging the spray of stones. 'In Christian charity it seemed to me . . .'

'And who will cook for you? Who will clean?'

'I can fend fer meself.'

'You've seen the cottage. Where would I be expected to sleep? It's madness, Father. If I didn't know better I'd think you'd been drinking.'

'Mr Byrne has signed the pledge. I'd never let ya work for 'im else.'

'A kitchen-maid. A nurse to that queer little girl.'

'Nothing was signed,' Ab Potter sighed, pulling the horse back to a trot. 'We only talked.'

Two weeks later, Jessie and her father drove back to Kilkenny. Strapped to the back of the cart was a trunk containing Jessie's skirts, jackets, bodices, stays, aprons, chemisettes, stockings, boots, bonnets, nightgowns, the rags to tie up her hair at nights, a framed photo of her mother, and the copy of the Bible given to her on passing her Sunday School examinations. They drove through blinding snow without exchanging a single word. 'A separate room,' Ab had assured his daughter. 'Till such time as the house is built.'

'A separate room *where*?' Jessie had shouted.

'Attached to the cottage. I insisted. He, of course, saw right away . . .'

'They say May Byrne killed herself because of that house. The one he never built.'

'Mr Byrne is a man of his word, Jessie. If he says the room will be built, then it will be. You should show a little respect.'

4

The bar of the New Brunswick Hotel was packed. It was the Saturday before Christmas, and there was an air of celebration. Bill Cairns, the licensee, had been measuring drinks since he opened the doors at eight o'clock in the morning. Now it was evening, and though some of the faces had changed, the regulars remained: Willie Inglis; Ted Erihana; Spotty Malone; Ab Potter; Old Champagne Sam, who'd struck gold back in 1887, and refused to leave his hut up country ever since. Bill knew all the yarns. He'd been pouring beers and hearing confessions for upwards of twenty years. There wasn't much he didn't know about lucky strikes and fights over claims, and the near starvation of men driven by the dream of gold. Though these days it wasn't the gold in rocks and rivers men fought over, but the gold in the soil. Men like Pearse Byrne, who'd turned desert into pasture, and at yesterday's Sale Day not only took top price for his wool, but was paid a record twenty-five guineas for a yearling filly he'd bred himself.

Bill Cairns would have welcomed a yarn with Pearse Byrne. The man was something of a talking point in the district. The drowning of his wife and children earlier in the year had stunned a community accustomed to tragedy. But Pearse Byrne didn't encourage sympathy. He was the type who picked himself up after a fall, dusted himself down, and got on with the job. Look at the way he'd got himself a housekeeper within two weeks of his wife's death. No other man Bill knew could have pulled that off. Jessie Potter had gone to Kilkenny under protest. That much was common knowledge. The way Bill heard the story, she was persuaded only when her father revealed the extent of his debts. 'Either you work for Mr Byrne, or ya see yer father in gaol,' was how Spotty Malone reported it. Whatever the truth, Ab Potter, with Pearse Byrne's pounds in his pockets, was now a regular at the New Brunswick. 'Drownin' me sorrows,' he'd inform anyone who asked. 'What else is there to do in this godforsaken country?'

'Same again,' Ab shouted now, above the din.

'So what's this?' a voice Bill recognised as Harry Bordeaux's answered. 'You have no longer signed the pledge?'

There must have been forty men in the bar that evening. Enough to raise a gust of laughter that shook the lamps hanging from the rafters. 'Harry the Frenchman', as he was universally known, was by way of being a travelling salesman: a hawker of pots and pans, nails and timber, cotton and calico. He'd not been in town since last August. He couldn't be expected to know what had happened in the intervening months.

'You'll take a whisky with me, Frenchman?' Ab called back. 'It's celebratin' we're about. Isn't that right, Ted?'

The Maori grinned. Son of a Ngai-Tahu woman and a Welsh miner, he'd grown up on the fringes of both cultures, belonging to one or both or neither as the mood took him. Tonight he was Pakeha. Tomorrow, if the spirits of his ancestors keened loudly enough, he'd make his way downriver to the coast, where what was left of his mother's people lived. 'Right, Ab. Yup,' Ted agreed. 'Celebratin', eh.'

Heads turned as the Frenchman made his way across the room. Interest in Ab Potter had risen sharply with the departure of his daughter for Kilkenny. Rumour had it Jessie Potter had taken the surly Irishman firmly in hand. Those few who had visited Kilkenny, on one pretext or another, confirmed that the house was all but finished; the child, whose early recklessness had been the subject of a dozen cautionary tales, subdued into a state of sullen obedience.

Bill Cairns rested his head in his hands. The mood of the men was jovial. He didn't anticipate trouble. Across the room a photo of the New Brunswick as it had been in the time of the gold fever was reassurance, had he needed it, that these days the hotel, like the town, wore a settled, respectable air. Other mementoes of the past served a similar function: a rifle that had seen service in

South Africa; the bell that was used still to warn of fire; a report from the *Goldfields Gazette* of the apprehension, in this very room, of a notorious highwayman. They'd come a long way since those days. It would take more than Ab Potter, unpredictable though he was, to stir tonight's crowd to mutiny. Which didn't mean Bill could relax. A man who'd led a riotous youth, been sober for ten years following the death of his wife, and was now, after another turn of the wheel, on the whisky again, had to be watched.

'Gentlemen!' Ab shouted, raising his glass above his head. 'I give you – Mr 'n Mrs Pearse Byrne!'

There was a hush, as if each man had swallowed at the same moment and was temporarily deprived of speech. Old Sam, feeling the saliva rise in his throat, shuffled to the door and spat loudly. The Frenchman combed his beard with his fingers. Bill Cairns developed a sudden interest in wiping down his beer-soaked counter. Ted Erihana whistled between his teeth. Only Ab seemed indifferent to the change in the atmosphere. 'Out with the old, in with the new,' he continued cheerfully. 'I told Jess she should nail 'im, and she has. First day o' the New Year they'll be wed. Mr 'n Mrs Pearse Byrne!'

'There's a kid, i'n't there?' Spotty Malone mused, when it seemed no one was going to respond. 'That's why, I reckon. Kid needs a mother.'

'Kid's got nuthin' to do with it,' Ab contradicted. 'All that little madam needed was a taste o' the belt. No, my Jessie's got her head screwed on, make no mistake. I told 'er, Pearse Byrne'll be a rich man one day. Ya'll not get a second chance.'

'I wish 'er luck,' a voice with a soft Scottish burr volunteered. Bill, peering round, identified Archie Drummond of Glenory. Archie, a widower with a young daughter, was not a regular at the New Brunswick. Christmas, or yesterday's Sale Day, must have drawn him out. ''Tis a brave wee lass as goes to live at Kilkenny,' he said quietly.

'Yer right there,' Spotty Malone concurred.

'The kid'll be startin' school soon,' Willie Inglis informed the company. Willie's wife, Florence, was infant mistress at the parish school. 'Queer wee youngster. Only gotta look at 'er.'

'Seen too much, shouldn't wonder,' Archie murmured.

'Jessie get on with her all right, does she?' Willie asked Ab.

'"Children should be seen'n not heard,"' Ab answered. 'I told 'er, don't you stand fer no nonsense.'

'Good on ya,' Bill Cairns approved. He was anxious to get Ab off the subject of Deidre Byrne. Something told him that child was bad for business. 'How about it then?' he invited, gesturing around the room. 'A toast to the bride an' groom?'

'Drinks are on me!' Ab encouraged. 'And yer all invited to the weddin'. We'll have ourselves one hell of a celebration.'

From that moment till closing time, Bill's hands were never still. Reason enough, he admitted wearily, as he bolted the door behind the last recalcitrant customer, to be grateful to Pearse Byrne, who'd never once crossed this threshold.

'Don't need to tell me, I already know,' his wife muttered from her side of the bed, when he started to tell her the night's news. 'Whole town knows. Poor woman. Out o' the fryin' pan into the fire.'

'What's that supposed to mean?'

'Ya wouldn't understand.'

'At least the child'll have a mother.'

'Men,' Violet Cairns sighed. 'Ya don't know nuthin'.'

5 ∫

'Kill, Kenny! Kill, kill, kill . . .'

'Whatever do you think you're doing?'

'Nuthin'.'

'Come here at once!'

Deidre picked up the doll she'd been thrashing with a stick, and scuffed her way across the yard. Between her father's hatred of the English, and the presence in the house of Miss Jessie Potter, English to her finger-tips, Deidre's world had become horribly confusing. 'For generations,' she'd heard her father tell Miss Potter, 'the Byrne family lived an' suffered in or near Kilkenny. Our branch was poor. Potato peasants. But there were rich Byrnes too. Enemies o' the English . . .' It was the repetition of the word Kilkenny which chiefly puzzled Deidre. Till she worked out it must be a coded instruction to her Irish forbears to 'Kill Kenny!'; Kenny of course, being English . . .

Jessie Potter, standing on the steps of the newly-built porch, looked down at the child who would, in a matter of hours, be her step-daughter, and allowed herself the luxury of a sigh. She'd vowed, when she first came to Kilkenny, never to strike the girl. But there were times, like now, when her fingers itched. Barefoot, hair a-tangle, face streaked with dirt, Deidre Byrne was enough to drive a saint to distraction. 'If you could see yourself,' she said. 'How ugly you are!'

There was no answer.

'Well, you're not coming inside to wash. You can make do at the pump. And don't dawdle, or we'll go without you. We leave in quarter of an hour.'

Deidre closed her eyes, counted to ten, then looked up at the porch. In that instant her face was transformed. Gone was the downward turn of the lips, the shifting, resentful expression of the eyes. 'I can make *anyone* disappear,' she announced to the still open door. 'So *there!*'

Her faith restored, Deidre skipped across the yard to the pump.

'*"She was lovely and fair as a rosebud in summer . . ."*' Her father had been singing that for weeks now. She'd hear him when he was out on Eddie, or working with one of the horses people had started bringing him to break in.

'*"But 'twas not her beauty alone that won me . . ."*' Sometimes, when her father had got the horse to trot on the end of a long rope, and Deidre could tell by the expression on his face that he was pleased, she'd come out of her hiding place and sit on the gate to watch.

'*"Ah no, 'twas the truth in her eyes fondly beaming . . ."*' If he spoke a few words to her she'd be happy for days. But she'd be satisfied if all he did was glance in her direction.

'*"That made me love Mary, the Rose of Tralee."*' One day, when her mother came back, her father would talk to her again as he had that day riding down from Fenian Heights. Till then Deidre knew she had to be patient. She had to endure his anger which, she'd reasoned, was only directed at her because it couldn't be directed at Miss Potter.

'Your mother's *never* coming back.' Her father's words, spoken the day he took her aside to talk to her about Miss Potter, were burned on her brain. 'Get that into your head once an' fer all.'

'But you can't marry her,' Deidre had whispered. 'You're married to Mother.'

'Jesus'n Mary! What am I to do with you?'

It was the kind of thing he said when he was going to hit her. But nothing was normal about that day. When the blow didn't come, and she opened her eyes, the expression on her father's face made her wish she was a good girl, and not the wicked person he was always telling her she was. 'Miss Potter is your mother now, girlie,' he said, in the voice he used to calm a frightened horse. 'You have no other.'

Deidre wiped her face on her sleeve, forced her muddy feet into the boots she was supposed never to take off outside, and walked, one slow foot in front of the other, towards the house.

'There's a clean pinafore on your bed,' Jessie Potter called, as she pushed open the door. 'Hurry up now!'

The house smelt of newly-cut timber and carbolic soap. For days after they moved in Jessie Potter had scrubbed and polished, as if fighting off an infectious disease. She would have nothing in the house from the cottage. 'I'd rather go without,' she'd snapped, when Pearse protested.

As for Deidre, she was *in the way*. 'Outside's where you belong, young lady,' she was told. Which suited Deidre just fine. *Outside* she was free.

Her room was at the end of the corridor. Three other rooms separated it from the one she'd been told her father and Miss Potter would be sleeping in after today. Eventually, her father had explained, the upstairs rooms would be finished. 'Kitchen, laundry, dining room, parlour, downstairs; bedrooms upstairs,' he'd said. 'With room for additions, of course.'

'But we don't need any more bedrooms,' Deidre had pointed out.

Her father had looked across at Miss Potter with the particular expression he reserved for her. Soppy, Deidre considered it. Sick-making.

'You should be grateful to your father,' Miss Potter had said. 'Not many girls your age have their own rooms. Most have to share with brothers and sisters.'

When *my* brothers and sisters come back, Deidre had silently resolved, we'll all sleep in the same bed. And you, Miss Bossy Potter, can go back to your own house.

Once inside her room Deidre pushed a chair against the door, and began to undress. It was a precaution she'd learned to take when they were still living in the cottage. Miss Potter, who slept in the newly-built lean-to, seemed to think she could barge in on Deidre whenever she pleased. Since there was no door Deidre could bolt, her only protection was to pin down with a chair the curtain that screened off her part of the room. That way she was assured some warning, at least, of invasion. What she couldn't protect herself against was the weekly ritual of the bath. Sitting in water that Miss Potter had already used, suffering the indignities inflicted by her soap-filled hands, Deidre's vow to run away took on fresh urgency. Already her stash of treasure behind the chicken-run had been augmented with a peg-bag full of sugar, six sprouting potatoes, and a jar of currants, which had once been full but was now, inexplicably, empty.

Deidre looked at the blouse she was supposed to wear, and wrinkled her nose in disgust. Sailor collars were for boys, not girls. But Miss Potter had made it specially. 'I'll not have people saying I don't do my duty,' she'd said.

When the hated garment was on, and the pinafore pulled over it, Deidre sat down on the bed and examined her hands. Every evening, before bedtime, Miss Potter examined Deidre's finger-nails for signs of lingering dirt. There were nights when Deidre had to scrub her hands till the skin was raw and red. Her ears were examined too. Miss Potter would twist her head round to the light and yank the hair back as if what she really wanted to do was pull it out by the roots.

Deidre picked up her brush, and ran it lightly over her hair. Her dilemma was when exactly today she should make Jessie Potter disappear. Should she do it now, before they got into the buggy? Or should she wait till they were in town and do it then? Deidre liked going to the town. She didn't even mind the smells. On one magical occasion she'd persuaded her father to take her to the railway station to watch the express arriving from Dunedin. Oh the wonder of that moment! The shiny black engine, screeching like a mad horse, gusting steam and smoke into the sky; the long, slow squeal of the brakes; the faces at the windows; the piercing whistle when the train finally stopped; the doors banging open . . . She'd had to be prised away. Jessie Potter was waiting. But for the rest of that day she'd been consumed with happiness.

'Deidre! Shift yerself, girl, we'll be late.'

Her father's voice brought a veil down over her favourite scene. But it was still there. She only had to close her eyes for the veil to be lifted.

'When we have children of our own,' she'd heard Miss Potter say last night (living in the cottage had made Deidre an expert eavesdropper), 'the girl can have that hovel to herself. She prefers it to here anyway. She told me so.'

'You don't think . . .' her father had started to protest.

'She *likes* being on her own. Haven't you noticed? She really is the most unsociable creature.'

Deidre pushed the chair away from the door, and inched her way out into the corridor. If she tip-toed, avoiding the cracks, she would reach the parlour safely.

'Look at her!' Miss Potter said, when the hazards were successfuly negotiated. 'Mr Byrne, will you *look* at your daughter? What *am* I to do with her?'

'She looks all right to me.'

'I suppose you're going to tell me you brushed your hair?'

'Yes, Miss Potter,' Deidre said.

'Run and fetch your brush. Quickly now. And what happened to that ribbon I put out for you? I know you like it long, Pearse . . .' Miss Potter's voice followed Deidre down the corridor '. . . but you can see for yourself what a tangle it is. I really must insist on cutting it. She behaves like a boy. She might as well look like one.'

When, at last, Deidre's appearance was declared satisfactory, the wedding party climbed into the buggy and set off for the town. The child sat on one side of the groom, his bride on the other. Deidre's eyes were still watering from the pain of the brushing, but that didn't prevent her noticing the shine on her father's boots, or the way his eyes kept straying to the woman seated alongside him. He was wearing the suit he'd worn the day Jessie Potter first came to Kilkenny. The day of what other people called the funeral. Did that mean anything? Deidre wondered. Perhaps they were going to fetch her mother? In that case she ought to be nice to Miss Potter, since it would mean she wouldn't be coming back to Kilkenny. But if that *were* true, why was Miss Potter wearing a new dress? It was the colour of butter and felt, to Deidre's exploring fingers, like the dress she'd found once in a box and glimpsed again, with horror, in the box they'd called a coffin.

'Sit still, child!' Miss Potter admonished.

Deidre retrieved her hand, which had strayed behind her father's back, and sniffed the finger-tips. *That* dress had smelt of vinegar. Miss Potter's smelt of lavender. 'What have you got on your head?' she asked, craning her neck to get a better view of the puzzling object.

'It's a veil. Nottingham lace. My mother wore it when she got married.'

The look Deidre gave her was one of pure hatred.

'Father?' she enquired next.

'What is it now?'

'Is Father Driscoll dead?'

'Questions, questions,' her father muttered.

'Curiosity killed the cat,' Jessie Potter laughed.

Deidre turned her head away. She wanted nothing to do with either of them.

They'd left Kilkenny behind now and were bouncing past Mr Drummond's paddocks. Deidre had heard her father say Mr Drummond was behind the times. He was opposed to machinery on the land; in particular the new McCormick harvester which had become available for hire in the district. But Deidre liked Mr Drummond. She'd bumped into him, literally, on one of the days when she was locked outside. She'd been trying to work out how far she could run from Kilkenny without getting lost, when she stopped for breath and there he was, grinning down at her. He'd let her drink from his flask, and promised not to tell her father how far she'd strayed. She wondered if it was him she could see now, driving his team of horses. The harvest was early this year. Six weeks of hot dry weather had seen to that. But her father was going to wait for the machine. 'Thirty bushels an acre,' he was predicting confidently. 'Double what that old trout Drummond'll get.'

The words had offended Deidre. Mr Drummond wasn't old. He was young, like her mother.

By the time they reached town Deidre had constructed a fantasy for herself in which she ran away from Kilkenny and was rescued by Mr Drummond. But this time it wasn't a drink he gave her but a ticket to travel on the train. 'Your mother'll meet you in Dunedin,' he told her. 'She'll be on the platform with your brothers and wee Molly. She's been waiting such a long time for you.'

The Church of the Holy Trinity was on a hill overlooking the town. A long way, Deidre realised sadly, from the railway station. But there were compensations: a glimpse of the main street with its verandahed shops and hotels; a building engraved with the letters, MASONIC LODGE which Deidre, who'd only just begun to read, decided spelt 'MANS LOG'; the rose-hung window of MADAME MIGNONETTE'S DRESSMAKING ESTABLISHMENT, where her mother once stopped to gaze on her way to Jonas Garvie's to be fitted for a pair of boots. She wanted to ask her father to slow the horse down. She wanted to ask him about the man with a pigtail, who raised his hand as the buggy sped past. But her father was cracking his whip. He was in a hurry to get to the church. She could see it now, moored like a tall ship in a picture book, at the end of an avenue of poplars. To Deidre, who'd not been here since the day everyone wore black and spoke in whispers, the presence of so many people outside the church was a puzzle. They were more cheerfully dressed than on that other occasion, but they were staring at her, as they had then, and talking behind their hands. 'Poor child, God preserve you, poor lost infant,' the priest, who was not Father Driscoll, had said to her that day. But this morning he was smiling and holding out his hand to help her from the buggy, and the words he spoke were to welcome her and tell her how happy she must be. 'We'd like to see the child at Sunday School,' he said to her father. 'Miss Potter, as you doubtless know, was one of our star pupils.'

'I'm here to be married, Dr Withers,' her father answered. 'I take it there are no obstacles.'

At a sign from her father Deidre set off on the path that led to the back of the church. Jessie Potter had vanished. A man with a nose like an old carrot had appeared from nowhere and taken her arm. Now there was no sign of either of them. Deidre was puzzled. Could the magic have happened by itself?

She glanced over her shoulder. A voice floated down the path. 'Stuck up little madam she looks, don't she?' Deidre waited till her father had disappeared round the corner, then she poked out her tongue. The gasp that went up from the crowd was intensely satisfying.

It was curiously cold behind the church. A path led through a gap in the hedge to what looked to Deidre like an overgrown garden. Her quick glance took in broken slabs of concrete, a scattering of crosses buried in long grass, and a pile of leaves, that experience told her would be full of nasty-smelling things like

dead birds and rats' nests. Then Dr Withers called her name, and
she was ushered into a small brown room, hung with portraits
of bearded men.

'Mr Drummond's already in church,' the minister said. 'I'm
correct in thinking he's to act as your witness?'

'He is, he is. And his daughter's supportin' Miss Potter.'

'Then I suggest we take our places.'

Pearse Byrne straightened his waistcoat, ran his hand over his
hair and beard, and followed Dr Withers through the door. It
took a few moments for Deidre to realise she'd been forgotten.
Someone would come back for her. That was what she thought
when the door slammed shut. But then she heard a grumbling
noise that reminded her of horses, followed by the whine of
an organ, and she realised this thing called a wedding was
happening, and she was no part of it.

She walked to the door and pressed her ear to the crack. She
could hear Dr Withers's voice, but only with difficulty make
out his words. 'Beloved' was one she caught, and 'instituted'
But she could tell, from the stillness, that the church was full,
and everyone was listening.

After a while Dr Withers stopped talking, and her father said
something. That was a further puzzle. Her father hadn't read the
Bible since the day her mother went away. She'd listened each
night for his voice, but it never came. Not even after Miss Potter
arrived. He'd stopped seeing Father Driscoll too. *His* absence
Deidre construed in physical rather than spiritual terms. But she
did wonder what it meant. And what her father's words, spoken
in a church, meant now . . . Then, to confuse matters further,
she heard Jessie Potter's voice. That was when she knew there
had been no magic, only a trick; a terrible trick played by the
whole world against her.

'Deidre! In the name of . . .! Have you been here all the
time?'

To the child huddled in the corner it was as if a whole night
had passed, and she was being forced, now, to *live* her nightmare.
She'd been crouched like this – eyes closed, ears covered with
her hands – since the moment she heard Jessie Potter's voice.

'I told you she should have come with me,' Jessie said. 'You
see what I mean about her, Nellie?'

'Can we go home now, Father?' Deidre risked.

She felt a hand on her head. But it wasn't her father's, it was Mr Drummond's. 'There's a fine feast waiting for you,' he encouraged. 'Fresh scones and Dundee cake and shiny red apples. You're hungry, aren't you?'

'Mr and Mrs Byrne, if you would just sign here?' Dr Withers said.

Deidre spun round. Mr and Mrs? *Mr and Mrs!*

'Mr Drummond? Miss Drummond?'

Deidre closed her eyes and summoned all her powers of concentration. She had no interest in Miss Drummond, or anyone else in the room but Jessie Potter. Make her disappear, she prayed. Make her disappear *now!*

'You must kiss your mother,' her father said.

'My mother isn't here.'

'Open your eyes.'

'No!'

'I won't tell you again.'

Deidre tensed every muscle in her body. As her eyes slowly opened, Jessie Potter's face swam into view.

'Now . . . kiss your mother.'

She pressed her lips together, and waited for the hated flesh to touch hers. When it was done, everybody, even Mr Drummond, laughed.

'Come along, girlie,' her father said. 'We'll take you home.'

6

13 November 1913
 Police clash with striking workers in Wellington.
 Mrs Byrne safely delivered of a daughter.

Deidre was asleep when the child who would be christened
Elizabeth Ivy was born. Mrs Robinson had come from the
town that evening. She'd stood with her back to the fire and
announced in her whistling voice that babies nearly always
arrived at night, causing maximum inconvenience, in order to
prepare the household for the broken nights and exhausting
days ahead. She seemed to think what she said was funny.
But Pearse Byrne hadn't laughed. Nor had Deidre, who was
too busy nursing her ancient grudge against the woman who
smelled, more strongly than ever, of lard.

In two months' time Deidre would be six. Old enough, she
reasoned, to run away *successfully*. Her three attempts so far had
ended in disaster. The first, the day after the wedding, was
triggered by the thrashing her father had given her when he
caught her hovering in the corridor outside his room. She hadn't
meant any harm. She'd heard him singing, and crept out of bed
to get closer. She liked to be near him when he was happy.

'If I ever catch you spyin' again,' he'd shouted, 'I'll tan yer
hide so hard ya'll not walk for a week.'

'Weren't spyin', Father,' Deidre had protested.

'Jessie's right about ya. Yer a little sneak. I'll break that spirit
o'yourn if it's the last thing I do.'

The thrashing hadn't been nearly as bad as others Deidre had
suffered. In fact, looking back on it now, she wondered if it

hadn't been administered more for Jessie Potter's benefit than her own.

'Didn't hurt,' she'd taunted, loud enough for her step-mother to hear. 'Didn't hurt one bit.'

Five minutes later, having wiped the snot and tears from her face, and gathered up her bundle of treasure, she was running as hard as her legs would carry her along the road that led to the town. The day had barely begun, but she could feel the heat all around her. It wasn't just in the air, it lay like a hot tray from the oven over the dusty ground. 'Look at her!' the voice she was running away from shrilled in her head. 'Will you *look* at your daughter, Mr Byrne? Out in this heat without a hat! How many times have I told her?'

When she judged she was far enough from Kilkenny, she threw herself into the tussock at the side of the road. Her heart was hammering so hard she thought it would jump out of her mouth. If only she'd remembered to bring water. Water and a sun hat. But running away, in her imagination, had always been associated with cold and hunger, not sweating and thirst.

It was then she remembered Mr Drummond. The day he found her she'd not been running away seriously, just exploring. But he'd been kind to her. He'd dipped his flask in the icy stream that ran by his house, and promised not to tell tales to her father.

The memory brought her to her feet again. She could see Glenory across the paddocks. An enchanted place it had always been for her, with its wide lawns sloping down to the river, its shady trees, and a thing called a 'conservatory', which her father dismissed as 'flummery', but to her was a source of magic, shooting sparks at the sun, warming her hands, mysteriously, in winter. If Mr Drummond saw her now he'd be kind, wouldn't he? He'd take her to her mother in Dunedin.

She was just about to cross the lawn when a voice that definitely wasn't Mr Drummond's hailed her from the window. Deidre, panicking, looked round for a means of escape. Nellie Drummond was only twelve, but she'd *supported* Jessie Potter at the wedding. Nellie Drummond would tell tales.

'What a nice surprise,' the voice said.

Half an hour later, after a breakfast of porridge and hot milk, Deidre was driven back to Kilkenny in the Drummonds' gig. It was an ignominious return. The first of three. But at least, on that occasion, she wasn't punished. She had Nellie to thank for that. She'd refused to leave till she'd got Miss Potter to promise there'd be no more chastisement.

Deidre's second attempt at escape took place the day Miss Potter cut her hair. She hadn't planned it. But from the moment the basin was jammed over her head she knew what she was going to do.

'I'm *not* Miss Potter,' the voice at her shoulder insisted. 'I'm Mrs Byrne.' Jab went the scissors, jab, jab. 'Your father and I have been married three weeks.'

'Yes, Miss Potter.'

'Yes, *Mother*.' Jab. 'Say it, Deidre.' Jab. 'Yes, *Mother*.'

'Yes . . . Mother . . .'

When the ordeal was over, Deidre turned her streaming eyes from the sight of her hair, lying like a dead thing at her feet, and ran out of the house. Her only rational thought was that this time she should avoid the open road. She'd heard her father say there was a track on the other side of the river which had been used by miners. 'Goes all the way to the Junction,' he'd said. Deidre wasn't sure what a Junction was, but she thought it had something to do with trains. As she bundled up her belongings, remembering, this time, to fill one of the bright blue bottles with water, she saw herself being lifted by invisible hands into the waiting carriage. What would happen after that was shadowy. She tried to imagine her mother at the journey's end, but all she could *see* was a blur of faces on a platform.

Deidre never did find the Junction. Sliding down the bank to the river, she was overcome by fear. She'd not been this close to the water since the day her mother and the babies disappeared. *'Do I have to thrash you to get you to speak?'* her father had thundered. But she wouldn't speak. She wouldn't *remember*. 'There's magic in that water, *bad* magic,' she'd tried to tell him. But that had only made him rage more.

By the time she'd scrambled up the bank again her teeth were chattering. If her father had been at home she might have slunk back to the house. But Pearse Byrne had left before dawn to take the culled ewes to the new freezing works on the coast.

He'd not be back till nightfall. Since she couldn't row across the river ('No one in their right mind risks a boat on those rapids,' she'd heard her father say) she'd have to walk along the bank till she got to the flying fox. That was how Widow Eichardt used to cross; sitting in the bucket built for miners, swaying over the white water.

This time it was Jimmy Fook who found her. She'd been walking an hour when she saw him, crouched by the river, sifting gravel through a wire mesh. Her father had impressed on her she must never speak to strangers. 'There are devils out there, in men's clothing,' he'd warned. 'Devils who lie in wait for young girls.'

'What do they do to them?' she'd asked.

'Terrible things. Worse than terrible.'

'Do they kill them?'

'That would be merciful.'

She'd been too afraid to enquire further. But the words came back to her now, signalling danger, as her feet, crunching on the gravel, signalled her presence to the stranger on the riverbank.

'Know who you are, yes, sir, yes, missie. You're the Byrne girl.'

Deidre froze. If he knew her name did that mean he *wasn't* a stranger? What did devils look like? Did they have pigtails, and wear funny clothes? Whenever Jessie Potter talked about *Chinamen*, her nose twitched, as if in the presence of a bad smell. But Deidre's mother hadn't been like that. She'd liked the man who, once a month, trundled his cart full of vegetables up the dusty track, and stood beaming at the children playing in the yard. She'd called him Mr Lain, and taken him into the cottage for tea and scones.

While Deidre stood in frozen indecision the man who knew her name, who wasn't Mr Lain but looked like him, put down his dish and began to climb up the bank. As he came into clearer view she recognised him. He was the man who'd waved at her the day Jessie Potter turned into Mrs Byrne.

'Jimmy Fook at your service,' he panted.

'Have to go,' Deidre mumbled.

'Go?' Mr Fook laughed. He was wearing a long, mud-stained

tunic and wide baggy pants. Deidre wondered if they were his pyjamas. 'Nowhere to go round here,' he said.

'Have to get the train.'

'Ah . . .'

'Can you take me?'

It was a few moments before Mr Fook answered. He was sweating from the effort of climbing the bank. Deidre decided he was very old. 'Look over there,' he said, pointing to the land on the other side of the river. 'Whadd'ya see?'

Deidre looked. Her father owned that land now. He'd bought it from Widow Eichardt soon after Jessie Potter moved in. What was Mr Fook pointing at? The sheep on the hills? The ruined cottage her father planned to restore as a haybarn? 'Is that where the train goes?' she asked.

Mr Fook sighed. 'Nil Desperandum,' he said. 'It's all there. Broken dreams.'

Deidre clicked her tongue against her teeth. Why couldn't grown-ups answer questions properly?

'Too soon for you to be running away, missie,' Mr Fook said. 'You'll understand when you're older.'

'I'm six,' Deidre lied.

'Look again,' Mr Fook instructed. 'See there, where the scrub grows, those are tailings. Leftovers from the search for gold. And there, against the hill, that's an old battery. What's left of it. You'd be surprised what you find. Bones of this and that. Your father's bought himself a graveyard.'

'What's "Nil Des . . ."? Those words. Whadda they mean?'

'There was a mine in those hills. Shaft went all the way down to the river. The men called it "Nil Desperandum". They were running away too.'

'Will you take me to the train?'

'I hope you find your dream, Miss Byrne,' Mr Fook said.

Deidre was never sure whether the beating she got that day was because she'd run away, or because it was Mr Fook who brought her back.

'Wicked child,' Jessie hissed, when the door opened in response to Mr Fook's knocking. 'Get inside at once.' There wasn't even time to say goodbye. 'Off you go now!' Jessie spat over her shoulder.

Not one beating, but two. When her father came home she was thrashed all over again.

After that, for several months, Deidre was a model of good behaviour.

'I do believe your daughter's learning sense at last,' Miss Potter said, one evening early in winter. She was dishing out vegetables from a large blue and white dish, while her husband, at the other end of the table, carved the mutton. Deidre sat silently between them. 'She's doing well at school too. I met Flo Inglis in town today. She was telling me.'

'Well o' course she's doin' well. Her mother . . .' The carving knife clattered on to the plate. 'She's an intelligent child, so she is,' Pearse Byrne muttered.

'What's your favourite subject, Deidre?' Jessie Potter asked.

You wait, Deidre vowed, as she had done every day since Miss Potter arrived, when I'm older, you'll see . . . 'Spelling,' she answered.

Miss Potter laughed. 'Do you hear that, Mr Byrne? *Spelling.*'

'And history and arithmetic and writing and grammar and geography and music . . .'

'All right, Deidre,' her father growled. 'That'll do now.'

Deidre looked down at her food. She'd started school the week after her encounter with Mr Fook. Though she would never admit it to anyone, she *loved* it. She'd only been in trouble once, and that was on her very first day, for ringing the bell. Mrs Inglis had threatened to strap her. 'Whatever possessed you, child? No one touches that bell but me!'

'Wanted the people back,' Deidre had scowled.

'War. Flood. Fire. *That's* when we ring the bell.'

It hadn't made sense. It was rung every day. At the beginning and end of lessons. But at least she wasn't strapped. Not once she'd promised Mrs Inglis she'd never *play wolf* again.

'Holy Father, bless this food to our use, and us to your service, amen.'

'Father?'

'Yes, child?'

'Can I help you tomorrow?'

Her father smiled. 'No school. Poor Deidre.'

'I could ride the new pony.'

'Biddy? She's a bit fiery.'

'*Please*, Father.'

'Oh let her go, Pearse, we'll never hear the end of it, else.'

Deidre jabbed her knife into her meat. Jessie Potter couldn't ride Biddy. Jessie Potter couldn't do anything. She was too fat. Her tummy had grown big as a hill.

The next day was the happiest Deidre had known since her mother went away. Though she loved school she was almost as isolated there as she was at home. She didn't seem to have the knack of making friends. But alone in the hills with her father she forgot the playground taunts; forgot Miss Potter's cruel words, and the stinging blows to her flesh. She even forgot the failed magic.

At the end of the day her father lifted her off Biddy, and told her she was as good a rider as any man he knew. It was enough to keep her happy for days.

Her third attempt at escape came as the snow was beginning to thaw. For days she'd been watching the bulge under Miss Potter's apron, trying to match it with the memory of her mother's similarly swelling body. She couldn't remember Sean's birth, but she remembered the day Molly was born, and the way her mother looked before little Seamus came along. So did that mean Miss Potter was going to have a baby? The thought sent Deidre running to her hiding place behind the chicken-house.

This time she got no further than Parnell Gully. Judging herself a safe distance from the house she stopped to rest by a patch of gorse, which her father was always complaining had been 'seeded by the devil'. A solitary sheep, separated from the flock, grazed among the stunted manuka to her left. Something was wrong with this patch of land. She'd heard her father say so a dozen times. It was unresponsive even to lime.

Every time Deidre lifted her eyes she saw the snow on top of Fenian Heights. The sight chilled her. Where was she going to spend the night? She'd not had time to make a plan. Her only instinct, once she'd gathered up her treasure, was to avoid the routes she'd taken before.

The more Deidre thought about this journey, the more

reluctant she became to continue with it. Her two previous attempts at escape had been in summer. If she'd failed then, what hope did she have now, when there was snow on the ground? Then another thought struck her. What if Miss Potter wasn't having a baby at all? What if she was just getting fat?

Half an hour later Deidre crept in through the back door, and made her way to her room. Miss Potter was in the kitchen, singing. Deidre hugged herself with relief. She wouldn't be singing if she was going to have a baby. Babies made people sad.

The relief lasted three weeks. During that time Deidre contrived to ignore Miss Potter's stomach. It was no concern of hers if people got fat. But then something happened which convinced her she would never feel relief again so long as Miss Potter remained at Kilkenny.

It happened the day of the move upstairs. Pearse, nagged every mealtime by his wife, had been working through the winter on the upper storey of the house. 'I will *not* have my confinement where *she* can hear,' Jessie had complained, flicking her ferret eyes at Deidre. 'Either you finish those rooms, or I move back to town.' Deidre had never heard the word 'confinement' before, but she understood what Jessie Potter wanted. She wanted to be *upstairs*, away from *her*.

The more Deidre pondered the significance of this, the more puzzled she became. Did it mean the threat to banish her to the cottage had been lifted? Her father had been using the building to store surplus hay. But come the spring, it would be empty again.

Deidre's question was never answered. The morning of the move upstairs she was told she would not be going to school that day. She was required at home, to help. Indignation pulsed blood into her normally pale cheeks. It was common practice in the district to keep children home during harvest and planting, but it had never happened to her before. 'I can help *after* school,' she pleaded. 'Please, Miss Potter.'

'Please *Mother*!'

'Please . . . Mother.'

'If you really were a boy, instead of just looking like one, you'd be seeing far less of your precious Mrs Inglis, let me tell you,' Jessie grumbled. 'Now come along, carry these sheets upstairs. We've a lot to do. And don't drop them. They belonged to my mother.'

Deidre's mouth turned down at the corners, and stayed that way for the rest of the day. By the time everything was done, it was dark.

'Your father'll be in any minute, expecting his tea,' Jessie announced.

Deidre's mouth opened in surprise. The voice was the one Miss Potter used when speaking to someone she liked. Nellie Drummond for instance. She'd never spoken to Deidre like that before.

Jessie picked up the lamp from the dressing table and shone it round the room. 'All it needs now is pictures,' she declared, sighing the way people do when they're satisfied.

Deidre was afraid to speak in case she broke the mood. The fear of being kept home a second day clutched at her throat. She'd agree to anything to avoid that. She'd call Miss Potter *God* if she wanted it.

'Men are such strange creatures,' Jessie said, putting the lamp back on the table. 'If I didn't know better, I'd say they were afraid.'

Deidre took a deep breath. One, two, three . . . she counted.

'My father's the same,' Jessie said.

The room looked pale in the lamplight. The blues and golds of the new curtains had faded to a creamy haze. Only the bed looked substantial. Deidre had polished its shiny brass orbs herself.

'We're supposed to be afraid of *them*,' Jessie confided. 'But I sometimes think, for all their power . . .'

Twelve, thirteen, fourteen . . .

'I told Mr Byrne, I won't have anything of hers. I won't have it in the house. Those months in the cottage were quite bad enough.'

The way she swayed on her feet; the way she rubbed the small of her back – Deidre had seen it before.

'They're babies themselves really,' Miss Potter said.

Twenty-nine, thirty, thirty-one . . . Had she forgotten who

she was talking to? When she remembered, would she be angry?

'Oh for heaven's sake, don't just stand there!'

'I'm sorry.' The words shot out of Deidre's mouth. She put her finger to her tongue. It felt rough, and tasted of blood. 'I'm thorry,' she lisped.

'What is it about you? Is it your eyes?'

'Can I go now?'

'You might as well get used to it. You'll be staying home a lot from now on.'

'I'll help with tea, shall I?'

'Once the baby comes . . .'

'No!' Deidre screamed. 'No, no, no . . .'

'That's right, Miss Smarty-pants.' The voice pursued the fleeing child down the stairs. 'There are going to be babies in this house, and *you're* going to mind them.'

Deidre's silence that evening was construed by her father as good behaviour. But that was not how Deidre would have described it. There were two things she knew now for sure. The first was that her magic didn't work: the second was that her mother was never coming back. These were terrible things to know, but they were not the end of her knowledge. She knew, for instance, that Jessie Potter was not God; and neither was Pearse Byrne. As she chewed her mutton and vegetables, Deidre determined to make this knowledge her faith now. One day, when her treasure was large enough, she would run away from them both, forever.

7

'Deidre Byrne, would you step up please? I'd like you to read for us. Luke, Chapter Four, Verses 1 to 13. The Temptation of Christ.'

It was the winter of 1914. Despite many absences Deidre's school work was of such high standard she was regularly paraded in front of visiting Inspectors. Her reading skills, mental arithmetic, grammar and spelling were held up as examples, not just to officials, but to her fellow classmates. This, inevitably, won her no friends. But Deidre had long ago accepted she wasn't like other children. She was absent more often for one thing. Miss Potter's ugly baby saw to that.

'"And the devil said unto him, If thou be the Son of God, command this stone that it be made bread . . ."'

Eliza, the baby was nick-named. 'After my mother,' Jessie Potter kept telling people. In Deidre's mind there was now a picture of a screaming, red-faced, toothless old woman, who dribbled foul-smelling liquid down her dress, and soiled her pants three times a day. 'I'll never have babies. *Never, never,*' she vowed every day. It was the only magic she had left now, the strength of her will.

'"And the devil said unto him, All this power will I give thee, and the glory of them . . ."'

Eliza wasn't the only new thing at Kilkenny. The Bible-reading had started again. Only now it took place inside, and Deidre was forced to listen. She blamed Miss Potter for this, as she blamed her for everything she didn't like. The month after Eliza was born Miss Potter had dragged Deidre and her father to hear the Reverend Samuel Jefcoate preach at the Baptist Church in

Caledonian Street. Everything changed after that. Miss Potter declared she'd 'done with' Holy Trinity, and would be a Baptist from now on. Deidre's father said nothing at the time. But when the next Sunday came he rode with his wife and daughters to the dingy, back-street hall, where, despite Eliza's wails, the Reverend Jefcoate preached a three-hour sermon, exhorting his congregation to renounce the devil and all his doings. The following day, Bible-reading returned to Kilkenny.

'"For it is written, He shall give his angels charge over thee, to keep thee . . ."'

Between Pearse Byrne and his elder daughter there was now almost no contact. When Pearse wasn't working outside he shut himself up in the room he called his office, emerging only for meals, and the daily round of readings and prayers. But Deidre took comfort from the fact that her father took even less notice of Eliza. 'Can't you do something about that child?' he'd snarl at his wife. 'What's the matter with her?'

'Thank you, Deidre. That was splendidly done. You may sit down.'

It was easy to ignore the looks on her classmates' faces. *Playing dead* still had its uses. What was less easy to ignore was the suspicion, fast becoming a conviction, that Miss Potter was going to have another baby. For weeks now she'd been complaining of being tired. Some nights she'd ask Deidre to rub her back. 'Say this for you,' she'd mutter at such times, 'you have strong hands.' But what Deidre wanted to do was rub out of existence the tell-tale lump under Miss Potter's apron.

While she waited with the other country children for the horse-drawn bus that would carry her to the gates of Kilkenny Deidre thought again about escape, weighing the bitter experiences of the past against the temptations of freedom. She'd meant to run away on her sixth birthday but, thanks to Nellie Drummond, the day had proved unexpectedly happy. Nellie, no longer a schoolgirl, had come to visit Miss Potter, who'd let slip it was 'that brat's birthday'. An argument followed, not all of which Deidre, lurking outside the window, could hear. But the upshot was, Deidre was taken back to Glenory. What followed – a tea that included chocolate cake; a brooch wrapped inside a silk handkerchief, a present from Nellie; a story told by Mr

Drummond, in his lilting voice, that had nothing to do with sin or punishment – left Deidre more puzzled than ever about the ways of humankind. Mr Drummond was a father. Nellie Drummond was a daughter. But between the worlds of Glenory and Kilkenny there stretched a gulf as wide as the sky.

That night Pearse Byrne prayed for peace. Deidre, joining in the Amens, wondered how you could have peace in a house where a baby cried all the time. But her father seemed more concerned with *Great Britain* and *Germany* and the *Empire*.

'I don't like it,' Pearse said, when prayers were over. 'It's not our fight.'

'You mean it's not Ireland's fight,' Jessie Potter sniped.

'You'd know all about that, I suppose.'

'I know a traitor when I see one.'

Deidre, glancing at her father, saw his fist close, and for a long moment thought he was going to bring it down on her head. But it was Jessie Potter he was staring at, not her. When he stopped staring, and turned to his daughter, Deidre obeyed his order to leave with alacrity. She knew that look on his face. 'You defy me again and I'll take the belt to you, so I will,' she heard through the imperfectly closed door.

'You'd strike a pregnant woman?' Jessie mocked.

'You are my wife.'

'You don't need to remind me.'

'What is it with you, Jessie? You're no different from . . .'

There was an odd, gurgling sound that might have been a laugh; then Jessie Potter said, 'Go on, Pearse, say it. Say what you think. I'm no different from *her*.'

The silence that followed seemed to Deidre to stretch like a wire from the lighted room to the dark hall where she stood, shivering. She longed to be in her own room, but her feet were nailed to the ground. 'If only I knew what you wanted,' her father said, so softly Deidre had to strain to catch the words.

She leaned forward, and squinted through the sliver of light. What she saw paralysed her completely. Her father and Miss Potter were kissing.

In bed that night Deidre screwed up her eyes, and prayed with all the force of her being for Miss Potter to have no more babies. 'It's what Father wants too,' she reminded the Almighty. 'You heard him tonight. He wants peace *badly*.' But peace, she learned next day at school, had been banished from the world. 'New Zealand has joined Great Britain in declaring war on Germany,' Mrs Inglis informed the class. 'Let us pray . . .'

In the play ground that day, instead of the usual games of *tiggy touch wood* and *kiss-in-the-ring*, the boys picked up sticks and shot at one another, and the girls tended imaginary wounds. Suddenly Deidre knew what her life would be. She *would* run away from Kilkenny, but for the first time she knew what she would be running *to*. She was going to be a nurse.

On the night of 28 January, 1915, Jessie Potter screamed for five hours. Occasionally there were lulls, when Eliza's screeches made themselves heard. But mostly it was Jessie's terrible voice Deidre tried to drown, covering her head with a pillow, chanting multiplication tables, reciting poetry, listing words beginning with all the letters of the alphabet. When at last the screaming stopped, and the house became a place of whispers, Deidre lay, exhausted, waiting for sleep. Next morning her father told her Miss Potter's baby had died.

For over a year after that Deidre didn't speak a word. At first little notice was taken of the sullen child who sat silently at table, or went about her chores with a blank look on her face. But with the start of the school year the situation could no longer be ignored. Pearse Byrne's response, when forced by outsiders to confront his daughter's dumbness, was to reach for his razor strap. Jessie Potter, too exhausted to muster the energy for action, chose sarcasm as her weapon. The girl was just like her mother. She would come to a bad end as sure as God made little green apples.

As for the wider community, their responses varied from the sympathetic to the morbidly curious. Florence Inglis blamed the war. 'Takes people all ways,' she confided to her husband. 'But I never expected a child to be so sensitive.'

'Stuff'n nonsense,' Willie replied. 'Child doesn't know war from whisky. How old is she? Six? Seven? If it's her tongue she's lost you'll find the cause at Kilkenny.'

But since the war was a reality, and news of it on everyone's lips, Flo Inglis's theory gained some credence among the citizens of the town. Mothers whose sons had sailed with the First Expeditionary Force were all too willing to consider connections between events otherwise unrelated. Why shouldn't a child be affected by the war? Already there were people saying they knew in advance who would be killed because the names had come to them in dreams. Who was to say Deidre Byrne wasn't having dreams too? After what she'd gone through as a wee tot it would hardly be surprising.

Of such interest was the subject, Willie Inglis decided to raise it in the bar of the New Brunswick. But the one person who might have been able to shed light was curiously unforthcoming. 'Each to his own,' Ab Potter muttered, when Willie asked his opinion. 'I don't interfere.'

'They've gone over to the Baptists,' Bill Cairns put in from behind the bar. 'Funny place for a Holy Roman to end up.'

'Dunnow so much about that,' Willie mused. 'Pearse Byrne was always a kill-joy.'

'Kid don't say nuthin'. That right?' Spotty Malone asked. This was Spotty's last night at the New Brunswick. News was coming in every day now of the fighting at Gallipoli. Spotty, a single man, reckoned it was only a matter of time before conscription was introduced. 'Get in first, that's my motto,' he'd contended, the day he volunteered.

'Not one word,' Willie said, in answer to Spotty's question. 'All my old lady can get out of her is what she writes down.'

Spotty put his empty glass on the bar, and nodded at Bill Cairns. All his drinks were paid for tonight. It was enough to make a man glad there was a war. 'Anyone thought to ask Archie Drummond?' he enquired. The beer was making him feel generous. He'd like to do something to help that poor kid. Wasn't right the way she was treated.

'He don't know nuthin',' Ab muttered into his glass.

'He's a neighbour. The girl goes there. You forget, I've worked for Archie. Ya hear things when ya work for a bloke.'

'Stickin' 'is nose in . . .'

'What's that?'

'Her too. Miss High'n Mighty Nellie. What age is she? Fifteen? Sixteen? 'Bout time she were wed. Ain't natural livin' out there with only 'er father for company.'

'That why you married off your Jessie?' Spotty challenged.
But that was a question Ab would never answer.

On the morning of 12 March, 1916, Deidre's voice returned. The long night just passed had been punctuated by Jessie Potter's screams, but this time Deidre hadn't tried to block them out. I promise, I promise, I promise, she'd vowed, over and over again. Only let this baby live. *Please* let this baby live.

Next morning, when she opened the kitchen door and saw Mrs Robinson sitting with a live baby in her arms, she fainted. When she came to, her father was looking down at her. 'I'm going to be a nurse when I grow up, Father,' she said, lifting her head. 'I'm going to look after sick people.'

'Are ya indeed?' Pearse Byrne replied. And for the rest of her life Deidre was to wonder whether the tears that came into his eyes then were for her, or for the little girl just born.

8 ∫

In Pearse Byrne's diary, discovered after his death in the winter of 1937, almost all the entries for the years 1914–18 concern the progress of the war. On page after page the facts of the Gallipoli campaign, and the bloody encounters of the Western Front are recorded. It's as if, his daughter thinks, turning the pages in her room in the Nurses' Home, nothing else, for those four years, existed for him. Not Jessie Potter, not his children, not even Kilkenny. What *did* he believe in? Was the entry for 24 April, 1916, a clue? 'IRISH REPUBLICAN BROTHERHOOD SEIZE GENERAL POST OFFICE IN DUBLIN.' The words, the only ones written in capitals, stand out starkly. Half a dozen lines later the rebellion has collapsed, and its leaders have been executed. Was that the start of his despair, or were the seeds sown earlier?

28 January, 1915.
Mrs Byrne delivered of a stillborn child, a son.

The word 'son' stops Deidre's breath. Her shoulders slump. She should have obeyed her instincts: left the diary where it was. She should never have *promised* to read it.

She takes off her spectacles and rubs them on the hem of her uniform. So it had been a *boy*. A *son*. A *brother*.

A few moments later Staff Nurse Byrne, in charge of the Isolation Ward at Christchurch Hospital, replaces her spectacles, and resumes her study. She'd not been able to read her father's diary straight through. The fear she'd had of him as a child had turned into fear of his secrets. But she won't flinch now. Amid news of battles and the death of men, she'll find what she's looking for.

> *12 March, 1916.*
> *Mrs Byrne safely delivered of a daughter, Dulcie Isabel.*
> *30 April, 1917.*
> *Mrs Byrne safely delivered of a daughter, Muriel Beth.*

It isn't easy extracting the private record from the public. Jessie Potter, Deidre acknowledges, was right to want the diary burned. She and her children scarcely feature in it.

> *September 22, 1916*
> *Brendan Malone killed in action on the Somme.*
> *February 11, 1917*
> *William Cairns dies of wounds received during the Somme offensive.*
> *June 25, 1917*
> *Edward Erihana killed at Messines.*

Again Deidre is obliged to stop. Bill Cairns, Spotty Malone, Ted Erihana, they were the lucky ones. It's the broken *survivors* she feels for, one in particular . . .

She turns another page, and the diary falls from her hands.

> *November 17, 1918*
> *My son born today. Clarence Abraham. God be thanked!*

Clarrie. My beautiful baby. My love . . .

Deidre throws back her head, the habit of years asserting itself to stem the flow of tears. Nine daughters were born to Pearse and Jessie; nine reasons, in Deidre's mind, never to have children of her own. Two of those babies died: one from scarlet fever; the other from diphtheria. But Deidre can recall no special grief when those tiny coffins were laid in the ground. It was part of the life they led. It was part of Kilkenny. But there'd been only one son, Clarence Abraham. In those three words, *God be thanked*, Pearse Byrne's daughter begins to understand.

'Seamus, my little bu-bu . . .' Deidre is ten years old. She knows she shouldn't touch, but she can't resist. This baby is different.

'You've come back to me,' she whispers, cradling the precious bundle in her arms.

The infant's small fist clasps her finger. Deidre is certain he's smiling. It's as unexpected as snow in summer, this surge of love. She looks across at the bed. Miss Potter's eyes are closed. Spots of moisture glisten on her forehead. 'I'll look after him for you,' Deidre promises. 'You can keep me home as much as you like.'

9

On 2 February, 1920, Deidre starts at the District High School. She's passed her Proficiency Exam with the highest marks ever recorded in the district. The war is over, Kilkenny is prospering, motorised transport has arrived in the town. The only cloud on the horizon is the spread of a virulent form of 'flu already rumoured to have claimed three thousand lives.

Deidre, at twelve, is tall and skinny, with flyaway hair which she wears in two plaits. The only outward sign of the woman she will become is the spectacles she puts on to read. Like all the other female students she is wearing a pleated skirt, matching jacket, white blouse and straw hat. On this hot, dry day, her skin glows with sweat.

The school is on the edge of the town, next to Varcoe's Livery Stables. By the end of 1924, when Deidre matriculates, those stables will have gone. So too will the horse-drawn coaches of Cobb and Co, the offices of the Blue Ribbon Society, and Frederick Cashell's blacksmith's shop. But the Athenaeum will live through another war; as will the brickworks and the Bank of New Zealand.

None of which is of concern to Deidre on that terrifying first day. It's her own future she's preoccupied with, not the town's. To be a nurse she knows she must do well in all subjects. Not since the morning of Dulcie's birth has she spoken of her ambition. But she's made it her business to learn all she can about the world of medicine: a safe, white, sweet-smelling world which she'd live in now, if she could, if Clarrie could live there with her.

Deidre's love for her brother has surprised everyone who

knows her. Since the birth of Clarence another daughter, Lynnea Ann, has been born, but Deidre has shown as little interest in this sister as she has in all the others. Lynnea is a good baby. She almost never cries. But no one can displace Clarence in Deidre's affections. Her greatest joy is to be alone with him, pretending he's *her* baby, and they'll live together forever. She takes him riding; reads him her favourite stories; shows him where her childhood treasure is still safely hidden. What Clarence has learned from all this is that Deidre is there to serve him. He's not a particularly attractive child. His hair sticks out in gingery tufts, and his face, thanks largely to Deidre's attentions, is plump and pasty. But he's a good-natured toddler, who knows, at fifteen months, exactly how to get what he wants.

To Deidre's dismay she discovers, on her first day at school, that she's expected to attend a sewing class while the boys study chemistry. Her protest over this lays the foundation for her later reputation as a *difficult* pupil. But Deidre has suffered too long under a despised authority not to know the rules of survival. When her protest gets her sent to the Headmaster she quickly rephrases her initial outburst, claiming to have been upset solely because of her ambition to be a nurse.

'And where did that idea spring from?' Mr Frank Larkworthy wants to know.

'The war,' Deidre answers.

'I see.'

'I can make people better. I know I can.'

Mr Larkworthy is holding a cane in his hand. He taps it on the edge of the desk. Deidre decides to concentrate on the picture of the King, hanging above his head. That way she won't have to wonder if he intends to use the cane on *her*. 'Attention, punctuality, courtesy, obedience. Those are the rules of this school, Deidre. Obey them, and you may well achieve your ambition.'

'Yes, Mr Larkworthy.'

'But I suspect you'll end up getting married.'

'No!'

'There are those who believe education is wasted on women. I'm not of their number, but I have to say . . .'

'I'm never getting married. *Never*.'

'You sound very sure.'

'I'm going to be a nurse.'

To her surprise Mr Larkworthy smiles. 'Then you'd better get back to class,' he says.

24 April, 1920
   Prince of Wales arrives in New Zealand.
2 May, 1920
   Prince of Wales thanks the New Zealand people for their sacrifices during the war.
30 May, 1920
   Glenory purchased.

The day Nellie Drummond came to say goodbye to Jessie Potter, Deidre was home from school minding the children. 'She's in bed,' Deidre told the woman, for that was what Nellie was now, standing at the door.

'It's not right, Deidre,' Nellie said. 'You've your school work to think of.'

'She's had a miscarriage.'

Nellie's eyebrows shot up. 'So soon?' she exclaimed.

'Shall I come up with you?'

'If your father can afford to buy Glenory he can afford to pay for a maid,' Nellie said. It was the only time Deidre ever heard her bitter.

Later, when she'd got baby Lynnea to sleep, Deidre carried tea and cakes upstairs on a tray. Two-year old Clarence waddled behind her. The two older girls, Dulcie and Muriel, were playing in their room. Though Deidre knew they were safe enough, it didn't stop her listening out for them. She might *wish* them dead sometimes, but she would never say so. Not out loud. God had a nasty habit of answering that kind of prayer. Eliza, to everyone's relief, had started school. In her first report Mrs Inglis referred to her as a *whining child*. Some things didn't change.

'Thank you, Deidre. Just put it down, will you?'

'Stay and have a cup with us,' Miss Drummond urged.

'Deardy, Deardy, Deardy,' Clarence chanted.

'What *has* he got on?' Jessie Potter complained. 'Really, Deidre, how many times do I have to tell you? Those trousers are for best.'

'I thought . . . with Miss Drummond here . . .'

'You make too much fuss of him. No doubt the girls are still in their old tunics.'

'These are delicious, Deidre. Did you make them?'

'Leamingtons. They're easy.'

'Your father will have to have corned beef tonight, Deidre. We finished the mutton last night.'

'I've been hearing great things about you, Deidre,' Nellie Drummond said. 'Mr Hislop tells me you have a real flair for Latin.'

Nellie Drummond and Mr Hislop were to be married in the spring. Deidre didn't like to think about it. Miss Drummond was her friend. And she wouldn't wish marriage on anyone but an enemy.

'I like Algebra better,' Deidre said.

'More!' Clarence shouted from the floor.

'You've been giving him cake!' Jessie Potter accused.

Deidre lifted her brother into her arms. 'Come on, piglet,' she said. 'I'll wash your face.'

'He follows her about like Mary's little lamb,' she heard Jessie say as she went out the door. 'One of these days she'll find him on the school bus. We'll see how she copes then.'

In the last six years a number of improvements had been made to Kilkenny one of which, an upstairs bathroom, enabled Deidre now to overhear the rest of the conversation between Miss Potter and Nellie Drummond. She'd never quite given up her habit of eavesdropping. Now that she was older, and knew it to be wrong, she justified it as a form of insurance. While adults still had power over her life, she owed it to herself to discover their plans. The days when she protested at being kept home from school were long past. Being with Clarence more than compensated for the hours of extra study she had to do to catch up. But she was curious to see if Miss Drummond would bring up this question of a maid. She knew Jessie Potter wanted one. She'd had several arguments with her husband about it. But Pearse Byrne had set his sights on Glenory. Once he had possession of that, he'd told his wife, they could talk about domestic servants.

'Will you live there, Jessie? I hate to think of the house standing empty.'

'What would we do with this place?'

'I don't know, my dear.' Deidre heard the sadness in Miss Drummond's voice, and felt a sudden anger against her father. Why did he have to *own* things? He could have bought the Drummond land and left them the house. Now Mr Drummond was going to live in Dunedin and Nellie, after her marriage, would live in the town.

'Mr Byrne has an idea about using it for shearers.'

'Glenory? But he can't. It's . . . You have the cottage for that. Surely he wouldn't. Not Glenory.'

'He wants to put George McKay in the cottage. George is working for us full-time now.'

'George has a family. The cottage is too small.'

'You know what men are like, Nellie, once they get hold of an idea. If I'd had my way, *Deidre* would be living in it.'

'She'd not be such a help to you down there.'

Jessie Potter laughed. 'Yes, yes, I know. You've always championed her. But you only see her good side. You've no idea what *I* have to put up with.'

Deidre moved Clarence to the other arm, and tip-toed past the open door. She didn't want to hear any more. Clarence looked up at her adoringly. So long as he had her undivided attention he was happy.

'What did the doctor say?' she heard Miss Drummond ask. 'I mean, don't you think, so soon after Lynnea . . .'

Deidre stopped. She couldn't be sure whether the sound Jessie Potter made was a laugh or not. She wasn't a laughing sort of person. In the beginning she'd smiled quite a bit, mostly at Deidre's father, but that, like Pearse Byrne's singing, had stopped long ago. 'Try telling that to Mr Byrne,' she said.

'But surely . . . there are things you can do. You know, Jessie. I don't have to tell *you*. To stop getting pregnant.'

'What would *you* know about such things?' Jessie Potter snapped. 'You're not even married.'

Miss Drummond's reply, much to Deidre's disappointment, was inaudible.

'God put us on this earth to bear children, Nellie,' Jessie Potter insisted. 'It's a sin to thwart His purpose.'

'You talk like a Catholic.'

'If you'd only come with me on Sunday . . .'

'Tickle under *there!*' Clarence piped.

'Clarrie, *don't,*' Deidre hissed.

But it was too late. 'Shut the door will you, Nellie? That wretched girl's eavesdropping again.'

11

The night of Nellie Drummond's visit Pearse Byrne summoned his daughter to his office. Deidre was puzzled, not just by the order, but by the expression on her father's face. He'd been wanting to own Glenory since the war ended. Surely he should be happy? But then she remembered Jessie upstairs in bed. What had Nellie meant when she said there were things you could do to stop having babies? Did her father know?

'Ah, Deidre . . .'

The moment she heard that note in his voice she knew it wasn't babies he had on his mind. Perhaps he was going to pray with her. These days praying was almost the only thing they did together.

'How much do they tell ya at school?' he asked, when she was seated opposite him. 'Do they teach ya about the world? Or is it all Latin and Greek, and the Kings and Queens of England?'

'We're learning about Canada,' Deidre told him.

'Canada . . .'

'I've been asked to give a reading in aid of the hospital,' Deidre blurted out. She hadn't meant to tell him about this yet, but she couldn't help herself. It might be weeks before another opportunity presented itself. 'They want me to do something from *The Letters and Speeches of Oliver Cromwell*,' she explained. 'Can I, Father? For the hospital.'

'Oliver Cromwell . . . Now there's a name.'

'Peter Sing's doing *Pilgrim's Progress*.'

Pearse Byrne sat back in his chair, and closed his eyes. Deidre watched for signs that he was praying. The Reverend Jefcoate believed a person should be 'open to God' at all times. 'Private prayer,' he was forever telling his congregation, 'is every bit as important as what we do here, in church. I know you pray together as families, as brethren in Christ, but remember, God hears your private voice too. Even your most secret thoughts are known to Him.'

While Deidre waited for her father to speak, she examined his face with the curiosity of one whose vision has been long dulled by familiarity. She couldn't remember when she'd last been alone with him. She still, occasionally, helped him on the farm. But her role in the household was domestic now. She was, as people constantly reminded her, almost a *woman*.

When had her father got those flecks of grey in his beard? When had his hair thinned, exposing those patches of mottled skin? She'd got used to the way he walked, throwing his weight on to his heels so that his spine curved back on itself. But now she realised, looking at him, that his posture was a sign he was ageing. He was often in pain from his back. You didn't have to be a nurse to see that. But he never complained. Not like Jessie Potter. He just drove himself, in the saddle and out of it, harder than ever.

'You're fond o' your little brother,' Pearse said.

'Yes.' Should she ask again about the reading? Or should she wait till he'd confided what was on *his* mind? She wanted very badly to do it. It was to be held in the Athenaeum Hall on the first Saturday in August. She was indifferent to any fame it might bring her. It was the hospital she cared about.

'I wanted to call him Patrick,' her father told her.

'Seamus,' Deidre whispered.

'What's that now?'

'Sometimes I call him Seamus. After the baby.' Deidre's heart beat louder than the clock. Not once in eight years had the names of the dead children been spoken. Deidre had long ago forgotten Seamus was *her* name for the baby.

'He was never christened,' her father said softly. 'May the saints preserve him.'

'Where are they buried, Father? No one's ever told me.'

'Buried?'

'The babies. My mother.'

'No business of yours.'

'Are they in the churchyard?'

Pearse Byrne flung his arms across the desk. His daughter flinched; then turned her head, instinctively, towards the door. How could she have asked those questions? She never thought about that time, not if she could help it. She slid forward on her chair, perching, ready for flight. If she stayed, she risked making her father angrier. If she left, she would never get his permission to do the reading.

'Never forget who you are,' Pearse Bryne said suddenly.

'I'm your daughter,' Deidre answered him. 'I'm a New Zealander.'

'You're Irish. You have an Irish name.'

'But you said . . .'

'Great crimes have been committed against the Irish, Deidre. They'll not teach you that at school. Oliver Cromwell . . . Never could abide the thought o' that man. But the English poison is in this country too. In all countries where the Union Jack flies.'

Deidre nodded, though she was far from sure she knew what her father was talking about. The only thing that was clear was that he didn't like Oliver Cromwell.

'You'll not hear about it except as a *lie*,' Pearse Byrne said.

'Hear about what, Father?'

'The Black and Tans. The *reprisals*.'

Deidre, struggling to make sense of her father's words, found herself remembering the priest with the bad breath, and the strange words, which she knew now to be Latin, that he'd mumbled over her head. 'We were Catholics once, weren't we, Father?' she hazarded. 'Is that what you're talking about?'

Pearse Byrne turned his remarkable eyes on his daughter. The room was lit by electric light. Thanks to a pioneering hydro scheme on the river, Kilkenny had been one of the first homes in the district to benefit from electricity. But Pearse was not a man to waste resources. His office, and the sitting room (a recent addition) where he sometimes sat with his wife in the evenings, were the only parts of the house not in darkness.

'You tell me,' he challenged. 'Which is the greater fiction? King and Empire? Or the One True Church?'

Deidre, finding answer impossible, turned her head to the window. A morepork cried in the darkness. She registered it with surprise. She'd trained herself long ago to ignore the voices of the night.

'It's not been easy for you, girl. I'm sorry for that.'

'Father?'

'When you have children of your own you'll understand.'

'I don't want children.'

'That's a fine way to talk.'

'I don't.'

'You love your brother, don't you?'

'That's different.'

Again those eyes. Deidre felt the chill of disapproval. But though she could tell a lie when it suited her, she couldn't lie *now*. Not about this.

'I don't want babies,' she persisted. 'I want to be a nurse. That's why I want to do the . . .'

She was stopped by the look on her father's face. When he pushed his chair back, and stood staring coldly down at her, she knew her cause was lost. Anything she asked for now would be denied.

'No daughter of mine is going to spend her life cutting toe-nails,' Pearse Byrne snarled.

'But it's not like that, Father. It's a profession.'

'Obscene! Other people's bodies.'

'I'll be helping them to get better.'

'You've enough o' that to do here.'

Deidre, knowing she should hold her tongue, play the submissive female, stood up. She was tall for her age, though still some inches shorter than her father. 'You can't stop me,' she defied. 'Once I've finished school . . .'

'We'll see about that,' Pearse Byrne interrupted. 'Aye, indeed! Now get along with you. It's past your bedtime.'

It wouldn't have surprised Deidre if, in the weeks following that encounter, her father started referring to her again as a *child of the Devil*. But he was curiously silent in her presence. Occasionally, and always when Miss Potter was in earshot, he would reprimand her. But the repercussions she'd anticipated didn't occur. Not that there was warmth between them. The only warmth shown to Deidre in that house came from Clarence.

It was possible then for Deidre to concentrate on school. To excel at everything except music and sport; to pursue knowledge as the only sure way of escape; to annoy and impress; to greet, early in 1922, the birth of twins, Winifred and Beatrice, with almost complete indifference; to hear her father condemn the rise of the Labour movement and the election of 'Red Feds' to Parliament; to see another Massey Government sworn in, and glean, from the newspapers she had now begun to read, that poverty was on the increase in New Zealand; to pass exams, and go on church picnics, and suffer the agonies of her first school dance. To grow up, in fact.

12 ∫

August 2 1923
My daughter, Lynnea, died this morning.

Deidre was fifteen when they carried her three-year-old sister to the grave. Death had come suddenly, from diphtheria. Now Jessie was fearful the other children would catch it. But Deidre's concern was all for Clarence. He was to start school in a week. Diphtheria wasn't the only danger. Poliomyelitis had been reported in different parts of the country. Deidre had been making it her business to learn about such things. The children must be immunised, she told Jessie. And if poliomyelitis got anywhere near their part of the country, they must be quarantined. But Jessie put her faith in God, and the Reverend Samuel Jefcoate. 'If you're so worried, stay home and help me,' she snapped.

'You've maids to do the work now. You don't need me.'

'Always got an answer, haven't you?'

But as the days passed, and the snow melted from the hills, Deidre's heart too began to melt. Why Lynnea? she asked the God whose existence she was beginning to doubt. She was the nice one. But just in case there *was* a God, and He chose to punish her, she added, Thy will be done.

On Christmas Eve of that year a seventh daughter was born to Pearse and Jessie Byrne. Pearse wanted to call her Lynnea, after the child he'd loved the best. But Jessie, whose word, increasingly, was law at Kilkenny rejected the suggestion as macabre. 'She's to be Amy, after my maternal grandmother,' she said. 'Amy Patricia.'

The sight of her all-powerful father meekly nodding his agreement, filled Deidre with shame. Jessie Byrne, at twenty-eight,
was a woman of substance. Her hips and breasts bore witness
to her many pregnancies. Her still-unlined face had filled out,
emphasising her lower jaw which, in Deidre's mental picture,
was almost always thrust out in irritation. But it wasn't just
physical substance Jessie had acquired. She was a force to be
reckoned with in the community as well. As wife of the owner
of both Kilkenny and Glenory stations, shopkeepers deferred
to her as of right. At Dwyer's General Store her order was
always attended to first. Especially since Pearse Byrne had
had a telephone installed, and the maid could ring the order
through.

'I've spoken to Madge Jefcoate,' Jessie informed her husband,
when she was well enough to come downstairs again. 'Amy will
be christened the second Sunday in the New Year. I've asked
the Mothers' Guild to do the tea. I'm too tired to think about
it myself.'

Deidre shifted restlessly in her chair. In nine days' time she
would be sixteen. Old enough, her father had decided, to sit
with him and his wife of an evening. Most nights Deidre
pleaded homework, and escaped to her room. But this was
the long summer holiday. She could hardly claim pressure of
work five days after Christmas.

'Deidre, I'll need you to run some errands for me in the town
. . . Deidre! Are you listening?'

'Yes, Mother.'

Deidre lifted her eyes to the clock on the mantelpiece. Ten
more minutes and she could excuse herself.

'You can take the older girls with you. Get them out from
under my feet. And there's no need to look like that, young
lady!'

Deidre corrected her expression. There was never any point
in offending Jessie Potter. She'd learned that lesson years ago.

'Now, what I want you to do . . .'

If only, Deidre thought, I could control my *mind* as easily as I
can my body. These last few months her thoughts had developed
a life of their own. She wondered if it could be the fault of the
weather. A warm wet spring had left the hills coloured with

foxgloves and dog daisies and swathes of gorse and broom. Even in Parnell Gully there were patches of green where grass had seeded for the first time. Pearse Byrne, who prided himself on the successful eradication, elsewhere on his land, of gorse and scabweed, had observed the new growth with amazement. 'Devil take me!' he'd exclaimed, forgetting himself sufficiently in front of his daughter to swear in the old way. 'We'll make a garden of this desert yet.'

But of course it wasn't the weather. How could it be? The coming of spring was nothing special. To Deidre it had always meant more and harder work: the frenzy of planting; the race to protect the lambs from late snowfalls; Jessie Potter's manic spring-cleaning. So how was she to account for this sense she had of something stirring inside her? This feeling that she too, like the land, was waking from a long sleep? Riding to school on the bus she'd press her nose to the window and observe, with mounting excitement, the newly planted orchards that had transformed a wilderness into a food bowl. Peaches, apricots, plums grew where once Archie Drummond had struggled to harvest oats. Sheep grazed where men had drilled and dredged for gold. The river she still saw as a place to be avoided, but at least she could acknowledge its part in the emergent beauty of the land. One day, perhaps, she'd be able to look at its white rapids, its swirling, teal-blue waters, and accept that its power was neither good nor evil, just *there*. But she wasn't ready for that yet.

'Now, you've got all that?'

'Yes, Mother.'

Jessie sighed. 'I don't know, honestly I don't. The way you *are* sometimes . . .'

'I'm the same way I've always been,' Deidre answered.

But she was not the same. Though she would have denied it vehemently, there was a dreaminess about her that hadn't been there before. There was even a hint of beauty. Her teachers had noticed it. So too had her stepmother.

'I do believe your ugly duckling's in love,' Jessie had confided to her husband, in Deidre's hearing. 'I could almost feel . . .' ('Sorry for her,' she'd been going to say. 'I was her age, near enough, when I met *you*.') But though Jessie had long ago stopped deferring to Pearse Byrne she wasn't ready yet to say the things that would finally separate them.

As for the staff of the High School, the feeling among them was that Deidre Byrne's powers of concentration were on the wane. There was, as yet, no falling off in her work, but voices were heard predicting a speedy decline in her fortunes. Others, less resentful of her cleverness, were more compassionate.

'Things all right at home, are they?'

The Headmaster's voice had startled Deidre. He'd come on her, alone in the classroom, the week before break-up. She was writing Latin verses on the blackboard.

'Yes, thank you, Mr Larkworthy.'

It was not a good beginning. The expression on the girl's face, Mr Larkworthy decided, was far from encouraging.

'Mr Hislop tells me you're a great help to him.'

The expression didn't change. But then there was no way Mr Larkworthy could know that Deidre had vowed to talk to no one about her friendship with Mr Hislop, and his wife, Nellie Drummond. It was part of her new, intangible store of treasure. Nellie had two babies now. Like Jessie Potter she'd become a woman of substance. But Nellie's manner towards Deidre was as friendly as it had always been 'If ever you need us, dear,' she'd said, 'you know where we are.'

Mr Larkworthy ventured a few steps closer. 'Where's everyone gone?' he asked.

'Highland Dancing. I've been excused.'

'You don't like dancing?'

'Not that sort.'

'Didn't I see you dancing with Peter Sing? At the School Dance. I did, didn't I?'

Deidre had had to turn to the blackboard to hide her confusion. The very mention of Peter Sing's name was enough to redden her cheeks. He'd come over to her the Monday after the hospital readings and told her the girl who'd replaced her wasn't nearly as good as she would have been. That had been the start of it. Then, at the School Dance, he'd filled in all the blanks on her card, escorting her to supper in full view of staff and pupils. 'I should be called Peter "Neither-one-thing-nor-the-other",' he'd joked, as they'd stumbled round the floor. She'd known at once what he meant. Chinese father, English mother, he was even more of a misfit than she was.

'Tell me,' Mr Larkworthy said. Having made up his mind to get something out of the girl, he thought he knew the way to reach her. 'We haven't talked for a while. You still want to be a nurse?'

'Of course!' Deidre answered indignantly.

It could hardly be described as a satisfactory conversation. Mr Larkworthy returned to his office little the wiser, and Deidre spent the rest of the day in a fury, convinced she'd been an object of ridicule ever since the dance.

'Peter Sing, if you must know, is a very nice person,' she answered the Headmaster, retrospectively. 'He doesn't call me names like most of the other boys in school. Do you know what it's like, Mr Larkworthy, to be called *Brain-Box*, as if there was something wrong with you? Or *Skinny*, because you don't have bosoms like the other girls? Peter Sing calls me by my name.'

What she didn't give voice to were the feelings Peter Sing had roused in her the night of the dance: the way her skin had tingled when his hand settled on her back; the distinctive smell of him which she tried, and failed, to conjure up when he wasn't there; his eyes, dark, crescent-shaped, teasing . . . *Nothing must get in the way of nursing. Nothing and no one.* They were the only words she knew to keep the feelings, and the panic they induced, at bay. But not even that spell worked when faced with the daily reality of Peter, striding across the schoolyard to greet her, enquiring, in his soft voice, whether she'd finished her homework, grinning delightedly when she blushed.

'What did I tell you?' Jessie Potter's laugh jolted Deidre out of her daydream. 'In love, or my name's not Jessie Byrne.'

Deidre sprang to her feet. 'It's nearly nine, Father. If you don't need me for anything . . .'

'Run along, child.'

'*Child?*' Jessie clutched the sides of her head. 'She's not been that for *years*.'

When she was safely in her room, and the door shut tight, Deidre threw herself on the bed, and pounded the pillow with her fists. *In love, or my name's not Jessie Byrne.* How dare she? How *dare* she? Deidre knew what being in love meant. She knew where it led. Never before had she hated Jessie Potter so much. Hated her because she was right: because she could see Deidre falling into the same trap as her, and was glad.

13

The following morning Peter Sing telephoned to ask Deidre to accompany him to the Caledonian Sports on New Year's Day. Deidre's first reaction was surprise. Peter had never shown any interest in competitive games before.

'I don't know,' she hedged. 'I'm not sure if I . . .'

'We could go for a walk,' he said. 'If you're not so set on the games.'

'I'll ask my father,' Deidre shocked herself by saying.

The next twenty-four hours passed in an agony of confusion. Her only hope was that her father would refuse to let her go. But when, egged on by his wife, he gave permission, Deidre felt the trap spring.

She met Peter at the entrance to the Sports Ground. The crowds eddying around them were in festive mood. But the expression on Peter's face was stern.

'I've got the tickets,' he announced, slapping the pocket of his jacket.

Deidre nodded.

'Throwing the hammer,' he informed her, gesturing in the direction of the fence.

'Yes,' Deidre agreed, though the grunts and shouts and sporadic applause reaching her ears could have signified any of a dozen different activities.

'Shall we go then?' Peter said. His meaning was unmistakable. The hand he held out pointed in the direction of the hills.

Deidre signalled her acquiescence. She had no desire to spend the afternoon watching sweaty men in singlets tossing the caber, or hurling themselves, with the aid of a pole, over high jumps.

On the other hand she didn't want to go with Peter Sing either. He'd become a stranger.

They set off briskly in the direction of the town, passing without comment the Celestial Hotel, owned by Peter's father, eventually reaching the river, and the flat known as Maggotty Gully. A warm dry wind blew in their faces. Deidre knew the low, cone-shaped hills lining the riverbank were not hills at all but tailings, formed from the tons of gravel dredged up half a century ago. Just for a moment she wished it were Jimmy Fook standing beside her. He'd have talked to her about these things. He wouldn't have *stared*, as Peter Sing was staring.

'My family weren't miners,' Peter said, as if to reassure her it was the past they'd come here to find, not the future. 'My great-grandfather ran a gambling den.'

Deidre giggled. Gambling, the Reverend Jefcoate never stopped reminding his congregation, was one of the major sins.

'You've heard of Fan Tan?'

Deidre shook her head.

'It was made illegal,' Peter said. 'But that didn't stop my great-grandfather. He introduced dominoes instead.'

'I remember my mother telling me . . .' (My real mother, Deidre added silently. The one I never talk about) '. . . that the Chinese used to send their old people back to China. Did your great-grandfather . . . ?'

Peter grinned. 'Not him. He didn't even want his body sent back. Don't ask me why. P'r'aps he was like me. A square peg in a round hole.'

The conversation made Deidre feel better. When Peter took her hand, she smiled. They were the same height so their eyes were level. 'I've never kissed a girl before,' Peter admitted.

'Me neither. I mean . . .'

Suddenly Peter grabbed her arms, and pushed his lips hard against hers. The action was so precipitate, Deidre almost lost her footing. So this is what it's like, she thought. Well, well . . .

The kiss went on for several seconds. When it stopped, Deidre took a gulp of air, shook her head, and dragged her sleeve across her mouth. Only then did she register Peter. He was scuffing his shoes through the gravel, as if searching for something. When he glanced up she saw that his normally smooth skin had gone blotchy.

'Sorry,' he muttered.

'S'all right.'

'Can I . . . ?'

Deidre touched her throat, conscious of the saliva trapped at the back of her mouth. He wanted to kiss her again, didn't he? He wanted to mingle his spit with hers. 'I ought to get back,' she said.

'Right.'

'Someone might . . .'

He laughed; then, as if regretting his levity, translated the sound into a cough. 'No one here but ghosts,' he reminded her.

They walked back to the town in silence.

I like him . . . I hate him . . . I wish I'd never set eyes on him, Deidre anguished on the drive back to Kilkenny.

'Cat got your tongue?' Jessie Potter taunted.

Deidre fixed her gaze on the steering wheel, and her stepmother's gloved hands. 'Thought Father was going to fetch me,' she said.

'Your father's got better things to do.'

That night Deidre crept upstairs to Clarence's room. This nightly ritual was another of her secrets. Clarence had his own room now, next to the one shared by Dulcie and Muriel. The diptheria epidemic was over, but poliomyelitis was still a threat, as was scarlet fever. Every day Deidre examined Clarence for signs of incipient illness. Every grumble, every pout, every change in his complexion was subject to her patient scrutiny. But Clarence was a healthy child, freckle-faced and full of himself. Mrs Inglis, at the end of his first term at school, had reported he was lazy. But like everyone else who came into contact with him, she found it impossible to be cross with him for long. 'He's not like you, Deidre,' she'd laughed. 'No ambition at all.'

'I love you,' Deidre whispered, brushing her lips over the plump cheek. 'Love you, and no one else,' she added fiercely.

At the start of the new school year Peter Sing left for Dunedin.

He'd been accepted at the Medical School, one of the first Chinese students to gain admittance. His last words to Deidre were a promise to write. But no letter came.

By the end of that year Jessie Potter had been elected president of the Country Women's Institute, Pearse Byrne had been prevailed on to join the Masonic Lodge, and Deidre was being talked of as the next Dux of the school.

These days, when Jessie Potter went to town, she drove the latest Ford. Sometimes Deidre accompanied her, her presence required to carry parcels or run errands. The embarrassment she felt at these times was heightened by the attention they attracted as they drove down the quiet main street. 'That's Mrs Byrne,' Willie Inglis might inform an enquiring stranger. 'Husband's a good friend of mine.' 'Drinks are on me,' Ab Potter would announce from his vantage point outside the New Brunswick. One of Deidre's errands was to see that Ab had money in his pocket. 'She's a good girl, my Jessie,' Ab would confide, as Deidre handed over the wad of notes. 'Pity ya can't join me, lass. Though things aren't the same with Bill Cairns gone. I had some hopes o' this new bloke, but he's bog Irish. No earthly good at all.'

Deidre had no feelings for the man she'd been told to call Grandpa. He simply didn't figure in her view of the world. She knew how he spent his money, and thought Jessie Potter a fool to support him. But it was no concern of hers.

What did concern her was what was happening in the rest of the country. From the wireless and newspapers, from the faces of those who'd already begun to suffer, Deidre knew something had gone badly wrong with the nation her father once insisted she call her own. Farmers were being forced off the land; factory workers were bring thrown on to the streets. Deidre, who knew her family was wealthy, and unlikely to suffer, studied the photographs of men in shabby suits and hats, queueing for soup, and looked in vain for signs of what her father dismissed as *mollycoddling*. As yet she had no framework for these feelings of outrage, but everything she saw, everything she heard and read, confirmed her suspicion that Pearse Byrne was wrong.

2 April 1925
  Mrs Byrne safely delivered of a daughter, Charlotte Louise.

14

At the ceremony in which Deidre May Byrne was presented with the medal for Dux of the School Mr Larkworthy made special reference to his star pupil's ambition to become a nurse. 'From her very first day at this school,' he told his soberly attired audience, 'I was aware of Deidre's single-mindedness. Her intelligence, her application to work, need no further praise from me. This medal is both proof of those qualities, and their reward. But those of you who know her will testify there's more to Deidre Byrne than academic ability. She is that rare thing, a young woman with a mission. Many of you will have heard of Grace Neill, whose tireless labours in our hospitals and asylums at the turn of the century won for the nursing profession full legal recognition and lasting respect. So it will come as no surprise to be told that Deidre has made it her business to learn all she can about Miss Neill, and the other pioneer women in whose footsteps she will be following. I only hope,' Mr Larkworthy concluded, amid laughter, 'that if I ever have the misfortune to land in hospital, Nurse Byrne will be there to take care of me. And now' – the Headmaster turned to the blushing young woman on his left – 'Deidre May Byrne, I have great pleasure in presenting you with your medal as Dux of this School. May God watch over you, and bring you good fortune.'

In Pearse Byrne's diary the year 1925 opens with a one-line account of the new binder-harvester which he introduced to the district in January. The rest of the year is taken up with politics – the death of Massey; the election of Gordon Coates as leader of the Reform Party – and the falling price of wool.

The only personal entry concerns the birth of Charlotte Louise, the baby who would be dead before the year was out of scarlet fever. Deidre's triumph (which was also the school's since, in the wake of Deidre's success, it was upgraded to a Grammar School) is unrecorded.

'You needn't think this makes any difference,' Jessie Potter sniffed. 'I need you at home.'

'I'll be eighteen in January,' Deidre protested. 'I can't stay home all my life.'

'You'll find yourself a husband, that's what you'll do, girl,' Pearse Byrne muttered.

They were driving past the gates of Glenory. Deidre could see, through the darkness, the lights of the house which she continued to associate, all these years later, with a rare domestic happiness. The family who lived there now were called Brannigan. They were tenants of her father's. These days Glenory produced fruit and fat lambs, helping to make Pearse Byrne one of the richest runholders in New Zealand. Kilkenny, long renowned for the quality of its wool, had become even more famous in recent years for its stallions and brood mares. When school work and Jessie Potter allowed, Deidre still took pleasure watching her father put a two year old through its paces. 'A horse is never vicious by nature,' he'd told her. 'But if badly treated, he'll retaliate.'

The car bumped over the cattle stop Pearse had recently had installed at Kilkenny. Deidre, watching the headlights play over the gabled roof of the house, saw, in sudden, bitter memory, her mother bending over the tub in the yard, heaving sheets through the mangle. Jessie Byrne, whose clothes came from the city, and were made of crepe-de-chine not calico, had a maid to do the washing. Her days in the cottage had left no scars. It was as if the place had never existed. The McKays were living there now. And the pines Pearse had planted on his wife's insistence had grown tall enough to hide it from view. But Deidre knew, though you could *hide* the past, though you could make yourself forget it, you could never *bury* it. Jimmy Fook had taught her that. Every autumn, after ploughing, the evidence was there: bones, bottles, shattered tools, fragments of china, the spokes of an old wheel, *broken dreams* . . .

'I'm going to be a nurse,' Deidre said quietly, when the car came to a halt. 'There's nothing you can do to stop me.'

That night, when Deidre crept up the stairs to say goodnight to Clarence, she heard a groan from Pearse and Jessie's bedroom. It was a sound she'd heard before, late at night, and ignored. But Deidre knew things now. She knew what that sound signified. 'Not another baby, please God, *please*,' she prayed. The last baby had died when only five months old. It meant the youngest child was now two. With three servants to help her, Jessie Potter could hardly justify keeping Deidre at home. But another baby would change all that.

By the end of January Deidre, and everyone else at Kilkenny old enough to understand, knew a child was coming. Jessie Potter was ill. She screamed at the children; ignored her husband; scribbled daily lists of things for Deidre to do.

1. Take twins to Garvie's. Be sure shoes FIT.

2. Take Dulcie to Dr Macandrew. Tell him the tooth will have to be pulled.

3. Take Eliza to Paaskeson's for new school jacket. Tell him to put it on the account . . .

And so the months passed. The baby was due in September. Deidre never prayed for it to die, but if there was a God, and He knew her secret thoughts, He'd know she had no wish to see it *born*.

7 September 1926
Mrs Byrne safely delivered of a daughter, Mathilda Gabrielle.

15 ∫

The day of Mathilda's birth Deidre slipped out of the house and ran through the pine trees to her old hiding place behind the chicken-run. Almost ten years had passed since her last attempt at escape. The birth of Clarence had changed everything for her. She'd still wanted to run away, but only if she could take him with her. Now Clarence was eight. She adored him as much as ever but he, for all her attempts to woo him over the long months since her schooldays ended, was no longer her shadow. The Brannigan boys from Glenory were his preferred companions now.

For days Deidre had been braced for Jessie Potter's screams. When they started, just before breakfast, she took her coat and scarf from the hook in the porch, and walked out the door. She didn't care that it was her job to get the children off to school. She didn't care that the midwife was new to the household – Mrs Robinson having recently, and reluctantly, retired – and might need assistance. She didn't care what her father or Jessie Potter might do to punish her. She was nearly nineteen years old. It could be years before Pearse Byrne gave permission for her to leave Kilkenny. What choice did she have? Sooner or later, with or without her beloved Clarence, she would have to escape.

The chicken-run was derelict, but recognisable still as the secret place of her childhood. The McKays had built a new run closer to the cottage. Peering through the trees Deidre could see the eldest McKay child tossing grain on to the ground. 'Here, chook chook chook,' the girl called. 'Here, chook chook chook.' The hens squawked and flapped. Deidre, watching, was reminded of the day her father put one of her mother's hens on the wood-block, and chopped off its head with an axe. It had run, headless and bloody, straight towards her. 'Make it better, make it better,' she'd screamed. Her father had roared with laughter.

When the squawking died down, and the child began to amble off in the direction of the cottage, Deidre moved out from the trees and stood by the fence that had once separated the run from the rest of the yard. Two of the McKay children had died in the last scarlet fever epidemic. But there were babies a-plenty still. The clothes line was full of little patched shirts and dresses, and sheets that had been turned so many times they looked liked thin paper on which intersecting lines had been drawn. There was almost no contact between the Byrne children and the McKays. Jessie Potter considered the family *unhygienic*. But Deidre liked them. The mother and father, despite their sorrows, were almost always cheerful.

As soon as the door of the cottage had closed, Deidre began to investigate her surroundings. The run wasn't so derelict after all. Apart from the fence, the shelves where the hens had nested were still more or less intact. Some of the wood had been removed, presumably to build the new run, but the skeleton remained. Deidre hooked her fingers through the wire. It had been her job as a child to gather the eggs from the nests. She could feel their warmth in her hands still; smell the straw where the hens had lain. Had she never witnessed that terrible execution she would have been happy for that task to be hers forever.

A slight turn of the head, and the old lavatory, long since converted to a tool shed, came into view. No temptation to explore there. Its smell may have been banished, but the memory hadn't. Closer to the cottage were the cowshed and dairy. Their function too had changed. These days milk was delivered to Kilkenny. But Deidre had only to close her eyes to recall the cool touch of her hand on the separator, and the strong sour smell that clung to her skin long after her chores were finished.

There was no sign of her stash of treasure. A pile of timber marked the place where it had been buried. The only person she'd ever shared that secret with was Clarence, but he'd had better things to occupy him. Perhaps one of the McKay children had discovered her hiding place. The thought pleased her. The treasure had never really been hers anyway. It belonged to the people whose stories had been buried with the flotsam and jetsam of their lives.

When she'd seen enough, Deidre made a cushion of pine needles and sat down under the trees. Jessie Potter's rules were deeply ingrained. 'Don't sit on the ground, you'll get piles.' 'Don't dirty your skirt . . .' The midwife was called Miss Sinclair. She'd trained at the State Maternity Hospital in Christchurch. Had the screams not come Deidre might have stayed to talk to her. But this baby was the cause of her being imprisoned at Kilkenny when she should have been in a Training Hospital herself. She could have accepted it, just, if she were getting a wage. Every penny would have been put aside to pay for the life she'd been dreaming of now for more than a decade. But her father hadn't offered payment, and she hadn't asked. She wasn't even given pocket money. If she wanted anything – a comb, a new blouse, her shoes repaired, a visit to town to see the weekly picture show – she had to *ask*. And Deidre *hated* asking.

It was the middle of the afternoon by the time she returned to the house. The place was quiet. Either Amy and the twins were asleep, or else one of the maids had taken them to meet the older children off the bus. Deidre advanced cautiously. Now that she was back on enemy territory she felt exposed. The courage of her dream had deserted her. But at least the screams had stopped.

To her astonishment no one seemed to have noticed her absence. She met Miss Sinclair on the stairs and was informed, casually, that Mrs Byrne and the baby were sleeping.

'Is it . . . ?' Deidre hesitated. She didn't want to advertise her absence. 'Boy or girl?' she mumbled.

'Why, a little girl, didn't anyone tell you?' Miss Sinclair smiled. 'Pretty as a picture she is too. Don't often see that. Most babies come into the world looking like boiled carrots.'

In the year that followed Mathilda's birth, Deidre returned many times to her hiding place behind the chicken-run. She found she could think better there. And now more than ever she needed to think. Something had happened the day of Mathilda's birth. Before that time her father's indifference to her had been leavened by occasional signs of interest. Now it was as if she didn't exist.

For a while Deidre blamed this worsening of the relationship with her father on the new baby. Mathilda was an enchanting child; sunny-natured and picture-book pretty. Pearse Byrne, like his wife, was delighted with her. But then Deidre realised something else going on. Not just the absorption of doting parents, but a new phase in their struggle for ascendancy. Jessie Potter wanted no more children. Mathilda Gabrielle was to be her last. Not till ten years later, when the diary came into her hands, did Deidre understand the nature of this conflict between her father and step-mother. But she saw enough to realise they were estranged. Even the sharing of meals was a torment to them. As was the daily ritual of prayers and readings, which Deidre had feared as a child, been bored with in adolescence, but now profoundly hated. For the rest of her life she would associate the Bible with black looks and unrelenting silences.

By the end of 1927 husband and wife had stopped talking to one another. Household decisions were made by Jessie alone without reference to Pearse. She drove the car, wrote cheques, issued orders, marched her children to church on Sundays, and had a lock put on her bedroom door. No one commented when Pearse began sleeping in the lumber room downstairs. But what Deidre saw in her father's face filled her with rage and pity. The pale blue eyes had grown cold as the river. Only Clarence brought a smile to his face now; and Tilly, when he was allowed near her.

10 January 1929
Deidre May Byrne turned 21 today.

16

'Ah . . . Deidre.' Pearse Byrne, turning in his chair, smiled at his eldest daughter. Deidre couldn't have been more surprised. Her father seldom smiled these days, and never at her.

She'd asked for this interview to discuss her future. A year had passed since her twenty-first birthday. A year, for Deidre, of agonising indecision. She knew what the world was like. Every day the numbers of unemployed rose. With so many seeking work, her chances of being accepted at a Training School were small. Hospitals were no different from other places of employment. Too many people were chasing too few jobs. And nursing, with its live-in life, and its ten shillings a week remuneration, was as good a job as any.

But Deidre wasn't needed at Kilkenny anymore. There would be no more births. And Clarence, her lovely roly-poly baby, would be starting at the Grammar School in February. These days, if she tried to hug her little brother, he'd push her away. 'Leave me alone,' he'd mutter. 'Don't be a *girl*!'

'Am I disturbing you, Father?'

'Not at all. Come on in. Sit down. A while since we've had a talk, you and I.'

Deidre closed the door. This was where her father spent every evening now, locked away in his office. The sitting room had become his wife's territory, exclusively. No one was allowed in this room without Pearse Byrne's permission. He wouldn't even have it cleaned unless he were present. His authority, overruled elsewhere in the house, had remained absolute here.

'What were you working on?' Deidre asked. She felt tongue-tied. The room was so small, so private, so filled with her father's presence. On the shelves above the desk were books on horse breeding, assorted religious tracts, and pamphlets describing the latest developments in grass seed production. Deidre had heard her father say he wanted to write his own book on the breaking and training of horses. Was that what he did in here each night? The lumber room, where he slept, was next to her room. She'd grown used to the sound of him moving about long after the rest of the house was silent.

Pearse indicated the page of figures in front of him. 'Wages,' he told her. 'Nothin' for you to worry your head about.'

'I *am* interested, Father.'

'Aye.' Pearse raked his fingers through his beard. These days he wore it close-cropped. It was almost completely grey, unlike his hair which had merely faded and thinned. 'The brains o' the family,' he said. 'If only it'd been Clarence now.'

Deidre said nothing. Any denial, any contradiction, might spoil her chances. There was only one reason for this conversation, and that was to get her father's permission, his help if possible, for her to train as a nurse.

'Country's in a bad way,' Pearse said. 'Wages can't be protected forever. The Government should stop blatherin', and stand up to the Arbitration Court.'

'*You're* not in difficulty, are you, Father?'

'I've bin lucky, so I have.'

'The McKays . . .'

Her father must have sensed what she was going to say because he picked up his account book and snapped it shut. 'When prices fall, wages must fall,' he said. 'Individual circumstances are irrelevant.'

The McKays, Deidre decided sadly, must fend for themselves. Other battles were to be fought here tonight.

While she waited for her father's irritation to subside, she watched the play of his fingers on the desk. His hands were covered in callouses. It had been many years since he'd used them to thrash her, but they could still induce fear.

'I was wondering,' she began. 'I'm not really needed here now. I was wondering . . .'

'It's good that you've come,' her father interrupted. 'I've somethin' to give you.' He took a key from his waistcoat pocket, and opened the drawer of his desk. Not even Jessie Potter had a key to that drawer. When she first became aware of its existence she demanded to be given one. Her husband's refusal, Deidre remembered, was for many months a source of grievance. But all that lay in the past. These days Jessie was as indifferent to Pearse Byrne's secrets as she was to the man.

The drawer was only open a moment, but for Deidre it was as if a photograph had been taken, and printed on her mind. Years later, when that drawer was opened again, she knew without looking exactly what she would find there: a bundle of letters tied with a blue ribbon; an exercise book, which she would discover, on closer scrutiny, was a diary; a string of beads, which she would subsequently identify as a rosary; some loose papers; a small, tattered, leather-bound book, familiar to her in that first, brief glimpse, but only recognised later as her father's missal.

When the drawer was closed Pearse placed a small box in her hand, and instructed her to open it. The moment she lifted the lid the cottage, with its coal-black range, and its windows glazed with calico, came flooding back to her. Lying in the box was the ring her mother used to wear in the evenings when her household work was done. It was one of Deidre's earliest memories, watching the light from the lamp play on the coloured stones.

'You should have had it when you were twenty-one,' Pearse said. 'I was meanin' to give it to you . . .'

'I can't wear it.'

'And why not?'

'It's too precious.'

'It belonged to your grandmother. Your maternal grandmother.'

Deidre put the lid back on the box, and closed her hand over it. Was this going to be one of those times when her father told her things? Should she *play dead*, or press on with her petition? She knew nothing about her mother's parents, other than that they were English, and had lived in Christchurch. There'd never been any talk of uncles or aunts. 'Thank you,' she said.

'It's yours now. Do what you like with it.'

Deidre's heart sank. Her father *angry* she could cope with. Her father *indifferent* filled her with despair. 'I'm sorry,' she said, knowing no other way to win him back, falling into the trap – assuming blame for his unhappiness – that her mother had laid for her. 'I'll take great care of it.'

Pearse locked the drawer, and returned the key to his pocket.

'I wanted to talk to you about my future,' Deidre said. The look on her father's face was not encouraging. 'I'm over twenty-one. You can't keep me here against my will.' It was the wrong note to strike, but it was too late to call the words back. 'What I mean is, what I'd like, is to leave with your blessing.'

There was no reaction. Pearse, as was his habit these days, stared at a fixed point of his own.

'I mean to train as a nurse,' Deidre said. 'I don't know how. I've no money, as you know . . . It's a three-year course. I've found out all about it. Christchurch would seem to be the best place. ('My heroines were there,' she'd have said, if she'd been honest. 'Grace Neill, Miss Maude.') 'If you were to help me,' she ventured instead, 'I'd repay you. Once I'm earning. But I'm not asking for that. I'm asking for your blessing. Please, Father . . .'

'Is that all?' Pearse said, when she'd run out of words.

Deidre nodded.

'Then I suggest you go to your room and pack.'

'What?'

'You heard me.'

'But I can't go *now*.'

'Why not? Since you're so anxious to be gone.'

'It's . . . it's late. It's . . . I've nowhere . . . I've no money.'

'Ya shoulda thought o' that before.'

'Father . . .'

'Get out!'

Deidre sprang to her feet. As she backed towards the door, her only thought was to escape her father's hand.

'I never want to see your face again,' Pearse Byrne said.

Deidre pulled the door behind her, remembering to close it quietly for fear of waking the children. Her fingers, clutching her face, felt like ice. It was gone nine. She couldn't *walk* to town, not with a suitcase. But it was a fine evening. She could shelter somewhere till morning. With luck a passing motorist, or farm cart taking produce to the market, would pick her up. The train for Dunedin left at midday. How many times, in imagination, had she travelled on it? How many times farewelled her father, or Jessie Potter, on shopping expeditions? Yet not once had she been invited to go herself. She'd never seen the city. Never seen the sea. The farthest she'd travelled from Kilkenny was twenty miles, for a church picnic.

As she folded her few clothes, nesting among the singlets and bloomers, the box with her mother's ring, and the brooch Nellie Drummond had given her for her sixth birthday, Deidre listened, with that sense of awe that comes from knowing it's for the last time, to the crackle of the wireless from the living room. Those evenings when Jessie Potter wasn't at a meeting of the Women's Institute or the Mothers' Guild, she sat turning the knobs on the wireless, searching for the music, or voice, that would bring her peace. Would she mind when she discovered in the morning that her unpaid help had fled? Would she feel anything at all? In her strange, calm state, Deidre found herself smiling at the thought that for once in this house Jessie Potter might be at a loss for words.

When her packing was finished, Deidre turned her attention to the question of money. There was no use pretending she could manage without it. Her father didn't keep cash in the house. That left Jessie Potter. The thought that she would be *stealing* temporarily disturbed her calm. But it wouldn't be stealing, it'd be *borrowing*. She'd leave a note promising to repay as soon as she was able.

It was while she was upstairs searching through her stepmother's handbag that the possibility she might never see Clarence again hit her. The purse fell to the floor, scattering its contents in an arc around her feet. This room was the hub of Jessie Potter's universe. No one entered it unless summoned. With a sickening lurch of her stomach, Deidre acknowledged her own powerlessness. In this house, which had been her home for nearly two decades, she was no better than a thief. She couldn't even lay claim to her only brother.

Scooping up the spilled money, Deidre stumbled out of the room, and made her way blindly towards the stairs. The children were all in bed, but they weren't asleep. She could hear Clarence tapping a message on the wall, and Dulcie, on the other side, giggling. 'Goodbye, my darling,' she whispered, forcing the words past the fire in her throat. 'Goodbye my dearest, my baby, goodbye . . .'

She reached the bottom of the stairs, grabbed her suitcase, and ran out into the night.

Part Two

The view from the drawing room of Cheyney Grange was spectacular. The winter of 1936 had been hard. Stock losses throughout the province were being numbered in the thousands. But a long winter brought one advantage. The mountains, splendidly framed in the Grange's generous bay windows, were still, three weeks before Christmas, shrouded in snow.

Sarah Rose Dutton, sixteen years old, and as restless as the sparrows flitting on the lawn, pressed her nose against the window, and made a face at the young man striding past. Richard Arthur Cecil Dutton, her brother, was eighteen, and in five weeks time he would be sailing for England. Sarah, who adored her handsome brother, was already in mourning for his departure. 'Why can't I go? Why *can't* I?' she'd pouted to her father. Sir Arthur, as he'd been titled these last ten years, seldom denied her anything. So why couldn't she get her own way now?

'All in good time, sweetheart,' he'd comforted.

'If it's boring old school you're worrying about,' she'd persisted, 'I can go over there.'

'And where would you live? Richard will be in college. You couldn't live with him.'

'Boarding school. They have them there, don't they? What would be the difference? I'm at boarding school now.'

'And in the holidays?'

'I'd be with Rich.'

Sir Arthur had patted her behind. 'You think I'm made of money, don't you?' he'd laughed.

'You are,' Sarah had retaliated. 'Everyone says so. You're the richest man in Canterbury. One of them anyway. And *I* think you're *mean.*'

'Wait for me,' she mouthed through the window. She knew where her brother was going. Every morning since his return from school, he'd saddled up his horse and taken off into the hills. He told his father he was checking for ewes. There were still a great many unaccounted for. But Sarah knew what he was really looking for. 'Wait!' she yelled, as her feet hit the gravel.

Richard grinned over his shoulder, and increased the length of his stride.

'Pig!' she grumbled when she'd caught up with him.

'What's the hurry?'

'You tell me.'

'Mother said you were going into the city.'

'Mother *wants* me to go to the city, you mean.'

'And you don't?'

'What's in the city?'

'Shops. Shopping. That's what you girls like, isn't it?'

Sarah gave her brother a shove. 'Not this girl,' she retorted.

The stable, where they were headed, was Georgian in style, with a clock tower at its centre. It stood behind the house, across a paved courtyard. Like her brother, Sarah had been raised on horseback and was as comfortable in the saddle as she was sitting in an armchair. Her present mount, a five-year-old gelding bred at Kilkenny station in Central Otago, had been intended for stock work, but Sarah had fallen in love with him, and persuaded her father to let the horse be hers. She called him Caesar, and for the two years he'd been in her life she'd ridden him every day she was at home. Not even the blistering nor'westers deterred her. Her letters from school were full of instructions as to his feed and exercise. Sarah's mother, who longed to be closer to her impetuous daughter, would scan the rambling paragraphs of dos and don'ts, and shake her head. 'As if we needed to be told,' she'd sigh.

'Same place?' Sarah called out, when she and her brother were mounted.

'Back around midday,' Richard informed the groom, who'd helped them saddle up. 'Follow me!' he shouted to his sister, and took off, dangerously Sarah thought, in view of the loose gravel, and the dogs barking on the ends of their chains, at a fast trot.

Cheyney Grange had been built in the 1870s by Sarah's great-grandfather, the first Richard Arthur Dutton. The house had been completely re-designed since that time, but the pastoral style had been preserved in the long sloping roofs, and the verandahs that so charmed their English visitors. Otherwise the Grange, with its twin turrets, the first things to be seen from the long approach road, could have been a city house. Certainly it had as many comforts. Marble fireplaces adorned all the reception rooms; heavy brocade curtains banished draughts; a chandelier imported from France in 1892 lit the now seldom-used ballroom; a Bechstein grand piano graced the music room, along with the more recently added gramophone; leather-bound books filled the library, Persian rugs lay scattered over polished kauri floors; and servants, no longer wearing uniform, but easily distinguished by their air of preoccupation, bustled from room to room, cleaning and warming and bringing light.

For Sarah and Richard these comforts were part of normal life. Which didn't mean they took them for granted. Their brief, albeit privileged contact with the outside world had taught them to see, with new eyes, the beauties of Cheyney Grange. Not just the house, but the *land*. The majestic rim of mountains; the dark stain of the native beech forest, creeping up the valleys to the snow-line; the brilliance of the gorse in spring; the way the light moved across the tussock, now gold, now pink, now purple. On this bright morning, when their path to the hills took them past paddocks drenched with daffodils (spring was late this year), along the willow-lined shores of a lake, home to dozens of geese and swans and muscovy ducks, through a stand of greening oaks, onto the first of a series of rising plateaux, brother and sister were of like mind. Such wonders were a gift. A gift they accepted with gratitude, but without undue surprise. Gifts of this kind had been coming their way since birth.

'Where are we going?' Sarah yelled, when her brother turned his horse off the track they'd been taking every day for the last week.

Richard waved an impatient hand. The condition on which Sarah was allowed to accompany him was that she didn't ask questions. Didn't talk at all, preferably, though that, Richard privately acknowledged, was too much to ask of a chatter-box like his sister. Still, he had to be allowed to concentrate. The purpose of these daily rides was not frivolous. Not to him. It was as serious as life itself.

The new track led to a plateau, from where they could see, snaking through the valley, the river which gave this bleakly beautiful region its name. Usually at this time of year the river was a trap for sunlight; as clear as the crystal glasses in the cabinets of Cheyney Grange. But today, swollen by the melting snows, frothing foully at the edges, it was the colour of mud.

Above them rose the jagged peaks of Ghost Ridge, last resting place of Paddy O'Connor, who died in 1872 trying to find a pass across the mountains. The story of Paddy's death, and subsequent ghostly wanderings, was first told to Sarah and Richard by Fred Tutengaehe who came to the Grange each spring with the shearing gang. For years after that brother and sister demanded an annual re-telling. Then they decided to take matters into their own hands. Several people had attested to the presence of the ghost. One, an old shepherd, known to everyone as Grey, who'd scoffed at the very idea of ghosts, told Sarah *his* mind had been changed one windy, January night. 'I'd swear on the Holy Bible,' he asserted, 'what I saw were real.'

'If Paddy O'Connor appeared for Grey,' Sarah had argued, 'he'll show for us, sure as eggs!'

But despite hours of patient watching no ghost was sighted. Not even when brother and sister stole out of the house one moonlit evening and rode to their chosen lookout, determined to hide in the tussock till dawn if need be. Paddy O'Connor proved as elusive under the stars as he had in broad daylight. His spirit, the exhausted pair were forced to conclude, was either at rest, or of a mind not to show itself to them.

'This'll do,' Richard announced, when they'd ridden for another twenty minutes.

'Where are we?' Sarah wanted to know.

'Nowhere. Which is exactly where I want to be.'

'Well done, Caesar,' Sarah murmured, burying her head in her horse's mane. 'Good boy.'

'You did bring something to read?'

'It's too cold. Honestly, Richard, how you can . . .'

'Sarah!'

'Sorry.'

'Here . . .' Richard rummaged in his pack, and handed his sister a pencil and pad. 'Now no more talking, all right?'

When she'd seen to her horse, Sarah spread her saddle blanket on the spongey ground, eyeing with distaste the mounds of dirty snow still lurking under the rocky ledges, and settled down to emulate her brother. The trouble was, she was no artist. She couldn't even draw a tree without making it look like something scribbled by an infant. No one knew where this talent of Richard's came from. Their mother claimed to have an aunt in Paris who did something artistic, but as no one had heard from her in more than three decades, the connection was considered tenuous. Sarah had tried to find out more about this aunt. Why had she gone to Paris? How had she got there? Was she married? But all her mother would tell her was that she'd gone on a tour of Europe with her parents before the war, and never come back. 'We assumed some kind of scandal, a married man perhaps. She *disappeared*, if that's the word. My grandparents never spoke of her.'

'But she *was* artistic?'

Sarah remembered her mother's smile at that moment. 'Wistful was the word for it. Margot Dutton, nee Ainsley-Bower, was a wistful personality. It was not a quality Sarah admired. Whenever she thought about her mother, which wasn't often, she felt a vague, guilty irritation. Her mother was 'not strong.' That was her father's description. But Sarah couldn't see there was anything wrong with her, other than this tendency to be wistful.

'Aunt Clara could draw anything,' Sarah was told. 'She drew me.'

'Do you have it? That drawing. I'd love to see it.'

'It's nothing like what Richard does, if that's what you're thinking. Richard . . . *imagines*. Aunt Clara drew what was there. A likeness.'

Which left the mystery of Richard's talent. Sarah was in no doubt it *was* talent, despite the lack of interest shown in him by his teacher at school, an artist himself, with an international reputation as a watercolourist. The intensity with which Richard pursued what their father persisted in calling his 'hobby', worried Sarah at times. She was afraid of losing him to it. But when he talked of what he wanted to do, to transform, no less, the way New Zealanders saw themselves and their country, she was awed. '"Colour is Light, Light is Love, Love is God",' he'd said to her once, quoting an earlier painter whom he admired. 'That says it all, I reckon.'

Sarah glanced at her watch. Only fifteen minutes had gone by. It felt like a hundred! She looked across at her brother, and bit the end of her pencil. 'If I was your wife instead of your sister,' she'd said to him once, 'I'd be jealous.'

'What of?'

'That.' She'd pointed to his sketch pad. 'It's all you ever think about.'

'Rich?' she ventured now.

'Huh huh?'

'Doesn't matter.'

Sarah looked down at the blank page. Nothing to stop her writing a letter. She hadn't answered Prue's last yet. Prue Coleridge was her best friend. She'd already left school, lucky her, and would be coming out next autumn. Another reason, Sarah realised, pushing the pencil backwards and forwards across the page, for seeing the immediate future as *dim*. No Richard, no Prue to natter to at school, cut off from Caesar for weeks on end. The thought of the return to school, the ghastly uniform and even more ghastly food, filled her with despair. It had been tolerable while Richard was around, a boarder himself, at Christ's College. They'd been able to meet on exeat days, and take tea at Ballantyne's. Or go to the pictures at the Majestic. They always preferred each other's company to that of their friends. Though Richard, whose looks Prue had compared to Errol Flynn's, was in great demand among Sarah's schoolmates as a dance partner. 'You don't know your own luck, having a brother like that,' Prue had pouted. But Sarah did know. She knew it now, looking at the slope of his shoulders, and the way his hair fell into his eyes.

'Can I see?' she asked.

There was no answer. 'No artist lets anyone see his initial drafts,' he'd said to her, first time she'd asked that question. 'All this is, is a trigger for memory.' But she'd stolen a look, and had to bite her tongue to stop herself speaking out. The land was there, tangible on the page. She could feel the slipperiness of the water; touch the rock that jutted like some ancient ship's head out of the side of the hill; see, and marvel at, the misty outline of a house, or was it a castle? shimmering in the hollow of the hill. There was no house there in reality of course. This was uninhabited country. But as she'd stared over her brother's shoulder she'd felt a kind of horror at their own occupation of the land. Cheyney Grange had no business existing. No one could own this country. Or tame it. It was God's. It was the Light's. Later she'd dismissed these thoughts as fanciful. The result of too much exposure to scenery. But she'd never quite been able to forget them.

'You know, you'll have to tell the parents sometime,' she said now. 'If it's going to be your life, I mean.'

Her brother looked up. His lips moved slightly as if he were talking to himself. He must have heard her though. The silence round here was like an extra presence. No trees, so no birds. Only the occasional hawk, swooping noislessly on its prey.

'You sure know how to pick your times,' he muttered.

Sarah flashed her most charming smile. This time in five weeks he'd be at sea. He could paint all he liked then. 'I'm right, aren't I?' she persisted.

'Perhaps I'll look up Great Aunt Clara. Join forces with her.'

'You can't. We don't know where she lives.'

'She's got a name, hasn't she? She must live somewhere.'

'She could be dead.'

'God, you're morbid, Sarah. What have you been reading?'

Sarah pulled a face. A devourer of historical fiction, she'd grown used to the jibes of her father and brother, both of whom preferred newspapers to novels.

'I'm doing what they want,' Richard reminded her irritably. 'I'm going to Oxford. Bet I get myself a lower second too, just like the old man. Once that's done I'll be twenty-one. Legally on my own.'

'What about the Grange? Won't you have to . . . ? I mean, it'll be yours, won't it, when Daddy dies?'

'I doubt it'll be anybody's.'

'What?'

It was Richard's turn to pull a face. He loved his sister, but he couldn't stand the way she was always asking questions. 'What do you think of Prue, really and truly, don't you think she's pretty?' 'Why do you want to be an artist, *why*?' 'What's God like, do you reckon? I mean, *God is Love*, what does that *mean*?'

'We've been lucky, our family,' he explained. 'We've clung to our acres when others have had to sell. Father would say it was the result of hard work and business acumen. But he's been lucky, and don't you doubt it. Director of the only mining company not to go bust. Principal shareholder in the Christchurch Coke and Coal Company, which has never stopped making a profit. Cabinet minister when wool prices were at their lowest. Married to money . . .'

Sarah waved a protesting hand. 'You make it sound . . . I don't know . . . sordid,' she complained.

'Money isn't sordid, Sarah. It's real.'

'But you're an artist. You don't want to think about money.'

Richard jammed his pencil into the palm of his hand. He'd wanted to fix a particular image in his mind this morning. To juxtapose the two seasons, winter and spring, in a fusion of snow and yellow gorse. 'Do you imagine,' he said moodily, 'that I'd be sitting here daubing if our father was a plumber, say? Or a tram-driver? Money isn't just real, Sarah. It's necessary.'

His words silenced her. Sarah's life was not so protected that she didn't know, hadn't seen, how things were for the thousands who'd been thrown out of work by what her father called this 'unfortunate recession'. The road home from Christchurch took them past one of the province's relief camps. The sight of men, some of them without coats, hacking away at the riverbank in the pouring rain, filled her with guilt. When she learned what they were paid – seven and six a day – guilt turned to shame. She thought nothing of spending twice that amount in one visit to Ballantyne's. Her father had tried to talk her out of her nonsense. 'If I were as poor as those men,' he told her, 'as you seem to want me to be, there'd be five hundred more people out of work. The staff at the Grange, the miners at Kaikoura, the employees of the Coke and Coal Company . . . Think about it, Sarah. You've got a head on your shoulders.'

'There must be something we can do,' she'd answered help-lessly.

Now her father was talking of the Red Threat, and accusing the present Government of spreading the disease of *socialism*. Sarah, who hated arguments, agreed with her father on one thing – she wouldn't want to have dinner with the little man currently ruling the country either.

'Damn it to hell!' Richard bellowed, tearing off the page, and screwing it into a ball.

'What's wrong?'

'Everything!'

'It's me, isn't it? I'm disturbing you.'

'I can't do it, Sarah. I can't get it.'

'Get what?'

'Landscape. That's all I'm good for. Decoration. Something to hang on your wall to show how rich you are.'

'You don't paint those sort of paintings.'

'How would you know?'

Sarah flinched. She hated it when her brother was like this. She never knew what to say to him. 'It'll be different when you're in England,' she said, though it hurt to admit it. 'You don't know how lucky you are.'

'That's a pipe-dream too. I'll end up doing exactly what the old man wants.'

'But why? You'll have money, won't you? Daddy wouldn't cut you off.'

She couldn't fathom the look he gave her. 'Love doesn't come into it,' he'd told her once, when she questioned him about his feelings for their father. 'Now if you were to ask me if he were my enemy . . .'

'What about you, old thing?' Richard said suddenly. 'What are you going to do with your life?'

'Me?'

'No one else here that I can see.'

Sarah laughed. This was the Richard she understood. The one who spoke fondly, and teased her. 'I'm going to ride Caesar,' she told him. 'Then, when Daddy's come to his senses, I'm going to travel to England and trail round art galleries with you. What do you think about that?'

He didn't answer. She watched him rise, and move towards the horses. As he passed behind her, he ruffled her hair. 'You'll get married, I expect,' he called back to her.

She was about to say, 'Not if I don't want to,' when she felt a sharp pain in her chest, as if she'd been stabbed by a matagouri thorn. By the time she'd caught her breath, Richard was back, leading the horses.

'Might as well head home,' he said.

'It'll be all right, Rich,' she comforted.

'You reckon?'

'You will be an artist.'

'Not on today's showing I won't.'

'I believe in you *absolutely*.'

'Ah, but you're my adoring little sister. You're prejudiced.'

2 ∫

On 9 January, 1937, the *Christchurch Press* carried the following report: 'Among the passengers sailing for England yesterday on the *SS Rangitane* was Richard Arthur Cecil Dutton, till last December a pupil at Christ's College. Mr Dutton is the son of Sir Arthur and Lady Dutton of Cheyney Grange, Oxford county, and Rosevilla, Fendalton.

'A large crowd of family and friends gathered to farewell this popular young scion of one of Canterbury's oldest families. A dinner, hosted by Sir Arthur, and attended by among others his brother, Mr Justice Dutton and his family, was held at the United Services Hotel the night before the sailing. It's understood Mr Richard Dutton will be studying law at Balliol College, Oxford . . .'

Sarah cut out the article, and pasted it in the scrapbook she'd vowed to keep till she saw her brother again. Every letter, every snippet of information about the life he'd gone to lead, would be hoarded, for comfort. She'd told no one about her plan. Not even her mother, whose eyes were still red from crying, two days after her son's departure. 'Never mind, Mummy,' Sarah had soothed, coming on her in the rose garden. 'You've still got me.' It was meant as a joke, but like most exchanges between mother and daughter, it backfired. 'I'll stay home from school if you like,' she'd gone on, adding insult to injury. 'If you think you'll be lonely.'

'You'll do nothing of the sort,' her mother had snapped. 'Whatever will you think of next?'

The long summer holiday had always been the happiest part of

109 •

Sarah's year. But with each day taking Richard further away, it was difficult not to feel there would never be a time of unclouded happiness again. Not that there weren't distractions. There was Caesar for a start. A gallop into the hills was a guaranteed cure for the blues. Then there were the picnics and tennis parties and race meetings that constituted the social calendar for this time of year. Usually Sarah attended these functions with her parents, but since Richard's departure her mother had more or less taken to her bed, and her father, claiming pressure of business, spent most of his time in the city. Sarah had never questioned what her father did before. But her brother's words – 'We've been lucky. We've clung to our acres when others have had to sell' – had sown the first seeds of doubt. What if her father were not the good man she'd always believed him to be? What if his wealth was the result of *greed*? His wife's wistfulness the result of *neglect*?

But Sarah couldn't sustain such introspection for long. Cheerfulness, as natural to her as the comfort she was born to, kept breaking out. How could she be miserable with so many nice things to do? She couldn't even claim to be lonely. Most days the Linwood twins, Desmond and Daisy, who lived a mere twenty miles away, came to the Grange to play tennis. Sometimes they stayed over, and there was music and dancing and talking late into the night. At Richard's farewell dinner, Sarah had found Daisy in the Ladies' Room, crying her eyes out. She'd thought it faintly ludicrous, in view of the fact that Richard had never shown the slightest interest in her. 'You don't know how I feel,' Daisy had sobbed. 'You don't know anything.' Sarah had puzzled about that, then decided Daisy was just another female with a crush on her brother. Definitely not the sort of person to tell about the scrapbook.

As for Desmond, he was a puzzle of a different sort. He'd been away at university in Dunedin, and had acquired mannerisms which both fascinated and irritated Sarah. He wasn't handsome, but the year away had definitely changed him. Sarah remembered him as a creature of arms and legs, clumsy to the point of embarrassment. Now it was she who felt embarrassed in his presence. Either he ignored her, which made her mad, or she'd catch him staring at her as if she'd just sprouted a set of wings.

Once, on the tennis court, during a game of doubles, they both lunged for the ball, and fell against each other. He was abject in his apologies. 'Sarah! Oh God, I'm sorry, my fault entirely. Are you all right?' He'd wanted to help her from the court. He'd wanted to pick the gravel from her grazed knee. He'd wanted, she realised, blushing deeply at the thought, to *touch* her.

Towards the end of January Prue Coleridge came to stay. It should have been the highpoint of Sarah's holiday. Prue was definitely someone she could show the scrapbook to. Not that there was much in it as yet. The family were still waiting for their first letter. But Prue, who used to want to talk about nothing *but* Richard, had other things on her mind. Other boys, specifically. Each night she'd inveigle Sarah into the music room and play, 'It's Only a Paper Moon', and 'I've Got You Under My Skin' on the gramophone. Between times she'd rabbit on about ball gowns and invitations, and the utter heaven of no more school. By the time she left, Sarah felt Richard had been gone for years.

The last day of January the harvesting gang arrived to bring in the wheat. Next morning Sarah, at a loose end without Prue, watched from the fence as the tractor belched smoke and dust into the air. If Richard had been here she'd be on first name terms with the men by now. They were housed in the cottages behind the wool shed. Some of them she recognised, from past seasons. But there were many new faces, and not a few who'd looked at her from under their hats as if they'd met her before, and disliked her. Richard would have known how to talk to them. He knew how to talk to everybody.

Sarah shaded her eyes, and lifted them to the mountains. The snow on the lower slopes was long gone. Only the peaks still raised white fingers to the sun . . . Less than a week of holidays to go. And not even the Linwood twins to distract her. Desmond had returned to Dunedin to do some work for his professor, and Daisy had gone on a tour of the North Island with her parents.

Sarah had been relieved when Desmond told her he was going. The awkwardness between them hadn't diminished. If anything it had increased. What with Richard's departure, and Daisy's inexplicable tears, and Desmond's odd behaviour, and Prue's apparent migration to another planet, not to mention her father's absences, and her mother practically living in bed, Sarah's world had become inexplicably threatening. She was stranded – that was how it felt – in a no-man's land between old assumptions and terrifying new perceptions.

It was an irritable Sarah who, shortly before midday, got down off the fence, and made her way back to the house. This was the nor'wester season. The headache season, some called it. Sarah's mother, who each year viewed the clouds of dust rising from the river bed with weary loathing, had been finding unexpected solace in the novels her daughter had been bringing her to read.

'Are you asleep?' Sarah whispered, peeping round the door of her mother's room.

'Come in, dear,' Margot Dutton answered.

Sarah pulled up a chair, and sat down close to the bed.

'What have you got for me today?'

'Another Georgette Heyer.'

'Bravo. She's my favourite.'

Sarah smiled. She'd chosen the book specially. A romantic plot, a cast of aristocrats, a guaranteed happy ending. Sarah had never been in any doubt as to what her mother would like.

It was pleasant in this room. It still induced feelings of safety. Sarah liked the soft blue walls, and the view from the chaise longue in the window. There was a room adjoining which was called the dressing room, but in reality it was her father's bedroom. Sarah had never seen her parents in bed together. Until recently she'd assumed all married people slept in separate rooms. It had come as a shock to discover some couples actually shared a bed.

'Walter Scott's *my* favourite,' Sarah said.

'He's a little heavy for me.'

'Do you want me to open the blinds?'

'No, thank you, dear. I prefer the electric.'

Sarah looked at her mother's pale face, and the fan of dappled hair on the pillow. In town her mother wore her hair in two rolls, one at her forehead, the other at the nape of her neck. In town, Sarah always thought her mother beautiful. She wore elegant, calf-length skirts, with jackets and coats to match. For Richard's dinner she'd worn a striped silk evening gown with no back. Even Sarah's father had commented. 'Is that the fashion nowadays?' he'd asked. But Sarah could tell he was pleased.

It was a different story in the country. The only concession Margot Dutton made to fashion at Cheyney Grange was the lounging pyjamas she put on in the evenings. 'I'd stay in them all day if I could,' she'd confessed to her daughter. 'Never set foot outside.'

'I wish . . .' Sarah began.

'Yes, dear?'

It wasn't often she felt close to her mother. Something should be said. Some acknowledgment. 'I do love you, Mummy,' she mumbled.

'Goodness me. Anyone would think I was dying.'

'Don't say that!'

Margot reached out for her daughter's hand, held it for a moment, then let it go. 'I think I might sleep,' she said. 'Would you tell Betty not to bother with luncheon?'

Sarah was tempted, as she tip-toed out of the room, to slam the door behind her. Since she couldn't seem to cheer her mother up, she might as well try and *shock* a reaction out of her. 'What's the matter with her?' she exploded to Caesar, the only creature left now at Cheyney Grange in whom she could confide. 'Doesn't she want me to love her?' She dug in her heels, and spurred Caesar to a gallop. At that moment she could think of nothing to be glad about. Richard was gone. The holidays were almost over. None of the questions she'd been asking herself had answers. 'Nothing will be right till Richard comes back,' Sarah informed Caesar's ears, and was rewarded with a sympathetic whinny.

The day before Sarah was to return to school two letters, post-marked Port Suez, turned up in the weekly mail bag. Sarah could hardly contain her excitement. One of the letters was addressed to her parents; the other was hers.

There was a protocol surrounding the opening of mail at Cheyney Grange that had been practised since Great-Grandfather Dutton's day. The family would wait for the servants to clear away the breakfast; then, still seated at the long mahogany table, they would open their letters and read aloud passages of common interest. Occasionally letters were held back for private perusal. This was considered perfectly natural. The Duttons valued personal privacy. But Sarah knew her parents wouldn't regard a letter from Richard as *private*. Pleased though she'd been to welcome her father back home, and see her mother out of bed for a change, at this moment she wished them both miles away. Already her father was reading aloud the letter addressed to him. How could she explain that she couldn't read hers? 'Anything you write to me will be for my eyes only,' she'd promised her brother.

Richard, it seemed, was having a splendid time. Lots of jolly people on board. A girl he'd taken a shine to. And a chap his own age who was going to England to join the RAF. 'Rather fancy having a shot at flying myself,' he'd written. 'Always wanted to, actually. Ray's promised to see what he can do. Private lessons, that sort of thing. Don't worry, Dad, I'm not going to chuck college. But if there's an aerodrome near Oxford, and Ray's pretty certain there is, then I might as well give it a go . . .'

It was almost an hour before Sarah could get to read her own letter. 'It's only a note,' she'd said, weighing the envelope in her hand, ignoring the pleading in her mother's eyes. 'He probably wants me to send things. You know what he's like.'

'Why don't you open it?'

'Plenty of time. Who's driving me in tomorrow by the way? Not Frank I hope. He'll talk the whole way.'

'I've got a meeting of the Progress League at three,' her father said. 'I can take you.'

'Goody. That'll make it bearable.'

'I wish you wouldn't talk like that,' her mother sighed.

'Like what?'

'As if you had a difficult life.'

When Sarah finally got to her room, she slammed the door shut and threw herself on the bed. 'You try being cooped up in a car with Frank McNichol for three hours, and see how *you* like it,' she challenged her absent mother. But Margot Dutton never bothered herself with the running of the station. Frank McNichol, manager and indispensable right-hand man to Sir Arthur, was of no interest to her.

Sarah tore open the envelope, and fell on her brother's letter. The palms of her hands were sweating. What had he been doing?

Painting the sea? Painting his fellow-passengers? Painting his memories? Her parents knew nothing about him. The real Richard, the one she'd sworn to protect, was in this letter.

'Dear Sis,' it began, 'Expect you've already heard the parents' letter so I'll spare you the boring details. Oh God, I can just see you, stuffing this down your dress, or wherever you females hide incriminating documents. Poor Mother. Her nose'll really be out of joint. Be nice to her, Sis, won't you? I hate having secrets from her actually, but if I told her, she'd feel she'd have to tell Father, and then I'd really be in the cactus . . .

'Sis, you MUST travel. It's IMPERATIVE! You're only half alive till you do. All the things I'd imagined, they're so much MORE, on so much LARGER A SCALE than I could ever have dreamed. The way the light plays on the sea. The thousand and one changes of mood. The extraordinary, unbelievable love affair between water and light. God, Sarah, I'd got it all wrong before. The LAND defeated me. But now, every day, it's as if scales have fallen from my eyes . . .'

There was more like this, lots more, words treasured by Sarah because she knew he shared them with no one else. Then he wrote, 'Suez, where I am now, has taken possession of my senses. I can't think. Can't begin to find words. Can you paint SMELL, I wonder? There's the most seductive smell in the evenings here. Oleander or jasmine or something. By day it's a mixture of spice and filth (Oh God, the FILTH!) and sweat (mine included!!) and dust . . . My eyes hurt. There's the glare from the sand for a start. But mostly it's the shock of everything. Imagine if Paddy O'Connor's ghost materialised at this very moment in front of you. Well, that's how I feel every minute in this place . . .'

Sarah's hand shook as she put the letter back in its envelope. 'I dread and look forward to and hope for and fear everything that lies ahead,' Richard had written at the end. They were just words, but they brought back that same sharp pain she'd first experienced talking with him in the mountains. Was it fear for him, or for herself, she was feeling? Or were the two fears indistinguishable?

That night Sarah cried into her pillow, and cursed the long year (minimum) she knew she would have to wait before daring to raise the subject of England with her father again. She must finish the year at school, matriculate (since that was what her father wanted), be the pretty playful daughter Sir Arthur so dearly loved. He couldn't deny her a second time. He wouldn't dare. She'd be eighteen years old, near enough. This time next year, she promised herself. And promptly fell asleep.

The night of her seventeenth birthday Sarah was woken by a dull pain across her stomach. Her dormitory at Rangi Ruru Girls' School was shared by three other girls, all of whom she liked, but none of whom she'd been tempted to confide in. The pain she still occasionally experienced in her chest was not worth bothering anyone about. It was, she'd decided, like wind, disconcerting, but natural. This pain though was different. It didn't go away for one thing. In fact, as she lay staring at the ceiling, listening to the muted sounds of the city at night, it began to get worse. 'Blastation!' she cursed under her breath. She mustn't be sick now. She couldn't. In three days' time she had weekend leave. In three days' time Prue Coleridge was going to be presented to the Governor General.

Ten minutes later she had a thermometer in her mouth. Vanessa Pitt-Aitken had heard her groan, and gone to fetch Matron. 'I'm all right, honestly. Probably ate too much cake.'

'Hurt?' Matron asked, prodding her stomach.

'A bit . . . Ow!'

'Hmm. Thought so.'

'What is it?'

'Appendix. Grumbling at the moment, but we'll have to keep an eye on you.'

'I won't have to have it out, will I?'

'Too early to tell. Now, drink this, it'll help you to sleep, and we'll see how you are in the morning.'

But by morning Sarah was worse. The pain, which was now acute, had spread to the other side of her abdomen. Matron didn't even bother to examine her. 'Right then, hospital for you,' she announced. Sarah, looking up at her through a fog of pain, groaned in protest. 'We'll ring your parents, don't worry,' Matron said. 'Expect you'll wake up to one or other of them.'

'There's no need,' Sarah insisted. Or thought she did. Since no one answered she couldn't be sure.

'I've always wondered what the inside of an ambulance looked like,' she said, to the men who arrived soon afterwards with a stretcher.

'Well, you'll find out now, won't you?' the younger one grinned.

'Where are you taking me?'

'Christchurch Hospital.'

'They'll soon put the colour back in your cheeks,' his partner encouraged.

The next thing she registered was the face of the nurse lifting her from the stretcher to the bed. 'Who are you?' she enquired groggily. She couldn't think where she was. Was she at sea? Why was everything so white?

'I'm Staff Nurse Byrne,' Deidre answered briskly. 'And you must stop talking now.'

3

For almost a year now Deidre had had her own room in the Nurses' Home, overlooking the river. It was one of the rewards for passing her State Finals. Staff Nurse Byrne, as she was titled, was no longer subject to the Night Nurses' curfew. She could read till dawn if she wanted, or had the energy after a long day on the ward. But the only use Deidre had for personal freedom was to push herself harder. She'd topped her year in both the Junior State exams, and the State Finals. She'd won the coveted Dutton Prize. She was admired, if not loved, by the other nurses. She was trusted by her patients; respected by her superiors. But something was missing. There was a gap in her life which honours and prizes and praise could not seem to fill. 'I do solemnly pledge myself before God and in the presence of this assembly, to pass my life in purity, and practise my profession faithfully,' she'd promised at her graduation. The magic she'd attributed to the words was the same she'd believed in as a child. But it hadn't worked. The restlessness, the sense of incompleteness, persisted.

'When I'm a Sister, then I'll have peace,' she said out loud, watching, with detached interest, a young man in white flannels and straw boater hat row his – sister? girlfriend? – along the leafy Avon. 'My own ward. My own patients to care for.'

It had been a long day. Deidre couldn't remember when she'd last worked the statutory nine hours. There was always a crisis somewhere, demanding extra of the nurses. In Deidre's opinion many of these crises could be blamed directly on the Government. What could you say to a mother who, having failed to take her sick child to a doctor because she had no money to pay the fees, was then forced to watch that child die from peritonitis? It was the accumulation of such miseries that had taken Deidre, during the last election campaign, to Sydenham Park, to listen to the speakers for the Labour Party. The excitement she felt, mingling with the large crowd, watching the red banners flap in the wind, had reminded her, curiously, of the way she used to feel in the company of Peter Sing. She hadn't thought about Peter in years. She'd been far too busy. But she thought of him every time she bicycled to the Park, and caught the infection of hope generated by the promise of Utopia ahead.

Nearly four months had passed since that time. It was too soon to tell whether Michael Joseph Savage, New Zealand's first Labour Prime Minister, would succeed in changing things, permanently, for the better. But he'd honoured his promise to the relief workers; launched a nationwide programme of state house construction; taken the first steps towards the establishment of a national health service. There was so *much* to be done. Children covered with scabies, or suffering from rickets due to Vitamin D deficiency; children who couldn't hear because of curable ear disorders, or couldn't see because their parents couldn't pay for spectacles, were a stain on the nation. Peace of mind – the missing element in her life – would come, Deidre revised, when she no longer had to tell a mother that her child, who should have lived, was dead.

The couple in the dinghy had disappeared. Deidre picked up her spectacles, and rubbed them on the hem of her uniform. Tomorrow was her day off. She didn't look forward to it. She supposed she should go somewhere on her bicycle; get the fresh air she was always urging on her patients. But aimless movement depressed her. If she was travelling, she liked to have a destination.

At the beginning of this month Deidre had learned from Matron's duty roster that she was to be moved from the Children's Ward to Women's Surgical. The change had come as a relief. Sick and dying children triggered too many painful memories. She'd not seen any of her family for almost a year now. Her last contact with Clarence was on a bitter day last May, when she'd gone back to her old school to try and persuade him to stay on and matriculate. It wasn't the first time they'd met there. Where else was she to see him, when her father, true to his word, continued to bar her from Kilkenny? But Pearse Byrne's power didn't extend to the Grammar School. Her friends there – Mr Hislop, Mr Larkworthy – made it their business to keep her informed of the progress, or lack of it, of her siblings. Clarence's sudden decision to leave had come as a bitter blow. It meant the end of her plans for him. It meant the end of their meetings.

'Your older sisters have all matriculated,' she'd reminded him gently. 'Don't you think . . . ?'

But her brother, who'd been dragged from his classroom with obvious reluctance to the Headmaster's office, told her he wanted nothing more to do with school. 'I'm gunna work on the farm,' he said. 'I'm gunna help Father.'

'Is that your idea, or his?'

'Mine.'

'I don't believe you, Clarrie.'

'Yeah, well . . .' She could still see the look in his eyes as he muttered his next words. 'You're the one he hates, not me.'

Women's Surgical was the domain of Sister Marigold Twopenny. Sister Twopenny had served in the Great War, and believed women to be not just the equal of men, but their superior. Traditionally, nurses looked up to doctors. But not Marigold Twopenny. In her presence even consultants, the Gods of the Hospital, quailed.

Deidre's first day on the new ward had fulfilled all her expectations. Sister Twopenny's discipline would not have been out of place in the toughest army platoon. There were no excuses for an overflowed steriliser (a common occurrence); none for sheets not properly mitred, or bed-pans less than mirror-bright. On Sister Twopenny's ward the rules of Hospital Economy were rigorously obeyed. Every bandage, every item of linen, every surgical mask, every tin of Chemico and Clever Mary was accounted for. Rubber gloves were washed and mended till they were nothing but patches. False teeth, removed during operations, were meticulously labelled. Things did not go missing in Women's Surgical. There was a place for everything, and everything was most assuredly in its place.

By the end of her first week Deidre felt she had come home.

It was the most gratifying and surprising of feelings. Nurses and doctors might fear Sister Twopenny, but her patients loved her. It was, Deidre realised, the way she'd always wanted the world, her world, to be.

But Marigold Twopenny was not without fault. As the days went by Deidre began to notice something which, by the end of the third week, she was forced to concede was a flaw. Sister Twopenny admired the rich. Deidre first suspected this weakness the day Mrs James Merivale, wife of the President of the Canterbury Club, was admitted for emergency surgery. It wasn't just the Sister's manner, or the way she hovered over the Junior Nurse making the bed, it was her insistence on preparing the patient for theatre herself. Deidre was horrified. It was the job of the Senior Nurse, not the Sister, to sterilise the skin and paint it with dye. Deidre didn't want to find fault with someone she'd made up her mind to emulate. But when a second 'Mrs Merivale' was admitted, she had to conclude, sadly, that Sister Twopenny was less than perfect. For the rich there was a special manner, a suddenly available supply of flower vases, and a blind eye turned to the striking of the bell at the end of visiting hour.

Only today there'd been another example of this. A pupil from the Rangi Ruru school had been admitted with appendicitis. The surgeon had decided the operation should take place immediately. Deidre, in the absence of the Senior Nurse, who'd been summoned to help with an emergency in another ward, prepared the girl for theatre herself. But that wasn't good enough for Sister Twopenny. 'I'll just take a look,' she'd said, pulling back the sheet to examine Deidre's work. Deidre had had to swallow hard to hold back the words of protest. 'Very good, excellent,' she'd murmured, running her finger along the edge of the sterile guard. 'Thank you, Nurse.'

'You know whose daughter she is, don't you?' Deidre was asked, when they were out of earshot. Her nod, intended to discourage further conversation, was ignored. 'Sir Arthur Dutton's,' she was informed.

Deidre got up to draw the blind, then changed her mind. There was still light over the river; enough to see the gold tips of the poplars, and make out the hunched figures of the men working late on their allotments. There'd been a howl of protest when the

Council decided to allow part of Hagley Park to be used as gardens for the city's poor. Sir Arthur Dutton had been one who'd let his voice be heard. Presumably he regarded the growing of vegetables on Council land as a subversive activity.

Though Deidre would never have admitted it to Sister Two-penny, she knew perfectly well who Sir Arthur Dutton was. Seeing him this afternoon, when he came with his wife to visit his daughter, took her back to her first two years in Christchurch, when she came close to despairing of ever becoming a nurse. Like other daughters of the country, seeking her fortune in the blighted capital of Canterbury, she'd gone to the slums in the south of the city to find board and lodging. She'd been luckier than most. She'd found, in Mrs Flight, a kindly landlady. For a guinea a week, all found, she had a home, till such time as she was accepted at the Nurses' School.

It was Mrs Flight who first alerted Deidre to the existence of Sir Arthur. Every washing day Deidre would watch her landlady examine the sky, not for rain clouds, but for a sign the wind might change. Half a mile from Mrs Flight's cottage, the Christchurch Coke and Coal Company, owned by Sir Arthur, belched smoke and soot into the air. During the nor'wester season it was not uncommon for the women of the neighbourhood to have to do their washing twice. 'All right for some,' Mrs Flight would mutter, as she lugged the wet sheets back inside. 'Sir High 'n 'mighty Dutton! 'E wouldn't know a mangle if 'e fell over one.'

It wasn't long before Deidre was familiar not just with the name, but with the look of the man as well. She'd first caught sight of him the week she started work at the hosiery mill. Mrs Flight, thinking to cheer her at the end of a long day, had come to meet her off the tram. It was, Deidre remembered, a particularly lovely spring evening. The usual fetid smells from open drains and outside lavatories had yielded, temporarily, to the scent of jasmine and wild rose.

'That's 'im!' Mrs Flight had shouted, grabbing Deidre by the arm.

'Who?'

'Sir Arthur Dutton. In that car, see? And that's 'is son sittin' next to 'im.'

Deidre, standing on the edge of the pavement, had watched the shiny black Rover Meteor glide towards her. She hadn't been the only person staring. Cars of any kind were as rare in this part of town as hot running water. But as the object of Deidre's interest drew near, instead of the hawk-like face she'd imagined, she saw a young-looking man, with dark, sleeked-down hair, chatting animatedly to his son.

'Stuck-up pig,' Belle Golightly, a neighbour of Mrs Flight's, yelled from the other side of the street.

At which the car accelerated, and disappeared round the corner.

After that Sir Arthur's name seemed to crop up at regular intervals. Either Deidre would read about him in the papers, or she'd see his car approaching, and stop to gawp. In May 1931, when the Government lowered public service wages by 10%, Sir Arthur was one of the first to follow suit. Only he went even further. He reduced by *17%*.

'If wages have to be lowered to maintain profitability,' he said, in a speech reported in the *Press*, 'then it's my contention, however painful that course of action may be, we, the employers, have no choice . . .'

'Better to cut labour by 10%,' he said, on another occasion, 'than see your business fail, and the entire work force thrown on Relief.'

It was hardly surprising then that Deidre should hold Sir Arthur personally responsible when, at the beginning of December 1931, she lost her job at the hosiery mill. Along with thirty other women she was given a week's pay, and dismissed. Three months passed before she found another job. To pay for her board during that time she had to sell her mother's ring, and Nellie Drummond's brooch. She blamed Sir Arthur for that too. By September 1932, when she received notice of her acceptance, for the following year, at the Nurses' School, Sir Arthur Dutton's name had become synonymous with everything Deidre despised.

'Your daughter'll be right as rain in no time,' Sister Twopenny had informed the anxious parents this afternoon. 'You've had a word with Mr Fitzgerald?'

Deidre hadn't been able to resist, later in the day, an entirely unnecessary examination of Miss Sarah Dutton's bindings. 'No tighter, Nurse, please,' the girl had pleaded.

It was a gratifying moment. Ignoring the girl's discomfort, turning to offer Mrs Parmenter, in the next bed, an extra pill to relieve her pain, Deidre felt she'd scored a political victory.

'Spoiled brat,' she said now, jumping up to pull down the blind. The light was gone. She'd wasted enough time. 'You'll be off with Mummy and Daddy to the country to recuperate, will you?' she challenged her absent patient. 'Tell you what. Why don't you take Mrs Parmenter with you? She's got six children, did you know that? And she's never had a holiday in her life.'

4

'What made you want to be a nurse?' Sarah asks.

'Some of us have to earn a living,' Deidre answers briskly.

'Yes, but why nursing?'

Deidre shakes the thermometer and places it back in the patient's mouth. The girl's temperature is normal. There's no need to check it again. But she prefers to complete this particular examination in silence.

In two hours' time Sarah will be going home. She's made a rapid recovery. Her youth and good health, not to mention the devotion of friends and family, have all combined to restore the bloom to her cheeks. From now till the beginning of next term she'll be convalescing at Cheyney Grange. She can't wait.

'Thank you, Nurse,' she says, when the thermometer is taken out.

Deidre looks at her over the top of her spectacles. 'You better get some rest,' she advises. 'You've a long journey ahead of you.'

Sarah starts to protest. She's not tired, she's too excited, she'd much rather talk. But Nurse Byrne puts a finger to her lips, and moves away.

The gesture, and the smile that accompanies it, confuse Sarah. Where Nurse Byrne's concerned, she's used to sterner treatment. From everyone else on the ward, Sister Twopenny especially, she's had nothing but kindness. But Nurse Byrne has acted from the beginning as if she disliked her. Sarah can't understand it. Mrs Parmenter, who has the bed next to her, has been treated far more gently. She's of the opinion Staff Nurse Byrne's the best there is. 'You can feel it in the hands,' she's confided to Sarah. 'She's a healer. I said to her, Nurse, you're wasted in this hospital. You could join a Mission, and heal people by the thousand.'

'So, you live at Cheyney Grange,' Nurse Byrne remarked, on Sarah's first day out of bed.

Sarah was both pleased and surprised. She'd been trying to engage the nurse in conversation for days. 'It's named after a place in England,' she explained. 'In Dorset. Our family comes from there.'

'Don't you mean your father's family?'

The vehemence of the question startled Sarah. She felt she was being accused of something. 'My mother's family comes from Essex,' she answered. 'There aren't many of them left now.'

'And what are you going to do with your life, Miss Dutton? No, don't tell me. Let me guess. You'll marry the son from the neighbouring estate. The one you told me about yesterday. What was his name again? Linwood?'

Thinking back on it now Sarah realises that was her first mistake. She should never have confided in Nurse Byrne. But she'd not been a patient before. How was she to know she'd feel so powerless? 'I'm going to England,' she informed the nurse. '*That's* what I'm going to do with my life. I'm going to live with my brother.'

'Your brother . . .' Sarah couldn't account for what happened then. It was as if the stiffening had been removed from Nurse Byrne's spine. 'Your brother,' she repeated. 'You're close to him, are you?'

'I love him more than anyone else in the world,' Sarah confirmed.

When the nurse pushed up her spectacles, and rubbed her eyes, it struck Sarah how much prettier she looked without glasses. 'They say there's going to be another war,' she said. 'Perhaps your brother will come home.'

'Why should there be a war?'

'Not that he'd be any safer here.'

'Richard's very brave. He was the leader of the cadet corps at school. If there's a war he'll want to fight.'

It had been the wrong note to strike, Sarah saw that at once. 'You don't know what you're talking about,' Nurse Byrne snapped.

'I didn't mean to boast.'

'You wouldn't know about Spain, would you? It wouldn't be discussed at the Grange. Or at that school they send you to.'

'Of course I know about Spain. As a matter of fact, only the other day my father said . . .'

But that was a wrong note too. The nurse scooped up her tray of instruments, and stared accusingly at her patient. 'At your age, all I dreamed of doing was making people better,' she scolded. 'If I'd been able to start my training when I wanted I'd have gone to Spain myself.'

Was she speaking the truth? Sarah couldn't tell, then or now. Could women have the same dreams as men? If they could, it was no wonder the nurse despised her. *Her* dreams were all of relationships: being with her brother, falling in love, being happy . . .

'But I'll have to wait for the next war,' Nurse Byrne finished. 'As you will, Miss Dutton. Whatever role you decide to play.'

For the rest of that day Sarah's mood swung between indignation – what had she done to make the nurse hate her? – and dissatisfaction – something was wrong, wasn't it? Wrong with her, wrong with her life. But a good night's sleep had restored her spirits. It's a free country, she concluded. We're all entitled to our opinions.

So what is she to make of this morning's volte-face? It doesn't make sense. Does the nurse want to be friends after all? Sarah watches her as she moves up the ward, checking charts, issuing instructions to her junior, soothing and encouraging. Her name, Mrs Parmenter has divulged, is Deidre. Come and talk to me, Deidre, Sarah wills, the old desire for approval taking hold of her again.

Half an hour later her wish is granted. Nurse Byrne walks over to the bed, plumps the pillows, and asks, 'Are you any relation to Bertram Dutton? Bertram Eli. I've been meaning to ask.'

'Not that I know of,' Sarah answers.

'Good,' Deidre says, and grins.

It's an encouraging start. Sarah smiles back 'Who is he?' she asks.

'There's a prize named after him. He fought in the war.'

'The Spanish War?'

'The Great War. Before you were born.'
'I know all about that,' Sarah says. 'An uncle of mine was killed.'

Deidre doesn't answer. Sarah, who's seldom at a loss for words, can think of nothing to say. She looks round the ward, seeking inspiration. But it would be wrong to ask about the other patients, wouldn't it? And what can you say about four white walls and a line of beds?

Fortunately Deidre comes to the rescue. 'You read a lot, don't you?' she observes, fingering Sarah's copy of *Ivanhoe*.

'Would you like it? I've got the complete set at home. It was my grandfather's.'

'I've no time to read.'

The words shock Sarah. Suddenly she is standing on the edge of a chasm; the same chasm that opened up the day the harvesting gang arrived at the Grange. It's as if, she thinks, looking at Nurse Byrne, we speak different languages. She tells herself it isn't her fault, she didn't make the world the way it is, but that doesn't make her feel any safer.

'You should get a job, you know,' Deidre advises. 'It would be a mistake to imagine your life will go on in the old way. Things are changing. This hospital for instance. You've been better cared for here than you would have been in a private hospital. Your parents were right to bring you.'

'I'd like to do something with horses,' Sarah answers.

'You could teach. Have you thought of that? You're intelligent. You express yourself well. You'd make an excellent teacher.'

Sarah knows she should be flattered, but it's irritation she feels. What business is it of anyone else's what she does with her life? 'I can't imagine it somehow,' she protests. 'That's the trouble, isn't it? Until you can imagine something . . .'

'So what *do* you imagine, Sarah? At night, before you go to sleep. Marriage?'

'I see myself with children,' Sarah admits. 'But whenever I try to see their father . . .'

'You don't dream of love then?'

Sarah grins. 'Not with Desmond Linwood anyway.'

Deidre rubs her aching back. The last few days have been frantic. A dozen new cases of tuberculosis, all of them too sick for the sanatorium, have stretched the hospital's resources to breaking point. With more than twenty nurses off sick, several of them with TB themselves, Deidre can't help wondering how much longer it will be before the whole system collapses.

'I must get on,' she sighs.

'You look tired. I'm sorry. I . . . I wish I could help.'

Deidre laughs. Sarah can't decide if it's friendly or not. 'Let me tell you something,' Deidre says. 'This love you dream of, it's a delusion. A dangerous delusion. If you want my advice, you'll have nothing to do with it.'

They're the last words nurse and patient exchange. When Sir Arthur arrives to collect his daughter, Deidre Byrne is nowhere to be seen.

By the end of the day Sarah is back in her room at Cheyney Grange. She's greeted Betty and the other servants, cried into Caesar's mane, and allowed her mother to tuck her up in bed. Sister Twopenny's immaculate white ward is a world away.

When the time comes to return to school, Sarah has all but forgotten Nurse Byrne. Her scrapbook is filling up with letters, and the cuttings and photographs Richard has been sending. One photo, taken by his friend Ray, shows him in flyer's cap and goggles, sitting at the controls of a plane. This is Sarah's favourite. 'Not long now,' she's written, in her most recent letter. 'Less than a year . . .'

5

There's only one way Pearse Byrne knows to rid himself of the black dog, and that's to ride to the top of Fenian Heights. The trouble is, these last few months the dog has been an almost constant companion. Pearse is a busy man. He can't ride off every day on what, in anyone else, he would dismiss as a whim. But inevitably the day comes when he can no longer ignore the monster at his back. That's when he takes to the saddle, spurring his horse on till he reaches the summit, and a view of the land he has so triumphantly mastered.

Today – 3 July, 1937 – it's something of an achievement just to have got here. The winter, which had set in early, has turned unexpectedly mild. Instead of snow there's been rain, day after day of it. The home paddocks have become lakes; the hills spongy traps for man and beast. Pearse has been glad of the new stable block, built last autumn, which has provided shelter for his brood mares, and the three nursing foals born at the end of May. These days he's content to leave the business of farming to his son, concentrating his own energies on the breeding and training of horses. Last August a stallion he'd schooled himself came in first at the Grand National Steeple Chase in Christchurch. It put Kilkenny, already well-known in Otago and Canterbury, on a nation-wide map.

'Race horses!' his wife had screamed, when the result of the Steeple Chase was announced on the wireless. 'You never told me you were breeding race horses.'

'What's it to you? So long as you have your money.'

'Gambling.' Jessie's mouth had twisted in disgust. 'You needn't think you can come to church with *that* on your conscience.'

The following Sunday, when the truck, packed with children, left for town, Pearse was not the driver. The decision was made almost without thought. Clarence would take his place now. The Baptist Church in Caledonian Street, like Father Driscoll's masses, and the Church of the Holy Trinity, was relegated to the past.

'Aye, but it's a grand sight, so it is,' Pearse sighed, as the mist lifted and a watery light illuminated his spread of acres. A bridge had been built close to the old flying fox. Pearse, using his contacts at the Masonic Lodge, had been instrumental in the choice of position. It was a great boon, that bridge. It enabled him to oversee his property on both sides of the Boyne without recourse to the town bridge, thirteen miles downstream. Only this afternoon Clarence had ridden across to rescue the ewes stranded on the former Eichardt lands, a job that would once have taken the whole day. Jessie had tried to stop him going. She always thought she knew best. But Clarence was a good lad. He knew what his father wanted.

Pearse glanced at his watch. It would be dark in an hour. Clarence should be home by now. With more rain threatened it would be foolish to try and move stock so near to nightfall.

The thought of Clarence triggered uncomfortable emotions in Pearse. There was pride – there'd always been that – but there was also regret, and a buried anger which he could neither explain nor dispel. Lately there'd been something else too. He didn't have a word for it, but it affected him like grief. He'd hoped for so much more.

The breakdown of his marriage, a more potent source of rage and regret in the months after Tilly's birth, was a fact of life which, for most of the time, Pearse accepted. Though he could still break out in a sweat, thinking back to the girl he'd made his second wife, how little she'd had, and how much he'd given her. Some days it was enough to see her, en route to town, marching on her well-heeled feet from porch to garage, for him to feel the hot breath of the dog on his shoulder, a murderous dog, tempting him to hideous deeds. Eleven years of celibacy, eleven years of wrestling with continuing desire, was enough to drive any man mad. But then he'd remember the children, Clarence in particular, and the dog would lose its power. Seven daughters and one son. A lot to be thankful for. Though the daughters, all but Tilly, too often seemed to him mere shadows of their mother. Their voices whined; their lips pouted; their eyes lit up only when their mother, to win peace, promised an outing to the pictures.

The other daughter, the lost one, Pearse preferred not to think about. Clarence had told him she was doing well as a nurse; winning prizes and promotions. Pearse had expected no less. But the time had come when he'd had to say to his son, 'I'll thank you not to mention her name again.' Between Pearse Byrne and his eldest daughter there could never be reconciliation.

Pearse shifted the weight to his other foot, and rubbed the sore spot in his back. The ache in his bones was permanent now. He woke with it, rode with it, slept in spite of it. But physical aches were of little account when a man's heart was sore. Jessie's disaffection Pearse could live with. He had to. What was tormenting him today was the thought that he was losing the regard of his son.

When Clarence declared his intention of leaving school and joining him on the farm, Pearse experienced one of the few moments of pure happiness he had known. Not since Jessie Potter agreed to marry him had he felt so hopeful. Between them, he and Clarence would make the name of Kilkenny known throughout New Zealand. There was no Glenory now. All the land had been merged under the one title. Clarence was a diligent worker. Though not quite the sunny-natured lad he'd been, he was far from morose. He'd grown tall, which pleased Pearse, and there was strength in his limbs, if not always in his eyes. What Pearse saw there some days troubled him. Clarence was Jessie's child. How then could he have acquired the *other's* melancholy? He blamed Deidre. She'd all but reared him. Another reason to ban talk of her. The boy should be encouraged to forget.

What Pearse had hoped for, as he and his son toiled together, was the gradual establishing of intimacy. But a year had passed, and if anything father and son had grown further apart. The *look* was still there too: the veiled accusation. It was that look, and Jessie's sneer – 'Why Clarence? Go yourself, if you must' – that had brought him here this afternoon. 'Have you looked at the glass?' Jessie had challenged. 'There's a storm on the way.'

Pearse wiped the sweat from his brow. He mustn't think about it. He'd come here to forget. Though he had to admit, watching the mist swirl above the river, he wished he *had* gone himself.

He was used to the vicissitudes of the weather. He could read the signs. And what he saw now, in mist and gathering cloud, worried him.

'Hey up then, Maeve,' he called. 'Time for us to be going.' The mare looked up from her grazing. 'Ah, but you're a fine figure of a woman,' Pearse murmured, as he heaved himself up into the saddle. Maeve's breeding days were over now, but she'd brought some first-class foals into the world. One of her last, a colt sired by Lord Leinster, he'd sold to Sir Arthur Dutton of Cheyney Grange. It had opened up a whole new market for him, supplying the runholders of Canterbury.

'Home, lass,' Pearse urged. 'Easy does it now.'

The rain started as he reached Parnell Gully. One moment it was dry, the next there was a crack in the sky, and the heavens opened. In the time it took to steady his horse, and glance over his shoulder, the Wicklow Hills had vanished, lost behind a wall of rain.

'Easy, girl, easy,' Pearse soothed.

Within minutes the ground beneath them was a sea of mud. Maeve skidded and stumbled, and snorted her dismay. But there was worse ahead. The mud turned to water, the water grew deeper, and Pearse felt the land slip from under him, as black waves began to break over his boots. Somewhere, in the encircling darkness, the eclipsed sun was sinking over the hills. But the only illumination came from the flashes of lightning splitting the sky.

'Whoa now, Maeve. Whoa now.'

The mare, whinnying in protest, slid to a halt. Pearse quickly dismounted, unbuckled the saddle, and heaved it, with the reins, into the torrent laying waste to his land. 'Off you go now!' he shouted, whacking the mare's flank. She'd have more chance without him on her back. But the more he shouted, the closer Maeve clung to him. 'All right, girl, you win,' he conceded. 'We'll do it together.'

He took hold of her mane, braced his body against the water, and lurched forward. But without light, there was no way of knowing which way forward was.

When they found Pearse Byrne next morning he was considered

lucky to be alive. Somehow he'd made it on to higher ground, and escaped the worst of the flood. The first words he spoke were of his horse. 'Maeve, is she . . . ?'

George McKay shook his head. 'It were a cloud burst, Mr Byrne. It's a miracle you've survived. The river broke its banks.'

No one dared tell him the rest of the night's news. That job was left to his wife.

'He's dead!' Jessie screamed, as they helped her husband through the door. 'Drowned. You sent him to his death.'

Pearse looked at the woman he'd loved, and loathed, registered her frenzied expression, wondered who she could be talking about, realised, cried out, and fell to the floor. As George McKay reported later in the bar of the New Brunswick, it was as if his wife's words had killed him. 'Never seen the like,' he declared. 'I was certain 'e was a goner. A dead faint, the doctor called it. *She* just stood there. Starin' like a mad thing.'

'Where were the kids?' Miki Donovan, the licensee, wanted to know.

'Upstairs, I reckon. Not visible anyways.'

'Just as well Old Ab's gone to his maker,' a voice from the other side of the bar volunteered. 'This'd be a bad day for him. His only grandson.'

'If you coulda seen the look on 'er face,' George said. 'There's been no love lost for years now, everyone knows that, but this was sumthin' else. Ask me, she *wanted* 'im dead.'

6

Jessie Byrne's decision to send a telegram to Deidre, informing her of her brother's death, was an impulsive one. Hysterical with weeping she'd made her way to Clarence's room. No one in the house could comfort her. Not even Tilly.

They'd taken Clarence to the morgue. They wouldn't bring him home, they said. No reason given, but Jessie knew why. Drowning was not a pretty death. Only by the greatest effort of will had she managed not to order the men, dripping water all over her kitchen floor, out of her house. Fools! Liars! Murderers! She'd made them tea; told them her husband was still missing; behaved as was fitting for a woman of her station. But the moment they were gone she ordered Eliza – reduced to silence, for once – upstairs with the other children. The tears began as Tilly was closing the door. She wept quietly at first, but then, as the pain spread, it was as if she too were drowning, with no one to hear her cries.

There was comfort in Clarence's room. It was more than illusion. She could smell it, touch it. He was an untidy lad, despite her nagging. His Sunday suit hung neatly from the rail, but the rest was a jumble of discarded clothes, and pieces of the crystal set he'd been building for the last six months. Since starting work on the farm a change had come over Clarence. He was no longer the cheeky, cheerful schoolboy. He'd spend long hours in this room, fiddling with his crystal set, or copying out maps, a hobby Jessie couldn't understand at all, but which occupied more and more of his time. There were maps, she saw now, charting every stage of Kilkenny's development. The one he'd been working on most recently was inscribed 'Deadman's

Flat'. Jessie held it up to the light, and saw that the river that had claimed the lives of Pearse Byrne's other family was called not by its European name, but by its earlier, Maori title, *Kaiwaka*.

Jessie had quarrelled with her son about this room. The memory of her anger, and his quiet resistance, shamed her now, forcing from her a cry that frightened her listening daughters far more than her earlier wailing. Clarence had wanted her to agree no one should come in here without his permission. He'd wanted his things left undisturbed. 'I'll clean it myself, I know what to do,' he'd assured her. But the thought of the dust that would gather under his bed, the untidied drawers and unwashed shelves, had filled Jessie with horror. The most she would concede was a promise to instruct the maids not to move the things on his desk.

'Forgive me,' she whispered now. 'I'll do what you wanted. It's not too late.'

This room, she resolved, sinking on to his bed, would be his shrine. The windy churchyard belonged to the lesser dead.

She'd been lying on the bed several minutes when she noticed something odd lying among the clutter on the bedside table. It was a letter, in Deidre's handwriting, addressed to Clarence c/o Mr and Mrs Charles Hislop.

It was a few moments before Jessie was able to read it. Her eyes felt as if they'd been scalded. But then the neat lines fell into place, and with them the reality of Deidre's continued existence.

When she'd got to the end she opened the drawer of the table and found, as she'd suspected, a bundle of letters stuffed at the back. For the next half hour Deidre was present in the room, her love for her brother as tangible to Jessie as the paper in her hand. 'I want her here,' she surprised herself by saying, when the last letter had been folded back in its envelope. 'I want her with me.'

The decision was made then. And with it came a bleak sense of satisfaction that the daughter whom her husband hated would stand alongside him as a principal mourner. Let Pearse Byrne see what havoc he'd wreaked. Let him suffer, as the cold of heart deserved to suffer.

CLARENCE DROWNED STOP COME PLEASE STOP JESSIE

But Deidre never received that telegram. The one that was delivered to her at the Nurses' Home read:

YOUR FATHER DEAD BY HIS OWN HAND STOP COME STOP JESSIE

By the time the mislaid telegram turned up, Deidre was on her way.

In Deidre's mind trains had always been associated with escape. To be returning by train to the place from which she had, albeit unwillingly, escaped, she saw as a trick of fate; one of those quirky coincidences which convince some people their lives are part of a Grand Design. Pearse Byrne had driven her from Kilkenny. Now his widow was summoning her back. There *was* a certain symmetry to it, Deidre supposed, but that was no reason to ascribe special meaning. It wasn't as if she hadn't made this journey before. Though then, admittedly, she was headed for the school, not Kilkenny. On those visits she'd thought only of Clarence. She'd not bothered with the twins or Amy and Tilly, all of whom were pupils at the school. 'Best not to risk it,' she'd lied to her brother, when the truth was she had no interest in anyone but him.

Had it not been for Clarence she might have pleaded work today, and stayed away. She had no wish to see Kilkenny again. According to Clarence the only one of her sisters who still asked after her was Tilly. The rest had forgotten her, as she'd forgotten them.

She'd been travelling most of the day. At first her mind had been busy with the horror of her father's death, and the manner of it, which she tried hard not to imagine. But now, soothed by the clackety-clack of the wheels, she felt numb. She would have to change trains at Dunedin. She couldn't afford to fall asleep. But it was sleep she craved . . .

News of her father's death had reached Deidre at the end of a thirteen-hour day. Though she was not yet a Sister, she had a Sister's responsibilities. The high rate of illness among nursing staff had seen Deidre promoted to Nurse-in-Charge of the Isolation Ward, where the tubercular patients were housed. The challenge of nursing the dying had called up new strengths in Deidre. No attention was too trivial, no task too arduous. She simply couldn't accept that none of the patients in her care would recover. Such was her determination to reverse fate, there was even talk of a miracle or two. One man, Phineas O'Reilly, a veteran of the Spanish War, who'd been diagnosed tubercular after a gunshot wound, had begun to show signs of recovery. Staff Nurse Byrne's reputation as a healer, carried beyond the hospital's walls by such as Mrs Parmenter, encouraged talk of miracles. 'I never give up,' she was quoted as saying. 'There's always one more thing you can do.'

As the train crawled round the Otago coast, the thought of Phineas ('Friends call me Finn,' he'd told her, the day he was admitted) acted on Deidre's jangled nerves like a nostrum. She and he were of one mind, politically, but her interest in him was not solely political. Though he talked freely of his experiences in Spain, answering all her questions, educating her in the horrors and complexities of war, she'd never once felt burdened by him. It puzzled her. Usually when people confided in her she would experience a growing feeling of dread, knowing it was only a matter of time before the worm would turn, and she would be seen, not as a confidante, but as a plunderer of secrets. But with Finn it was as if he were telling her someone else's story. Never for a moment did he demand anything of her. On the contrary, he seemed grateful for her interest.

Finn O'Reilly had been wounded in the battle for Malaga. It was, he confessed to Deidre, a double blow: first the wound, then the discovery of his TB. Right up to the moment of embarkation, he'd resisted repatriation. If he was going to die, he reasoned, he might as well be put back in uniform and sent out to fight. 'But you nurses are a stubborn breed,' he'd complained, grinning provocatively at her. 'I could've got round the doctors. They know how a man's mind works. But you try telling a nurse you'd rather die among strangers. Either she doesn't believe you, or she thinks you're some kind of monster.'

'And which are you?' Deidre had wanted to know.

'Neither,' her patient had answered. 'I don't have any family so I might as well have stayed where I was.'

Deidre glanced at her watch. In half an hour the train would reach Dunedin. There was only a handful of people in the carriage, all of them glued to the windows on the seaward side. It is beautiful, Deidre acknowledged, turning to look at the surf crashing on the rocks, but I've no wish to gaze at it. It had been months before she could bring herself to look at even the gentle Avon with any pleasure.

If Finn O'Reilly were sitting opposite her, instead of the woman who'd given up trying to make conversation, and was now feverishly knitting, what would they be doing at this moment? They'd be talking, wouldn't they? She'd have told him where she was going, and why, and he'd have found exactly the right words to comfort her. She'd never wished her father dead, not even when he cast her into exile. He was fifty years old. He should have lived another twenty years. Now there could be no forgiveness, no reconciliation, no healing of wounds.

Deidre had never talked to anyone about the events of her childhood. She'd been tempted on occasion to tell Clarence, but had invariably thought better of it. Jessie Potter had made certain no hint of what had happened was ever breathed in her house. The gossips in the community could prattle all they liked. At Kilkenny, Jessie Potter's word was law.

The click-click of the knitting needles had stopped. The old lady was asleep. Deidre rested her cheek against the window and closed her eyes. Now the person sitting opposite her really was Finn O'Reilly. 'But how well you look,' she exclaimed. His gaunt cheeks had filled out; his papery skin had been touched by a kindly sun; his eyes, once bright with illness, smiled gratefully at the nurse who'd restored him, against all odds, to health. This new Finn had grown a moustache. Deidre, who found this detail troubling, ordered the image changed; till she remembered he'd told her once he'd worn a moustache for years. He'd shaved it off, he'd explained, because of the continual coughing . . .

'The worst thing about war,' Finn once said to her, 'is the licence it gives people to be cruel. I went to Spain because I believed in the essential goodness of man. I left doubting everything except the necessity of opposing tyranny. I knew what needed to be destroyed, you see, but I was no nearer, none of us were, the far more difficult task of construction. It's like your job really. You get rid of a poison, but there's no guarantee good health will follow.'

Finn was someone she could have talked to about her childhood. He was always questioning her about her life outside the hospital. But it was her job to listen, not confide. She was the nurse, after all. 'You still haven't told me about *your* family,' she reminded him, the last time he tried to quiz her.

'Yes I have,' he answered. 'I don't have one.'

'Nonsense! Everyone has a family. They can't all be dead.'

When he laughed, she saw in his eyes the spark that had taken him, at the age of twenty-two, to fight in Spain. 'I'm a bastard,' he informed her. 'Does that shock you?'

'Why should it shock me?'

'The sins of the fathers?'

'If that were true, there'd be no hope for any of us.'

'You don't have a high opinion of men, do you?'

The conversation might have ended there. Deidre didn't care to be teased. But Finn was not like other men. If he teased her, it was because he liked her. 'Do you know anything at all about your parents?' she asked him.

'I have my theories,' he replied. 'I was raised by nuns. It wasn't a bad life. Taught me discipline. There was a priest who used to visit the orphanage. Father Collins. I was his favourite. Well, it was more than that really. He wasn't interested in the other boys. Later on, when I knew a bit more about life, I began to wonder. But of course he'd never admit it. More than his job was worth.'

'Are you telling me the truth?'

'Don't you believe me?'

'A priest . . .'

'Know the breed, do you?'

'I remember one. It was a long time ago. He had bad breath.'

That had made him laugh again. It was a new experience for Deidre. No one had ever considered her witty before. She felt a brief, retrospective gratitude to Father Driscoll, whose existence she'd all but forgotten.

The train dipped into a grassy valley, then, in a flurry of smoke, began climbing again with the gulls. 'What you understand,' Deidre whispered, addressing her secret companion again, 'is the nature of infection. The way the innocent are infected through exposure to malice. The way *I* was infected. The cruelty of the world, which you talk about, Finn, the tyrannies, the dictatorships, they're not aberrations, they're reflections. They reflect the cruelty of the human heart.'

'So where does that leave society?' she heard him challenge. 'You're a socialist. You must believe in some sort of perfectability.'

'I believe in opposition,' she answered him. 'Like you. I'm opposed to men like Sir Arthur Dutton. I want to bring them down.'

'And then?'

'Out of my hands.'

'You're an anarchist.'

'I want the meek to inherit the earth, Finn. I want to bring my mother back to life.'

'You need God for that.'

'I don't believe in God. I believe in revenge.'

A shrill whistle announced the approach of a tunnel. Deidre wound up the window. She shouldn't be thinking about Phineas O'Reilly. There were seventeen more like him in the ward. It was wrong to favour, even in her head, one patient over another. She hoped Nurse Vale, who was filling in for her, was following instructions. What TB patients needed was a cheerful atmosphere. Any fool could empty a sputum mug. So long as no one dies during my absence, she prayed. So long as Finn doesn't die . . .

An hour later Deidre was seated on the branch-line train that would take her to the town, and the last leg of her journey to Kilkenny. Now that she was so close, instead of grief and apprehension she felt, to her amazement, something like hope. Jessie Potter had summoned her. That in itself was a miracle. Finn was a great believer in unplanned miracles. 'They happen even in war,' he'd told her. 'Just when you think the whole world's dark . . .' Clarence would take over Kilkenny now. He would grieve for his father, but he would recover. 'What you feel after a battle,' Finn had confided, 'is this desire for rest, for amnesty. Death is a great leveller. We hated the Nationalists, make no mistake. We were more than prepared to kill them. But death isn't the end, it's the beginning . . .'

Who knows, Deidre mused, as she drifted towards sleep, there might even be a place for *me* at Kilkenny. A welcome, occasional visitor . . .

She woke as the train was pulling into the station.

7

Deidre hadn't expected anyone to meet her. Her telegram to Jessie had insisted she'd find her own way. But there, on the station, wrapped in coats and scarves, were Charles and Nellie Hislop. Tears sprang into Deidre's eyes. She'd not seen Nellie since her last abortive visit to the school. Nellie had comforted her, and got her back on the train, and made her promise to write. But she hadn't written. What could she have said? That Clarence had refused another meeting? That there was no longer any reason for her to visit? She'd told herself it must be difficult for Clarence to get away now that he was working. Pearse Byrne was an exacting master. But it wasn't that, was it? She was an embarrassment to her brother, that was the truth of it. All she had left, to console her, were his letters.

'My dear!' Nellie's arms encircled the exhausted traveller. Deidre's appearance was a shock. Beneath her thick wool coat, there seemed to be no flesh on her at all. And the face, never pretty, – 'striking', Nellie called it – looked so hollowed out, so drained of all but line and shadow, Nellie had to remind herself this was a grieving woman she was holding in her arms. 'Oh, my dear,' she whispered. 'I'm so sorry. So very very sorry.'

'It was good of you to meet me,' Deidre said.

A hand was placed on her shoulder. Deidre looked up at her former teacher. 'Car's outside,' Charles Hislop said.

The town looked smaller than Deidre remembered. And shabbier. The Depression, which Mickey Savage had pledged to end, had struck this farming district, as it had every other in the country. There were electric lights in the town centre now, but they only served to sharpen the aura of decay. The sign for the New Brunswick swung loose on its hinge, its drum-beat against the wall shattering the peace of the all but deserted street. As they drove past, Deidre saw a huddled form in the doorway. As good a place as any, she supposed, to bed down for the night. A few blocks further on the twin lanterns of the Celestial Hotel threw out their familiar orange light. Deidre smiled briefly, imagining four hunched, pig-tailed figures sitting at a table playing Fan Tan.

'Do you ever see . . . ?' she began, then thought better of it. Peter had gone to London to sit his surgery exams. She'd seen his name on a list in one of the medical journals she made it her business to read. He would be *Mr* Sing now.

'You must have known Amelia, Peter's sister,' Nellie said. She'd seen Deidre's head turn, and guessed the direction of her thoughts. 'She matriculated last year. A clever girl, like her brother. Peter's back from England now. You know he's married?'

Nellie glanced at her husband. Deidre, who'd refused to ride in the front, was seated behind them. Charles caught his wife's look, and by the merest flicker of his eyes indicated he understood. They'd anticipated a difficult journey. Deidre, they'd assumed, would be prostrate with grief. Both of them were convinced Clarence was the reason Deidre had never married. Would never marry. All the love she was capable of had been lavished on that one, in their opinion, rather moody young man.

'Married?' Deidre echoed. 'But of course. He'd want that. Did he marry a Chinese girl?'

'English, I believe. He met her over there.'

'English . . .' Deidre sighed. 'How appropriate.'

They drove on in silence.

'You'll notice some changes,' Charles said, as they turned on to the road that would soon be known, officially, as Byrne Avenue. 'Your father was never one to leave things as they were.'

Deidre registered that *was*, and felt a moment of panic. More than seven years had passed since she last drove through the gates of Kilkenny. What was she coming back to? Why had Jessie Potter summoned her? Had Clarence asked for her? Was that the reason? Around her loomed familiar shapes, and some she couldn't identify. There, on her right, were the lights of

Glenory. And that sleeping giant on the horizon, its nose and chin outlined in the swaying headlights, was the start of the Wicklow Hills. Any moment now the bars of the cattle stop would rattle beneath them, and it would be Kilkenny's lights that beckoned.

'How did it happen?' she asked suddenly. 'The telegram said he'd died by his own hand. How? Why? Was it something to do with the storm? I heard about that on the wireless.'

Was it just her impression, or did the car slow down?

'He shot himself,' Charles said. Deidre couldn't see his face, but she saw the turn of his head, and caught the look of horror in Nellie's eyes. 'I'm so dreadfully sorry, Deidre,' he comforted. 'We both are. This is a terrible tragedy for you.'

'I don't understand. I mean, I knew there'd be damage, it said so on the wireless. But he had insurance. He was fanatical about things like that. Why would he kill himself? He was never . . . Not Father . . . The opposite really.'

The car slowed almost to a halt. Nellie turned to look at her. 'Deidre,' she said.

'Worse things had happened to him. Much worse. He and Jessie . . .' Deidre turned away. She couldn't stand the look on Nellie's face. She didn't want people to suffer on her behalf. 'They hated each other, you know,' she said.

'It was nothing to do with Jessie.'

'But there *was* a reason . . .'

'Yes.'

'Then it must be Tilly.' Deidre's mouth went dry. 'Tilly was the one he loved.'

'There were two telegrams,' Nellie said. 'Jessie sent two. The one about your father was the second.'

'And the first?'

The car bumped slowly over the cattle stop. In the spread of light from the house Deidre saw a scene of devastation, which, for a split second, she couldn't explain. Then she remembered. 'It's too early to assess stock losses,' the newsreader had announced. 'But there's been considerable destruction of property along the whole of the Central Valley. So far there's been no report of loss of life.'

'The first?' Deidre prompted.

The shed where the tractor was housed had lost its roof. The garden had become a tip. In place of Jessie's tidy shrubs, and the neat beds of roses and hydrangeas, there were broken pieces of timber, and snapped branches, and shreds of what looked like the remains of a line of washing.

'Clarence,' Nellie whispered. 'He was drowned. The bridge . . .'

The sentence was never finished. Deidre clamped her hand over Nellie's mouth, and let out a scream that caused Charles, a man of normally unflappable temperament, to brake so suddenly the car veered off the drive into a tree. Fortunately no serious damage was done. Charles regained control, and continued on to the house.

8

The funeral of Pearse Byrne and his son was held in the Baptist Church in Caledonian Street on the morning of 7 July, 1937. Only a few among the large congregation remembered the other funeral, a quarter of a century ago, when a mother and her three children were buried behind the church of the Holy Trinity, and an entire community mourned. The Reverend Samuel Jefcoate, long-time incumbent of the Caledonian Street Church, had heard rumours, but thought it inappropriate to refer to an earlier, and possibly greater tragedy. Though he couldn't resist mentioning Mr Byrne's regrettable absence from church in recent months. 'God will not be mocked,' he warned his stunned congregation. ('He's not suggesting, is he,' Nellie whispered to her husband, 'that Clarence's death was a *punishment*?') '"He that is not with me, is against me."'

Everyone present on that melancholy occasion was struck by the change in Deidre Byrne, who had aged, it was agreed, far beyond her years. Those familiar with her history were further struck by the apparent harmony that existed between her and her stepmother.

'God moves in mysterious ways,' the Reverend Jefcoate commented, when Flo Inglis remarked on the situation.

'It's like when two women love the same man,' Flo volunteered. 'Only in death can they be friends.'

But that was not a concept the Reverend Jefcoate was equipped to entertain.

After the service the mourners drove back to Kilkenny, where they were given a funeral tea judged as lavish a meal as any ever served in the district. It wasn't, Nellie confided later to her daughter, only Deidre who had changed. Jessie Byrne was not noted for her generosity. The merchants of the town knew her as a woman with a keen eye for a bargain. Others, with less at stake, called her stingy. Yet here she was, bestowing on her guests a feast that would not have been out of place in the grandest home in the land. Grief became Jessie Byrne. That was Nellie Hislop's conclusion. In her determination to honour her son, she inadvertently did honour to herself.

When the last guest had departed, Deidre and Jessie turned their backs on the mountain of dishes, and walked upstairs to Clarence's bedroom. Eliza would supervise the cleaning up. Though Deidre was still too dazed to absorb the many changes in Jessie's household, she had observed the change in Eliza. There was no way of knowing whether it was the result of shock, or the prospect (she was twenty-four, and engaged to be married) of imminent escape. Whatever the cause, Deidre was grateful for it. She could only be at Kilkenny three days. When she'd asked for compassionate leave she'd thought that quite long enough. Now she longed for those days to be weeks.

'He kept all your letters, did you know?' Jessie said, after they'd sat in silence for a while.

Deidre didn't answer. Had she been able, she'd have thanked Jessie for her words. 'Time heals,' she'd said so many times to the numbed relatives of patients who'd died. She was ashamed now. Time didn't heal. How could it, when the loved person was gone forever? But Jessie's words healed. They told her Clarence had loved her after all. He'd kept her letters. That was proof.

'Do you want them?' Jessie asked.

Deidre shook her head.

'He'll always be here, Deidre, in this room. No one can take that away.'

Deidre reached out for her stepmother's hand. Tomorrow she would be on the train back to Christchurch. There were things to do. Practical things. The only way she could repay Jessie, for those words, for wanting her here, was to make certain her life at Kilkenny would go on as before. 'We should go through Father's papers,' she said.

Just for a moment the old Jessie surfaced. She stuck out her chin; flicked her head impatiently.

'It's important,' Deidre insisted. 'You can't leave everything to the lawyer. Why not do it now, while I'm here to help you?'

Jessie covered her mouth with her hand. 'I've spoken to the bank manager,' she said, stifling a yawn. 'You remember Mr Tedcastle? There's nothing to worry about, he told me. Mr Byrne left his affairs in perfect order.'

'You're in charge now, Mother. Kilkenny's yours. Clarence would want you to make the decisions, not Mr Tedcastle.'

Deidre wasn't sure whether it was the mention of Clarence, or the fact that she'd called Jessie Mother which made the difference. She'd learned to use the word in the past from sheer self-interest, but it had never slipped out naturally before. Whatever the cause, Jessie got to her feet, and allowed her step-daughter to lead her downstairs.

In what excellent order Pearse Byrne *had* left his affairs was obvious the moment Deidre opened the door of his office. His desk had been stripped of everything but a single blank sheet of paper, on which he'd placed a key. Deidre understood at once. That key was to unlock the drawer her father had opened the night he banished her from Kilkenny.

She closed the door quietly, and pulled up a chair for Jessie. It was a measure of Pearse Byrne's power in this room that neither of them had wanted to come here before. Deidre could feel that power still, in the neat shelves of books, in the memory of her father's voice, in the challenge of that key.

'The lawyer has the will,' Jessie reminded her. 'There won't be anything here.'

Deidre picked up the key, and unlocked the drawer. The first thing she saw was her own name, written in capitals on a large envelope. She took up the package, weighed it in her hand, judged it to contain a manuscript of some kind, and placed it to one side. Jessie watched her out of dull eyes. Underneath the envelope was an exercise book with a battered cover and torn edges. Pearse Byrne's name, and the dates 13 August, 1887 – 4 July, 1937 were printed in large capitals at the top.

Deidre's hand shook as she removed the book from the drawer. She'd recognised it the moment she saw it. It was one of the objects she'd glimpsed on that fateful night. She hadn't known what it was then. Now she saw it was a diary. The first entry read:

29 March 1909
After a five-day journey, reached my land at sunset. Pitched tent.

The last, dated 4 July 1937, read,

Clarence drowned last evening. God have mercy on our souls.

'What is it?' Jessie asked.

Deidre put the diary in her hand. 'It's for you,' she said.

For a few moments the only sounds in the room were the ticking of the clock, and the rustle of turning pages. Deidre fixed her eyes on the empty grate. She didn't want to see what was in her step-mother's face. As a child she'd begged her father for stories. But she had no wish to hear his story now. She'd worked too hard at forgetting.

'I don't want this,' Jessie said, snapping the book shut.

'He meant *you* to have it,' Deidre pointed out.

'Get rid of it! Burn it! I don't want it in the house.'

'But why should *I*? He was your . . .' The book was thrust into her hand. Her fingers tightened round the familiar soft cardboard. How often had she written in books like this herself? History, Geography, Spelling, Comprehension . . . Steps on the way . . . 'I can't burn it,' she whispered.

'Then do what you like with it,' Jessie yawned. 'Just so long as I never see it again.'

9

Two weeks after Deidre returned to duty, Phineas O'Reilly suffered a haemorrhage. The suddenness and severity of it shocked Deidre out of the numbed state she'd been in since her departure from Kilkenny. Charge Nurse Byrne knew about grieving. She'd seen too much of it not to recognise the stages. Had it not been for Finn she might have gone on indefinitely, with every sense but that of duty dulled. But Finn was her *special* patient. On him she'd lavished not just her skills, but her faith. His affection for her, and her belief in his recovery, had anchored her to the future. She'd never been foolish enough to imagine there was more to his feelings than gratitude. But her loneliness had been assauged; the gap in her life unexpectedly filled.

'You should take your own advice, you know,' Finn had urged, on her first day back. 'Remember? It helps to talk . . .'

'I'm all right. And so are you, I'm pleased to see. Nurse Vale looked after you, did she?'

'She's not as pretty as you.'

It was the first time anyone had called Deidre pretty. Numbed though she was, she took pleasure from the words, and the smile that accompanied them.

'And you needn't come the older woman with me either,' Finn had gone on to say. 'I don't believe you're older than me at all. I think you just say that to shut me up.'

All the symptoms were there, Deidre realised, looking back: the heightened colour; the flirtatiousness; the bursts of energy. Only *she'd* chosen to see them as omens of health.

'You're all right,' she soothed, when the fit had passed and the doctor had declared Finn out of immediate danger. 'A setback, nothing more.'

He smiled wanly up at her. They were alone in the curtained-off space around his bed. Everyone in the ward had expected him to die. He'd expected it himself. Only Nurse Byrne refused to accept that his death warrant had been signed. 'Do something for me,' he croaked. 'Get a transfer. You don't need this place.'

'And you, young man, need sleep.'

'Please, Nurse . . .'

Deidre picked up the bowl full of his blood, and stepped back from the bed. 'You don't know what you're talking about,' she said briskly.

In the weeks that followed Deidre was to long for a return to those numbed first days. This second stage of grieving was so much worse. For a time she found consolation in the letters she wrote each week to Jessie. But when a month passed with no reply, the old feelings began to re-surface. Jessie Potter had loved her son. For that Deidre had been prepared to forgive much. But she couldn't forget. And neither, it seemed, could Jessie.

Day after day Deidre trudged the path from the Nurses' Home to the Isolation Ward, eyes lowered for fear of Clarence's ghost, whose sudden materialisations had been making a nightmare of her waking hours. Finn had urged her to talk, but how could she burden a dying man? How hide from him her anger that he was leaving her? So acute was her unhappiness during this time she felt sure others must notice. But with the exception of Finn, no one treated her any differently. The truth was, her other patients, and the doctors and nurses she came into contact with, chose to see what they'd always seen: a more than competent nurse, dedicated to her work, bringing hope to a place of hopelessness. Under Deidre's guidance the Isolation Ward had lost its institutional character. Despite initial opposition, she'd won permission for her patients to bring with them some of their personal belongings. Now, in addition to the neat rows of beds and lockers, there were books, wirelesses, pot plants, even a bird in a cage. It was on Finn's wireless that Deidre had heard the report of the cloudburst over the Central Valley. He'd guessed from her reaction that she had family there. But she'd assured him it was nothing to worry about. Such things had happened before.

At the beginning of September a change came over Phineas O'Reilly. It was the reprieve Deidre had been both expecting and dreading. No one talked of miracles any more. Everyone, including Finn himself, knew this reprieve would be his last. But that only made him the more determined to break down the wall Nurse Byrne had erected between them.

'Tell me about your father,' he said, the morning she wheeled him, at his request, on to the verandah. The other nurses often stopped by the open windows for a chat, but not Nurse Byrne. He'd have to think quickly to get her to stop now. 'You've time, haven't you?' he challenged.

The verandah overlooked the park. With its view of the river, and the greening trees, it was a favourite spot of Finn's. Today, as if to herald the thaw he was hoping for in his relationship with Deidre, there was a scattering of gold among the green. By the end of the week the park would be ablaze with daffodils.

'You've been like a ghost since you got back,' he went on. 'What do I have to do to bring out that Irish smile again?'

He sensed her irritation in the sudden, unnecessary braking of the wheelchair. 'You don't want to hear my story,' she snapped. 'It's not in the least enlightening.'

'All stories are enlightening.'

'You say that because you believe in human nature.'

'Don't you?' He looked round at her. Her hands were gripping the back of the chair. The expression on her face was meant to intimidate.

'Stories that confirm the existence of cruelty are best left untold, Finn,' she said.

If he'd had the strength he'd have reached up to her. That clipped way she had of speaking didn't fool him for a moment. But he was short of breath, so he closed his eyes, and waited for the spasm to pass.

Deidre, alert to every change in his condition, responded quickly. She moved to his side, and pulled the rug up over his chest.

'You're an angel, Deidre,' he whispered. 'An Angel of Mercy.'

Deidre sprang back. Not even in her most unguarded moments

had she imagined such words. She hadn't even realised he knew her name.

'Have you any idea what your kindness means in this Valley of the Shadow? How can your story be a cruel one when *you* are so kind?'

He should never have spoken to her like that. She should never have let him. The tears which tipped from her eyes were unprofessional. If she could have managed the words she would have scolded him. 'I'm a nurse,' she would have said. 'It's my job.'

'That's it,' Finn soothed, reaching for her hand. 'There's plenty of time . . .'

That evening, when Deidre got back to her room, she dragged her suitcase from under her bed, and took from it her father's diary, and the package with her name on it. Neither had been touched since her return from Kilkenny. The package contained, as she'd guessed, a manuscript. On the title page were the words, *The Breeding and Training of Horses* by Pearse Byrne. There were no instructions as to what was to be done with it. But Deidre knew what her father would have wanted. The book was to be his memorial.

For some time she sat with the manuscript in her hand, listening to the birds nesting down for the night, registering the approach of spring without interest or emotion. Her father had left this task to her, despite their quarrel, because he knew she wouldn't fail him. Somewhere in that knowledge she sensed comfort, but it was too soon yet to feel it.

The book was competently written. That much she could see at a glance. There on the page were her father's virtues: his devotion to work; his attention to detail; his feeling for animals. There too were his vices: his lack of humour; his self-righteousness. She had no doubt the book would be published. There was no other like it so far as she knew. Besides, the author's name was a familiar one. He was the owner of Cuchulain, the most successful racehorse in the country.

When she'd done with the book she picked up the envelope again, and tipped out the rest of its contents. A bundle of letters tied with blue ribbon, her father's rosary (the existence of which she'd forgotten), and a battered, leather-bound book, with the words *Latin Missal* barely distinguishable on the cover, fell into her lap.

Deidre's hand was steady as she picked up the letters. The first began, 'My dearest Pearse', and closed, 'Your sweetheart forever, May'. 'All stories are enlightening,' Finn had said. 'Very well then,' she answered him. 'Let's see if you're right.'

There were thirteen in total, none more than a page long. Nothing of consequence had been set down; no references to wars, or floods, or the politics of the day. But the story of a love affair was there. A warning, had Deidre needed one, never to go down that treacherous path.

They took only a minute or two to read, but Deidre sat with them in her lap for the best part of an hour. It occurred to her, had someone else stumbled on them, they might have formed the basis of a romance. She'd never read a romantic novel, but she knew enough of the form to guess the content. Her mother was no different from other women, after all. She'd seen romance as her escape from the confines of daughterhood. No one had told her romance was not concerned with truth. Or warned that marriage could be the worst prison of all.

When the letters were neatly tied up again, Deidre picked up the diary and let it fall open in her hand. 'You will read it, won't you?' Finn had insisted. And though her instincts had screamed, No! she'd given him her word.

For the rest of that long evening Deidre turned the pages of Pearse Byrne's life, stopping when the memories came too fast, jumping backwards and forwards, tormented by the thought that her father could see her. The language of the diary was curt and unemotional, but that was no protection. She was a child again, walking Kilkenny's acres, riding the hills, shielding her eyes from the river. She watched her mother's coffin disappear into the ground, and wept (for the first time) at the sight of those tiny, flower-strewn boxes. She was the shunned observer of her father's marriage to Jessie Potter: the silent witness to the births and deaths that followed. When she stumbled on the date 5 August 1914, it was as if her father were speaking to her, forcing her to remember the men who went away and never came back . . . The final entry was the one she feared the most.

But she'd promised Finn, so she persevered. She knew what he'd say. He'd tell her there was evidence, even at the end, of a connecting heart. Finn was always ready to think the best.

It was after midnight when Deidre crawled, exhausted, into bed. She couldn't imagine how she'd sleep. But one thought kept rising above the confusion. Grief, like winter, must recede . . . Grief, like winter, must recede . . .

She was woken at five o'clock with the news that Phineas O'Reilly was dead.

10

In the months that followed the deaths of her husband and son, Jessie Byrne bought eleven new hats, and put on two stone in weight. When Deidre's first letter arrived she tore it open eagerly, hungry for the consolation she'd convinced herself only her step-daughter could bring. The letter was a cruel disappointment. What comfort was there in talk of tuberculosis, or the changes in the condition of some man called Finn? If Deidre really cared, as she said she did, she'd give up her job and come home. Eliza was to be married in the spring, after which Dulcie was going off to the Teachers' College in Dunedin. That left only Muriel of companionable age at home. And she'd set her heart on a job in the city – any job, Jessie had heard her tell the twins, so long as it was away from Kilkenny. But of course Deidre wouldn't dream of giving up her precious career. She was as stubborn about that as she'd always been.

With the arrival of Deidre's next three letters, disappointment turned to rage. Deidre had betrayed her. The sympathy, the understanding, the companionship she'd promised had all been lies. Where was she? Where were the words of comfort? These letters were even worse than the first. They were all about politics. Who cared about the Government's plans for free hospital and medical services? If people couldn't pay their way they had no business falling sick. There was more about this man Finn, too, and his going off to fight in Spain. Deidre was just like her father, sounding off about war and tyranny and the just cause. Jessie knew what sort of people went to fight in Spain. Communists. The Reverend Jefcoate had made it crystal clear. Those men – and women! – seeking martyrdom in a foreign cause were a disgrace to the Empire. New Zealand should set an example and strip them of their citizenship.

The fifth letter, with more of the same, so infuriated Jessie she took herself off to the one place where she could find peace – her son's shrine. What she wanted to do was re-read the letters Deidre had sent to Clarence. The thought of them, tucked away in the drawer, had begun to agitate her, much as the thought of hidden dust or dirt.

For nearly an hour she sat on the bed, reading and re-reading the pages covered with neat blue handwriting. 'I've enough money saved,' Deidre had written, in a letter dated 3 April, 1936. 'You could board with Mrs Flight in Sydenham, and go to university here. We could spend my days off together . . .' So the betrayal had been there from the start. It was Deidre's fault that Clarence left school when he did. If she hadn't pressured him, he'd have stayed on; gone to university in Dunedin, which was what he'd always intended. Jessie's eyes filled with tears as she saw what Clarence would have become. Dr Clarence Byrne, the noted scientist. He was so interested, always, in how things worked.

'Please don't bother to communicate again,' she wrote, in the letter Deidre received the day Phineas O'Reilly died. 'I find your letters unbelievably insensitive. God knows what possessed me to expect anything different of you . . .'

As 1937 drew to a close newspapers began to talk of an end to the Depression. In the two years he'd been Prime Minister, Michael Savage had honoured his promise to buy the country's way out of recession. The Reserve Bank had been nationalised. Never again would the country be held to ransom by the vagaries of the money market. There was now a minimum wage, a 40-hour week, compulsory union membership, a revitalised Court of Arbitration, and a new deal, signed by Savage and Tahupotiki Ratana, addressing the wrongs suffered by the Maori. In September the first state house had been handed over to its tenants. Thousands more would follow. And though another nine months were to pass before Savage's dream of a free health service would become a reality, no one doubted that that most enlightened piece of social legislation, the first of its kind in the world, would soon be the law of the land.

Elsewhere in the world hope was in shorter supply. The war in Spain was all but over. Franco's troops controlled more than two-thirds of the country. In Germany, Franco's ally, Adolf Hitler, was poised to begin his march into Austria. In Italy, the Fascist dictator Benito Mussolini was celebrating the annexation of Ethiopia. Fascism was on the move. Prime Minister Savage knew it, and urged the League of Nations to take action to secure the world against aggression. His warnings were not heeded.

'Ring out the old, ring in the new,' the wireless in Deidre's bedroom trumpeted, as the bells of the city announced the birth of 1938.

Across the river, on the balcony of Rosevilla, city residence of Sir Arthur and Lady Dutton, a champagne cork popped. Sarah laughed, and raised her glass to her father. She was a grown woman now, almost. Her school days were over. If 1938 lived up to its promise it would see her sailing to England, to join Richard. 'To you, Daddy,' she said. 'And to you, Mummy. The best parents anyone could have.'

Deidre switched off the wireless and climbed into bed. She'd taken her leave of the old year earlier in the evening. In a solitary ceremony she'd confined to the hospital incinerator her father's missal and rosary, her mother's letters, and the diary Jessie Potter had told her to burn. When it was done, she washed her hands carefully, and climbed the stairs to her room. Tomorrow was a working day. And the day after, and the day after that. There was such a lot to be done.

Part Three

Margot Dutton was worried about her daughter. Worried enough to raise the matter with her husband over dinner. The last time they'd discussed Sarah, other than casually, was when she'd had appendicitis. Then it had been a matter of deciding, quickly, which hospital she should go to, and whether one or both of them would make the journey into the city to be with her. It was Margot's will which prevailed on that occasion. Sarah was admitted to the public hospital, not, as Arthur had wanted, to St George's. And they were both at her bedside when she woke from the operation.

'Sarah?' Arthur queried, from his end of the table. 'What's the matter with her?'

'Don't you find it strange she wants to stay on here? Usually she can't wait to get back to the Grange.'

'It's New Year. There's a lot going on.' Arthur's smile was indulgent. 'She's growing up, my dear. We both have to face it. She'll be coming out in August.'

'She doesn't even seem to care about Caesar any more.'

'Girls grow out of horses. It'll be young men she'll have on her mind now.'

'I wish you wouldn't say things like that.'

'Why not? It's true, isn't it?'

'I don't think it's that simple.'

Arthur wiped his mouth on his napkin. The expression on his face was not encouraging. 'We should have had more children,' he said.

Margot resisted the temptation to answer back. This was not

the time to re-open old wounds. 'If you're worrying about me, please don't,' she asserted. 'I've plenty to occupy myself.'

The words put the smile back on her husband's lips. 'Only wish I had your time to read,' he complained. 'Must be twenty years since I opened a novel.'

Margot spread her fingers on the white cloth, and examined her freshly manicured nails. At the start of this conversation she hadn't been sure what she wanted. Now she knew. She wanted to stay on at Rosevilla. 'Arthur . . . ?'

'That was a capital meal, my dear. The duck was splendid.'

'Thank Hazel, not me.'

'You manage the staff very well. I know how difficult it is in town.'

'I thought I might stay on with Sarah. She's a little young to be left with just the servants.' (You spend half your life here, she silently reminded him. Now I'd like a turn.)

'Sarah won't be unchaperoned, Margot. Have you forgotten? The Linwoods'll be here.'

'What?'

'I told you the other night. Surely you remember? They're having their place re-decorated.'

Margot rubbed her thumb over her polished nails. She had a poor memory. Arthur was always telling her so. But she'd have remembered if he'd told her *that*. She didn't care for Cynthia Linwood. A hearty woman, with an appetite for country life which Margot envied, but also, secretly, despised. The thought of sharing Rosevilla with her was enough to bring on a headache.

'Sarah'll be in good hands,' Arthur soothed. 'There's nothing for you to worry about.'

Margot reached for the hand bell, and rang it irritably. Of course Arthur wouldn't want her to stay on at Rosevilla. That's why he'd cooked up this little scheme with Cynthia. Arthur was the sort of man who liked to know what his wife and daughter were up to. With the Linwoods in residence he could keep tabs on the one, while the other was safely tucked up at the Grange.

'Just the coffee, please, Hazel. And for Sir Arthur. He'll take his here tonight.'

There was satisfaction in seeing her husband frown. Arthur

was nothing if not courteous. He would never countermand her instruction in front of a servant. But his ritual of an evening, when there were no guests, was to have coffee served in his den. Margot was never sure what he did there. Smoked a cigar; read the paper. Some nights she heard him on the telephone. She never questioned him about his business. There was a time when she'd had a genuine interest, but not any more. These days Arthur managed things on his own.

'Where *is* Sarah by the way?' Arthur asked, when the coffee had been poured.

'At a meeting.'

'At this time of year? Thought everyone was on holiday.'

'It's an art do of some kind. She's gone with a friend of Richard's.'

Arthur stopped stirring his coffee. It was ridiculous, Margot thought, for the two of them to be dining at this long table. When they were on their own they should be like other people, and eat casually. But Arthur liked to preserve traditions. This was the way his parents had dined, with candles lit, and silver polished. If he had his way he'd make it law for Richard to do the same, when his turn came.

'What friend of Richard's? Have I met him?'

'His name's Louis. Louis de la Tour. The family's from Akaroa.'

'French?'

'Originally.'

'What does the father do?'

'A timber business of some kind, I think. I'm not sure.'

'I thought she was keen on Des Linwood.'

Margot registered the note of anxiety in her husband's voice, and felt a moment of sympathy for him. It's not *I* who mind her growing up, she thought, it's *you*. 'Do you remember when you first brought me here?' she said. 'I was Sarah's age. The war had just started. Your mother was terrified you were going to go off and fight.'

'If I'd had my way I would have.'

'You were a farmer. You couldn't be spared.'

'So my two brothers went instead . . .'

'Sarah doesn't care for Desmond, Arthur. You can put that idea out of your head.'

'You seem to know a lot about it.'

'Besides, Desmond's not going to take over the property. Cynthia told me. He's going to be a mining engineer.'

'Is he indeed?'

'He's quite determined.'

Arthur reached for the jug, and re-filled his cup. Instead of his usual one lump of sugar, he helped himself to three. He stirred for several seconds before lifting the cup to his lips. 'This de la Tour fellow,' he said. 'Anything in it?'

Margot smiled. 'They've only just met.'

'Sarah confides in you. I'm glad, that's good.'

'I only wish she did.'

A puzzled look came into Arthur's eyes. Margot, observing it, had the curious sensation that it was *better* to be a woman. Men understand so little, she thought. 'I *am* Sarah's mother,' she pointed out.

'De la Tour . . .' There was a faint, whistling sound as Arthur sucked in his breath. 'Richard never mentioned him, did he? Is he at the university?'

'He's a painter. An artist. There's quite a group of them, Sarah told me. They're the avant-garde.'

'The *what*?'

'Leaders. Experimenters.'

'I know what it *means*.'

'If you'd been home when you said you were going to be, you'd have met him for yourself.'

Arthur stared into his coffee.

'Prue introduced them, I gather. At Atholl Fitzgerald's lecture. You remember. We wanted to go ourselves.'

'Odd sort of place to meet.'

'Eugenics interests a lot of people, Arthur.'

'What I don't understand is what Sarah's doing going to a meeting – you did say it was a meeting? – of artists. She's a down-to-earth sort of girl. With no artistic talent that I've ever noticed.'

'I think she's doing it for Richard. You know how close they are.'

Arthur drummed his fingers on the table. His son's interest in art – a hobby he should have outgrown by now – was a subject he tried to avoid. Though that wasn't always possible, given Richard's enthusiasm, conveyed in his weekly letters home, for obscure Italian painters. He had had eight months to kill before college started. Arthur had hoped he'd use the time to look up English family and friends; to travel, in the way of young men, through Europe. But what had he done? Taken himself off to Italy to look at paintings! Now here was Sarah encouraging him. His wife too, judging from her expression. 'Strange Richard never mentioned this chap,' he grumbled.

'Not really.' Margot's voice was kind. She took no pleasure in her husband's discomfiture. They both needed to believe *he* was the strong one. 'They were in different houses,' she explained. 'And Louis told me tonight he'd didn't really discover art till he left school. Mathematics was his first love.'

'Pity he didn't stick to it.'

'He says he has. It's integral to his work, he says. You really must meet him, Arthur. He's a most interesting young man.'

Arthur plunged his thumbs into his waistcoat pockets. What he wanted now was a cigar, but smoking at the table, with ladies present, was against the rules. It wasn't just *this* conversation that was unsettling him. It was the memory of others he'd had in recent weeks, with his daughter. 'I can go to England now, Daddy, can't I?' Sarah had piped, the day she left school. 'You *promised*, remember?' He didn't recall doing any such thing, but when she kept on about it, he undertook to give her an answer on her birthday. It was the only way he could get any peace.

'Seems to me,' he complained, frowning at his wife, 'young women nowadays want the best of both worlds. They want the parties and the romance and the happy-ever-after marriage. And they want to lead their own lives too. You should tell her, Margot. Put her right. It's either one or the other.'

He might, Margot reflected, have been talking about Aunt Clara. 'Chasing after rainbows,' he'd declared, first time he heard her story. 'That sort of thing always ends badly.'

'Sarah's a bright girl,' Margot reminded her husband. 'She should go to university.'

'I've no quarrel with that.'

Margot pushed back her chair. It was ludicrous to be having this conversation with a table length between them. 'Then talk to her,' she urged, as she made her way up the room. 'She'll listen to you.'

Arthur rose slightly, acknowledging her arrival. 'You know what she *wants* as well as I do,' he muttered.

'You must tell her no.'

'I suppose we could all go . . .'

'To England?'

Arthur nodded.

Margot looked at the chair she'd just vacated, and wondered why she'd bothered to move. The day she and Arthur married he asked her what she wanted most in the world. She answered: 'To travel.' He made a promise to her then. As soon as the war was over, they'd sail for England. At the end of the war Richard was born, followed, two years later, by Sarah. After that, whenever Margot raised the subject, the time was never right. Till now, that is, on the eve of what looked like another European war. Only it wasn't an old promise to his wife Arthur was keeping, but a new one he'd made to his daughter.

'I wasn't going to tell you yet,' she said, 'but I've asked Richard to come home.'

'You've done *what*?'

'I don't want him trapped, Arthur. You said yourself, you don't like the way things are shaping in Europe.'

'You had no business . . .'

Margot steeled herself against the look in her husband's eyes. She shouldn't have told him, should she? This conversation was getting out of hand.

'I don't care for this Hitler fellow,' Arthur allowed. 'I may have said that. But I never . . .'

'I know what you're thinking, dear. That he's wasted his time. But he hasn't. He's learned to fly.'

'One term. That's all he's had.'

Margot slid her hand across the table. When it touched her husband's, and he didn't pull away, she felt both irritated and relieved. She was still sufficiently in love to want to please. And Arthur, she realised, looking at him with mild surprise, was still, in all physical essentials, the man she'd married. 'What is it about you Dutton men?' she'd teased, during their courtship. 'You and your father could be brothers.

Did some fairy godmother bequeath you the gift of eternal youth?'

'I'm sorry, darling,' she murmured. 'I should have consulted you. But I assumed you'd agree.'

'Yes, well . . .'

'It won't make much difference anyway. Richard'll make his own decisions.'

'Talking of Germany,' Arthur said, 'Sarah gave me this.' He took a newspaper cutting out of his pocket, and handed it to his wife.

'FOR A HOLIDAY THAT'S DIFFERENT COME TO GERMANY,' Margot read. 'EUROPE'S HAPPIEST HOLIDAY LAND.' She smiled. 'Obviously no one's told her about Herr Hitler.'

'On the contrary. This was her answer to that very objection. She always has answers, that girl.'

'What did you say to her?'

'Oh, we had a very adult conversation. Come to think of it, I see now why she went to Atholl's lecture. She had quite a lot to say about the Nazi belief in a Master Race.'

Margot felt a familiar stab of frustration. If only she knew more. Sarah was always telling her she should read the newspapers. Lately they'd been full of articles about eugenics, and the concern of the medical profession to protect 'the future of the race.' Sarah had expressed herself volubly on the subject.

'It *is* worrying though, isn't it, Arthur? Europe, I mean.'

'Yes, old thing. I'm afraid it is.'

'I wasn't wrong to write that letter to Richard, was I?'

Arthur's fingers drummed. 'Don't suppose so,' he conceded. 'He can always fly home if necessary.'

'I still think we should go,' Arthur said, folding the newspaper cutting and returning it to his pocket. 'Richard can come back with us.'

'Is that what you told Sarah?'

'I haven't told her anything.'

'What about university?'

'She can start next year. She's not eighteen yet.'

'You're worrying about this young man, aren't you?'

'Aren't *you*?'

Margot hesitated. It had been a mistake to bring up the

subject of Richard. Arthur hated surprises, particularly when they involved his family. But the harm was done now. 'I don't think taking Sarah to England is the answer,' she said quietly. She must mollify him somehow. He still hadn't agreed to her staying on at Rosevilla. 'But I do think one of us should be here with her now.'

Arthur's eyebrows rose. 'You surprise me,' he responded. 'I thought a trip Home was what you'd always wanted.'

Margot laughed. What else could she do? Her husband's version of events was like written history – official. 'If you were to promise Sarah a trip when she has her degree,' she suggested carefully, 'England, Europe, America. Wherever she wants . . .' Arthur frowned. Margot registered the change, but refused to let it deter her. 'I don't want my children trapped overseas,' she stated firmly. 'I don't want *us* to be trapped. Wars are no respecters of persons, Arthur.'

To her relief, her husband smiled. 'Tell you the truth, my dear,' he said, 'travelling's the last thing I want to do right now. There's so much needs attending to here. Getting rid of this Government for a start.'

'You agree with me then?'

He nodded.

'And I can stay on here with Sarah?'

'Whatever makes you happy,' Sir Arthur Dutton said.

2 ∫

'Where are we going? Thought you said you had a car.'
'I'm an artist, Sarah, not a stockbroker.'
'But you said . . .'
'You never travelled on a tram before?'
'Don't be silly.'
'Then what's your difficulty?'
Sarah laughed. 'We're heading the wrong way, that's what.'
Five minutes later Sarah and her date for the evening ('Louis
de la Tour here,' he'd said, on the phone. 'I'm ringing to ask you
to be my date for the evening') jumped on to the Sydenham
tram, and joined the city's workers returning to their homes in
the suburbs. Sarah would have said yes to Louis even if he hadn't
been at school with Richard. Her father's refusal to discuss how
and when she was to get to England had cast a pall over the
New Year holiday. Going out with Louis would be a welcome
distraction. Besides, he'd made quite an impression on her the
night they met. *And* he was an artist. The only one she knew,
apart from Richard.
'You've heard of Beulah Dowling?' he'd said, when she asked
what the occasion was.
'*The* Beulah Dowling?'
'She's come back here to live. A friend of mine, Kitty Whyte,
she's an artist too, you know her? Well, you will soon enough.
She's putting on a shindig to welcome Beulah.'
As they talked, Sarah could see the words on the page. 'Dearest
Richard, you'll never guess who *I* met last night . . .'
'I'd love to come, thank you,' she'd said into the phone.
'Louis de la Tour,' her mother had reacted. 'Do I know him?'

'I told you, I met him with Prue.'

'At the lecture?'

'You should have gone to it, you and Daddy. You'd have learned something.'

('So, Mr Fitzgerald, you advocate a programme of *enlightened euthanasia*, do you?' Louis's voice would have attracted her attention anyway. It was almost as startling as his appearance. 'Can you tell me in what way your theories differ from Adolf Hitler's?')

Sarah grinned at the memory. 'You'll like Louis,' she'd assured her mother. 'He's very outspoken.'

'Can I hear the joke?' he asked now, leaning so close his breath tickled her ear.

The tram clattered to a halt. Sarah released the strap she was clinging to, and let the alighting passengers push past her.

'Move on down the car,' the conductor ordered. The bell clanged, and the tram lurched into motion again.

'I should tell you,' Louis said, his face swaying close to hers, 'in case it's a problem, I don't have any money.'

Sarah flashed him a warning look. Even had they not been packed in like sardines his words would have been easily overhead. He had what her elocution teacher at school would have called, approvingly, a 'carrying' voice. 'You mean now, tonight?' she whispered.

'I mean altogether.' Louis beamed at her. He seemed oblivious of the other people in the tram. Sarah, in her lime-green dress and jacket, and her second-best silk stockings, felt conspicuous. She had the impression the women passengers (she'd counted seven among a sea of male faces) made this journey every day. They had the blank look of the profoundly tired or bored. Some clutched baskets: others gripped ancient handbags. One woman, older than the rest, muttered incessantly to herself. 'I've quarrelled with my father,' Louis said.

'What about?'

His hand slapped into her back. 'You haven't travelled on trams much, have you?'

'Not at this time of day.'

'Better get used to it. You and I are going to be seeing a lot of each other.'

If they hadn't been in such a public place Sarah would have asked what made him so sure. It wasn't as if he was good-looking or anything. But they were attracting enough attention as it was. 'You were telling me about your father,' she prompted.

'Hopeless old reactionary,' Louis informed her cheerfully. 'Wanted me to be a lawyer.'

Sarah decided not to pursue the subject. *Her* father had fixed ideas about careers for sons too.

'He gave me an ultimatum,' Louis sailed on. 'Enrol at the university, or have my allowance stopped.'

'So what did you do?'

'I got a job.'

Sarah glanced at the man on the other side of her. He was about thirty, she guessed, with a bad complexion, and a disconcerting habit of sneering every time their eyes met. He was wearing a hat decorated with a feather. It assorted oddly with the rest of his clothes, which were torn and dirty. She was trying hard not to mind about his elbow digging into her ribs.

'I got a job so that I could do what I was born to do,' Louis said.

Sarah nodded. She would have to remember this conversation, to tell Richard.

'So, let's talk about you,' Louis invited. Sarah's eyes signalled panic. 'Where are *you* headed, Miss Dutton? Apart from Sydenham, that is.'

Sarah giggled. 'No idea,' she hedged.

'Why not?'

'You might as well ask me if I believe in God.'

'And do you?'

She shrugged.

'You don't strike me as a girl with no opinions.'

'I've plenty of opinions. Ask my mother. She calls me cussed.'

'Good word that.'

'I prefer stubborn.'

'And what are you stubborn about, Sarah?'

By the time they reached Sydenham Sarah had decided she didn't care if she never saw Louis de la Tour again. He was too inquisitive for a start. Personal questions of the sort he'd been asking were rude. Especially when you'd only just met. Who

did he think he was anyway? Short, red-haired, unemployed . . .
Almost the only distinguished thing about him was his name.

'We're making for that street ahead,' Louis announced, as they
jumped off the tram. 'Pine Avenue. Cripes, what a stink!'

Sarah looked at the cottages belching smoke into the air;
registered the grubby faces of the children playing in the street,
the stray cats, the dog defecating, the man on the verandah
opposite, smoking his pipe, the woman with the scarf knotted
round her head, bringing in the washing; registered, too, the
smell, which she knew came from the Christchurch Coke and
Coal Company at the end of the road. Did Louis know what
her father did for a living? Would he care? Since he'd quarrelled
with his own father it was possible the subject of fathers was of
no further interest to him.

'Have you sold any of your paintings?' she enquired politely.
The road was uneven, and mined with stones, but that hadn't
discouraged Louis from setting a brisk pace. She stopped to
remove a pebble from her pump, and noticed the leather was
scratched. 'Damn,' she muttered. The pumps were a Christmas
present from her mother.

'Selling's not the point,' Louis answered over his shoulder.

'So how do you live?' she persisted, when she'd caught up
with him.

'You can buy me lunch, if you like. Three times a week. That
should keep the wolf from the door.'

'You're joking.'

'Not about wanting to see you again.'

'I don't even know where you live.'

'Kitty Whyte lets me have a room.'

'You live with her?'

'I'm her lodger.'

Sarah's face must have betrayed her thought because Louis
laughed. 'Kitty's my friend and my landlady,' he assured her.
'That's all.'

'It's none of my business.'

'It will be. If I have anything to do with it.'

Sarah picked her way among the grass and stones. If you
were any kind of a gentleman you'd have warned me what
to expect, she thought sourly. It's not as if I've ever walked

these streeets before. 'My brother wants to be an artist too,' she told him.

The look of incredulity on Louis's face gave her a fleeting satisfaction. He didn't know everything then. 'You're kidding,' he said.

Sarah shook her head.

'*Grenadier* Dutton? It's not possible.'

'*What* did you call him?'

'Grenadier. I'd have picked him for the military. Sure thing.'

'Well, you were wrong, weren't you?'

'I do recall . . .' He scratched his head. 'Gladys, our worse than useless art teacher, did say something . . .'

'Gladys?'

'Mr Carter-Boyes. Paints charming little watercolours of a distinctly English hue.'

'Richard had another name for him.'

'Unflattering, I hope. The man's a liability.'

The two young people stared at each other. Sarah's hand was on her chest, monitoring her suddenly increased heartbeat. Louis had put his hand up to his eyes, though the sun was troubling Sarah, not him. His index finger flicked at the hair which had fallen over his wrist.

'I've written to Richard about you,' Sarah said. 'I write to him every week. As a matter of fact . . .'

'You're beautiful,' Louis said.

'Strange you not knowing. About Richard, I mean.'

'I've never said that to anyone before.'

'We're going to be late.'

'Does my admiration bother you?'

'You don't know me.'

'I know your eyes. I've seen them before. Better artists than me have painted them.'

Sarah squinted into the sun. She didn't know whether to be flattered or irritated. And hadn't anyone ever told him it was rude to stare?

'You all right?' Louis asked.

'I get this pain sometimes. In my chest.'

'What sort of pain?'

'It's nothing. A stitch. It's gone now.'

'How long's it been happening?'
'Are you a doctor as well as an artist?'
'Tell me!'
'If you must know . . . since my brother went away.'

Louis's face came closer. When the evening was over Sarah was to remember the look he gave her and puzzle over it. It was a kind look. She was in no doubt about that. But it was also curious. As if he were trying to make sense of something. Later she was to regret her self-consciousness, and wonder what would have happened if she'd returned his gaze. Might he have kissed her? And what would she have done if he had?

A yelp from the dog reminded Sarah where they were. She peered over her shoulder on the pretext of checking her seams. She felt mildly out of control. As she had the night she'd decided, on impulse, not to return to the Grange. She hadn't been able to explain that to herself, any more than she could explain now the rogue pain in her chest. 'We really are going to be late,' she scolded.

'What did you tell your brother about me?'
'What?'
'In your letter.'
'Oh . . .' Sarah grinned. She was on safe ground with a question like that. 'I told him you were a very impertinent person,' she answered. 'You asked embarrassing questions of nice Mr Fitzgerald, who took my appendix out.'

Louis let out a hoot of laughter. In that moment Sarah knew she liked him. She bent to pat the dog, which had trotted hopefully up to her. 'Yuk!' she said. 'He pongs.'

'Come on,' Louis urged, cupping his hand under her elbow. He pointed to a cottage halfway down the Avenue. 'You'll like Kitty,' he pronounced confidently. 'She's an interesting painter. Sensual. Or do I mean, *sensuous*? One or the other.'

This street was exactly like the other. Rows of cottages with lean-tos at the back, and gardens in varying states of neglect. A couple of boys wearing trousers held up with string pushed a makeshift cart along the centre of the road. When they drew parallel, they pulled their caps down over their ears, and giggled.

'I'll tell you what I think about your friend Fitzgerald,' Louis said, nodding at the boys. 'I think he's got a skeleton in his cupboard. More than one, like as not. When an intelligent human being blames criminality on poor breeding . . .'

Sarah turned to follow the boys' progress. Their cart was full of potatoes. It clattered over the stones, tossing its cargo on to the road. 'I thought he was more concerned with mental defects,' she said.

'Mental, physical, moral – they're all grist to his mill.'

'He's got a point though, hasn't he? I mean . . .'

Louis grabbed the shock of hair which had fallen over his face, and plastered it behind his ears. The gesture, which Sarah was beginning to see was habitual, made her smile. Richard had exactly the same physical impatience. 'The only *point*, Sarah,' he said, 'is that babies born into economically deprived homes haven't a hope of thriving in the way you and I have thrived. Look around you. A breeding ground for crime, wouldn't you say?'

The boys had reached the corner. When Sarah glanced over her shoulder again they put their thumbs to their noses, and poked out their tongues. She waved back defiantly. 'Not everyone born into a poor home becomes a criminal,' she attested.

'And you think that proves something? What about the criminals of the wealthy class? Look at the figures, and you'll see what I mean. And those are just the ones who are caught.'

By the time they reached their destination Sarah had decided to invite Louis to Rosevilla for dinner. 'He needs feeding,' she'd tell her mother. 'He's very poor.' She wouldn't say anything to her father. He'd be bound to disapprove. If it weren't for the Linwoods coming to stay she'd wait till her parents were back at the Grange. But the thought of Desmond and Louis together deterred her. Desmond had become a real pain lately.

'You're doing it again,' Louis said, as he pushed open the gate.

'Doing what?'

'Grinning.'

'You must come to dinner,' Sarah said. 'How about tomorrow?'

'Louis! There you are. What took you so long?'

Standing in the doorway was a tall, bony woman, wearing a

purple turban round her head, and scarlet evening pyjamas. 'So you're Sarah,' the figure said.

'Meet Kitty,' Louis instructed. 'Is everyone here?'

'*Tout le monde*,' Kitty answered. 'You're the last. Did you bring any food?' she asked Sarah.

Sarah shook her head. Her hand had been pumped, her appearance scrutinised, now she was being held responsible for her failure to bring food.

'My fault,' Louis beamed.

Sarah followed him down a narrow passage, into a room so crammed with paintings and sculptures it resembled, not a living space, which Sarah supposed it was, but a public gallery. In addition to the dizzying display on the walls, there were bronze animals in various poses, semi-human figures, and carved objects of Polynesian derivation. There was almost no furniture. What there was seemed to exist solely to show off works of art. It occurred to Sarah, in those first vivid seconds, that the people in the room could well be taken for works of art too. They were draped about on cushions, clutching glasses and cigarettes, and gazing animatedly at one another. Striped blazers and paisley scarves knotted at the neck distinguished the men; embroidered boleros and flared trousers, the women. For the second time that evening Sarah regretted the clothes she was wearing. She'd know better next time.

'*Attention*, everyone,' Kitty called. 'I want you to meet Sarah.'

'No, I'm not an artist,' she explained, when the inevitable question was asked. 'I'm here with Louis.'

For most of the people in the room that put an end to their curiosity. They weren't exactly rude, but they made little or no attempt to include her in their conversation. The exception was Beulah Dowling. Sarah was looking round for a place to sit when Beulah motioned her to join her. Any doubts Sarah may have had as to her motives were soon dispelled. Beulah Dowling's friendliness was genuine.

'Just for once, Richard, I think *you* might have envied *me*,' she wrote next morning. 'I mean, she's *nice*, as well as clever and brilliant and all those things. When I told her about you, she seemed genuinely interested. She said you were absolutely right to spend your time just looking. Time enough to paint when you get back here, she said. Because you are coming back, Richard, aren't you? I don't want you to be like Aunt Clara, and stay away forever . . .'

'Enjoying yourself?' Louis asked, when the evening had progressed to the point where most people, Sarah included, were mildly drunk.

'I'm having a ball!' Two glasses of sherry had made Sarah feel euphoric. She'd been imagining herself, mature at eighteen, waving to her parents from the deck of the *Rangitane*.

'*Mes amis* . . .' Kitty clapped her hands for silence. 'Fellow artists! Beulah has asked me not to make a speech, and I'm not going to, I promise. But I can't let the occasion pass without expressing how I feel, how we all feel . . .' She turned to Beulah, and opened her arms wide. 'You're here, *merveilleuse femme*, here among us. It's more than we dared hope, more than we could ever have asked for . . .'

Beulah punched the cushion on which she was sitting, and adjusted her comfortable frame. 'Come now, Kitty, let's not pretend. I'm lucky to be back, and you know it.'

'But think what you've left. Your studio. Your patrons. Those marvellous friendships . . . Paul Klee, Georges Rouault, Pablo Picasso . . .'

'Fifteen years. It was time to come home. And in case you haven't noticed, there's going to be a war.'

Sarah's eyes spun back to Louis, but there was nothing in his expression to correspond to the sudden pain in her chest. That nurse in the hospital – what was her name? – the bad-tempered one – she'd said something about a war. And of course there were things in the newspapers. But when you want something as badly as Sarah wanted this trip to England, you take no notice of signs and portents.

'I made the decision to save my skin,' Beulah insisted. 'Don't any of you, please, underestimate what's brewing in Europe. If you have relatives there, or friends, tell them to get out.'

No! Sarah wanted to contradict. You're wrong. It's not like that. Don't you see? Hitler may not be a very nice man, but he's made Germany safe for holidays.

By the time the evening came to an end Sarah had a headache. She blamed it on the sherry, and the fact that she'd been smoking, a practice she'd only just taken up. But of course it was more than that. The word 'war' had punctured her euphoria.

'Beulah talked about a magazine,' she wrote to Richard next day. 'I think it was called *The Studio*. Do you know it? I should have paid closer attention. A lot of what she said reminded me of you, of things *you* say. Like, a painting should have a life beyond the frame. I remember you saying that. And lots of stuff about line and tone, and the need to think spatially . . . Louis said he'd take me to Beulah's exhibition when it opens. It's bound to be controversial, he says. She changes her style every few years . . .'

Louis was quiet on the journey home. Perhaps he'd noticed her preoccupation, and was angry. The thought troubled Sarah, but not enough to make her speak of it. It was past ten, but there were still glimmers of light in the sky. Sarah tried, and failed, to imagine a January night in Oxford. She couldn't even picture Richard clearly. She could see the back of his head, or the curve of his shoulder as he painted, but she couldn't see him *whole*.

'Till tomorrow then,' Louis said, when they reached the gates of Rosevilla.

Sarah listened to the tram clattering in the distance. It would be a long ride back to Sydenham.

'Dinner,' Louis reminded her. 'You invited me.'

'Oh . . . yes. Can I telephone you? I should check with my parents.'

'I'll call round. Kitty doesn't have a phone. Midday all right?'

Sarah nodded. 'Thank you for taking me,' she said, to Louis's retreating back. 'I enjoyed it.'

He lifted his hand.

'So how was it?' Margot called from the sitting room.

Sarah tossed her jacket over the banisters and crossed the hall. 'You're still up!' she exclaimed.

'Enjoy yourself, did you?'

'I've invited Louis to dinner tomorrow. Is that all right?'

Margot smiled at the young woman framed in the doorway. She was her father's daughter all right. Same hazel eyes, same self-absorbed expression. Richard shared their features, but not that *look*. She'd often wondered where it came from. Shyness? Arrogance? A secret life? Whatever its cause, it was a form of protection, she was certain of that. How else to account for her husband's continuing youthfulness? 'I was going to suggest it myself,' she said.

'He's quite poor. He could do with a decent meal.'

'I see.' Margot resisted the temptation to ask questions. Though she would need answers, sooner or later, for Arthur. 'Why not sit down a moment?' she suggested.

Sarah stretched against the door jamb. 'I'm dead beat,' she yawned. 'We went on the tram . . . You and Daddy aren't going home till next week, are you?' she asked.

'*I'm* staying. I've persuaded your father.'

'Whew!' Sarah leaned into the room.

'I hope that means you're pleased?'

'What about the Linwoods?'

'It'll just be the twins. I telephoned Cynthia after your father had gone to bed. She suggested it, luckily. I don't think I could have coped with the four of them.'

'Me neither.'

'Do you want some cocoa?'

'No, thanks. I'm stuffed.'

Margot winced. She'd had words with her daughter about slang, but it had done no good. 'Oh, Mummy, you're such a *dinosaur*,' Sarah had wailed.

'Cynthia and Harold will stay at the club,' Margot disclosed. 'It's a much better idea.'

'Beats me why they have to move out at all,' Sarah grumbled. 'What's so terrible about a few painters and decorators?'

'You know Cynthia.'

'Why doesn't she go back to the country?'

'And miss the race meetings? My dear, I'm ashamed of you.'

Sarah laughed. 'I'm glad you're staying, Mummy,' she said. 'We'll have fun.'

Margot, who was experiencing a sudden constriction in her throat, nodded. Expressions of affection from her daughter were rare. '*Rose Marie*'s on at the Tivoli,' she murmured.

'Super! We'll go.'

'Oh, and your father would like a word in the morning. If you wake up in time, that is.'

Sarah blew a kiss. 'Goodnight, Mummy,' she trilled.

3

When Louis arrived at Rosevilla, as instructed, he was shown into the drawing room by a maid. 'Lady Dutton will be down shortly,' he was told.

'It's Sarah I've come to see,' he stated, dismissing the room and its contents in a glance.

The maid frowned. She was new to the job, and not at all sure she liked it. But it was room and board, and money in her pocket at the end of the week. Other people would tell her she should be grateful. 'Don't know nuthin' about that, sir,' she said.

'Louis's the name. What's yours?'

'Pamela. Pam. I'm not really a maid. I'm a tailoress.'

'Don't tell me. Laid off, were you? Bad luck.'

'Weren't just me. There were dozens of us.'

'And they say things are getting better!'

'The people who say that, sir, write it in the papers, they should take themselves off to Armagh Street, to the soup kitchen. Ever been there, sir? It's run by the Salvation Army. Some days ya can't see the end o' the queue.'

Louis looked at the girl standing just by the door, and tried to visualise the painting he would make of her. Her sensibly shod feet, planted on the carpet, assorted oddly with the expensive fragility of the objects in the room. What use would *she* have for the tapestried chairs with their finely turned legs? Or that pair of pale green vases, inlaid with gold, gracing the mantelpiece? 'Treat you all right here, do they?' he asked.

The girl shrugged. 'No worse'n anywhere else, I s'pose,' she said.

'It's not always going to be like this, you know,' Louis promised. 'Masters and servants. All that's going to change.'

The girl smiled.

'You don't believe me?'

'I like dreamin' too, sir,' she said.

Louis flicked the hair off his face. What was he doing in this house anyway? Sarah Dutton was a spoilt rich girl. He shouldn't be wasting his time. 'Is Sarah home then?' he asked irritably.

The maid's smile disappeared. 'She's home all right,' she answered.

'So when is she coming down?'

'She's in her room. Been there all day.'

'Look, Pam . . .'

'She's been cryin', sir.'

'Crying?'

'Dunno what about.'

Louis, turning his head, was confronted by his own image in the large gilt mirror above the fireplace. He'd taken care over his appearance: dampened his hair into place; knotted a sober tie. So how come he looked as if he'd been out in a gale? He put his hands to the sides of his head, and smoothed them over his scalp. Was *he* the cause of those tears? Somehow he didn't think so. When he'd called round at midday Lady Dutton had made excuses for her daughter, but the invitation to dinner had not only been confirmed, it had been warmly endorsed. He'd gone back to Kitty's in exuberant mood.

'Lady Dutton's been with 'er most o' the day,' Pamela said.

'And you've no clue?'

'What would *I* know, sir?'

Louis censored the words that jumped into his mind. None of this was the maid's fault. He walked to the window and found himself gazing, through fronds of wistaria, at a lawn shaded with tall trees and laced with roses. Even at this late hour there was a man working in the garden. Taking advantage of the weather, his employers would no doubt claim.

He must make amends to the maid. 'You can be very intolerant, you know, Louis,' his mother told him, shortly before she died. 'You've no patience with those less talented than yourself.

And since that's almost everyone you come into contact with, I fear you may end up friendless . . .'

He turned, and saw that Pam was gone. Next moment the door opened, and Sarah's mother entered.

'Louis! I'm so sorry. Have you been waiting long?'

The hand which Lady Dutton extended drew Louis back into the centre of the room. 'Good evening,' he said, positioning himself with his back to the mirror.

Lady Dutton pressed his hand lightly. 'Can I mix you a cocktail?' she asked.

Louis was good at reading faces, but he could decipher little of this one. If there *was* trouble in the house, *real* trouble, there was no sign of it in Lady Dutton's carefully made-up countenance. 'Thank you,' he said.

'Sarah will be down directly,' he was told, as his hostess made her way across the room to the liquor cabinet. 'I should warn you, she's a little upset. A disagreement with her father.'

'Ah . . .'

'Martini?' Sarah's mother smiled at him over her shoulder. 'That's what I usually have.'

'Fine. Thank you, Lady Dutton.'

'Margot, please. I hate titles.'

Louis nodded. He was being made welcome, wasn't he? Treated as a friend rather than a guest. So why did he feel uneasy?

'Sarah's used to getting her own way, you see,' Margot explained. 'She takes it hard when her father says no.'

'May I ask what the disagreement was about?'

Margot turned, cocktail shaker in hand, and smiled at him again. The impression he was getting was that she was pleased about this quarrel between father and daughter. There was definitely something gloating about her expression. 'Perhaps you should hear it from *her*,' she said.

Louis accepted the drink she offered him, and sat down. Mother and daughter, he'd observed, when he saw them together last evening, were not alike. There was a Mediterranean quality to Sarah's beauty: a hint of something unpredictable. The mother was an English rose, a little withered on the stem now, but Louis suspected that had more to do with disappointment than age. 'Will Sir Arthur be dining with us?' he asked.

'Oh, yes,' Margot chirruped. 'He's looking forward very much to meeting you.'

They sipped their drinks, and talked of safer things. Louis smiled when appropriate, and answered the questions Sarah's mother kept firing at him. But impatience was never far below the surface. 'I'm not arrogant, Mother, really I'm not,' he'd protested. 'It's just I can't seem to sit still for long.' Like now, he thought, struggling to find something to say about the Duke of Windsor, whose name had suddenly entered the conversation. I've come here to see Sarah, he wanted to protest, not exchange gossip about the ex-King of England.

Was this the sort of thing Sarah talked about when she was at home? He knew almost nothing of her relationship with her parents. With her brother, yes. He'd already twigged that one. Any man interested in Sarah would have to suffer comparison with that twit, Dutton. And if he failed the test he'd be out. Tricky. Louis didn't have a sister. Just a brother, six years younger. The last person in the world he'd choose to compare anyone with.

When, a few minutes later, the door burst open, Louis sprang to his feet. But it wasn't Sarah who materialised, it was Pam.

'Try and remember to knock, Pamela,' Margot reprimanded. 'She's new,' she explained, when the door had closed again. 'Shall we go through?'

'Shouldn't we wait for Sarah?'

'I think you'll find she's waiting for us.'

But there was no Sarah in the dining room. Just Sir Arthur, in suit and tie, standing in front of a portrait of a young man with handle-bar moustache (an ancestor, Louis assumed), wearing the uniform of an officer of the Canterbury Yeomanry.

'Good evening!' Louis's hand was vigorously shaken. 'My apologies for not joining you sooner. These are busy times.'

The face Louis found himself studying was familiar. So Sarah's dark good looks came from her father. 'Pleased to meet you, sir,' he said.

Sir Arthur indicated which of the dozen chairs at the table

was to be his, then sat down himself. 'My daughter's asked me to apologise to you,' he said. 'I'm afraid she's indisposed.'

'You mean she's not joining us?'

'Evidently not.'

Louis ran his fingers through his hair. What the hell was going on? Just for a moment he felt nostalgia for his childhood home overlooking Akaroa Harbour. Compared to Rosevilla it was a modest establishment, which hadn't stopped him turning his back on its comforts. His father, Ernest, had made his money during the war. Before that the de la Tours had been labourers and shopkeepers. Unlike the Duttons, Louis thought sourly, who'd been accumulating money and exercising power over people for *centuries*.

'Perhaps I shouldn't stay,' he mumbled.

'Good heavens!' The idea obviously struck Sir Arthur as comical. 'You must. I've been looking forward to getting acquainted.'

'It was Sarah who invited me.'

'You're an artist, she tells me. I'd like to hear about it.' Sir Arthur leaned back to allow Pamela to serve the soup. 'We have quite an interest in art in this family,' he said.

By the time the main course arrived Louis had fielded a dozen questions, not just about his work, but about his family, his future, and his views on everything from the economy to the display of daffodils in Hagley Park. It had all been very pleasant, on the surface. ('But how *interesting*, Louis. D'ya hear that, Margot? This young man thinks war is an *irrelevance*.') But the more he was grilled, the more uncomfortable Louis became. Sir Arthur Dutton, he decided, was a particularly noxious species of paternalist, all the more dangerous for being so charming. It was damnable having to explain himself to such a man.

'I really think we should let Louis eat his beef, don't you?' Margot remonstrated, when the questions started up again.

Sir Arthur beamed at his guest. 'It's just that I find your generation so interesting,' he said. 'So different from my own.'

'My father doesn't approve my choice of career either,' Louis retorted.

He'd intended to provoke, but the response he got was disappointing. 'The world needs artists,' Sir Arthur replied evenly. 'They have to come from somewhere.'

Louis made a note to curb his tongue in future. Offending Sarah's parents wasn't going to get him anywhere.

'Thank you, Pamela,' Margot smiled, when dessert was served. 'You and Hazel must have some too.' She turned to Louis. The look she gave him struck him as coquettish. 'Summer pudding,' she said. 'I hope you like it.'

'Looks great.'

'I'm sorry about Sarah. You could call tomorrow.'

'Is that what *she* wants?'

Margot glanced at her husband. 'I'm sure it is,' she answered.

It was as coffee was being poured that a way of seeing Sarah now occurred to Louis. He'd ask to be excused and find her room. It shouldn't be too difficult. And there was always Pam, if he got lost.

When the moment came he had the feeling Margot knew exactly what he was up to, and approved. 'Bathroom's upstairs,' she informed him. 'Third door on the right.'

'Why not the cloakroom?' Sir Arthur put in, from his end of the table.

'Back in a jiffy,' Louis called from the door.

He mounted the stairs three at a time, selected the door he guessed to be Sarah's, knocked, and pushed it open. 'Bull's eye!' he exclaimed.

Sarah's head shot off the pillow. She was wearing a red kimono embroidered with yellow dragons. A book lay discarded on the floor. Others were heaped on the bedside table. She was a reader then. Louis, temporarily at a loss for words, grinned.

'How did you . . . ?'

'You look terrible,' Louis said.

'Do they know you're here?'

'They think I'm relieving myself. Well, I am, in a way. You're alive. That's good. And you're not indisposed, as your father would have me believe. You've been on a crying jag. That's a different thing altogether.'

'I suppose I do look pretty dreadful,' Sarah sniffed.

'I'm sorry you're miserable. Is there anything I can do?'

'They didn't tell you?'

Louis sat down on the bed. It was a cheerful room, with fresh flowers on the dresser and an abundance of childhood toys. A portrait of Sarah's mother as a London debutante hung on the wall behind him. 'Nobody's told me anything,' he said. 'I'm the one who's been doing the telling. Your father would have made a good career in the Spanish Inquisition. Your mother too, come to that. Though she doesn't go in for quite such extreme forms of torture.'

Sarah's laugh was infectious. 'Poor you,' she giggled. 'I'm sorry. And I'm sorry I didn't come down. I couldn't face you. I felt so ugly.'

'You *look* ugly.'

'Thank you very much.'

'Don't mention it.'

'You better go. It doesn't take that long to . . .'

'Can I see you tomorrow? Not here. Anywhere else. You say.'

'We could go to the beach.'

'Do you like walking?'

'I prefer riding.'

'We could walk in the hills. There's a place I know . . .'

'All right.'

'I'll call for you in the morning, shall I?'

'Don't you have to work?'

Louis leant forward, and cupped her face in his hands. 'This *is* work,' he said. 'Only that's not the word I'd use. *Life* . . . Work, life, love. What is it about four-letter words?' He laughed, and dropped his hands. 'I want to *live*, don't you?'

A shudder passed through Sarah's body. Louis resisted the temptation to take her in his arms. There would be time enough for that.

'You don't muck about, do you?' she said.

'What are you afraid of, Sarah?'

'At this moment, everything,' she admitted. 'You especially.'

'I'm not your enemy.'

'Aren't you?'

'You've got that pain again, haven't you? The one you told me about.'

'How can you tell?'

'The look on your face.'

Sarah's head fell back on the pillow. 'I'll see you tomorrow if you want,' she said. 'But don't count on me for much, will you? It's all changed, you see. My life. It's not going to work out as I'd planned.'

4 ∫

The two people sitting in the fold of the hill would have struck a
passer-by, had there been one, as a typical young couple making
the most of the holiday season and the warm day. Later in the
month the nor'westers would blow, and a hike in the Cashmere
Hills would loose its appeal. Later too the holidays would end,
and the young pair (was it safe to assume they were lovers?)
would be obliged, surely, to return to work.

But speculation wouldn't end there. Our passer-by, observing
the girl's well-favoured appearance, her smart jodhpurs and
open-necked shirt, might wonder if she worked at all. Could
she be a student? Or a debutante daughter marking time before
marriage? She might be a nurse of course. More and more girls
from wealthy families were seeking careers in nursing: some to
establish their independence; others to avoid matrimony.

Unable to decide which category the girl fell into, our passer-by
would probably shift his attention to the young man. But *he*
would prove even more of a puzzle. His voice, which would not
have been out of place on the wireless, his gestures, which were
exaggerated, the motley nature of the clothes he was wearing
(striped trousers rolled up to the knee and a shirt which had
obviously never seen an iron), fitted no known pattern. Not a
worker. That much could be deduced from his hands. And not
rich, or at least not willing to appear so. What then? Foreign?
That could be it. A visitor from Home, since he spoke such good
English. And the girl assigned to show him the sights.

That there *were* sights to be seen would be obvious to anyone
who'd climbed as high as Louis and Sarah. There at their feet
lay the city, its mansions and factories, cottages and council

chambers, trees and spires reduced to a neat, impersonal design. There too lay the plain, stretching beyond the city to the mountains, blue in the distance. Sarah didn't want to think about the Grange, tucked away in those hills. She didn't want to think about Caesar, and what would happen to him now she'd decided, as she had, to live in the city. 'Rites of passage,' Louis had said, on the climb up. 'They're always painful.' She hadn't been sure what he meant, but she'd been comforted.

Sarah turned to the man sitting on the grass beside her. The expression on his face reminded her of Richard. 'It's too much, isn't it?' he complained. 'I mean . . . look!'

'I take it this is a favourite spot of yours?'

'How can I call myself an artist? It's tosh. As if the personality, *my* personality, can hope to capture . . .'

'But you *are* an artist.'

'I'm a painter. That's the better word. Truer. I want to reflect the world, not my own ego. You must help me to be less conceited, Sarah. We must talk of what I do as *work.*'

'One of your four-letter words.'

'Gauguin said we must paint like children. It sounds easy, but it's the hardest thing. I mean . . .' He swept his hand in an arc.' All this. This *immensity.* How would a child paint that?'

'Richard would love it here.'

Louis twisted a blade of grass around his finger, and thought how much he'd like to punch the nose of Grenadier Dutton. He was the uninvited guest on this picnic: the reason for those shadows under Sarah's eyes, and her gentle gratitude now. At this moment Sarah felt she had no friend in the world but the man in whom she'd just confided. Ever since her brother left for England she'd been living for the day when she would leave herself, to join him. But her father had said no. Not now, not in the foreseeable future. Louis had been sympathetic. He'd understood her anguish at being denied her dearest wish. He'd reassured her, if war did break out, her brother would not be stranded. But even while holding her hand, and drying her tears, he'd felt irritated by her devotion. What chance did *he* have when her dreams were centred on a man twelve thousand miles away? She was going to look for a job, she'd told him. Her father expected her to go to university, but she was damned if she was going to do what he wanted. 'I'm like you,' she'd claimed. 'Stubborn.'

Later, pausing on their climb to catch her breath, she'd confessed what lay behind her rebellion. 'I'm going to pay my own way to England,' she'd explained. 'I'll not be beholden to them . . . I don't believe there's going to be a war anyway,' she'd added, when he didn't respond. 'Why should there be another one?'

Louis yanked the grass up by the root, and tossed it away. 'It's all there, you know,' he said moodily. 'The vast generosity of it all.'

'Generosity?' Sarah queried. 'Whose?'

'I dunnow. God's, I s'pose. It's *there*. That's all I know.'

Sarah leaned forward and clasped her knees. If Richard had been here he'd have known what to say. He hated church as much as she did, but he talked about *God* all the time. She sighed. Louis had been so nice to her today, so understanding. Nevertheless the thought of the climb down, and the long tram ride home, chilled her. Since the conversation with her father yesterday morning she'd felt as if she were fighting off an illness. She hadn't wanted to do, or say, anything. But Louis's words mattered, didn't they? He was saying things Richard would want to hear.

'You don't think . . .' she began. What was it Richard used to say? About Light and Love? He was always using words like that, with capital letters. 'You don't think there's something missing?' she suggested. 'People perhaps? Immensity's all very well, but it's not very comforting.'

Her words were greeted with a surprised shout, at the conclusion of which Louis grabbed her hand, and pumped it up and down. 'But you're right!' he exclaimed. 'That's it exactly. The human dimension. Sarah, you're brilliant!'

'What have I said?'

'It's so obvious. We haven't possessed the land yet. That's our tension, our struggle. The reason we dream of other lands. Homelands. The Maoris do it too. Hawaiki. The place from which they were cast out. Oh, Sarah, if only . . .'

She watched the pulsing of his Adam's apple. It both attracted and repelled her. He'd told her earlier he wanted to paint her. 'When your eyes are sad,' he'd said, 'as they are today, you look like a New World Madonna.'

'Those hills aren't empty,' she said, with conviction. 'There are ghosts.'

'Exactly! The living and the dead. I can do it, Sarah, I know I can.'

Half an hour later, our passer-by, if he or she were watching still, would have seen the young couple scrambling down the hill, grasping at the tussock when their feet slipped, laughing, pausing to sip from the bottle the man carried in his pack. An enviable pair, the passer-by would almost certainly conclude. Young, healthy, in-the-pink. If – let's assume our voyeur is male – he were of charitable disposition he might wish them well. But if the bitterness of the age had entered his veins he'd probably curse them, and all their tribe. The Age of Anxiety, some commentators were calling it. Others referred to it as The Aspirin Age. Neither definition would have seemed relevant to Sarah Dutton or Louis de la Tour. But for all their gestures of independence, their conviction that they could *plan* their lives, like everyone else living in this time and place, their destinies would be shaped, not just by the prevailing mood, but by the large events waiting to happen.

Over the next six weeks Sarah and Louis saw each other every day. Mornings Louis spent painting, while Sarah tramped the streets looking for work. At midday they'd meet in town, and Sarah would buy lunch. For the time being she had money in her pocket. Her father still paid her an allowance, though he'd made it clear, if she went out to work, the allowance would stop. On the days when Sarah's spirits were low she'd want to turn her back on father, home, and money. But Louis would persuade her to be patient. 'If you leave home, you'll have to pay rent, then you won't be able to save a penny,' he'd point out. Sarah's suggestion that she move in with him he saw as a bitter joke. He was in love with her, had been from the start, but his feelings were not reciprocated. She'd let him kiss her. She'd even, on occasion, return his caresses. But her eyes didn't feed on him the way his did on her. 'The Madonna as Tease', he'd re-named her.

Afternoons they spent in Kitty's house, in Louis's untidy room; Sarah posing, while Louis sketched. As the weeks passed, the

Cezannes and Beulah Dowlings, which Louis had cut out of books and pinned on his walls, gradually disappeared, buried under drawings of the New World Madonna. But for every sketch pinned up, a dozen were discarded.

'It's me, isn't it?' Sarah would pout, at such times. 'You're disappointed in *me*.'

Some days they'd give up, and catch the tram out to Brighton for a swim in the sea. On the evenings of those days, after Sarah had returned to Rosevilla, Louis would draw a laughing Madonna, rising out of the waves like Botticelli's Venus, and for a short time he'd feel he'd got it right: the child's vision of the universe; the *human dimension*.

At the end of February Sarah landed a job as a corsetière in Beath's Department Store. The pay was only slightly more than the allowance her father had been paying, but it was her own money, and she intended to save every penny of it. 'I'm afraid this means no more lunches,' she told Louis.

'Pity.'

'You'll be all right, won't you? I mean, you won't starve.'

'Would you care?'

'Well, of course I would. Don't be stupid.'

'I'll tell you what's stupid, Sarah, this obsession of yours with getting to England. I mean, do you even know your brother wants you? Have you thought of that?'

It was their first quarrel. Louis cursed himself afterwards. Sarah was about to start work. For someone like her the daily drudgery would come as a shock. He knew. He'd worked himself, for ten months, in the wool stores. It had brought him, he'd calculated at the time, a year's independence. Now Sarah was going to experience at first hand what it was like to be part of the working population. He should have been supporting, not undermining. But he couldn't take back his words. Sooner or later he would have had to tell her what he thought.

'*Dear Sis,*

'*Perishingly cold here. My scout has just brought me some more coal, so hopefully my fingers will thaw and I'll get this finished before dinner.*

'*I have your last in front of me, and I must say I'm at a bit of a loss to know how to answer it. You and the pater always seemed to me to have a special thing going. I mean, how could you* QUARREL *with him? Wouldn't you have been better to do what he wanted, go to university, and see how things pan out? It's what I've done after all, and I have to admit it hasn't been so bad. There are some fine chaps here, and a female or two whose company I enjoy. Of course I'd rather be painting. That goes without saying. But I have my flying now. Did I tell you Ray and I got over to Paris at the weekend? Terrific jaunt. Flying over the Eiffel Tower gave me the biggest buzz of my life . . .*'

The letter came the day Sarah started work. Three days had passed since her quarrel with Louis, days in which she'd refused to see him or speak with him. How *dare* he suggest Richard didn't want her? Just because he wasn't close to his brother, or to anyone so far as she could see. All that first day at work, while the supervisor chanted instructions, and Sarah learned how to write out a docket and despatch it, with the payment, on the pulley suspended above the counter, Louis's words played over in her mind. By the time she got home, aching with tiredness, she was resolved never to see him again.

Richard's letter was waiting for her on the hall table. She ran upstairs, threw herself on her bed, and tore it open. It was the first she'd had since Christmas.

The tears started almost at once, angry tears, fuelled by her sense of the injustices done to her by her father and Louis. What did Richard mean by saying she should have done what the pater wanted? Didn't he see that was impossible? And who were these females whose company he enjoyed? At the bottom of the page she registered Louis's name, and Beulah Dowling's, but there was no comfort in reading about them. She and Richard had always agreed about everything. If *he* didn't understand why she'd taken this hateful job, who would? She might as well live at home, like her friend, Prue, or silly Daisy Linwood. All they ever thought about was having a good time.

Over the next week Sarah sweetened her workaday existence with massive doses of self-pity. Her job was tedious, and full of unexpected humiliations. Mrs Miles, the supervisor, kept hinting there must be a reason for the daughter of Sir Arthur Dutton to take a job in a department store. 'Romantic trouble?' she'd had the effrontery to suggest. 'You can confide in me, you know, dear.'

The customers were worse. Most of them looked at her as if she wasn't there. 'Isn't there someone else, someone a little more experienced?' they'd complain, when, as seemed to happen several times a day, she'd bring out the wrong article, a hip girdle, for instance, when what had been asked for was a side fastening corset. Travelling home on the tram Sarah would practise the smart answers she knew she could never make. Not if she wanted to keep the job.

'Good day, dear?' her mother would call out, as she came in through the door.

'Fine, thank you,' Sarah would answer, climbing the stairs towards the longed-for hot bath.

The only crumb of comfort was that Desmond and Daisy Linwood were no longer around to make jokes at her expense. Their visit, prolonged to the end of February, had fulfilled her worst expectations. Had she not been so preoccupied she might have mourned this ending of a childhood friendship: as it was all she could feel was relief that they'd gone. '*Why* do you want a job?' they'd probed a dozen times. 'What have you and your father quarrelled about?' 'Where do you go every day?' 'Who *is* Louis de la Tour?'

'Bully for you,' Desmond had chuckled, when she finally confessed what her job was to be. 'You can bone up on the matrons of Christchurch.'

Daisy had looked as if she were about to burst. 'Does this mean I can come to you for fittings?' she'd screeched.

But their cruellest jibes were saved for Louis. 'De la Tour,' Daisy had retorted, when Sarah could no longer avoid introducing them. 'Good name for an artist. Did you make it up?'

'Unkempt sorta fella, isn't he?' Desmond observed when Louis had gone. 'But then some women like that. Brings out the maternal instinct.'

'Who do they think they are?' Sarah complained to Louis every day. But Louis, who viewed Desmond as a rival, refused to discuss it.

A week after the arrival of her brother's letter Sarah decided to look at it again. Perhaps it wasn't as bad as she'd imagined. When this proved to be the case she felt both relieved and foolish. She still didn't like what Richard said about her quarrel with her father, but he'd written out of concern for her, hadn't he? He was unhappy thinking of her slaving away at a job she hated.

The rest of the letter, which she'd ignored, confirmed this view. Here was the brother she loved. The confidante she could write to about Louis and Beulah Dowling. The friend to whom she could send newspaper cuttings, knowing he'd share her glee at the frenzy generated by a recent article in the *Christchurch Press* on the subject of Trial Marriage.

What she wasn't prepared for was the bombshell on the last page. Richard had been on a visit to Lytton Cheyney, the family seat, so called, in Dorset. There he'd made a startling discovery. The Richard Arthur Dutton who'd migrated to New Zealand in the 1850s and built, twenty years later, the original Cheyney Grange, was not, as Sarah and her brother had been brought up to believe, the youngest son of the squire, but the child of his head woodsman. 'No doubt about it,' Richard wrote. 'The Duttons who live there now have done well – the old boy's a Lieutenant-Colonel. The pater was right about that. But their only connection, historically, with the Manor, was as a place of employment. Bit of a turnup, don't you reckon? The Colonel wasn't sure whether Father knew the true story or not . . .'

Sarah folded the letter carefully, and tucked it back in the scrapbook. Someone had been telling lies, and for not very noble reasons. Thing is, was her father the liar, or did it go back to the first New Zealand Dutton? If her father had been in residence she'd have asked him, but Sir Arthur was at Cheyney Grange. The only person at Rosevilla who could shed any light was her mother.

'Go ahead,' Margot instructed, when her daughter asked if she could read out something from Richard's letter.

When she got to the end, Sarah looked at her mother hopefully. She suddenly wanted very much to hear the lie was not her father's.

'I wouldn't say anything about this just yet,' Margot murmured.

'Does Daddy know, do you think?'

'If he does, he's not told me.'

'Doesn't it worry you?'

'That the Duttons aren't who they say they are? Not in the least. Why should it?'

Sarah thought about this for a moment, then smiled. 'You know, you're really quite a remarkable person, Mummy.'

They didn't speak of it again. Margot was leaving in the morning to join her husband. Neither of them wanted to spoil this last evening together. Sarah would be sad to see her mother go. They'd grown close in the last two months. 'Let me know when you've recovered from this madness,' her father had spluttered, the day she told him she'd been taken on at Beath's. But her mother had only smiled, and said, 'If it's what you want, dear.'

'I'll miss you,' Sarah said, when her mother asked if she'd be all right in her absence.

'That's what your father's been saying to *me*. He's not used to being on his own.'

'He hardly ever is.'

'Don't be too hard on him, dear, will you? This thing about his great-grandfather. Richard should keep it to himself.'

'We'll have to talk about it sometime.'

'Why?'

'Because it's important.'

Margot adjusted the combs in her hair. She was looking particularly lovely, Sarah thought. It suited her to live in town. 'I think you should be concentrating on the future,' Margot said, 'not the past. How much longer are you going to punish this nice young man of yours?'

'I'm not punishing him. Whatever gave you that idea?'

'Darling, he turns up here every night. What am I supposed to think?'

'You like him, don't you?'

'*My* feelings aren't the point.'

'I don't know, Mummy. Things aren't clear the way they used to be. I like Louis, I really do, but . . .'

'But you want to join your brother in England.'

Blood rushed to Sarah's cheeks. Was she such an open book then? Since her quarrel with her father she'd maintained a rigid silence on the subject of England. 'How did you . . . ?'

'You'll have children of your own one day,' her mother sighed. 'You'll learn what it is to watch, and say nothing.'

'I would have told you . . .'

'You didn't have to.'

'Has Daddy guessed too?'

'You've made your father very unhappy, Sarah. I'm not saying he's without fault. He can be as stubborn as you at times. But he loves you, more than you realise.'

6

Over the next week Sarah brooded on her mother's words, and wondered at the tolerance of women, Margot Dutton in particular, who so often looked sad, but who, these last two months, had seemed to acquire a new authority. By the end of the week she'd decided it was time to bring her quarrels to an end. She'd write back cheerfully to Richard. That was the first thing. And she'd say sorry to her father. She wouldn't give up her job, that was too much to ask. Richard's letter had made no mention of politics. Which suggested he was as convinced as she was there wouldn't be a war. So money was still the only thing stopping her going to England. Money, and Louis de la Tour . . .

Ending the quarrel with Louis was not so straightforward. She was still angry with him. But at least she could acknowledge that her anger had more to do with the fear he might be right. Richard had never said in so many words that he wanted her to join him.

Tomorrow was Saturday. If she felt the same way in the morning she'd take the tram to Sydenham, and knock on Kitty's door. Louis had made so many attempts to see *her*. At first, until she asked him to stop, he kept turning up at work. The excitement his appearances generated in Mrs Miles revolted Sarah. She could hardly pretend he was a customer. After that, he took to calling on her at home.

'It's him again, miss,' Pam would announce. 'What shall I say this time?'

She could have begun the process of reconciliation today. True to form Louis had rung the bell within minutes of her return from work. But Desmond Linwood was coming to dinner, and the last thing Sarah wanted was to be piggy-in-the middle. She had no idea why Desmond should want to see her. As she understood the situation they were barely on speaking terms. But he'd phoned her at work, and said he had something to tell her. He'd come up from Dunedin specially, he said.

'Get rid of him, *quick*,' she'd instructed Pam, when informed of Louis's presence. 'If he catches sight of Desmond . . .'

'You should tell him yourself,' the maid had grumbled.

Now, hearing the door bell ring again, Sarah braced herself for the encounter with Desmond. 'Be down in a sec,' she yelled.

She glanced in the mirror, jammed a clip in her hair, and wished, not for the first time, that her mother was still in residence. An entire evening alone with Desmond Linwood was a depressing prospect.

'How's varsity?' Sarah enquired, when drinks had been poured, and she and her guest were seated by the fire.

Desmond shrugged. It was a bad start.

'Aren't you missing lectures?' she persisted.

He managed to reply to that, and to the other routine questions she felt obliged to ask. But as they moved to the dining room, and the meal was served, the silences between these exchanges grew longer.

Finally, over dessert, Desmond found his voice. 'Now that you're a member of the working classes,' he said, leering at her across the table, 'I s'pose you're going to vote for that frightful little weasel?'

Sarah clattered her spoon in the bowl. 'Do you mean our Prime Minister?' she retorted coldly.

'You're just doing it to spite your father, aren't you?'

'Doing what?'

'This job. That wowser you go round with.'

'I don't go round with him. Anyway, you don't even know him.'

'I've seen him. That's enough.'

Sarah felt a spasm of pure hatred. Right, she thought. That's it! From now on I *do* go round with Louis de la Tour.

'It's getting late,' she announced briskly. 'What did you want to talk to me about?'

Desmond wiped his mouth on his napkin. 'Can we go somewhere else?' he asked.

'Out of the house, you mean?'

'Somewhere we won't be interrupted.'

Sarah pushed back her chair. 'You've changed, d'you know that?' she complained, as she led him through to her father's den. 'Varsity's changed you.'

'I'm not the one who's changed.'

When the door was closed, and they were seated opposite each other in large leather chairs, Sarah surprised herself by feeling a brief moment of compassion for Desmond. When had he become handsome? Surely not in the last few weeks? He'd thickened out, that was what she'd failed to notice before. His height was no longer at variance with his arms and legs. But it wasn't his looks that moved her to pity him. It was the compulsive way he kept cracking his knuckles. She'd ignored it through dinner, but here, in her father's sanctuary, there were no other sounds to distract her. She wondered about offering him a cigar (her father kept a box on his desk), but thought better of it. It would only prolong an already wretched evening.

'Daisy's getting engaged,' Desmond announced suddenly. 'It'll be in the papers next week.'

'What?' Sarah's mouth hung open in surprise. 'Who to?'

'James Mountford. You met him at the Creichtons. His father's a KC.'

'I didn't even know they were seeing each other.'

'Well, you and Daisy aren't exactly . . . not any more.'

'That's not my fault.'

'Isn't it?'

'Look, Desmond . . .' Sarah fixed her gaze on the row of framed awards and citations hanging above her father's desk. 'Given at Our Court of Saint James's under Our Sign Manual . . .' she read. It irked her that Daisy was to be engaged. It gave her far too much importance. 'Why can't the three of us be friends again?' she said sweetly. 'I hate all this bad feeling.'

'Daisy doesn't love James,' Desmond shot back at her.

'Then why . . . ?'

'Because she loves your rotten brother, that's why!'

An invisible fist punched Sarah in the chest. Daisy had cried for Richard in the Ladies' Room of the United Services Hotel. 'You don't know anything,' she'd sobbed. The next day Richard sailed for England.

'If he was here now, in this room, I'd strangle him,' Desmond snarled.

Sarah took in a breath. The pain in her chest was making speech difficult. 'But it's not his fault if Daisy . . .'

'You don't understand, do you?'

'Lots of girls . . . I mean, he's very good-looking, even if I say so myself. He can't help it if girls get crushes on him.'

'God, you're an arrogant lot, you Duttons. I mean, listen to yourself.'

'What have I said?'

'The assumption, the sheer bloody arrogance of it . . .'

'I suppose you expect me to believe it was Richard who had the crush?'

'It was rather more than that.'

Sarah tilted her head so that Desmond was no longer in her field of vision 'Most Excellent Order of the British Empire . . .' she read.

'He told her he wanted to marry her.'

'What!'

'He said she could join him in England. They'd be married there.'

'That can't be true.'

'He slept with her. *That's* what's true. He ruined her life. Everything else about him is a lie.'

Sarah sank back in her chair. 'Why are you telling *me* this?' she struck back. 'If it's true, which I don't believe, you should be saying it to Richard.'

'And how am I supposed to do that?'

'You can write a letter, can't you?'

Desmond laughed scornfully. 'You think he's God Almighty, don't you? You think the sun shines out of his arse.'

'Whereas We have thought fit to nominate and appoint . . .' Sarah read.

'Daisy came down to Dunedin to tell me about the engagement,' Desmond went on. 'We had a few drinks, and it all came

out. You should have been there, Sarah. I've never seen anyone
cry like that before.'

'I'm sorry . . .'

'Not half as sorry as your brother's going to be when I've
finished with him.'

'But you can't . . . I mean, it's over, isn't it? If it's true at all.
What point is there in . . . ?'

Suddenly Desmond leapt out of his chair, and lunged at her.
Sarah's first impulse was to laugh. They'd had plenty of physical
tussles as children. But then she felt his hands pulling at her
clothing, and she drew the breath down past the pain in her
chest, and pushed him to the floor.

For a few seconds after that all she was aware of was the
thumping of her heart. She felt no fear. Desmond may have
wanted to hurt her, but he'd never have been able to go through
with it. As he picked himself up off the floor she noticed he'd
torn his shirt.

'Sorry,' Desmond muttered. 'I'm sorry.'

'It's all right.'

'No, it's not.'

Sarah hauled herself out of her chair. She felt as if her bones
had been filled with lead. 'It doesn't matter, Desmond. Really.
We were both upset.' She tried to smile, but he looked so
wretched her intention faltered.

'What's happened to us, Sarah?' Desmond asked. 'It wasn't
meant to be like this.'

Before she could think of an answer, he was gone.

'Dear Rich,
    I'm at a bit of a loss to know how to reply to your letter . . .

'Dear Rich,
    *Sorry I haven't written. Now that I'm a working girl I don't
have much time . . .*

'Dear Rich,
    If I ask you something, will you tell me the truth . . . ?

That night Sarah dreamed she was back in hospital. 'Are all men the same?' she asked the nurse who came to check her dressing. 'Is my father? Is Louis?'

The nurse pulled the binding tight. 'Ow!' Sarah protested.

'A little pain never hurt anyone,' the nurse scolded.

'You haven't answered my question,' Sarah reminded her.

The nurse smiled. 'Love?' she said. 'It's a delusion. If you want my advice, you'll have nothing to do with it.'

7

When Louis saw Sarah standing on the doorstep his first thought was, something's wrong. She's been refusing to see me for two weeks. Why would she suddenly turn up now? But then he registered the look in her eyes, the Madonna as Tease, and he grinned at her and said, 'You'd better come in.'

'Hang on a jiff,' he instructed, as they neared his door.

'You've got someone in there,' Sarah accused. The words were out before she could censor them. What was the matter with her? She'd made up her mind to say nothing to Louis about last night's events. It would only confirm his suspicions about Desmond, for one thing. But that wasn't the real reason for her decision. She'd told Desmond she didn't believe him. His accusations about her brother were figments of Daisy's imagination. But she'd woken this morning with the familiar pain in her chest, the same pain she was experiencing now, and she'd known, as surely as if Richard had told her himself that Desmond's words were true.

'Abracadabra!' Louis shouted, throwing the door open, and ushering her in.

The room was in its usual state of colourful chaos, but it was the easel at its centre that caught Sarah's attention. A woman's face, painted against a hill crowned with three wind-bent trees, stared back at her. The woman's eyes were familiar. They rose out of the stark hillside like pools, giving and reflecting light. Were they her own eyes she was looking at? If so, where did that weight of sorrow come from?

'You've finished the painting,' she said softly.

'Do you like it?'

'*Like* it? Louis, it's marvellous.' She moved closer, then changed her mind and stepped back again. On the way here she'd resolved to make it up to Louis. She'd treated him badly. No point denying it. Now here she was, confronted with his vision of her, fighting back self-pitying tears.

'It's yours,' Louis said.

'What?'

'A birthday present.'

'But it's not . . .'

'Does it matter?'

'Not for another three weeks.'

'I showed it to Beulah. She wants me to exhibit it. I told her that would be up to you.'

Sarah took out a handkerchief and blew her nose. All the time she'd been angry with Louis he'd been working on this painting. For her. She didn't need Beulah to tell her it was good. She could see that for herself. 'You're going to exhibit?' she asked.

'It's Beulah's idea. There's to be a Group exhibition in September. She's persuaded the others to take me on.'

'But that's wonderful.' Sarah glanced at him, then looked away. She didn't want to have to explain her tears. They were for herself, which was shameful given the sheer good luck of her life. But they were also – and this was what she couldn't explain – for those nameless sorrows she saw in the Madonna's eyes, sorrows known to every woman who'd ever borne witness. 'It could be the start, couldn't it?' she said brightly. 'I mean, everyone's heard of the Group. Richard always said . . .'

'The picture was painted for *you*, Sarah.'

She gulped. If he was going to go on saying things like that she really would be in trouble.

She gestured at the Madonna. 'How do you know these things?' she demanded.

'You do like it then?'

'It's the most moving painting I've ever seen.'

Louis tossed his head, like a dog with a stick, then let out an exuberant whoop. Sarah was here, in his room. She'd come to him of her own free will. She *liked* his painting. 'I was going to paint you as a spirit,' he confessed. 'You know that story you told me? About the ghost in your hills? I had this idea of you finally seeing him, in a dream, and him turning out to be the Angel Gabriel.'

'I never knew you were so religious.'

'Isn't everyone?'

'I'm not.'

'Rubbish. You just *think* you're not.'

'I don't like church.'

'That's not what I mean by religious.'

They were standing a yard or so apart, facing the easel. Louis wanted very badly to kiss Sarah. Her tears had given her eyes an extra brightness. He wasn't so vain as to imagine those tears were for him. But his painting had inspired them. That was enough. 'You're a fool if you ever let this out of your sight,' Beulah had said. But Louis knew what he was doing.

'I've taken a job,' he announced cheerfully. 'Matter of necessity.'

Sarah looked stricken. 'But your work,' she protested.

'It's only part-time. Coaching maths. I quite enjoy it actually.'

'It's my fault, isn't it? If I hadn't been so pig-headed . . .'

'What are you talking about?'

'I used to buy you lunch.'

Louis flung his arm across his forehead. His hair lay back a moment on his scalp, then fell over his face again. 'What *about* lunch?' he grinned. 'Don't suppose there's a picnic in that basket, is there?'

Sarah's eyes sparked. 'Corned beef, tomatoes, my father's specially imported Stilton cheese, a bottle of South African wine, a cigar . . .'

'Don't,' Louis groaned. 'I'll die of bliss.'

'Where would you like to go?'

'Mountains or sea. You choose.'

'Mountains. More private.'

'Where we went before?'

'Why not?'

His hand reached out for hers. 'God, I've missed you,' he said.

'There's so much to tell you,' Sarah responded.

8 ∫.

Now began a time when Louis and Sarah could hardly bear to be out of each other's sight. Sarah had no idea it was possible to be so happy. When she wasn't with Louis she dreamed of his caresses. When she was with him, she wondered how long it would be before their loving took them over that threshold she'd always identified with marriage. She was even able to talk to him of Richard – the *real* Richard – and feel he understood both her continuing love, and her deep disappointment that her brother hadn't seen fit to confide in her.

Filled with this new emotion, Sarah looked on familiar things with the eyes of one miraculously healed from blindness. Even Mrs Miles took on a new significance. Her interest in her assistant's romantic life began to seem perspicacious. Sarah fought the temptation daily to confide in her. She wanted to tell everyone of her happiness. But she was still sufficiently in the world to see the folly of this. She was seventeen years old; Louis not yet twenty. It wasn't difficult to imagine what people would say should they make their feelings public.

As winter neared, and snow crept down the sides of the distant mountains, cooling the hot plains wind, and emptying the beaches, Sarah grew more and more certain that Louis was her destiny. Yet when she tried to follow that belief to its logical conclusion, her imagination failed. How could *he* marry *her* when he had no money and no job? How could *she* marry *him* when her father was sure to say no?

'I'm glad you've made it up with Louis,' her mother remarked, when she came back to town.

'Will you tell me the truth if I ask you something, Mummy?'

'Goodness, so serious.'

'Will you?'

'I'll try.'

'What's it like to be in love?'

But the answer Margot Dutton gave disappointed. 'It's like the weather,' she said. 'You have no control over it.'

As for Louis, the feelings Sarah roused in him were so bound up with his work he could barely distinguish the one excitement from the other. From the day of the picnic, when they ate her father's cheese and drank his wine, he existed in a daze of the senses. He was incapable of thinking rationally about her. His only rule was never to do anything she didn't want.

'When I asked to paint you, that first time,' he said, when there was nothing left of their picnic but the cigar he'd attempted to smoke, 'I saw you as unobtainable. I loved you, I was in love with you, but I didn't believe you'd ever let me close.'

'And now I have,' she said, smiling up at him.

'You're beautiful . . .'

'You want to paint me like this, don't you? That's what you're saying.'

'Are you a mind-reader?'

'I think I must be in love too,' she acknowledged.

When Beulah Dowling saw the drawings Louis had made of Sarah she was quiet at first, so that Louis feared they weren't as good as he'd imagined. But then she turned to him, and clapped her hands. 'You must exhibit these too,' she said. 'I'll speak to the others.'

'You don't think Sarah will mind?'

Beulah looked at him over the top of her glasses. In her shapeless tunic, long green cardigan, and scarf knotted round her head, she looked like the woman come to clean, not an artist of international reputation. 'If Sarah's half the girl I think she is,' she said to him, 'she'll be proud.'

Some nights Louis couldn't sleep for excitement. Images of Sarah crowded his brain, compelling him to take up his pencil and draw. The curve of her hip, the soft cushion of her stomach, the long line of her back, the sharp peak of her knee, became, for him, emblems of the land. Sometimes he painted her as a geometrical shape, a dislocation of the human form to match the tumbling mountain rocks. At other times he saw her as fluid; face dominated by its eyes, arms extended, streamers of cloud floating above her head. Because he loved her he could grasp the paradox that had been eluding him all this time: that in order to paint he must work from his ego; but to paint well, to catch the truth, his ego must die.

At the end of March Sarah turned eighteen. Her father, with whom she was now reconciled, had insisted the occasion called for something more than a celebratory dinner.

'A party. Here at Rosevilla,' he'd announced. 'With all your friends.'

Sarah's protests had proved a waste of breath.

'Make a list,' her father had instructed. 'Desmond, of course. And Daisy and her fiancé. Then there's the cousins . . . Oh, and your friend, Prue. What's she up to these days? We don't see nearly enough of her.'

Only at the very last had he mentioned Louis. 'Mustn't forget our struggling artist,' he'd chuckled.

'Dear Rich,

'Sorry it's taken so long to write. The parents are insisting I have a party for my eighteenth birthday. Can't say I want to much. It'd be different if you were here . . .

'Rich, I have something to tell you. It concerns Daisy. She's engaged, did you know? To James Mountford. They're to be married in the Cathedral in August. Will you write back to me about this, tell me what you think? Perhaps you know James? He's coming to my party. He seems nice enough, but how can you tell? How can you tell about anybody really . . . ?'

'If it's marriage you want,' Louis whispered, as they danced to the music of the band Sir Arthur had hired, 'you must tell me. I don't see it as important myself. Why involve other people? But you, your family . . .'

Sarah glanced over her shoulder. The party was a success. The dining room, converted to a ballroom for the evening, decorated with fern fronds and white lilies, swayed to the music of Duke Ellington, played by five musicians disguised as negroes. Prue, her best friend, was dancing with Desmond. What were they talking about? So far Desmond had avoided her, for which Sarah was grateful. But Prue had sought her out, to confide a secret, and Sarah had returned the favour. 'So we're *both* in love,' she'd marvelled. 'Remember how we used to wonder about it? What it would be like? Well, now we *know*.'

'So whadda ya say?' Louis insisted. 'Shall we get married?'

'We're too young,' Sarah answered him. 'How would we live?'

Louis drew her close. 'We'd find a way,' he promised. 'We're both working class now.'

On 4 April Beulah Dowling's exhibition opened at the McDougall Gallery. The public, confronted with a melange of paintings ranging in style from the extremes of Expressionism to the barely recognisable forms of Beulah's personal Symbolism, reacted with polite expressions of interest, and the display, wherever possible, of knowledge.

'Ah yes, you can see it there, in the juxtaposition of those shapes, the influence of Braque . . .'

'Mondrian, without a doubt. Almost a copy, wouldn't you say?'

'Now what would you call *that*? Homage to Kandinsky?'

Louis, stalking the paintings like a hungry lion, seethed. 'Whadda they know?' he muttered to Sarah. 'Of course other artists are present here. Painting is a form of dialogue.'

But Sarah, dizzied with looking, said nothing. Where, among all this confusion of shape and line, was Beulah's comfortable presence? Where her kindness, her ordinariness? Some of the paintings seemed to have been deliberately disfigured. The trunk of a tree, smooth as bone, rose out of a dark swamp into a tangle of foliage that made Sarah think of dried blood. 'Is this how you see life here?' she wanted to ask. 'Is it really so terrible?'

*   *   *

Two weeks later the letter Sarah had been longing for, and dreading, arrived. But none of the things she'd anticipated – explanation, confession, some sign of contrition – were there. All Richard had to say on the subject of Daisy's engagement was, 'Hope this Mountford chap has a good supply of handkerchiefs. She's a great little crier, our Daisy.'

The rest of the letter was even more dispiriting. Richard had joined the RAF Volunteer Reserves. 'Everyone here seems to think there'll be a war,' he wrote. 'If there is, then I want to be in from the start . . .'

'Yes,' her father sighed, when she went to him with the news. 'It was in our letter too.'

'Is that why Mummy's crying?'

Sir Arthur gestured his helplessness in the face of female emotion. 'Richard's not a child any more,' he said sternly.

'But you promised. You said, if there was a war, he'd come home.'

'And I'm not saying he won't.'

'You know what *your* trouble is, don't you?' Louis said, when Sarah went to him for comfort. 'You take everything too literally. Of course your brother'll come back. Why should he fight for England?'

'It's not just England, it's the Empire.'

'But he's a New Zealander.'

'P'r'aps he feels English now. Dadddy said he did, when he was there.'

'Talking of your father, did you ever confront him with that stuff about your great-grandfather?'

'Mummy asked me not to.'

Louis ran a hand through his hair. Flecks of green paint marked the trail of his fingers. 'What is it about families?' he brooded. '*Your* family anyway. Have you always protected each other? Or is it *The Family* you're protecting? The institution. I don't much like it, love, sorry. It smacks of Empire building.'

'I'll have enough money saved by the end of the year,' she wrote back to her brother. 'So there'd better *not* be a war . . .'

What she didn't divulge was the change in her relationship with Louis. That was her revenge. Richard hadn't confided in her about Daisy, so she wouldn't about *her* love life. There were plenty of other things to tell him: Beulah's exhibition; *Blockade*, the new Henry Fonda movie; the wonders attributed to the Slimform Girdle; Prue Coleridge's engagement to a widower with two young sons . . . Sarah had no idea it was possible to write so much about so little.

But the subject of war, for all Sarah's determination to ignore it, refused to go away.

'Those who see war as an option are deranged,' Louis declared, when Sarah visited him on the eve of Anzac Day. 'You don't expect me to watch the parades, do you?'

'Why not? They're about remembering, aren't they?'

'Celebrating, more like.'

'An uncle of mine was killed in the war.'

'What does that prove?'

'I don't know.' Sarah looked at him crossly. She wondered why he was speaking so loudly, till she saw the cotton wool in his ears. The local band was practising in the street outside. 'It has to mean *something*, doesn't it?' she challenged.

Louis put down his brush, removed the plugs from his ears, and kissed her. 'It's you I'm thinking of,' he said. 'The less people see war as an option the better for your brother. That's what you want, isn't it? For him to be safe.'

'*He* wants to fight.'

'He doesn't know what he's talking about.'

'He's not a coward.'

'And I am. Is that what you're saying?'

She didn't answer. For the first time in weeks she felt the old pain in her chest. She blamed Louis. She should have been concentrating on getting to England, not spending her time with a man she couldn't, for all her efforts to visualise it, see herself marrying.

'Look,' he soothed, 'my objection to Anzac Day is very simple. It's nothing to do with denigrating past sacrifice. That would be crass. But you tell me, honestly now, when you hear the bands, see men marching, what happens to your pulse rate? It's exciting, that's what it is, sending men off to war. No one thinks of the consequences.'

'People don't *want* to die.'

'Course they don't. But you never think it's going to happen to you.'

Sarah's face set in an expression of mute resistance. Louis had seen that look before, most recently the night he foolishly asked her if she still intended to go to England. When he heard her answer, he'd had to bite back the words that jumped into his mind. There was something deranged about her attitude to her brother.

'Think about it,' he said. 'One good Anzac parade, and at the end of the day a few hundred more men will want to go off and fight. Anticipating war is the same as wishing it into existence, Sarah. You can't have it both ways. The ultimate failure of the political process, that's what war is.'

It could have been a quarrel. The fact that it wasn't did little to allay Louis's anxiety. They'd quarrelled about Sarah's brother before. Now, with other differences building up between them, it seemed inevitable they would quarrel again.

10

The arrival of winter put an end to picnics, but otherwise made no difference to the amount of time Louis and Sarah spent together. Sarah no longer bothered to tell her parents where she was when she didn't come home for dinner. There was only one rule: she must be in by ten. Otherwise, apart from Sundays, when she was expected, if her parents were in town, to attend morning service at the Cathedral, she was left free. This in itself was something of a puzzle. It wasn't customary for girls of her class to go about unchaperoned. Louis was of the opinion her parents were hoping she'd get sick of him. He cited the long tram ride home from Sydenham and his singular failure to provide glamorous evenings out as evidence of what Sir Arthur and Lady Dutton would be bound to see as his shortcomings. But Sarah suspected her parents' liberalism sprang from an entirely different cause. 'Know what I think?' she confided. 'I think they *like* having the house to themselves. They're always together now, whether at Rosevilla or the Grange. I swear to you, Louis, the nights I am home with them, Mummy just mopes about, listening to the wireless.'

But there were times when Sarah wished there was a place she could go, just to be on her own. The news from Europe was increasingly depressing: what with the German Army mobilising along the Czech border; every day Jews being expelled from their businesses and homes. Caught between her father's militarism and Louis's growing pacifism, desperately anxious about her brother, Sarah began to see it as a matter of survival to have a view of her own, one by which she could navigate the twists and turns of her daily life. Her father had joined the Defence League soon after it was set up in 1936. At first he'd been prepared to give Hitler the benefit of the doubt, at the same time arguing that peace was best served by the maintenance of a strong army. Now he was convinced of the need to re-introduce conscription. 'If we don't watch out,' he'd been warning, publicly and privately, 'that bunch of crypto-pacifists in Wellington will lead us all to the slaughter.'

Sarah listened to what her father had to say, but kept her thoughts to herself. There was to be an election in November. For the first time in her life she'd be voting. If her father knew she'd decided to vote Labour he'd choke on his cigar. 'It's that renegade you keep company with, isn't it?' he'd splutter. 'My God, Sarah, when I think what you're throwing away! I'm just glad your grandfather isn't alive to witness this betrayal.'

'You're wrong about Louis, Daddy,' Sarah would have been able, with perfect honesty, to answer. 'My politics were formed years ago, with you, when I asked you to explain the relief gangs on the riverbank. The image of those men has haunted me ever since. Now, of course, I see the same gaunt faces every day on the trams. It was what I saw, and failed to recognise, in the eyes of the shearers peering at me from under their hats. And it was what disturbed me in hospital, talking to the woman in the bed next to mine. You remember her, Daddy? I introduced you. Mrs Parmenter. The lady with all the children.'

'What on earth are you talking about?' her father would be bound to explode. 'What's this Parmenter woman got to do with anything?'

She could hear him as if he were in the room with her. As, when her mind was troubled like this, she could hear Louis.

'Make your own decisions, for God's sake!' he had shouted the night they nearly quarrelled about Richard. 'Marry me, or don't marry me. Make love to me, or drive me crazy, but do it for *you*, not for your brother . . .'

'Why *don't* you marry him?' Prue had demanded, after church last Sunday. As an engaged woman she viewed marriage as the gateway to happiness. 'You love him, don't you?'

'It's not that simple.'

'Why should it be simple?'

'Oh, I don't know. You're different from me. You take risks.'

'I don't think it's that at all. I think you're still stuck on being with Richard. You're an idiot, Sarah. He's your brother, not your goddam' keeper.'

Could Prue be right? The thought gnawed at Sarah, infecting her happiness. But then she'd see Louis again, and her doubts would vanish, and she'd answer Prue in her head, I only want to *talk* to Richard, that's all. Put things right. Then I can get on with my life.

'Now, young lady,' her father said, on the eve of Daisy Linwood's wedding, 'since we're talking ceremonies, we should be making plans for your coming out.'

'I'm not coming out, Daddy. I told you.'

'Nonsense. Dutton women have always been presented. At Court preferably, though the present situation rules that out, I'm sorry to say.'

Sarah looked at her mother. Surely she would come to her defence? Last time the question had been raised, Margot Dutton had agreed with her daughter. Sarah was a working girl. She was in love with a penniless artist. How could she possibly be a debutante?

'Mummy agrees with me, don't you?' Sarah said, forcing her mother's hand. 'I'm sorry if it upsets you, Daddy. But I won't change my mind. Please don't let's quarrel about it.'

To her surprise her father, a few moments later, capitulated. His wife had a point, he conceded. Their daughter was not following her pre-destined path. He didn't like it, but given the changed world they were now inhabiting he supposed he'd have to lump it.

Next day, as Sarah was dressing for the wedding, her father handed her a parcel. 'Something I picked up for you in town,' he said, smiling in approval of the hat she was pinning to her head. 'Is that an ostrich feather?' he asked.

'Do you like it?'

'Very becoming.'

She didn't open the parcel till her father had gone. She knew, more or less, what would be in it. It amused her father to buy historical romances for her. He'd been doing it for years.

But it wasn't a romance. It was some kind of equestrian handbook. Its title was *The Breeding and Training of Horses*, and it was by a man called Pearse Byrne.

'Coming,' she shouted, in answer to her mother's call. She turned to the first page. 'A horse is like a child,' she read. 'He must be treated with firmness and kindness. If he is disobedient, it is the fault of the master . . .'

She closed the book, and ran downstairs. She hadn't been to Cheyney Grange since Christmas. She'd told herself she'd go back when Richard came home. But that wasn't an answer she could give her father, who never stopped trying to persuade her to return. Caesar had been put to stock work. He was no longer her horse. If this book was meant to press that particular nerve, it had succeeded. Though there was something else troubling her as she climbed into the waiting car. The book had only just been published, so why did she have the feeling she'd seen it before?

The thought kept recurring through the farce of Daisy's wedding.

'You're not still planning to go to England, are you?' her mother asked, as they took their seats at the reception. 'Because your father will stop you. He can, you know, you're under age.'

It was typical, Sarah thought sourly, for her mother to choose such a moment to bring up the subject she'd been avoiding for weeks.

'He can't stop me forever,' she snapped back.

When, after hours of tedium and forced jollity, Sarah finally made it round to Louis's, she threw herself on his bed, and vented her pent-up feelings.

'If we were engaged,' he comforted, nuzzling her ear, 'I would have been there with you.'

'What's that got to do with it?'

She felt his arm behind her back stiffen. 'What's the matter?' he asked.

'Nothing.'

'Yes, there is. You've got that look on your face.'

'Oh, for heaven's sake!' Sarah's hands shot out, simultaneously pushing him away and grabbing her discarded coat. 'If you're going to be like that, I'm going.'

'What have I said?'

'You don't need me anyway. You can get Kitty to pose for you. You're always telling me how sensual she is.'

'Sarah . . .'

The door slammed. 'Damn and blast!' Louis shouted, loud enough for Sarah to hear.

The long honeymoon had come to an end.

11

Spring brought a change of mood to the country. The winter had been hard. Stock losses were being compared to the disastrous freeze of 1936. But now the snows were melting, and the flood waters were receding. On the domestic front the Government's Social Security Bill held out the promise of universal prosperity, while beyond New Zealand's shores there was talk of the need to contain Germany, not by war, but by treaty.

'This is more like it,' Louis declared, grinning over the top of his paper at Sarah. They were friends again, much to their mutual relief. Their quarrel, this time, had lasted only a few days. 'You know something?' he went on. 'I read somewhere, in the *Peace Record* I think it was, that Britain is spending two hundred pounds a minute on armaments, and tuppence halfpenny on peace. Well, maybe they'll start to get things a little more balanced now . . . Sarah?'

'Sorry. What did you say?'

'You don't *want* war, do you?'

''Course not.'

'I wish you'd come with me tomorrow night. Dick Sheppard's a good speaker.'

'If my father knew you were going to these meetings . . .'

'It's a free country. I don't interfere with him.'

'He says, if you have your way, people like you, pacifists and such, the freedoms you take advantage of will be destroyed.'

'Is that what *you* believe?'

Sarah leaned across the table and kissed him. They were having tea in the Square before she caught her tram home. These days Louis was too busy preparing for his exhibition to see much of her. All the works he'd submitted to the Group had been accepted. The drawings of her, done in those heady weeks after their picnic in the Cashmere Hills, had excited considerable comment for their frank sexuality. Sarah was delighted. She didn't mind a bit that Beulah and the rest of them knew it was *her* body displayed across the walls. Others wouldn't find her so easy to identify. 'I believe in *you*,' she answered. 'In your work. And I don't want to quarrel.'

Six days later, on 15 September, the Group exhibition opened. The headline in the *Press* that day read, 'CHAMBERLAIN FLIES TO GERMANY'. The exhibition was not mentioned.

Sarah, arriving at the Gallery during the opening speech (Mrs Miles had *not* been sympathetic to her leaving early), felt conspicuous among so small a gathering. There were the other artists, most of whom she recognised, and a clutch of strangers, friends or relatives of the exhibitors, she imagined, since the public, it was all too apparent, had stayed away.

'I'm sorry, darling,' she whispered, as she and Louis drifted round the room, 'it's not fair, your first show . . .'

'I'm not the only one affected.'

'The others are all right. They're established.'

'Hardly. Louise Henderson maybe. The rest . . .'

'I'm *furious* with my parents. They said they'd come.'

Louis smuggled a hand inside Sarah's coat, and squeezed her breast. 'Think what they would have said,' he breathed.

'Serve them right!'

'They'd be sure I'd deflowered you.'

'Well, you have, almost.'

'Ah . . . but what a world's contained in that *almost*.'

Next day the *Press* announced, 'BERCHTESGADEN SCENE OF VITAL MEETING'. Underneath, in smaller letters, were the words, 'Pitfalls of State Ownership Described by Leader of Opposition'. No matter how many times Sarah scanned the pages, the result was always the same. Nowhere did the exhibition get a mention.

Never had she hated her job more. Mrs Miles was worse than the worst house-mistress at school. The women who wanted years taken off their lives and inches off their waists were vain fools, indifferent to the suffering of their fellow human beings. All Sarah could think about was being with Louis, and comforting him.

But Louis, when he opened the door to her that evening, looked cheerful. 'I've had an idea,' he said. 'Come and tell me what you think.'

'Bloody Hitler, bloody Chamberlain, bloody bloody, bloody,' Sarah exploded, when the door was closed.

'Never mind about that,' Louis laughed. 'Tell me what you think of this?'

He grabbed her elbow, and steered her towards the unmade bed. Then, still with a grin on his face, he picked up his sketch pad, and sat down beside her. 'The creation story, here, in New Zealand, whadda ya think?' he gabbled, flicking the pages so rapidly the drawings became a blur. 'Garden of Eden, serpent, expulsion, Cain, Abel, the lot.'

'Slow down, Louis. I can't see.'

'I thought a mural, or a series of panels covering a whole wall . . .'

'Louis!'

His fingers fluttered to a halt. 'Look!' he commanded. 'D'ya recognise that face? Isn't he the perfect Adam?'

'It's Desmond Linwood!' Sarah exclaimed.

'And this,' Louis went on, jumping back a page. 'I struggled for hours with this little fella. How in tarnation d'ya paint the devil? Then I hit on the moustache.'

Sarah laughed. 'Louis de la Tour, you're a genius,' she said.

'Now, here we have the world *after* Eden. I'd like to get Mickey Savage in there somewhere. A sort of small town problem-solver, you know the type?'

'Who's this?' Sarah asked, when another page was turned. 'It looks like Desmond, but . . .'

Louis grinned. 'You don't imagine Adam was *white*, do you?'

By the time they'd examined all the sketches, they were both exhausted. 'Sorry sweetheart, sorry,' Louis breathed in Sarah's ear. 'I'm a selfish swine.'

'I thought you'd be depressed. I came round to comfort you.'

Louis dropped his head into her lap. 'I wish you could stay the night,' he murmured. 'I wish we were married, and I could make love to you.'

Thirteen days later, when news of the Munich Agreement broke, Sarah came to a decision. Two months had passed without a letter from Richard. He'd been on holiday in Europe, that could explain it. But if anyone had asked her, now, what her brother was going to do with his life, she'd have had to answer, 'I don't know. I don't know what's important to him any more.'

'Richard, I so want to talk to you,' she'd written in her last, long letter. 'I feel I can't *progress* till I do. Does that make sense to you?' Now, with Mr Chamberlain's guarantee of peace, there was no prospect of her brother's coming home for another year at least. She was glad, of course, that there wasn't to be a war. She'd never been convinced it would bring Richard back anyway. But with the clearing of the air, internationally, came a revival of the belief in normal life. Overnight Sarah found herself looking at her own life, and judging it, by the standards of the day, as anything *but* normal.

She didn't reflect for long. With her usual impatience she dismissed the last nine months as a dream, *ab*normal, because she'd deluded herself into thinking she could do nothing, decide nothing, till she'd seen Richard. The irony was, she'd saved almost enough to get to England. Till now she'd persuaded herself her father's opposition wasn't a problem. She'd lie about her age. Or run away. But Louis had pointed out, in one of their painful discussions on the subject, that it wasn't just money she needed. There was the little matter of a passport.

'I won't be in for dinner, Mummy,' Sarah said, on the phone.

'You've heard the news?'

'Terrific, isn't it?'

'Darling, it's a miracle. If you knew how worried I've been . . .'

'Does Daddy know?'

'He's on his way home now. We thought we'd go out to dinner.'

'Don't wait up for me. Louis and I'll probably go out too.'

On the tram to Sydenham all the talk was of Chamberlain and Hitler, and what the agreement meant to New Zealand, and whether it really did guarantee peace, or just postpone the evil day. Listening to her usually silent fellow-passengers Sarah wondered how any two people could ever agree about anything, since there seemed to be as many shades of opinion as there were travellers on the tram.

As she walked up the now familiar street she waved to Kitty's neighbours, and greeted those she knew by name. There was talk here too: relief and scepticism and rejoicing. Sarah was glad of the charged atmosphere. It would explain the heightened colour in her cheeks, and the way her feet kept running ahead of her.

'You're early!' Louis beamed at her over a dripping paint brush. 'Don't tell me the dragon lady let you off?'

'Have you heard what's happened?'

'I caught it on the wireless at lunchtime. What are we going to do to celebrate?'

'I brought this.' Sarah took a bottle of sherry out of her basket. 'And these.' Cream cakes followed. 'Then I thought we might make love.'

'What?'

Sarah laughed. Now that she'd arrived her nervousness had vanished. The excitement she'd sensed in the streets was the wake of a storm that had passed. Here, in this room, she was buoyed with certainty. This man, this moment, were all that mattered.

She removed her coat, rinsed a couple of glasses, and poured the sherry. 'Well, don't just stand there,' she scolded.

'Sarah, I'm confused. Does this mean you'll marry me?'

'Cheers!' Sarah grinned.

'I see. You've been worried about Richard, and now you think . . .'

'It's nothing to do with Richard.'

'Isn't it?'

'Well, yes, in a way. But it's not what you think.'

Louis held out his glass. 'I need more,' he said, frowning.

'I still want to see Richard,' Sarah admitted. 'Talk to him. But I can't wait for that to happen to . . .'

'You make it sound as if you were going to ask his permission.'

'Louis, don't make this difficult.'

'Difficult? Jesus!'

Sarah sat down on the bed. This wasn't at all how she'd imagined it. 'Can I have a cigarette?' she requested.

There was silence while they lit up, then Sarah asked, 'Where's Kitty?'

'Out. She's got an admirer. Didn't I tell you? A doctor. I suspect he's married.'

Sarah sipped on her sherry. She was tempted to follow Louis's example, and swallow it all. 'I think Richard's going to stay in England,' she said, acknowledging the need for an explanation. 'Whether there's a war or not, I mean. Not that he's said anything. I'm just guessing.' She stopped. It was clear from Louis's expression that he needed more. 'If he comes back here he'll never be an artist, will he?' she went on irritably. 'He's not like you. He wouldn't be able to turn his back on his family.'

'You almost persuade me to like him.'

'You would, if you knew him.'

'Go on.'

'He loves Cheyney Grange, I know he does, but it's not his destiny to live there. It's not mine either . . .'

'What if he decides *not* to be artist? What if he isn't . . . good enough, lucky enough, whatever?'

'I don't know. I can't think that far ahead. I only know what it's like to be his sister.'

'And what *is* that like?'

Sarah swallowed the rest of her sherry, coughing as it burned its way down to her stomach. She was beginning to regret removing her coat. It was cold in Louis's room. 'I'd always imagined,' she said, 'before I met you that is, that I'd live near Richard. With him even. From earliest childhood that was how I saw my life. I know it sounds crazy, but we were, are, close. There weren't any other kids around when we were growing up. Perhaps that explains it. I don't know. It's just how it was.' She shivered. For some reason she found herself thinking of Paddy O'Connor, and the night she and Richard camped on the mountain waiting for his ghost. She'd been cold then too.

'Do you love me, Sarah?' Louis asked. He was standing by the easel, a glass in one hand, a cigarette in the other. Sarah, who'd never thought of him as handsome, saw him, in that moment, as something much more. He was irresistible.

'You know I do,' she answered.

'Because if you're doing this for any other reason . . .'

Sarah stubbed out her cigarette in one of Louis's abandoned palettes. 'Come here. Please,' she pleaded.

'Jesus Christ, Sarah . . .'

'Don't you want us to make love?'

There was no answer.

'Louis, I'm *freezing.*'

She couldn't take her eyes off him. Why had she never seen him like this before? If they had a child, would it be freckled like him? she wondered. She was startled, but not at all embarrassed, by the direction her thoughts were taking. In books it was always the man who did the persuading.

'There's something I want to tell you first,' Louis said. 'It's about your brother.'

Sarah pulled the eiderdown up from the end of the bed, and wrapped it around her. She was glad Kitty was out. Sometimes, when she and Louis were cuddling, he'd let out a groan, which she felt sure Kitty must hear. It was always more exciting when they had the house to themselves.

'That business with Daisy,' Louis said. 'I wanted to say this to you at the time. I mean, I'm not making excuses for your brother or anything, but most women don't know, don't realise, how difficult it is being male. I mean, no one tells you how it will be, past puberty. There are these girls you've know all your life, and suddenly you want to make love to every single one of them. I'm not exaggerating, Sarah. These are biological facts. Men between the ages of fourteen and twenty, fourteen and thirty for all I know, think about sex every minute of the day. All girls have to do is preserve their virtue. Boys, on the other hand . . .'

Sarah pushed back the eiderdown, and slid her feet on to the floor. 'Don't talk any more, darling,' she implored, pulling him towards the bed. 'You're making me nervous.'

12 ∫

The year between Munich and the outbreak of war would be variously described by historians as the Year of Dreams, or the Year of Delusions, or even, given what followed, the Year of Madness. But for Sarah, confiding in her friend, Prue, there was a different label. 1938–9 was her Year of Destiny. Not that she imagined, at the time, that her destiny would be anything but glorious. She and Louis would overcome all obstacles to live happily and colourfully ever after. Later, when the temptation to blame – society; her parents; the Government – was part of her daily struggle, she would concede that the momentous decisions taken by politicans and generals during those twelve months did deeply affect her life. But she would never deny that she too made choices; choices moulded by the opinions she was at such pains to forge at the time.

None of which cast more than the palest shadow over the days immediately following her eager relinquishing of her virginity. She was certain people must notice the difference in her, and was vaguely affronted when they didn't. (When, two years later, her mother told her she *had* noticed, Sarah felt betrayed. How many others had guessed, and said nothing?) She was equally certain the gods were on her side. It was more than just personal. There was the Munich Agreement, enshrining the desire of the German and British peoples 'never to go to war again', and there was the Labour Government's landslide victory in the election. Sarah and Louis, celebrating with the crowds on that crisp October night, hugged one another, and cheered till their lungs hurt. Now there would be peace *and* justice. What a world in which to be in love!

'I've taken a flat,' Louis announced, at the beginning of December. 'It's in the next street. Well, when I say "flat", what I really mean is a room. But it's got the lot – two good north-facing windows, stove, tub to wash in, dunny outside. All for two guineas a week. Whadda ya say? Will you come "live with me and be my love?"' He picked her up, spun her round, and breathed warm laughter over her face.

'Put me down!' Sarah laughed back. 'You know I can't.'

'Why not?'

'We're not married.'

'And whose fault's that?'

'Don't start, Louis . . .'

'Once upon a time you said I couldn't make love to you. Now look at you. Hungry for it, brazen hussy.'

'I don't notice you discouraging me.'

'Who discourages happiness?'

'That's what I mean. We're happy the way we are. Why change things?'

But change was not subject to agreements, personal or otherwise.

'. . . Don't want to alarm the parents,' Richard wrote, in the letter Sarah received at Christmas, 'but Munich isn't worth the paper it's written on. You probably only hear the good news out there. How the policy of appeasement is working, tommy rot of that sort. No one here believes that any more, not even Chamberlain . . .'

In a later paragraph he talked of his weekends training at the RAF base at Northolt, and his first taste of flying the single-seater Hawker Hurricane. 'But you know, Sis,' he wrote, 'now that war looks inevitable, I've rediscovered my passion for painting. God knows why, or how, I lost sight of it. Reckon I must have gazed at too many marvels on too many European walls. Inspiring at first, but finally intimidating. How could I ever hope to match even the least of it? But when I got back to Oxford this time I suddenly started drawing again. Not the view from the window, but home, Cheyney Grange . . .'

Sarah's heart missed several beats when she read that. She wanted to be glad. It meant he was thinking of home, of *coming* home even. But how could she be glad when the rest of his letter talked of preparations for war? 'They're digging up Hyde Park,' he wrote. 'It's a right mess, I can tell you. Sandbags strewn everywhere, planks of timber, red-faced men up to their waists in mud. At least no one complains about unemployment any more . . .'

Louis, when she told him, shook his head and looked melancholy. He'd been in his flat for over a month now. It was even more cluttered than his room at Kitty's. 'Come with me tonight,' he said, seizing Sarah's hand. 'You don't have to do anything, just listen.'

'And stand with you on a corner handing out subversive literature? You must be joking.'

'Ormond Burton'll be speaking. How can you be so sure you're against him if you've never heard him?'

'See what I mean?' Sarah's hand twitched. She wanted to *shake* Louis. Hardly a day went by now when he didn't speak or listen or write on behalf of the pacifist movement. Yet when she accused him of lack of patriotism he had the gall to answer, 'There are more ways to love your country than putting on a uniform, Sarah.'

'How can we ever be married?' she challenged now. 'We have nothing in common, nothing at all.'

At the end of the New Year holiday Sarah handed in her notice at Beaths. Her father was jubilant. 'You've come to your senses at last!' he beamed. 'Now perhaps we'll see something of you at the Grange.'

'Only if I can bring Louis,' Sarah answered him.

'Don't you see enough of him during the week?'

'You might as well get used to the idea, Daddy, one of these days I'm going to marry him.'

Seven weeks later Sarah enrolled at the university. The two decisions – to give up her job, and to start studying for an Arts degree – were taken separately. The first was a natural consequence of the relinquishing of her dream of going to England. The second followed from the first. But there were other factors of which Sarah was only partly conscious. She wanted to make her own mind up on the subject of war, and peace. It was too easy for Louis to accuse her of thinking like her father. Easy and wrong! She'd proved her independence. Voted against her father's interests. 'You're really no different from *him*,' she'd retaliate, whenever they argued. 'You want me to think the same as *you*.'

'That's drivel, and you know it. I want you to think for *yourself*.'

Which is exactly what I'm doing, Sarah told herself, as she made her way, among throngs of strangers, to her first lecture. Though that argument too was flawed, since thinking for yourself was clearly *not* the point of attending university. She discovered that during her first tutorial.

'I don't understand you,' a radiant, newly married Prue complained. 'You say you love Louis, yet you don't want to marry him. Is it because he's got no money?'

'Don't be silly.'

'It is, isn't it?'

'My father wouldn't let me. I'm still only eighteen, you know.'

'So was I, when I met Ivor.'

'Yes, but . . .'

'You don't think *I* had opposition? Ivor's forty-one years old. My parents weren't exactly thrilled at the idea of having him for a son-in-law.'

'You can twist your parents round your little finger.'

'So can you.'

'Not over Louis I can't. They blame him for all my . . .' Sarah had to search for the word. 'Deviations,' she decided.

'So you'll wait till you're twenty-one.'

'I expect so.'

'You don't sound very sure.'

'Oh, give it a rest, Prue. I love him, isn't that enough?' They were talking in the quadrangle of the university. Sarah was between lectures. Prue had come looking for her, wanting to talk curtain materials and recipes and the advantages of permed hair. 'I'm scared of marriage, if you must know,' Sarah admitted. 'I don't want to turn into my mother.'

In the middle of March news of the German invasion of

Czechoslovakia broke. It was all a long way away from Christ-church, but Sarah, listening to her father talk on the wireless of the need to bring in conscription *now*, felt the familiar tightening of the muscles in her chest. The Japanese were advancing into China; the Germans were striding across Europe; while Louis de la Tour held aloft a placard proclaiming, 'WAR IS A SIN AGAINST GOD AND A CRIME AGAINST HUMANITY'.

'I don't see killing people as a solution to anything,' he insisted, during one of their interminable arguments on the subject. 'And no, it's not because I'm a Christian. That's your department. You're the one who goes to church.'

'They've got conscription in England now. It can only be a matter of time before we have it here.'

'Don't let's talk about it, darling. You said yourself . . .'

'I don't *want* you to go to war . . .'

'Of course you don't.'

'But if everyone else does . . .'

'Sarah.' Louis cupped her face in his hands. 'I love you with all my heart and soul,' he said. 'But I can't change the world for you.'

So Sarah, navigating by her own star, wrote essays on the Albigensian Crusade, and the novels of Thomas Hardy, and tried not to dwell on things she couldn't change. But every time she opened a newspaper she was reminded: 'BRITAIN AND FRANCE GUARANTEE POLAND'. 'LONDON SCHOOL CHILDREN ISSUED WITH GAS MASKS'. 'GERMAN TROOPS MOVE ON ROMANIA'. Even if she quickly closed the newspaper again, the photos would linger in her consciousness. Now, in addition to the images of suffering in her own land, there were other sights to haunt her: General Franco leading his victorious troops through the ruined streets of Madrid; the faces of Jewish refugees clambering down gangways on to American soil; the devastated city of Canton . . .

'We are united in a common love of Empire and of Home,' the President of the RSA pronounced.

'Men who refuse to fight should be made to do so,' Sir Arthur Dutton fulminated, in support.

'Heaven is crammed with laughing boys,' the Chairman of the National Service Movement informed the country. 'If war comes, it will be the chance our young men have been waiting for.'

At the end of August a shocked world read of the signing of a treaty between Russia and Germany. In the days immediately following bets were laid as to how soon war would be declared. In the event it came sooner than the punters anticipated. On the evening of 3 September Prime Minister Savage broadcast these words: 'Both with gratitude for the past, and with confidence in the future, we range ourselves without fear beside Britain . . .'

New Zealand and Germany were at war.

13 ∫

Sarah had put on her plaid suit (the one with the fur trimming on the collar and cuffs), and her green velour hat with the upturned brim (her 'Greta Garbo', Prue called it). She'd painted her lips, powdered her nose, and sprayed herself with eau de cologne. Her mother was crying in her bedroom along the passage. Her father was out. He'd left the house before breakfast. 'Tell your mother I'll be late,' he'd instructed his daughter.

It was Monday, 4 September. Sarah had three lectures on a Monday: Anglo Saxon with Professor Noakes; the English Reformation with Mr Curtin; and the plays of Molière with Miss Delaunay. She would not be attending any of them.

'You look nice,' Pamela encouraged, as she came down the stairs. 'Going somewhere special?'

'Act of persuasion,' Sarah answered.

'Not joining up, are you?'

Sarah pulled a face. She and Pamela had become friends. They told each other things. What Sarah liked most about Pamela was her ability to listen without passing judgement. Things happened. That was her view. Sometimes they happened *to* you. Sometimes you made them happen. Either way there was no point complaining.

'Keep an eye on Mummy, will you, Pam? She's practically consigned Richard to the grave.'

'Who'd be a mother, eh?'

'Nothing's going to happen to him, I'm absolutely certain of it.'

'I'll tell ya something for free, Sarah. This war could be a good thing for the likes o' me. If the men go off to fight, the women'll have to do their jobs, won't they?'

'Don't know. Will they? I can't think that far ahead.'

'Bet yer life on it!'

'This house'd fall to bits without you, Pam.'

'Yeh, well . . .'

Sarah glanced at herself in the mirror. The hat was too much really, but she felt better with it on. 'Funny, isn't it?' she mused. 'I woke this morning expecting everything to look different.'

'Me too.'

'Daddy thinks it'll all be over by Christmas.'

'Doesn't sound like Sir Arthur.'

'You think he just said that to comfort?'

'He's *your* father, Sarah.'

'What am I going to do, Pam? If conscription comes . . .'

Pamela clicked her tongue against her teeth, a habit of hers when thinking. She knew what was worrying Sarah. She could read her like a book. Personally, if she were in Sarah's shoes, she'd have married Louis de la Tour by now. Sir Arthur would come round soon enough. He doted on his daughter. Pamela had made no secret of her liking for Louis. She'd never forgotten what he'd said to her at their first meeting, about a time coming when there would be no more masters and servants. 'Only one thing to be said for war,' her father used to mutter, when the pain from his gassed lungs got too much for him, 'it makes everyone equal.' Was that what Louis had meant? That it would need a war, a second one, to bring equality?

'Your Louis's not like other men,' she cautioned now. 'Don't be too hard on him.'

'It's not my judgement that matters.'

'It is to him.'

'I didn't tell you, did I? He was nearly arrested last week. There was a scuffle in Hereford Street. If Daddy knew . . .'

Pamela put a hand on her friend's arm. 'You're going to have to make up your mind whose side you're on, Sarah,' she said softly.

But to do that, Sarah reflected, as she walked towards the tramstop, I'd have to tear out a part of myself. She knew who's side she was on in the war. She was on Britain's side. The Empire's side. Richard's side. The fact of war made some things very simple. But with Louis – she quickened her pace, imagining she heard the tram – with Louis, *nothing* was simple.

'Wow!' Louis exclaimed, when she walked in through the door.

'What are you doing?' Sarah asked.

Louis shoved a piece of drawing paper under her nose. 'Like it?' he demanded.

'What is it? I mean, I can see it's a dove, but what's it for?'

'It's a design for a poster.'

'A peace poster?'

Louis nodded.

Sarah thrust the paper back into his hand, and sat down on the bed. The streets outside were quiet. Men and women were going about their business as if nothing had happened. There were no drums, no flags. The only differences Sarah had noticed, on her way here, were the looks on people's faces, and the line of men outside the recruiting office in Colombo Street.

'D'you want to go out somewhere?' Louis suggested. 'I can do this later.'

'Haven't you got to teach?'

'Not till the afternoon.'

'It's too cold for a picnic.'

'Tell you what.' Louis crouched in front of her, and pressed her hands between his warm, paint-stained palms. 'We'll go on the river. Why not? We'll be the only ones probably. A cold spring Monday . . .'

Sarah's eyes filled with tears.

'Now now,' Louis protested, touching her cheek with his finger. 'None of that.'

'I love you most dreadfully, Louis. I wish I didn't.'

'You'll spoil your face.'

'What's going to happen to us?'

Louis's smile sent Sarah diving for her handkerchief. 'We're going to float down the Avon, that's what,' he said. 'Then I'm going to buy you a slap-up lunch at La Scala, after which we'll come back here and make love.'

'Perhaps I should move in with you. Perhaps that would solve things.'

'Don't you want to marry me first?'

Sarah pulled away from him. What right did he have to grin at her like that? Didn't he understand anything?

'You know what you've done for me, don't you, Sarah?' Louis said, edging his hand back till it lay next to hers. 'I don't just mean' – he gestured at the easel – 'I mean . . . *everything.*'

Where their hands touched, Sarah's skin burned. She'd come here to cajole, but what she felt like doing was screaming.

'Think of us as characters in a play,' Louis went on cheerfully. '*Romeo and Juliet.* Only we won't make their mistakes, will we? We won't put our trust in family.'

'It's not family that divides us,' Sarah said.

'Isn't it?' Louis picked up her hand, and kissed the tips of her fingers. The burning sensation spread.

'You don't have anything to do with yours,' she reminded him.

'Correction.' Louis cleared his throat. His adam's apple, Sarah noticed, was protruding alarmingly. 'As from last night,' he said, 'my father and I are back in contact.'

'But that's wonderful!'

'Well, if *you* can co-exist with *yours* . . .'

'I'm glad, Louis, really I am. Perhaps your father will . . .'

'At least I can look him in the eye now,' Louis interrupted.

'But he's not a pacifist, is he?'

'I've started making money.'

'You've sold something?'

'The panel. The whole of it. I was going to surprise you this evening.'

'Oh, Louis . . .' Sarah's heart beat a sudden tattoo. What did this mean? Would it make her job of persuasion easier?

'I've Beulah to thank,' Louis went on. 'She chatted up this vicar she knows in Ashburton. He's buying it for his church.'

Sarah nodded excitedly. There'd be a public showing, wouldn't there? An unveiling. Louis was going to be recognised. 'I can't take it in,' she admitted.

'Beulah's writing an article about it. They'll publish it if it's by her.'

'It's what you've always wanted, isn't it? Your work will be seen, and not just by critics . . .'

Louis brought his face close to hers. When the expected kiss didn't materialise, she leaned back, and waited for him to speak. But words, for once, didn't come easily to him. 'This . . . *war*,' he began.

'Perhaps they won't, *you* won't . . .' Sarah shook her head crossly. The phrase she was looking for was on the tip of her tongue. 'You know what I mean,' she said.

'Exemption from military service?' Louis guessed. He smiled. 'That's what every woman will be hoping for.'

'But if enough people praise you, if you're acknowledged a genius . . .'

'Oh, darling.'

'You're an artist, Louis. Your work is *important*.'

Louis plunged his hands into his hair, and raked it back off his face. His adam's apple swelled and bobbed. 'You and I might consider painting vital to the national interest,' he muttered. 'But the majority . . .'

'You could be a war artist,' Sarah surprised herself by saying. 'That wouldn't be against your principles.' She'd no sooner uttered the words than she realised this was the idea to which she'd been struggling to give shape. There had to be something Louis could do that would allow them both to keep faith. 'Daddy has a book of paintings from the Great War,' she explained. 'Richard and I used to pore over it when we were kids.'

Louis touched the brim of her hat. 'Is that why you dressed up?' he asked. 'To charm me?'

Sarah dragged the hat off her head. 'It's Monday, in case you've forgotten,' she retorted. 'I've got lectures.'

'You know what war artists are for, don't you, Sarah? All those scenes of heroism and endurance . . .'

His hands slid up her arms to her shoulders. She could feel the pressure of his fingers under her fur collar. She'd never convince him, would she? The argument had been lost from the beginning. 'Is there nothing I can say?' she despaired.

'I love you,' Louis answered her.

Sarah retrieved her hat, and jammed it back on her head. 'Then we'll just have to hope enough men volunteer, won't we?' she snapped.

An hour later a lone dinghy drifted past the Nurses' Home,

attracting the attention of Sister Deidre Byrne, who'd come into the park on an off-duty hour to calm herself. She'd just accepted a proposal of marriage. It was the sixth time Fergus McLean had asked her, and she had no idea why she'd said yes.

Fergus McLean had come into her life because of her father. He was a publisher, based in Dunedin, whose list included religious tracts, royal picture books, biographies of famous men, and manuals designed to help the amateur gardener, cook, and mountaineer. Pearse Byrne's treatise on the breeding and training of horses fell into the latter category. Fergus had accepted it without hesitation, and promised to keep her informed at every stage of its progress. Deidre's protests – she'd hoped, with the handing over of the manuscript, to be free of her father – fell on deaf ears. Fergus began writing to her. At first it was occasional. Then, with the book out in the world and selling well, he found cause to write weekly. Eventually, when a second edition was being planned, he decided to drive to Christchurch. That was when Deidre realised she was being wooed.

Why *had* she said yes? She was happy as she was – a Sister now, with her own ward to manage. The death of Phineas O'Reilly had marked the end of her youth. She was thirty-one, nearly thirty-two; but the face she saw each morning in her mirror looked much older.

'You won't have to work any more,' Fergus had promised. 'You can be a lady of leisure.'

'But I *love* my work.'

'Those long hours? All that suffering? You've done enough, lass. Someone else can take over now.'

It wasn't what he said, so much, as the way he said it. The first time she heard his voice it triggered a long-buried memory. Standing with her mother in a hot kitchen; the smell of newly baked bread tickling her nostrils; two men, strangers, talking. 'Wee lass,' one of the men had called her. And she'd seen in her mind the future he'd predicted. A fine house, and a carriage to take her calling . . .

'No, Fergus, no,' she'd answered, each time he pressed her. 'I'll never marry.'

'I won't give up, Deidre. I'm fifty-seven years old. I've waited a long time for this.'

'Why now? Why me?'

But he'd never said the expected thing, that he loved her. Never, that is, till this morning.

Is that why I said yes? she asked herself, casting a cold eye on the couple in the boat. Usually she avoided this part of the park, a popular place with lovers. But today, with the city chilled by frost and the news of war, she'd assumed she'd be alone.

Trailing in the wake of the dinghy was a family of ducks. Sensing Deidre's presence on the bank they quacked excitedly, and veered off in her direction. 'Go away!' she growled, flapping her hands. 'I've nothing for you.'

The girl in the dinghy raised her head, and looked over her shoulder.

'It's her,' she said, her voice sharp with surprise.

'Who?' her companion asked.

'I've remembered.'

'What are you talking about?'

Sarah huddled back into the bow. 'It's not important,' she said.

The ducks had resumed their pursuit of the dinghy. Deidre pulled her cape tight around her shoulders. Those two – lovers, clearly – must be chilled to the bone. Or did love really do what the song claimed, and keep people warm? Love was no longer a word in Deidre's vocabulary. She'd buried it once with Clarence, a second time with Finn. She couldn't disinter it again. Fergus was a good man. Everyone said so. A pillar of the community. But she didn't, couldn't, *love* him.

'You'll be Mrs Fergus McLean,' he'd said. 'You'll be mistress of Iona.'

Iona, Glenory, Kilkenny . . . She chanted the names now, as the dinghy wove in and out of the willows. 'I have no family,' she'd told Fergus, when he asked. 'I'm quite alone.'

'My sister's looked after the house till now,' he'd explained. 'But of course if you say she's to go . . .'

'There's going to be a war, Fergus. We shouldn't be thinking of ourselves.'

'You'll be safe with me, my dear. Wait till you see Iona. Five acres. A couple of paddocks, an orchard, a large garden. We'll build a shelter near the house. It'll be for everyone. Family. Neighbours. We'll be safe as houses, you'll see.'

The dinghy emerged from the willows, rounded the bend in the river, and disappeared.

'So long as we keep on loving each other, we'll be safe,' Louis said to Sarah.

But Sarah was remembering Nurse Byrne who didn't believe in love, or safety.

14

31 March, 1940

'Dear Everyone,

'Well, here I am, in my new quarters. Can't tell you a lot about what's going on, but you'll see from the above address that I'm stationed on the coast, and I'm now officially a Pilot Officer. So far all we've done is train. But that's pretty exciting stuff I can tell you! Goering better watch his back. These new Spitfires are beauties to fly. Speeds of up to 300 mph, and a turn on them like a bird . . .'

Sarah, sitting at the breakfast table, listened to her father's voice, and tried not to show her disappointment that, once again, there was no letter for her. It was now the middle of April. People were calling this war 'phoney', and wondering why New Zealand had been so quick to send away its men. But this morning the headline in the *Press* read, 'NORWAY INVADED'. Sarah hadn't needed her father to point out the significance of this latest German advance. With the German Army threatening France, there could be no doubt as to Hitler's intention: to invade Britain, and destroy the Empire.

'I must say this place is a lot more interesting than Oxford,' Richard wrote. *'We've got chaps from Czechoslovakia, Poland, Canada, Australia. There's even a kid from Romania, not that anyone can understand him, his accent's so thick! And did I tell you, Ray's here too? Wangled it somehow after being sent to France first. It's wizard to have him around. We've bought a car between us so that we can get up to London and have a bit of fun . . .'*

He's never asked about Daisy, Sarah thought. Never mentioned her again.

'You mustn't worry about me,' the letter went on. *'The sooner the real show starts the better, far as I'm concerned. You know there's to be a New Zealand Squadron, don't you? Seems a lot of our chaps are coming over now. Ray and I have applied to be transferred. Might as well fight with the home team . . .'*

Ray, Ray, Ray. Sarah was sick of the name. If it wasn't for Ray, Richard would never have joined the Air Force. 'Ray really fancies you,' Richard had joked, in the last letter she'd had from him. 'I showed him your photo, the one of you with Caesar, and he reckons you're a bit of all right . . .'

'You listening?' her father wanted to know.

''Course.'

'Sounds like quite a party.'

Sarah glanced at her mother. She wished she could think of something to say to comfort her. Her father's determined cheerfulness was no help at all.

'Go on,' Margot urged.

'Thanks for all your letters. Sounds like you're putting a bit of muscle into the Patriotic Fund, Dad. Chairman for the Duration! Good on you! We need all the help we can get over here, what with rationing, and petrol worth its weight in gold. Though so far, you'll be pleased to know, there's been no shortage of beer . . .'

I've enough to worry about, Sarah thought, without seeing that look on Mummy's face all the time. What's the matter with Daddy? Since the war started he's had no time for her at all.

'By the way, a query for you, Sarah. Are you still seeing that chap, de la Tour? Wish I could remember him, but the mind's a blank. Hard to imagine school from here. It all seems so long ago . . .'

Sarah ignored the question in her mother's eye. What she'd told or not told Richard was her own affair.

'You informed your brother this young man of yours is a pacifist?' her father challenged.

But Sarah ignored that too.

By the end of May no one talked of the war being 'phoney' any more. Norway had fallen. So had Denmark, Belgium and Holland. France would follow in the first two weeks of June. The British Army, trapped on the continent, was even now being evacuated, a miracle of seamanship which Sir Arthur Dutton, among others, would hail as the salvation of the Empire.

Sarah, moving round the city, registered the changes that had been reassuringly slow at first, but now, with the news from Europe, were multiplying daily. By the middle of June it was commonplace to see men and women in khaki; commonplace to watch parades, and attend fund-raising drives, and answer questions about your contribution to the war effort; commonplace to see school children saluting the flag, and hear 'Roll out the Barrel' played on crackly public gramophones; commonplace to conserve petrol, and learn that freezing workers, or the Christchurch Carpenters' Union, had agreed to a voluntary cut in wages to donate to the Poles or the Finns, or the newly formed Spitfire Fund; commonplace to read posters urging citizens to 'WORK FOR VICTORY', or 'SUBSCRIBE TO THE LIBERTY LOAN', commonplace to pass queues of men in mufti waiting to volunteer . . .

'Conscription will not be necessary,' a colonel in the Canterbury Yeomanry had declared, 'if our young women refuse to play tennis or dance with *non*-volunteers.'

But conscription *would* come. Sarah's father had left her in no doubt. 'Forty thousand men have come forward so far,' he'd told her. 'It's not enough.'

On 18 June it happened. Under the National Service Emergency Regulations all males between the ages of 18 and 46 became eligible for service in the armed forces. By a perverse stroke of fate Louis de la Tour's first solo exhibiton opened, on the very same day, to enthusiastic notices.

'The work of Louis de la Tour,' the *Press* report read, 'first seen at a Group Exhibition in September 1938, has attracted attention recently for its powerful presentation of an essentially human religious mythology. Those who have seen de la Tour's Creation Panel in St John's Church, Ashburton, will not be surprised to learn that this new exhibition, which opens today at the McDougall Gallery, continues to explore the mystery of creation, and the burden of human suffering . . .'

Sarah stood in front of the painting entitled 'Comrade', and wept. It was the only painting in the exhibition in which the sea figured. She supposed it would be described as an abstract, though the sea was recognisable to her. The other works featured human figures, whited landscapes, hovering, larger-than-life birds, and the skeletal shapes of burnt-out buildings. But 'Comrade' was simple, and unbearably sad.

'You like it then?' Louis asked.

She turned to him, and in front of Beulah, Kitty, Prue, Ivor, and her parents, she kissed him.

'How long, do you think?' she whispered.

15 August 1940

'*Dear Everyone,*

'*Well, it's started! Goering has finally shown his colours, and the war, as far as we in 485 Squadron are concerned, has begun. I'll write as often as I can, but don't you go worrying if you don't hear from me because it's all pretty much go here, and we don't get a lot of free time. Jolly good to be with other Kiwis though. I've had a few games of rugger and become a bit of a whizz on the billiard table . . .*

'*The flying's a piece of cake. Hitler's Messerschmitts don't stand a chance against our Spitfires. I flew my first mission yesterday . . .*'

15

They were a ridiculous sight. They both knew it. Standing among the debris of torn Christmas streamers, and pine needles from the shedding tree, yelling at each other. How had it happened? And so quickly.

'I hate you!' Sarah shouted. 'Hate you, hate you, hate you!'

'Calm down, for God's sake.'

'Just when I was beginning to think . . .'

'I shouldn't have told you. I wasn't going to. What the hell did you expect, Sarah? You know what I am.'

'Oh, I know what you are, all right. You're a coward. Daddy's right. You'll let other people fight while you . . .'

'Go on, say it.' Louis thrust out his chin. The expression in his eyes was one Sarah had never seen before. 'Say what you think,' he urged. 'Don't be afraid. You think I consider myself a cut above other people, don't you? You think I want to save my life so I can paint.'

'I wish I'd never met you.'

Louis closed his eyes. When he opened them again, the anger had gone from them. 'God,' he muttered. 'I almost hit you.'

'Why didn't you? I'm an easy target.'

He smiled briefly. 'Against my principles,' he said.

'I think you'd better go.'

'I only came to wish you Happy New Year.'

'That's a *joke*.'

'Richard's survived the worst Hitler could throw at him, Sarah. You and your family have reason to be grateful.'

'He still flies, doesn't he? It's not finished yet.'

'Who knows? By the time you get back from the Grange . . .'

'You were invited too, remember.'

Louis bowed his head. She'd had the first word tonight, and she would have the last. She'd told him, when he arrived, that she was feeling on top of the world. She'd done well in her exams, Richard was safe, *his* pictures were selling. She hadn't noticed the look on his face. 'Don't suppose I'll ever get to see it now,' he said huskily. 'The legendary Cheyney Grange.'

Sarah leaned back against the wall. They were talking in the hall, the only part of Rosevilla where Margot Dutton permitted Christmas decorations. Tomorrow Sarah would drive herself to the Grange. These days she had her own car, a grey Ford Standard. Louis could have come, but he'd decided otherwise.

'What will you do?' she asked shakily.

'Wait,' he answered. 'Though I don't expect I'll be waiting for long. Once the authorities realise I've torn up my ballot paper . . .'

'Can't you say you're a Quaker or something? They're a designated sect, aren't they? You'd be let off automatically.'

'I'm not even a Christian, Sarah, not really.'

Sarah made fists of her hands, and rubbed them into her eyes. She'd imagined this moment so many times, searching, beyond its inevitability, for a miracle. Now it was as if a mist had come down, obscuring what was really happening, leaving her capable only of irrelevant observation. Louis was wearing the shirt she'd given him for Christmas. The shorts he had on she'd planned to burn. Bing Crosby was singing on the wireless in the kitchen – 'Life is Just a Bowl of Cherries'. The tune pulsed maddeningly inside her head.

'I'd understand,' she muttered, 'if you were prepared to do *something*. Anything. Stretcher-bearing . . . I don't know. But you won't even work in a factory.'

'War contaminates everything, Sarah. Even farming.'

'Don't you care what happens to people?'

'We've been through all this.'

'You don't, do you?'

Louis's answer was a groan. 'You read the papers,' he said, when he could find words again. 'You know what's going on. Everything we produce now is part of the war effort. You think Hitler's a dictator, and you're right. But our Government has the same sweeping powers as Hitler does. It can order me into prison for my beliefs, and you into a factory to make grenades.'

'I know where I'd rather be.'

'I'm not doing this to avoid danger, Sarah.'

'You don't love me.'

'Don't be stupid!'

'Then why are you betraying me?'

'Would you rather I betrayed myself?'

To her shame, afterwards, and to the astonishment of them both, Sarah threw up her hand, and hit him hard across the cheek. For a few seconds neither of them spoke; then Sarah, her cheeks flushed as if *she* were the one who'd been slapped, flung back at him, 'Not against *my* principles anyway.'

Louis put his hand where hers had been. His flesh stung, but he wasn't thinking of that. He was thinking, if we could laugh about this . . . But then he saw the expression on her face, and the thought died. She'd chosen her world. That's what he read in the set of her lips. Cheyney Grange, Richard, the University, the Patriotic Fund – those were her icons now, the stuff of her religion. The identity they'd forged together, the world of their love, was dissolving before his eyes.

'Do you want me to go?' he asked.

'You know what I want.'

'I c . . . I can't do what you want, Sarah,' he stammered. 'I'm sorry . . .'

'Then go to hell!' she shouted.

Louis's premonition that he'd never see Sarah again was not strictly accurate. He did see her, after the war, bustling into Hallenstein's with a basket on her arm. She looked – the word struck him like a blow in the stomach – *wifely*. She was wearing a tweed coat and a beret, and her hair he could see, even at a distance, was caught up in a roll, the fashion favoured by her mother. He called her name. He thought he called loud enough for her to hear, but she didn't turn. Then the doors opened, and she was gone.

For most of a minute he thought about following her. At least he could find out what had happened to her. None of his letters had been answered.

Louis had spent the war behind the barbed wire of Strathmore Detention Camp near Rotorua. Not all of it had been bad. He'd shared a hut with a writer called Maurice Goodman. They'd become friends. It was Maurice who'd taught him how to grow vegetables in the inhospitable pumice; Maurice who'd encouraged him when others left to serve as non-combatants; Maurice who'd almost persuaded him there would be no recriminations once the war was won; Maurice who'd guessed there was a woman, and it wasn't over yet . . .

The peacetime crowd swirled around him: women pushing prams; men in suits and hats pursuing their business in defiance of the nor'wester; a scattering of uniforms, khaki, navy . . . He didn't belong. Sarah had always known that, and wisely refused to marry him. What would be the point of following her? Like everyone else who'd survived the war, her heart would have hardened. There were no old friends now, only new ones. Beulah Dowling had brought that home to him. She'd greeted him, on his return to the city, with a mixture of embarrassment and contempt. He hadn't understood, till he learned she'd lost a favourite nephew at Tobruk. The day after he spoke to her he went into the office of Shaw, Savill and Albion, and bought a ticket on the *Dominion Monarch*. It was to sail for England in three days' time.

'Go,' Maurice had urged, in his letter. 'You have money. Your father's left you well set-up. If it weren't for the family I'd go myself . . .'

'Strange, isn't it?' Louis had written, in answer. 'My father's death hardly touched me at the time. Now it's as if a whole world died while we were up there in the mud . . .'

He pressed his hat to his head, and set his face against the wind. 'Goodbye, Sarah,' he called softly. 'Goodbye, my love.'

Part Four

15

The wedding of Deidre May Byrne and Fergus Rory McLean took place in the Nurses' Memorial Chapel of the Christchurch Hospital on 2 February, 1940. There were only two witnesses: Fergus's brother, Iain, and Peter Sing, who gave the bride away. The minister, the Reverend Hugh Mason, was puzzled at the lack of female support for the bride, but in these tense times he'd learned not to question departures from the norm.

The ceremony was brief, and might have seemed depressing were it not for the rays of coloured light from the stained glass windows. Perhaps, Hugh Mason reflected, the bride felt no need of an attendant maid in such a claustrophobically female place. The names of the nurses who'd died in the sinking of the *Marquette* in 1915 were enshrined in brass plaques on the walls. Other names – Matrons, Sisters, District Nurses – were honoured in the memorial windows. The bride, Hugh couldn't help noticing, seemed unduly aware of her dead companions. Her short walk down the aisle was punctuated by pauses.

Deidre Byrne was dressed sombrely, in a black suit and hat. Her only concessions to the occasion were the pale roses she carried, and the wispy veil over her face. The bridegroom, whom Hugh knew by reputation, wore the suit of a successful businessman. In a clear voice, warmed by a Scottish burr, he promised to endow his wife with all his wordly goods. She, less enthusiastically, promised to obey him. The bridegroom's brother, a slimmer, younger version of the groom, looked unhappy throughout the proceedings. The other witness, a surgeon of Chinese extraction, looked bemused.

The reception was to be held at the Christchurch Club in

Latimer Square. Hugh Mason would have liked to attend. He was not normally invited to such places. But he had a funeral to take, so was obliged to decline.

'A pity,' Iain McLean confided to Peter Sing, when the ceremony was over. 'As we're so few.'

'Afraid I have to bow out too,' Peter confessed.

'Ah . . .'

'I've explained to Deidre.'

'You work together, do you?'

'We're old friends.'

Iain wiped his brow with his handkerchief. They were standing outside the chapel waiting for the newly-weds. Iain, in a suit identical to his brother's, was feeling the heat. 'I'd assumed a professional connection,' he admitted.

Peter smiled. 'I've only been in Christchurch a few months,' he said.

'You're an eye man, my brother tells me?'

'I was at the Dunedin Hospital before this.'

Iain nodded, though he could have wished for more fulsome answers to his questions. He knew almost nothing about the woman who'd just become his sister-in-law.

'Your brother must be a very persuasive man,' Peter said. 'I could have sworn Deidre would never marry.'

Iain eyed the doctor from under the brim of his hat. What was the word they used about the Chinese? Inscrutable? Whatever the name for it, he could see he would get no more out of Deidre's enigmatic friend. 'I'll just . . .' He gestured at the chapel.

'Don't let me detain you,' Peter said.

In some distress Iain climbed the steps, and peered inside. Fergus and his wife were standing near the altar, deep in conversation with the minister. Iain removed his hat, and slipped in through the door. The family had grown used to Fergus as a bachelor. The days when his mother and sisters had tried to marry him off were long gone. As the eldest brother he lived in the family home, a place every member of the clan felt was his or her home too. Now Deidre Byrne would be in charge. To say that Dottie, their sister, who'd been mistress of Iona for seventeen years, was put out, was seriously to understate the case. Dottie was distraught. Her one meeting with the future Mrs

McLean had sealed their mutual dislike. From now on Dottie would be living, on her own, in the cottage at the bottom of the orchard. Built by their grandfather, it was only ever used at Christmas, when the big house filled up with family. 'You'll be living in a little bit of history,' Iain had comforted. But Dottie was a practical soul, rooted in the domestic joys of the present. History, for her, meant old photographs and tombstones.

'There you are,' Fergus greeted, coming on his brother in the vestibule. He took his wife's arm, and stepped out into the sunshine.

He's no business looking so pleased with himself, Iain thought, as he followed them out.

A few seconds later Hugh Mason emerged, waved, and hurried off towards his car.

'Sorry you can't join us, Mr Sing,' Fergus said.

'Peter, please.'

'I've been telling Deidre, I haven't been to the club for a year or more. Used to stay there on business trips. They keep a very good table.'

'I'm sorry to be missing it.'

'Thank you for giving me away, Peter,' Deidre said.

Peter smiled. 'You be happy now,' he commanded, leaning to place a kiss on the bride's cheek.

Deidre smiled her first truly natural smile of the day. She'd run into Peter Sing in the hospital corridor the week before war was declared. She'd heard he'd transferred to Christchurch but thought little about it. Seeing him changed all that. He was almost exactly as she'd remembered him. In fact, she'd thought afterwards, the only difference was in his manner: he was no longer shy. A few days later they met for tea. She knew, of course, that he was married. 'No,' he'd said, though she hadn't asked. 'The marriage isn't happy. She's English, my wife. I feel responsible, Deidre. I brought her out here.'

Deidre had been tempted to ask if there was someone else. She felt sure there must be. The man she was looking at didn't appear broken-hearted.

'And you?' he'd wanted to know. 'Tell me about *you*.'

So she'd told him about her work, and laughed when he

asked if there was anyone in *her* life. Next morning, when Fergus phoned and asked her to marry him, she said yes.

'Don't suppose I'll see you again,' Deidre said now. Over Peter's shoulder she could see her husband talking with his brother. How alike they both are, she thought. And how little I know them.

'You still wear glasses,' Peter said, fixing a professional eye on her. 'You can come and see me when they need renewing.'

'Don't be silly! I'll be living in Dunedin.'

Peter winced. She had a sharp tongue on her, Deidre Byrne, no doubt about that. What he'd been going to say was that they'd run into each other on home territory. He still visited his parents whenever he could. But a sudden doubt made him hesitate. Something had happened at Kilkenny, hadn't it? His sister had written him about it. A double tragedy, involving, if he remembered right, the father and the brother. Nor was that the end of it. There'd been some kind of falling out with the step-mother . . . Poor old Deidre. She didn't have much luck with family. Let's hope this McLean fellow, for all he looked to be twice her age, treated her kindly.

'We should be going, dear,' Fergus called

'Goodbye, Peter,' Deidre said.

Peter took the hand she offered him, and shook it warmly. 'Be happy,' he urged again. 'Don't let the past . . .' He stopped. He'd seen that look on her face before: blue eyes, piercing. 'Goodbye,' he said curtly.

Deidre watched him stride across the gravel to his car. Then she allowed herself to be escorted to her husband's Daimler, which he proceeded to drive, with no interruption to his flow of conversation, down Riccarton Avenue.

The following week, after honeymooning in the hotel at Lake Wanaka, Fergus McLean brought his bride home to Iona.

2 ∫

It was a matter of pride to the McLean family that Iona, built in the last century and added to over the years, was visible from both land and sea. Standing on the crest of a hill overlooking the Otago harbour, its chimneys were still used by some old salts as navigational aids. For landlubbers, the sight of the house rising above the trees was more likely to induce exhaustion. The winding drive which climbed from the street to the front door had been measured at three-quarters of a mile. It was the first thing Deidre learned to curse.

Mrs Fergus McLean, as she was called now, had settled into her new life with what the family, always prepared to think the best, considered remarkable ease. Three months after the wedding there was even talk of the marriage being a good thing. Hard on Dottie, of course, but Fergus was getting on, and with his history it was really rather fortunate he'd taken a nurse for a wife.

Domestically, Deidre was pronounced more than satisfactory. A methodical woman by inclination and training, her daily routine, established within days of her return from honeymoon, had taken on (as Dottie snidely remarked) the 'authority of Holy Writ'. Each morning Deidre would take her husband a cup of tea in bed; then, having quickly dressed, she'd hurry down the drive to collect the milk and paper. She could have taken a short-cut through the orchard, but that would have taken her past Dottie's door, and the consensus was, Deidre would rather walk an extra mile than risk confrontation with her sister-in-law.

In other parts of the world a killing war was being waged, but here, at Iona, Deidre's war was with dirt and dust, those elusive reminders of a messy past. The house was scrubbed down, room by room. Curtains, carpets, cushion covers, were all, at different times, seen hanging on the line. The shelves were still full of Dottie's jams and preserves, but Deidre was not one to let a good harvest go to waste. By the end of March the trees in the orchard had been stripped bare of their fruit. It was the one task for which Deidre agreed help was needed. She had no wish to be spied on by her sister-in-law.

'You've done magnificently, my dear,' Fergus complimented, on one of his rare visits to the kitchen. 'Let the Huns do their worst, eh? No one in *this* house will starve.'

Deidre didn't like to point out that at their present rate of entertainment the shelves would be empty long before the next crop of fruit was ready to be picked. Fergus had warned her his was a gregarious family. Every Sunday after church his four siblings (a fifth, who lived a two-hour drive away, in Oamaru, was an occasional addition), assorted nieces and nephews, cousins, and family friends, gathered at Iona for lunch. 'It's a bit of a tradition,' Fergus had explained. 'We put the extra leaves in the table, scoop up all the chairs, and sit down to a side of mutton, and Dottie's excellent . . .'

He'd stopped, at a loss suddenly. Fergus, for all his kindness, was not an especially sensitive man; but neither was he *in*sensitive. The state of war between his wife and sister was a cause of deep distress to him. 'If you feel it's too much . . .' he'd demurred.

After the first Sunday, when the last of the twenty-seven guests had departed, he'd asked her, humbly, if she still missed nursing. His anxiety moved her to tell the truth. 'I do, yes. I think I always will. But I've no regrets.'

A clutch of Sundays later she could tell him, with equal truth, that she hardly thought about nursing at all.

'You don't miss your friends?' Fergus had asked.

'Well, yes, there is one . . .' She could never have told him she had *no* friends. He'd not have believed her. He had so many himself. 'I miss Marigold Twopenny,' she'd said.

Iona was a large house. Five bedrooms, drawing room, dining room, small sitting room, kitchen, pantry, storeroom, washhouse, a bathroom on the grand scale, with the bath positioned like a throne in the middle of the floor. Across the front of the house was a verandah, which Fergus talked of glassing in should the house fill up with children.

'Children?' Deidre queried, the first time the idea was mooted.

Fergus took the pipe out of his mouth, and smiled at his wife. 'I thought we might adopt,' he said.

Deidre counted slowly to ten. Her old childhood trick of *playing dead* came back to her at that moment as if she'd never given it up. 'When you have children of your own, you'll understand,' her father had said, in one of his rare moments of kindness. But all Deidre had ever understood was that children were trouble and sorrow.

She bent her head over the sock she was darning. The idea of adoption was preposterous. Fergus was nearly sixty. With her help he'd see seventy, but he'd be lucky to get any further. Deidre knew more than he realised about his state of health.

'You're tired,' her husband soothed. 'We'll talk of it another time.'

Was she happy? It was a question Deidre constantly asked herself. As it wasn't one she'd ever bothered with before, she supposed it must have something to do with the expectations that surround marriage. She was a bride, and brides were supposed to be *radiant*. Once or twice, while brooding on this subject, she found herself thinking of Sarah Dutton. Funny how some patients stayed in the memory. She'd been hard on Sarah. It wasn't her fault she'd been born a Dutton.

Deidre spotted her once, at a public lecture, not the sort of occasion she'd have associated with that family. She'd assumed the girl was there because the speaker, a well-known surgeon, whose views Deidre had found alarming, had operated on her. But then a young man had started asking questions, and Deidre, seeing him talking, later, to Sarah and her female companion, was forced to revise her opinion. How did a girl with a passion for romantic novels come to be acquainted with so radical a youth? And what, she wondered, her mind pulled back to the war, were those three young people doing now?

Mostly though, what Deidre felt when she asked herself if she was happy, was surprised. It had all happened so quickly.

The meeting with Peter; Prime Minister Savage's broadcast announcing the outbreak of war; Fergus's warm voice on the end of the phone. What she remembered chiefly about those few crucial days was the sense of exhausted hopelessness. The thought of the suffering that lay ahead so diminished her, she felt ready to say yes to anything.

'A nurse,' one of her first lecturers had instructed, 'must at all times keep her personal feelings separate from her work. "Kind but brisk" is the nurse's motto. Sympathy, yes. You will make a poor nurse if you don't feel that. But the personal bond is taboo on the ward. That belongs at home, with your loved ones . . .'

But if there are no loved ones, Deidre had argued, after Clarence's death, what then? The answer was Phineas O'Reilly, and the ache she still felt when she thought of him. Another war, she'd realised, as she listened to Mr Savage's voice, will mean more young men like Finn coming, broken, into the wards. It will mean nurses putting on military uniforms and sailing off, smiling, to the horrors of the battlefield. Images from the film, *Blockade*, set in the Spanish Civil War, which she'd gone to see because of Finn, and had to leave because she kept glimpsing him, in ragged battledress, running towards his death, had flooded her mind, weakening her resolve never to leave nursing, exposing her to the temptations of safety, and the personal bond.

'Your future would be secure with me,' Fergus had urged. 'I'd make certain of that.'

It was a novel idea for Deidre, this concept of personal security. Up till then she'd always thought of the future in political terms: a juster society; a universal health service; a safer world . . .

'We've so much to tell each other,' Fergus had enthused, when he'd got over the shock of her acceptance. 'I want to learn all about you. What sort of childhood you had. Who your friends are. Where you went to school. That father of yours seems to have been a rum sort of cove. Not sure I'd have wanted him for *my* father.'

But Deidre, since her second exile from Kilkenny, was more resolved than ever not to talk about the past.

She'd hated the wedding, and the ridiculous palaver at the Christchurch Club afterwards. But she *liked* Fergus. More and more, as the days went by. She'd never met a human being so utterly free from malice. On the honeymoon he'd told her things which had made her understand, a little, why he'd chosen her. He was not as strong, emotionally, as he would like people to believe. Head of both a successful publishing house, and a large and respected family, he had, for most of his adult life, been plagued by doubts as to his fitness for these roles. In his late-forties these doubts drove him to alcoholism. At first he merely drank as an extension of his hitherto moderate daily habit. But then he began to drink secretly – in the office; the car; his glasshouse, where he grew his prize begonias. Then, at the beginning of 1938, returning from a family holiday at Wanaka, he drove his car into the river. The fact that he crawled out of the wreck, unharmed, was hailed as nothing less than a miracle. The accident brought him to his senses. He could, he admitted to his shocked and thankful family, so easily have killed someone. Five months in a sanatorium, and the drying-out process was complete. 'My courtship of you,' he told his wife, 'began soon after.'

Deidre never did tell her husband what passed through her mind as she listened to his story. The river that nearly drowned him was the same that took Clarence; the same that took . . . But there her memory faltered, as she had instructed it to do, and her will took over. She would protect this man, and keep him safe. That was her duty now.

'I asked for twin beds,' Fergus explained, on their wedding night. 'I thought you'd prefer that.'

It was the first indication Deidre had that theirs was to be an unconsummated marriage. I'll never have babies, never never! she'd vowed as a child. Had Fergus intuited that from the few things she'd let slip about her early life? Was this his way of protecting her?

'You know, of course, that it's possible to enjoy married life without risking an unwanted pregnancy?' she'd ventured, three days into their honeymoon. It cost her dear to speak so plainly, but the thought of his denial (and mine, she'd acknowledged, with a sense of shock) was causing her distress.

Fergus had cleared his throat, as he often did before speaking, and given her a look of such pained wistfulness, she'd quickly changed the subject. It was for him to speak, wasn't it? She should never have presumed . . . Afterwards, playing the scene over in her mind, she saw where she'd gone wrong. Fergus was an affectionate man. She should have used the language of endearment, not lectured him like Marie Stopes. The matter was never raised again. Fergus had the usual sensual appetites. He liked his food, his pipe, the sun on his face. But he was not, Deidre was forced to concede, as the honeymoon drew to a close, a *sexual* man.

Did she mind? That was another question she continued to ask herself. Mostly the answer was no. It's a relief, she decided, lying in her bed, listening to her husband's snores. Those other sounds, remembered from childhood, haunted her still: the groans from behind the closed bedroom door; the raised voices; Jessie Potter's screams . . . The rare moments when a different answer came she dismissed as a consequence, inevitable but irrelevant, of her deepening affection for her husband.

In the busy days that followed her arrival at Iona, Deidre's mind often returned to that quiet week of honeymoon. At first she'd dreaded the thought of Wanaka. She'd never been there, but as the source of the river that had haunted her since childhood it held a special, fearful fascination. She could have protested. Fergus was not one to insist on having his own way. But she'd discovered, even at that early stage, that Fergus McLean was the kind of man people liked to accommodate, and *she* was no exception.

'I can't believe you've never been there,' Fergus reacted, when she confessed her ignorance of Wanaka's charms. 'Kilkenny can only have been half a day's journey away.'

'We never had holidays,' Deidre explained.

'You'll love it, I know,' her fiancé encouraged. 'It's where we go every summer. The family. A home away from home.'

As things turned out, Deidre didn't fall in love with Wanaka, but she did feel peaceful there, and safe. Fergus read the papers, and listened to the news on the wireless, but Deidre had resolved, for those few days, to forget the war. It was even possible to forget the past. The dusty township, with its picture house, its rival milk bars, and its overflowing General Store, was sufficiently unlike her own home town to stifle memory. As for the lake, cradled by bare brown hills, and flung about with birds, it seemed an unlikely source for a river of such proven malevolence.

The journey back to Dunedin shattered that peace. Deidre hadn't realised their route would take them past the gates of Kilkenny. Fergus was a cheerful driver. When he wasn't talking he sang under his breath, or whistled. Deidre prayed his attention would not be drawn to the tall gates (Jessie, it was obvious, had been spending money), from the top of which hung a board carved with the words KILKENNY STUD.

'You have a cousin in Milton, don't you?' Deidre asked, as the tell-tale gates swung into view. 'Perhaps we should call?'

Fergus, turning to look at her, took his hand off the wheel, and squeezed her arm. She wished he wouldn't do that. His brother Iain had warned her Fergus always drove as if there was no other traffic on the road. 'When he learned to drive you didn't need a licence,' he'd told her. 'But don't worry,' he'd joked. 'Someone Up There is looking after him.'

'That's a nice suggestion, dear,' Fergus answered. 'Sure you're not too tired?'

'I have to meet them all sometime,' Deidre said.

When the last of Kilkenny's acres was behind them, Deidre leaned back in her seat, and closed her eyes.

'Byrne Avenue,' Fergus announced suddenly. 'That must be after your father.'

Deidre's eyes sprang open. Keep going, just keep going, she willed.

'We must be near his property then,' Fergus said.

'Sold, I expect,' Deidre murmured.

'Don't you want to find out?'

'I don't want to talk about it,' Deidre replied, in the clipped voice she'd used to discipline probationers. 'I'd be grateful if you'd agree never to mention my father's name again.'

Her husband gave her a curious look, but he didn't argue. 'We'll have to talk about him sometimes,' he reminded her gently. 'There's the book.'

'That's different,' Deidre said.

There was another sticky moment, passing through the town. 'All this must be very familiar to you,' Fergus observed.

Deidre, alarmed by the sudden increase in traffic, kept her eyes on the road. She'd never learned to drive, but had been wondering if it was something else she might have to take on in this unpredictable marriage. They were driving down the main street. Though Deidre had no wish to see, there, on her left, was Dwyer's General Store, only now it was called The Four Square. And ahead, on her right, was the New Brunswick Hotel, still in need of a coat of paint, still a magnet for the district's derelicts.

'Oh look,' she exclaimed, eager to distract, 'there's the recruiting office.'

'Every town in the country has them now,' her husband responded.

'It was the blacksmith's when I was a child.'

It was a relief when the town was behind them. If buildings could unhinge her, what might have happened had she recognised a *face*? She had no knowledge, and no curiosity normally, about her remaining siblings. Eliza would be married, and Dulcie a qualified teacher by now. But what the others were doing she could only speculate. Tilly, the baby, would be fourteen.

'Why did you never marry before?' she asked her husband, as they gathered speed on the open road.

'I was waiting for you,' Fergus teased.

'You don't expect me to believe that, do you?'

'I could ask the same question of you.'

'I'm not fifty-seven,' Deidre pointed out.

'You're thirty-two,' her husband sighed. 'You could have done much better for yourself.'

Deidre, recognising the note of self-reproach, reached over and touched his arm. It was one of the rare moments when she wished their marriage could be more. 'I'm very proud to be your wife,' she astounded herself by saying. Then further confused matters by adding, 'I'll do my very best to be what you want.'

3 ♪

At forty-nine, Dorothy McLean owned little in the way of wordly possessions, and laid claim to even less in the kingdom of belief. She was not at all convinced, for example, that God existed. Though this in no way interfered with her church-going (she was an enthusiastic member of the choir), she freely admitted, when asked, that the notion, so beloved of clergymen, of *knowing* God, was alien to her. 'I've never experienced Him personally,' she'd argue, 'so how can I be expected to *know* Him?'

Fergus called her his 'Doubting Thomasina'. 'You only believe what you see,' he'd chided. 'Which cuts out an awful lot, my dear.'

But Dottie had seen quite enough in her almost five decades. She'd nursed her mother and father, and watched them die. She'd been the busy bridesmaid at both her sisters' weddings. She'd 'held the fort' when her nieces and nephews were born, and mourned the deaths of two of those dear infants. Finally, and most gloriously, she'd taken her mother's place as mistress of Iona. For seventeen years she'd cared for the brother she regarded, privately, as the best man in the world. Anyone could cook and clean. It was not for those things she wished to be valued. What she'd done, for seventeen years, was *cherish*.

'Why, Fergus, why?' she'd shamed herself by shouting, when he announced he was going to marry. 'Haven't I always put you first? Listened to you. Held your hand when you . . . when things were bad for you?'

It was his distress that silenced her. To the best of her knowledge she'd never hurt him. She wasn't going to start now. 'You've been a guardian angel, Dottie,' he'd replied. 'I can never thank, never repay you. But perhaps it's time – I'm no spring chicken, after all . . .'

It was almost the entire extent of their conversation on the subject. But from that moment on, Dottie's small store of belief was boosted by the absolute conviction that her brother's marriage would end in disaster. 'You know me,' she wrote to her sister in Oamaru. 'I never speak ill of people. But I have to say, there's something not quite right about our future sister-in-law. You'll see for yourself when you meet her. It's nothing I can put a finger on. She's perfectly civil, and obviously, as she's a nurse, extremely capable. But I don't trust her. Don't trust her motives for marrying Fergus. They're not at all suited . . .'

After the marriage, Dottie's views, which the family, increasingly, refused to share, hardened into dogma. Deidre's domestic virtues, generously trumpeted by her other sisters-in-law, Dottie dismissed as evidence of coldness. She didn't go so far as to say Deidre didn't love her husband, but she implied that love was not an emotion easily felt by one of Sister Byrne's austere disposition. Take, for example, her obsession with cleanliness. The family saw this as a product of her nursing training and, on the whole, a thing to be commended. 'Cleanliness *is* next to Godliness,' Iain's wife, Enid, reminded. But Dottie, never one to worry over a bit of dust, observed Deidre's compulsive cleaning and tidying, and sensed the panic that lay behind it. 'It's as if she has to control every nook and cranny,' she complained in her weekly letter to Oamaru. 'It's been three months now, and she's still at it. God help poor Fergus if she gets started on the garden . . .'

'Well, of course you don't approve, dear,' Meg wrote back. 'She's so different from you . . .'

'Don't imagine it's because I'm jealous,' Dottie countered defensively, when Enid accused her of lack of charity. 'I *am*, as a matter of fact, but that's beside the point. I hope I can see past my own failings . . .'

'Lists,' Enid proclaimed, as if the word itself were a virtue. 'I've never seen anyone make so many lists.'

But what Dottie thought, and refrained from saying, was that those lists were a false trail. They gave no hint at all of what was going on in the woman's mind.

*   *   *

Towards the end of June, when newspapers were filled with reports of the heroism at Dunkirk, and conscription was a matter of days away, Fergus paid an unexpected visit on his sister. Since his marriage he'd made a point of calling on Dottie several times a week, on his way home from work. But this was Saturday morning.

'Well well well,' Dottie greeted, as he walked, dripping with rain, through her door. 'This *is* a surprise.'

Fergus turned to shake his umbrella. 'How are you?' he asked, closing the door behind him.

'Same as I was last time you enquired.'

'Good-oh.'

While Dottie hung up his coat, Fergus moved to sit in the rocking chair that had been his mother's. The sofa, the only other place to sit in this tiny room, was covered with Dottie's sewing.

Something's up, Dottie thought, as she cleared a space for herself on the sofa. Fergus was a creature of habit. Saturday mornings, hail or shine, he spent in his garden. Sometimes he did little more than pluck dead heads, or pull the occasional weed. There was a gardener to do the heavy work, though he, like his employer, was no longer young. A joke had long been circulating in the family that Fergus and Robbie were really twins, separated at birth, then mysteriously reunited through their love of the soil. Fergus liked nothing better than working alongside Robbie. The sight of the two men, hats pulled down over their balding heads, leaning over their spades, turning the rich brown earth, was as much a part of Iona as the macrocarpa hedges, planted the best part of a century ago to keep out the Antarctic winds. When Fergus and Robbie stopped to smoke their pipes, or drink the tea brought out to them from the kitchen, they were as alike, to a distant eye, as two peas in a pod. Illness apart, Dottie had never known her brother miss his Saturday communion.

'It's coming down in buckets,' Fergus explained, as if sensing her question. 'Not a lot I can do.'

'Robbie hasn't turned up then?' That too would count as a departure. Robbie, a bachelor, had never let bad weather stand in his way before.

'He's cleaning out the old harness room. Deidre needs the space.'

'What for?'

'Preserved eggs, I think she said.'

'What's wrong with the wash-house?'

When her brother didn't answer Dottie got up and walked through to the kitchen. Perhaps Fergus had come to escape his wife's scrubbing. Even on a Sunday, officially a day of rest, Deidre could still be found scrubbing an already clean bench, or polishing an immaculate sideboard. As if there wasn't enough to do preparing lunch!

Fergus, rocking gently in his mother's chair, listened to the soothing sounds of tea being made, and tins (containing scones, he hoped) being opened. He knew where he was with Dottie. She was the most predictable, the most reassuring person in the world. Even her response to Deidre, thankfully a matter of history now, had been in character. He knew how much it had meant to her to be mistress of Iona. He'd have let her stay, if Deidre hadn't objected. But Deidre had pointed out, quite rightly, that there was room for only one woman in a kitchen.

On the way down through the orchard this morning, Fergus had felt apprehensive. How would Dottie take the news he was bringing? He'd made a detour, ostensibly to inspect the now completed air-raid shelter, but really to rehearse what he would say to her. He often talked to himself like this. It boosted his confidence for public speaking. No one ever took any notice. Thinking aloud was a family habit.

The shelter had been built under a row of pear trees, some of which, sadly, had had to be sacrificed to the project. But now that the work was finished Fergus could appreciate not just the necessity of the thing (it could house, if need be, up to thirty people), but its symmetry. When it was nothing but an ugly scar across the hillside it had seemed to him evidence, however humble, of the disruptive power of war. But this morning, seeing it tucked under the trees, tidily camouflaged with branches, it had struck him as a symbol of hope. If we all do our bit, he'd thought, as he struggled to find the right formula for his sister, civilisation will survive.

Having mastered his 'speech', Fergus decided to examine the contents of the shelter. His wife, he acknowledged, as he lowered himself through the entrance, had worked a miracle here. The shelves, built into the sides of the bank, were stocked with tinned food and preserves, sealed jars of tea and sugar, candles and blankets. There were covered buckets for water storage, and a large wicker basket labelled FIRST AID, full of the paraphernalia of Deidre's profession. There was even a stash of books, wrapped around with corrugated iron to keep out the damp. 'No doubt about it,' Fergus had congratulated himself. 'I've married a fine wee woman.'

The thought reassured as he listened now to the whistle of the kettle. What was there to be worried about? Dottie would be delighted with his news.

He heaved himself out of the rocking chair, and threw another log on the fire. 'Aye, but it's cosy in here,' he said, watching the flames curl round the base of the log.

When Dottie moved into the cottage Fergus insisted she bring as many of her favourite pieces from Iona as she wanted. This rocking chair, for instance, had been her first choice. He could still see her at home, feet propped on the old fire-guard, fingers busy with her needle, swaying back and forth. He used to read or play patience while she sewed. Sometimes they'd listen to a talk on the wireless, or play canasta. More recently, as the world teetered on the brink of war, they'd begun tuning into the news. Of course he couldn't expect things to be the same with Deidre. She had no *patience* with cards (Fergus smiled at the pun). But he'd been surprised when she'd shown no interest in listening to the broadcasts, a recent innovation, transmitted each evening from the BBC. It was as if she'd made up her mind to distance herself as far as possible from the war.

Fergus ran his fingers over his moustache, checking, as Deidre had trained him to do, for pieces of stray tobacco. If he stretched out his hand in one direction he could touch the piano; in the other, the dresser, hung with his mother's cups. Fortunately Deidre had parted with both willingly enough. The top of the piano was cluttered with sheets of music, framed photographs of babies and family weddings, and the scattered contents of Dottie's upturned sewing basket. Fergus grinned. 'It may look messy to you,' he could hear his sister saying, 'but I assure you, I know exactly where everything is. Test me. Go on! Ask me to find something ... You see?' He laughed now at the recollection. 'You don't dare, do you? You know I'm right.'

Small, pokey, over-heated (even on warm days Dottie kept a fierce fire in the grate), all those words could be used to describe this room. But Fergus preferred *cosy*. Cosy and familiar. That chest, over by the window, Uncle Leonard's Chinese chest, had been a source of delight as a child. Full of musty smells, and materials cold as ice to touch, it had frequently drawn him and his sister, Meg, out of their beds, to explore its mysteries by candlelight. He was glad Dottie had chosen it. As far as he was concerned, if she'd asked for the entire contents of Iona, he'd have given them to her.

It had gone quiet in the kitchen. Dottie would be waiting for the tea to draw. Fergus took out his pipe, and banged it on the arm of his chair. If only he could be sure his sister was happy. She'd always liked this cottage. He remembered her, as a young girl, begging their mother to be allowed to sleep here. All the children, at different times, had come under its spell. Built to house the first of their clan to arrive from Scotland, it stood today, a century later, among apple and pear trees, its verandah looped with ivy, its windows framed by dark green shutters. There was still a problem with draughts, which Fergus had promised to see to. Those windows, opening like the doors on to the front verandah, were old and ill-fitting. He'd talk to Robbie about it at lunch time. Robbie was the man to fix things.

'Capital!' Fergus applauded, as a tray with teapot, cups, milk, sugar, and a plate of heavenly buttered scones was placed on the table beside him. 'No one can bake like you, Dottie.'

'Get away with you,' his sister demurred.

'That door could do with another coat of paint.'

Dottie glanced over her shoulder at the door Robbie had built to connect kitchen and living-room. It had been the way it was ever since she moved in. Why did it suddenly need painting? 'Have you talked Deidre out of redecorating the kitchen?' she couldn't resist asking. 'It's fine as it is. Everybody says so.'

'Deidre thinks it's dark.'

'Tell her to turn on the light.'

Fergus took a large bite out of his scone. He should tell his sister he approved of his wife's alterations. It was more or less true. He should tell her life was going to be different at Iona from now on, so change, a new broom as it were, was to be expected. But loyalty to his wife needn't extend to churlish treatment of his sister. She was entitled to consideration too.

'How did choir practice go?' he asked, when his mouth was more or less empty.

'All right,' Dottie answered.

'You don't care for Bill Gallagher much, do you?'

'It's his music I don't care for. Why can't he stick to the old tunes?'

Fergus grinned. 'Can't say I blame you,' he agreed. 'But then I'm tone deaf, people tell me.'

You and your wife both, Dottie thought sourly, helping herself to a scone. She was thinking of last Sunday when, voiceless from a cold, she'd abandoned her usual seat in the choir stalls, and joined the family in their pew. Fergus, typically, had insisted she sit next to his wife. If she hadn't known how much it would have hurt him, she'd have told him not to bother. It wasn't as if Deidre wanted it.

'How's Deidre?'

'I've got some news . . .'

Brother and sister laughed. They were so used to one another, long, companionable silences were often punctuated by the two of them opening their mouths at the same time.

'Deidre's fine,' Fergus said. 'Busy. We'll be twenty-four tomorrow.'

Dottie nodded. Her brother would be shocked if he knew what murderous thoughts she was having at that moment. Sundays, when she lived at Iona, were the highlight of her week. She was in her element putting the joint in the oven, calculating the roasting time while she was away at church, podding the peas to be ready for quick cooking on her return, basting the potatoes so they would be crisp and brown. In winter she would put a rice pudding at the bottom of the oven, and cook it long and slow, stealing a little of the delicious brown skin that formed on the top, before carrying it triumphantly to the table. In summer there would be fresh stewed fruit and junket, and jelly for the little ones. There was always enough. More than enough. 'I've eaten like a king,' Fergus would say, when asked if he wanted more. And the chorus would go up, from Iain and Enid and their five; from her sister, Heather, and hubby, Gordon, and those of their brood old enough to talk sense; from Tom, next to Fergus in age, and his ailing (but immortal, Dottie suspected) wife, Rona; from their two grown-up sons when they were at home; from the Oamaru clan, when they were in town; from everyone at the table, 'Another great meal, Dottie. *Well done.*'

'You said you had some news,' Dottie prompted.

'That's right.'

'More tea?'

'Just a top-up, thank you.'

A bitter smile touched the corners of Dottie's mouth. Fergus liked his tea to stand seven minutes in a warmed tea-pot. He could always tell when it had been poured too soon, or the pot hadn't been warmed. When Deidre first moved in, Dottie, in an effort to be friendly, confided this quirk to her new sister-in-law. Her thanks was a look that would have curdled milk.

'I *will* see to those windows, Dot,' Fergus said. 'I haven't forgotten.'

Dottie settled herself to wait. Since his illness Fergus had been prone to long periods of silence. She'd wondered sometimes if he were fighting the desire for a drink. That was one thing to be said for Deidre. She never touched alcohol. Had Fergus, Dottie wondered, confided his history to his wife? If Deidre had been a different sort of woman she might have asked. These days the family kept their whisky bottles discreetly out of sight. Not that Dottie had one herself. She couldn't stand the taste. If Fergus *had* told his wife, that might explain her excessive mothering of him. Breakfast in bed; cream, in defiance of rationing, with his porridge; carrots grated and sieved through muslin as a pre-meal drink; shoes cleaned; shirt-collars starched; blackheads expertly removed with tweezers.

'Won't catch me doing that for a man,' Iain's eldest daughter, Fiona, had giggled. 'I'd rather be single, thank you very much.'

Like me, Dottie had thought at the time. She knew what people said. *Poor old Dottie. A casualty of war. So many men of her generation killed.* Stuff'n nonsense, Dottie answered them now. I've never wanted to be any man's wife.

'What's that, dear?'

Dottie brushed the crumbs from her ample lap. 'Just thinking aloud,' she answered.

Her brother smiled.

'So, what's this news you've come to tell me?'

Fergus cleared his throat. Now that he'd finished his scone he could light up his pipe. Things were always easier with a pipe in your mouth. 'We've decided,' he began, seeing himself, for a second, standing at the entrance of the shelter. But this wasn't a speech, was it? This was conversation. 'Well that's not quite true actually,' he digressed. 'Deidre took a while to come round. But she's keen as mustard now.'

Dottie pushed the ash tray towards her brother. When she was in charge of Iona his habit of spilling tobacco everywhere never bothered her. Here it did. This was a cottage, not a family home. This was where people surplus to requirements were sent to live.

'We're going to adopt a child,' Fergus announced. 'There! I've said it! A son. Deidre insists it be a boy. Not too keen on girl babies apparently.' He grinned. When the expected response didn't come, he put his pipe back in his mouth, and sucked it noisily. 'Well, that's it,' he encouraged. 'My news. Whadda ya think?'

There was a loud crack from the fire. Dottie, stooping to pick up the glowing ember that had landed at her feet, answered, 'I'm absolutely flabbergasted!'

'Suppose it *is* a bit of a surprise.'

'Good God, Fergie, you're . . .'

'I know. Don't start, there's a good lass. I'm nearly sixty. Don't think I haven't thought about it. But Deidre's young . . .'

'Is she?'

'Well, you *know* she is. Almost half my age.'

Dottie retrieved her sewing from the other end of the sofa, held up the needle, saw it required thread, and plunged it into the pin cushion. 'How long have you been planning this?' she asked, measuring out a length of cotton. When she bent to thread it, she discovered, to her shame, that she was shaking. 'Is it because . . .? She glanced at her brother. He was busy lighting and discarding matches. She'd never felt embarrassed in his company before. It's *her* fault, she thought bitterly. His wife's. These things shouldn't have to be discussed at all. 'Is it because you and Deidre couldn't, can't . . .' She faltered. For all her determination the words refused to be spoken.

'There was never any question,' Fergus murmured. 'Children of our own. Not possible.'

Dottie shuddered. The thought of Fergus and Deidre . . . No. She wouldn't. She *mustn't*. When Deidre moved into Iona, Dottie viewed with approval her re-arrangement of the master bedroom. Instead of the one double bed, in which Fergus, since his mother's death, had slept, there were now two beds, on opposite sides of the room. Sex was a subject that perplexed Dottie. Not because of her own feelings, but because she didn't know what all the fuss was about. She'd assumed it was that way for her brother too. Till Deidre came on the scene.

'You won't be allowed to adopt, will you?' she pointed out. 'Aren't there rules about age?'

Fergus smiled at her through a haze of smoke. He needed her approval. It would surprise her, he thought, to know he always had. Dear, good Dottie, in her sensible shoes and homemade dresses. Someone must have pointed out her similarity to his wife. Dottie was plump, and high-coloured. She had blotchy brown spots on her hands, and an ugly black mole, from which hairs grew, on her lower left cheek. Deidre was a head taller, and thin. Her skin, which was colourless, had a stretched look to it. But the same modest way of dressing characterised both women; the same disdain for makeup and jewellery. They even wore their hair in a similar style, caught up in a net, fixed to withstand work and wind.

'I've had a talk with the lawyer,' Fergus answered his sister. 'He's going to look into the rules and regulations. I think we can get round it.'

'Have you told anyone else in the family?'

'You're the first.'

'And you're determined, both of you?'

'Absolutely.'

'When?'

'Well . . .' Fergus lowered his pipe into the ash tray. 'Quite soon as it happens. That's why I'm here. Could be as early as next week.'

'Crikey Dick!'

'Deidre's organised it. She didn't want me to say anything till we were given the green light. She's a remarkable woman, Dottie. She'd have been Matron of that hospital if I hadn't kidnapped her.'

Dottie kept her thoughts to herself.

'It was what persuaded her actually. The idea that she'd be *rescuing* a child.'

'Rescuing? From what?'

Fergus laughed. 'Religion, as a matter of fact. Deidre's a lot like you, Dot. All religions are suspect in her book.'

'That's a ridiculous thing to say, Fergus. I'm not like that at all.'

'You are about the Catholic religion.'

'I'm not alone in that.'

Fergus bent down to retrieve his sister's thimble. She was taken aback of course. Everyone in the family would be. But she'd come round. Dottie was a softie where children were concerned.

'I'd just about given up,' he admitted. 'Trying to persuade Deidre, I mean, when we got this appeal through the mail from the Catholic Boys' Home. You know the place? Next to the Little Sisters' Convent. Don't ask me to explain, you women aren't always rational, you know, but it struck a chord with Deidre right away. After that I had difficulty restraining her. She wanted to visit the Home that very day.'

Dottie's brain was racing. Something didn't make sense. Why would Deidre want to adopt a *Catholic* child? 'Byrne,' she muttered. Irish, of course. They all knew that. But that was only the half of it, wasn't it? Deidre Bryne, daughter of a horse trainer – horse *thief*, more likely – who'd had the effrontery to write a book. If it hadn't been for that book . . . 'You won't be allowed,' she repeated, more forcefully this time. 'I don't mean your age, I mean your religion. The child will have to be raised a Catholic.'

'That's just it.' Fergus flashed a mischievous smile. 'He can be, in theory. Deidre was baptised a Catholic. I had no idea.'

Dottie clamped her teeth together. What could you say about a woman who never talked about her family? Who refused to answer when asked if she had any brothers and sisters? Who was given away, not by a relative, but by a Chinese doctor? 'She's full of surprises, your wife,' Dottie muttered.

Fergus decided to treat the remark as a compliment. 'She's been amazing,' he boasted. 'It was she who wrote to the Mother Superior. God knows what she said, she wouldn't let me see the letter, but it did the trick.'

'She must have lied then. You know what the Mickey Doolans are like. They'd never let a Protestant adopt.'

Fergus retrieved his pipe from the ash tray. 'We've a final meeting with Mother Joseph on Tuesday,' he said, striking a match.

Dottie recognised the expression on her brother's face. It was the one she used to dread when he was struggling with his demons. It meant the conversation was effectively at an end.

She pushed the needle through the fabric, and yelped. It had gone straight into her finger.

'Use the thimble,' Fergus advised. 'You know what you're like when you're hot and bothered.'

For two pins, Dottie thought, flashing him a look, I'd speak my mind. But she contented herself with, 'Don't let Deidre carry this rescuing business too far, will you? Pick a cheerful baby, for goodness' sake.'

'My sentiments exactly,' her brother beamed.

4

The day she was to go with her husband to collect their son, Deidre looked at her reflection in the mirror and decided she was, after all, capable of radiance. She was wearing the suit and hat she'd worn on her wedding day. There was nothing else available in her wardrobe for so auspicious an occasion. But she'd have worn it anyway, her black suit, bought to last, and the hat with the veil, turned back now over the brim. Black's my colour, she confirmed, peering at herself through misted spectacles. I'm too pale, too sandy, to wear real colours; and too old, too married for pastels.

'Clarence William McLean,' she mouthed. The words were her mantra; her Open Sesame to happiness. Clarence William would be christened next Sunday in her husband's church.

Fergus was waiting for her on the verandah. It was one of those winter days when the sun creates unexpected pockets of warmth in the corners of rooms. Deidre could feel it in the bedroom and see it, through the verandah window, in the pool of light bathing her husband's chair. Fergus had come home from the city at lunchtime. He'd gulped down a bowl of soup, but was otherwise uninterested in food. It was all Deidre could do not to throw her arms round him. He was as excited as she was.

These last few weeks, with the planning and the shopping and the meetings with Mother Joseph, Deidre had felt a closeness with her husband she would have thought inconceivable at the time of the wedding. She'd known since winter started that she loved him. It was almost impossible to feel any other way about so kind a man. What she hadn't bargained for was the sense of complicity they would share once she finally capitulated over the adoption. She should have told him what changed her mind. It was nothing to do with religion, as he supposed. It was to do with Phineas O'Reilly, and Clarence Abraham Byrne, names that had never been spoken in this house.

'Marriage and children,' Fergus had mused, more times than Deidre cared to remember. 'They go together, don't they?'

She'd had to struggle not to remind him of the honeymoon, and the conversation they'd failed to have.

'Is that why you married me?' she'd asked, on one occasion.

'Of course not,' he'd reassured.

Later he'd said something about 'life going on', as if that explained his gentle obsession. Because it *was* an obsession. Deidre had been left in no doubt about that.

Then came the day when the letter from the Boys' Home arrived. Deidre could recall exactly what she was thinking as she hurried down the drive for the second time that morning. Her marriage was a sham. It made no difference that she now loved her husband. If anything that made it worse. Because Fergus didn't love her at all. He'd married the nurse in her, not the woman. He'd known she'd look after anyone, any *child*, entrusted to her care. Of course he liked her. She was not so sunk in depression as to deny that. But she was not his *wife*. He had no *desire* for her at all.

A routine letter, which she almost threw away . . . Deidre smiled into the mirror. 'Clarence William McLean,' she repeated.

She turned her head to the verandah window. Fergus had risen from his chair, and was peering at the watch he kept chained to his pocket. Deidre nodded in sympathy. It had become a matter of survival with her not to compare herself to her husband. The results, whenever she did, were too dispiriting. Six months of marriage had persuaded her Fergus was a man who hated no one, not even Hitler. 'Reject the sin, not the sinner,' was his answer to the world's evil. It was a mystery to her how anyone, male or female, could grow up without hating. Hate changed things; made things happen. The very word was charged with energy. Hating Jessie Potter had changed her from a sad child to a strong one. Hating the Duttons and all they represented had focused her mind on the evils of society. Without hate she couldn't have worked her small miracles of healing. Nor loved – she acknowledged the word reluctantly – the dying soldier, Finn.

Deidre took off her spectacles, and wiped them on her handkerchief. She'd never sat so long in front of a mirror before; though of course she wasn't really looking, just thinking. Love is my business today, she reminded herself, not hate. Love the reason I look . . . She laughed. *Shiny*, she decided. That's the word.

She opened the drawer of her dresser, and took out her ten-year-old box of face powder, a Christmas gift from Mrs Flight. Not even on her wedding day had she been tempted to open it. But this day was different. For her son's sake she wished to appear calm.

Love. The word sang in Deidre's mind, as she flicked the yellowy powder over her cheeks. Such a soft word, defenceless . . .

'So pretty you look, Deidre, like a picture . . .'

She shook her head, scattering the fine grains of powder over her shoulders.

'Do I have to thrash you to get you to speak . . .?'

'No . . .' she moaned, jamming the lid on the box, and flinging it back in the drawer. Her powdered reflection stared grimly back at her.

She tugged at her hat, pulling it down, in defiance of its style, over her ears. 'Clarence William McLean,' she chanted.

The smile returned to her face. Ghosts could always be made to disappear. Everything's in order, she reassured herself, as she adjusted her hat. Clarence's bedroom, next door, furnished with cot and buggy and baby clothes. She had Dorothy to thank for the knitted suits, in white and blue, the six embroidered night shirts, the lace-edged christening robe, hanging ready for Sunday's ceremony, in the wardrobe. Dorothy, in Fergus's words, had been an *angel*. But Deidre had known, even as she accepted the clothes, and murmured her thanks, that she and her sister-in-law hated each other still. She'd served too long an apprenticeship not to recognise the signs. Hate was both the strongest, and the most intimate of emotions. It bound human beings together forever.

'Say it, Deidre, say it! Yes . . . MOTHER!'

'STOP IT!' she shouted at the mirror.

'What's that, dear?' her husband called.

'Be there in a minute,' she answered him.

They were expected at two. The clock in the hall had just struck a quarter past one. At this time of day the journey into the city shouldn't take more than twenty minutes. Deidre had a fear of arriving early. She'd lied to Mother Joseph about religion. She'd said Clarence would go to a Catholic school. But of course Fergus would never permit that. Nor would she. If I had my way, she thought now, he'd have no religious instruction at all.

She picked up her handbag, snapped the clasp, and walked purposefully to the window. Robbie was in the rose garden, tying up the bushes broken by the recent winds. Deidre liked Robbie. She felt comfortable around men who spoke in his soft, slow way. They reminded her of Archie Drummond. I wonder where he is now? she thought. But speculation of that kind led nowhere.

She re-crossed the room, and glanced into the verandah again. Fergus was back in his chair, a Reader's Digest open in his lap. He looked up, and their eyes met. He pointed to his watch. But if we arrive early, Deidre silently protested, Mother Joseph might start asking questions. The prospect of being exposed as a liar in front of her husband sent the blood rushing to her cheeks. She glanced down, instinctively looking for the watch pinned to her uniform. What met her eye instead were specks of powder, betraying her momentary vanity. She hurried back to the dressing table, took up the clothes brush, and swept it vigorously over her shoulders.

'Patrick was baptised at birth, naturally,' Mother Joseph had told her. 'We put all our little orphans in God's hands.'

Patrick . . .

'Naturally we hope you'll keep the name he was given.'

Deidre, who was not used to lying, had taken a deep breath, and said what the Mother Superior wanted to hear. If Fergus had been with her it would all have been over. No one could tell a lie in front of Fergus.

'Do you know who his parents were?' she'd asked, on that occasion. Not that she minded. The moment she'd set eyes on 'Patrick' she'd known he was hers.

'His mother was a good Catholic,' she was told. 'That's all you need to know.'

'Was she young?'

Mother Joseph had looked at her over folded, arthritic hands. '*Too* young,' she'd answered.

'And there's no . . .' Deidre had hesitated, reluctant, as always, to speak about herself. 'I was a nurse,' she'd explained. 'I've been trained to ask about . . .' She'd been going to say 'hereditary illnesses', when she remembered the foul things Mr Fitzgerald had said in his lecture: that poor breeding was the root cause of criminality; that mental defects were bred into the species, and could be bred out. 'Health problems,' she specified instead. 'A history of diabetes, anything like that.'

'No,' Mother Joseph had assured her. 'Not from either side.'

What would I have done, Deidre wondered, her restlessness taking her back to the garden window, if Fergus hadn't chosen Clarence too? No other child was possible. It had been Clarence from the moment she walked into the dormitory.

'Well, I'm blowed,' Fergus had murmured, struggling, as she was, to take in the scene before them. 'So many.'

Mother Joseph had guided them gently along the rows of cots. 'These are our babies,' she'd informed them. 'The older children are down the corridor.'

'You mean there are boys here who never find a home?'

'Good care is taken of them, Mr McLean. You need have no doubts about that.'

'Fergus!' Deidre had had to draw her husband's attention to the curly-headed angel, peering at them over the bar of his cot. He was the only child she had eyes for. 'Oh, Fergus . . .'

'Let me introduce Patrick,' Mother Joseph had encouraged. 'One of our older children. Ten months,' she'd added, when Deidre looked at her enquiringly.

'Hullo,' Deidre had said, shyly.

'He's a good boy. Sleeps well. Likes his food. Don't you, Paddy?'

Clarence had smiled, on cue, and thrust his finger into Deidre's hand. There was no room for doubt after that. Clarence was *her* baby.

On the way home, barely able to speak for excitement, Deidre had explained to her husband that the name Clarence had been in her head from the beginning.

'Clarence,' Fergus had mused.

'You don't like it?'

'I'd imagined, well, a more *Scottish* name.'

'*My* father was Irish, Fergus.'

'I'm aware of that, my dear. But Clarence isn't an Irish name, is it?'

Deidre had been momentarily stumped. She'd wanted to say something about her mother, about her being English, but her words were pre-empted by Jessie Potter's voice. 'Cat got your tongue?' her tormentor had sneered.

'My mother was a New Zealander,' she'd proclaimed boldly.

'That's an odd way to put it.'

'Is it? Why? It's who we are, isn't it? Clarence will be a New Zealander.'

The discussion had gone on well into the evening. In anything else Deidre would have yielded. Pleasing Fergus had become a way of life with her. But in this one matter she wouldn't, *couldn't*, give in. Her son, her smiling, curly-headed son, *must* be Clarence.

'Very well, my dear, since it matters so much to you,' Fergus had at last conceded. 'Clarence it is. Clarence *William*, for my father.'

Clarence *Seamus*, Deidre secretly revised, but that could wait.

'Ready, lass?' Her husband's head appeared around the door. 'Not still tidying, are you?'

'Robbie's making a lovely job of the roses.'

Fergus smiled. The affection between Robbie and his wife was a comfort to him. It's an odd thing, he thought, moving into the room, but my wife seems to like men better than women. 'You look very smart,' he acknowledged.

'You should take a coat. It could turn nasty.'

'There are rugs in the car. We'll be warm as toast.'

Deidre picked up her handbag. 'One last look?' she pleaded.

Fergus nodded indulgently. He'd been called in to inspect the nursery half a dozen times in the last few days. The walls had been re-papered, the floor scrubbed, the furniture polished, the drawers lined. 'No self-respecting germ would dare show its face,' he'd teased.

'Smells clean, doesn't it?' his wife had answered. 'All my life I've loved the smell of *clean*.'

'Everything AI at Lloyd's,' Fergus reassured now, standing in the doorway while his wife smoothed the coverings in the cot. 'You've worked wonders, my dear.'

5

The approach of Christmas, 1940, was marked by relief that the threat of a German invasion of Britain had receded, gratitude for the miracle of Dunkirk and the RAF's defeat of the Luftwaffe, and an almost universal conviction that the war was about to intensify. In London, Winston Churchill had replaced the now despised Neville Chamberlain. In Wellington, Peter Fraser, a one-time pacifist, had inherited the mantle of leadership from Michael Joseph Savage, whose death from cancer earlier in the year had shocked the nation.

Though New Zealand was still far from the fighting, the commitment of its Government and people was such that reminders of war were everywhere. Billboards exhorted citizens to save, to give, to be alert to the operations of the fifth column. Wirelesses broadcast news of the Allied resistance in North Africa. Newspapers printed official propaganda. Sunday bands played military tunes in neat botanical gardens. Training camps sprang out of the mud; so too did camps to intern aliens and defaulters. Conscription was now the law of the land, but still young men and women were called on to enlist, to do their bit, to sacrifice . . . Every household had its rationing books. Soon blackout curtains would be the norm. There was food to eat, and fuel to keep people warm, but it was not uncommon, in those parts of the country where the puritan ethic held sway, for households to consume *less* than their entitlement.

'Amazing what you can do with a pound of dripping,' Dottie McLean encouraged her female relatives. To Deidre she added, 'I'll make the Christmas puddings for you, dear. You'll have your hands full with young Clarence.'

'Your first Christmas at Iona,' Fergus reflected, when his wife had finished what she had to say on the subject of Dottie and puddings. 'Our first as a family.'

'Enid and Heather have given me some of their coupons. We'll have more than enough.'

'The loaves and fishes, my dear. I never doubted your ability to provide.'

It was evening. With Christmas less than a week away Deidre had been busy in the kitchen till nearly nine. But she'd come, on her husband's insistence, to sit with him, and drink a cup of Ovaltine.

'Wee chap finally asleep?' Fergus enquired.

'He's excited. He knows something's going on.'

'You spoil him, ya know, lass. You shouldn't go to him all the time.'

Deidre, blowing on her drink, watched the skin snake across the cup and curl itself over the rim. She'd explained to Fergus, as calmly as she could, that she needed no one's help to make this the best, the happiest, the brightest Christmas Iona had ever known. Dottie's cakes and puddings could go elsewhere. The local orphanage, why not? They needed them far more than she did.

'Have you spoken to Tom?' she asked. Both Tom's sons were in the army now – one in Egypt, the other training at Burnham Military Camp.

'Good news,' Fergus answered. 'Wilfrid'll make it, after all. Rona had a call. It'll just be for the day though.'

'Well, that's better than nothing.'

Fergus smiled. His wife's willingness to feed and house his family was a source of continuing thankfulness to him. Were it not for the difficulty with Dottie, he would swear she was determined to get on with everyone. No doubt about it, he thought, remembering how it was in this house after the honeymoon, adopting Clarence was the right decision. Deidre still worked from dawn to dusk, but she'd lost that driven look. These days, when he walked past the kitchen, as often as not he'd hear her laughing. 'Got you, you little scoundrel!' And from Clarence would come a squeal of delight as his mother hoisted him into her arms.

The only sadness, for Fergus, was his own relationship with his son. Something that should have happened by now, hadn't. He'd play with him when he got home in the evenings; read to him at bedtime; take him on his lap and let him feel his moustache, or run his fingers over his bald head, but whenever he tried to hug him, the lad would wriggle away. Last night he'd used an old trick – pushing out his false teeth with his tongue – to try and amuse him. The boy had screamed, bringing Deidre running from the kitchen. 'She'll make a Little Lord Fauntleroy of him if you don't watch out,' Dottie had warned. 'For goodness' sake, Fergus, at least get her to cut his hair.'

'Don't worry,' his brother, Tom, had comforted. 'It was the same with my two. Your turn'll come later.'

'You don't think he's spoiled?'

Tom, conscious of his wife in the next room, had lowered his voice. 'You remember how it was?' he'd whispered. 'Worried every second disaster would strike? It made her ill. At least that won't happen to Deidre. She's made of sterner stuff.'

Fergus put his cup down on the tray, and took out his pipe. Clarence ... He would have preferred Andrew or Robert. Andrew Fergus William. That would have been nice. He opened his tin of Havelock Gold, and rolled the tobacco between his fingers. 'Now that summer's here,' he said casually, 'you don't think ... the lad's hair ... don't you feel it should be shorter?'

Deidre swirled the last of her drink in her cup. She wished she liked milk more. Something about its smell, and the way it formed a skin when cooling, repelled her. But Clarence loved milk. She'd never had any problems with him.

'Drop more, dear?' she asked.

Fergus shook his head.

'Doesn't *feel* like summer,' Deidre hedged.

'That's because you're always working.'

Deidre closed her eyes, and swallowed the last of her drink. After Jessie Potter cut baby Clarence's hair, it grew back in ugly gingery tufts. Deidre had wept tears of rage. Her golden-haired baby mutilated by that *witch*. But Fergus was not Jessie Potter. That look on his face now – kind, perplexed, anxious. Someone had been getting at him, hadn't they? Someone not very far from this house. Deidre knew what was being said. She'd heard

Dottie, in conversation with Heather, call Clarence a 'spoiled brat'. Eavesdropping, a habit Deidre had revived since coming to live at Iona, was proving as essential now as it had thirty years ago. Some of the most important lessons of her childhood had been learned behind closed doors.

'I suppose,' she conceded, 'if we're going to Wanaka . . .'

The smile on her husband's face was all the proof Deidre needed. 'I'll see to it tomorrow,' she said, banging her cup down on the tray.

While Fergus fiddled with the knobs on the wireless, searching for the BBC, Deidre planned how she would cut her son's hair gently, so gently he would think it was a game. Afterwards she'd sweep up the curls, and arrange them, between layers of tissue paper, in a box.

'Let's hope they're just baby locks,' Fergus said, when he'd found the right station. 'Boys can't abide curly hair.'

Through the static, Fergus and Deidre learned that the Italian advance had been stopped at Sidi Barrani. Good news, they agreed. But there was talk of sending troops to Greece. New Zealand troops. That was not so good.

'I've been thinking,' Fergus said, when the bulletin came to an end. 'The Home Guard. I think I should put myself forward.'

'You're fifty-eight years old, Fergus.'

'I can hold a gun.'

'Against whom? The Germans? Whatever would they want with New Zealand?'

'I was thinking more of Japan.'

'We're not at war with Japan.'

'We could be. They've signed a pact with the Axis Powers. What's to stop them?'

Deidre jumped up from her chair. Clarence was awake. She could hear him murmuring. She didn't want to think about the war. She'd hoped, over Christmas, a moratorium would be declared. What good did it do, talking about it? The deprivations, the calls for clothes and food parcels, she could cope with. They were a challenge. But when an old man like Fergus . . .

'I'm not quite in my second childhood, you know,' Fergus pointed out.

'It's your health I'm concerned with,' Deidre snapped. 'Not

your age. Out all hours, shooting at shadows. It's a nonsensical idea. You're needed here, Fergus. I need you. Your son needs you. You don't have to prove anything.'

I'll have a word with Iain, she resolved, as she hurried across the hall to the nursery. It isn't as if the family's failing in its duty. There's Tom's two, and Meg's girl, Amy, in the VAD. Philip'll be next. Iain said so himself. That boy can't wait to turn eighteen . . .

'There there, my darling,' she soothed her fractious son. 'Mummy's here. Did you think I'd gone away? Silly boy. I'll never leave you. Never. You're the only one, Clarrie. I keep telling you that. There'll never be anyone else.'

'Dwink!' the boy demanded.

Deidre reached for the bottle of rosehip juice, which she'd left ready for the night. 'Want Mummy to hold you?' she asked.

Clarence's fists grabbed the bottle. Deidre ruffled his curls in approval. 'You know what you want, don't you, little scallywag?' she teased.

It was after ten when she finally tiptoed into the room she shared with Fergus. Like her son, he too was asleep.

Deidre pulled the eiderdown up to his chin, and whispered goodnight. His snores wouldn't keep her awake tonight. She was far too tired. In four days' time it would be Christmas.

6

As Christmas Day drew to a close everyone agreed it had been a success. The traditions, as Iain kept telling people, had been maintained. Even Dottie, grappling with her green-eyed demon, acknowledged that Deidre had done well: the lamb cooked to a turn; the gravy dark and delicious; the peas and potatoes sweetly minted. By sleight of hand Deidre had made sure all the children had sixpences in their puddings. By a similar trick, the wedding ring had fetched up on bachelor Wally's plate, just as it had for the past thirty years. The teasing and laughter that followed were as traditional, at Iona, as the presents under the tree. Wally Reed was Fergus's oldest friend. Every Christmas Eve he drove up from Balclutha, and every New Year's Day he drove away again.

But this was 1940, so not everything that happened that day could be explained in terms of the past. For all Deidre's efforts, the subject of war would keep surfacing. There was Wilfrid, for a start, prickly in his uniform. To the younger cousins he was a magnet. Deidre, listening to their prattle, was thankful Clarence was too young to understand.

'Well now, doesn't he look the regular little soldier?' Dottie had gushed, when Clarence was brought out for the family to admire.

'Short back and sides,' Fergus had laughed. 'At least he's not as bald as his father.'

Later, when everyone had repaired to the garden, Deidre discovered two of Heather's brats teaching Clarence to fall down dead. 'Whatever do you think you're doing?' she'd shouted.

'He's a German,' the one called Ross, explained. 'He's got to die.'

At the end of the meal Fergus had proposed a toast to the King and Queen. Another tradition. Deidre, raising her glass of lemonade, had had her composure sabotaged by the sound, in her head, of her father's words. 'The English poison is in this country too . . .' She'd been quick to dismiss the voice as a trick – What poison? The McLeans were Scots, not English – but some minutes passed before she felt in possession of herself again.

The next toast, to absent friends, had unsettled that silly woman, Rona. Hearing her sniff, fearing the onslaught of tears, Deidre had thrust a handkerchief into her hand.

'Oh . . . thank you,' Rona had squeaked. Her husband and son, Deidre had noticed, paid no attention.

The afternoon, as tradition decreed, had been taken up with games in the garden. There was a treasure-hunt; a lolly-scramble; hide-and-seek; races involving sacks and wheelbarrows and legs tied together. Deidre had been glad of the excuse of the dishes. So glad she'd refused the help that was offered. She'd designated Meg's eldest, Amy, to be in charge of Clarence, donned apron and protective cuffs, and set to work. 'I'm not at all tired,' she'd insisted, when, having seen off the nieces, Dottie tried to butt in. 'You run along with the others.' But she *was* tired, she admitted later, listening to the shrieks from the garden. Tired enough to wish all but one of those children a thousand miles away.

By the end of the afternoon, when Fergus had mustered the whole company for a photo session, even the children were showing signs of exhaustion.

Looking at the family photo, a week later, Dottie was struck by the resemblance some of her nieces and nephews showed to her parents and grandparents. There was Gordon's middle boy, Kelvin, who'd shadowed Wilfrid for the entire day, looking uncannily like his Great-Grandfather Fergus. And Meg's little after-thought, Grace, the spitting image of Grandmother Frances. The only face that didn't fit, of course, belonged to the little dark-haired boy, sitting on his mother's knee in the front row.

With the coming of the New Year Deidre could no longer hide her exhaustion. There'd been eight extra staying at Iona – Meg and George and their four, Uncle Angus, who'd come with them, and stayed on, at Fergus's insistence; Wally Reed, whose snores had rivalled her husband's.

'Well, that's it for another year,' Fergus sighed, as Wally's car disappeared down the drive. 'Wonder how many we'll be next year?'

Deidre, shielding her eyes against the sun, tried, and failed, to imagine Christmas, 1941.

'Come on, lass,' her husband urged. 'You look tired.'

'It went all right, didn't it, Fergus?'

'It went splendidly. Everyone says so.'

Deidre put her arm through her husband's. Clarence would be two-and-a-half years old next Christmas. He'd be talking, running, sitting up at table.

'I've had an idea,' she said. 'I think we should get Clarence a horse.'

'Hector Crawford!' Fergus exclaimed.

'We've got the paddocks. Seems a waste not to use them.'

There was a pause, then her husband said, 'I was thinking of letting them actually. This war . . . Well . . .' He laughed. 'Fergus McLean Publishing can't expect to escape unscathed.'

'You mean, we're hard-up?'

'Well, I wouldn't go so far . . .'

'I wish you'd talk to me about your work, Fergus. I wish you'd confide in me.'

When he didn't answer, Deidre removed her arm from his, and set off at a brisk pace towards the house. This idea of hers, about the horse, it wasn't new. She'd been harbouring it for weeks. She could see Clarence now, grasping the reins in his little fists, laughing . . . The horse would be called 'Biddy'.

She was surprised when Fergus caught up with her. She'd not heard him approach.

'The lad'll be awake soon, won't he?' he asked.

Deidre took his arm again. She was always ashamed, afterwards, when she showed irritation with her husband. He was so unfailingly good-natured himself.

'Our son did well, don't you think?' she prompted 'His little cousins seemed to like him. Grace kept asking to have him in her bed.'

'*You* were the one who did well, my dear,' Fergus answered.

'So long as *you* think so . . .'

'I don't think. I *know*.'

'Well, it's over now. It's just the three of us.'

They didn't speak again till they were in the house. Then Fergus said something which Deidre, recalling his words a year later, was to curse herself for ignoring. 'Aye, Clarence had a high old time all right,' he acknowledged. 'He's a regular son-of-a-gun, that boy. But ya know, lass, I've been thinking – there's something not quite right about an only child.'

7

By the time the summer of 1940 came to an end talk of the war was as commonplace as talk of the weather. It was a long time since anyone had predicted an early end to the struggle. These days Sir Arthur Dutton peppered his speech with phrases like, 'the long haul', and 'necessary sacrifices', and 'the inevitability of victory', words which singularly failed to comfort his wife and daughter.

'At least Richard sleeps in his own bed at nights,' he'd reminded them recently. 'Soldiers have to *live* war twenty-four hours a day.'

Margot had responded by leaving the room; Sarah, by staring at him as if he were talking Chinese. 'God help me!' he'd been goaded into shouting. 'What is it you women *want?*'

Sir Arthur was not alone in his frustration. The air was so poisoned with rumours no one felt safe any more. The New Zealand Division, presently stationed in North Africa, was rumoured to be destined for Greece. Japan, victorious in China, was rumoured to have its sights set on the Pacific. The Battle of the Atlantic, currently raging in the North Sea, had revived the old fear that Britain would fall.

'If Britain goes, the Empire goes.' It had been said before, but now, with newspapers carrying daily casualty lists, fear came garlanded with the visible badges of suffering. The Allies were fighting for freedom, but everywhere freedoms were being eroded in the cause of victory. Tolerance, difficult enough to practise in peacetime, became a luxury few could afford. This was especially true in New Zealand, where isolation, and the long separation from sons, husbands, and fathers, fuelled resentment. 'HOLIDAY CAMPS FOR CONCHIES' a January headline in the *Press* proclaimed. Underneath were the words, 'While their fellow-countrymen sweat and die in the deserts of North Africa, our conchies, justly punished under the law, read and dig their gardens.'

It would not be that way for long.

'You don't need to tell *me*, Daddy,' Sarah snapped, when her father drew her attention to the article and accompanying photograph. 'And no, that isn't Louis. Though I agree there's a likeness. But then they all look alike, wouldn't you say? Stuck behind barbed wire . . .'

Sarah Dutton has ditched Louis de la Tour. For a few weeks, in certain select parts of Christchurch, *that* had been the hottest rumour.

'About time,' James Mountford, husband of Daisy, responded, when the story reached him. 'If ever I saw a coward, it was Louis de la Tour.'

'Can't be much fun in prison,' his wife observed.

'Prison? Health camp, more like.'

'You don't want to believe everything you read.'

'It's no fun being shot at either,' James countered.

'How would you know?'

James clasped his hands behind his neck. 'Here we go,' he sighed.

'Just because you're a lawyer, that doesn't mean you can go round judging people,' Daisy pouted.

Her husband smiled. 'You really do want me to join up, don't you? Like that precious brother of yours. You know they won't have me. You saw the report yourself. But that's not good enough for you, is it? You'd like me to get on my horse, and ride out of your life in a thunder of hooves and glory. You'd make a lovely widow, Daisy. I'm sure Richard Dutton'd find you irresistible.'

By the end of March, interest in Sarah and Louis had yielded to the persistent fear that Britain would be starved into surrender. If the convoys couldn't get through, if Britain's pilots, decimated by the battle for the skies, couldn't protect the seaways, Hitler would be the victor, and the Empire would fall.

In this atmosphere, as the lights, by Government decree, were being dimmed in every city and town in New Zealand, Sarah found herself walking along a familiar Sydenham street. It was late-afternoon. She'd just come from the university, where she'd enrolled for her third and final year. She was twenty-one years old, a fact which had gone virtually uncelebrated. 'Have it your own way,' her father had grumbled, when she'd insisted her birthday be private. 'Don't suppose you'll say no to a cheque though, will you?'

Sarah's destination was Kitty Whyte's house. She'd not seen Kitty to talk to since Louis's exhibition in June. But she'd seen her by chance a week ago, walking on Sumner Beach with a man. That sighting, Sarah had decided, was her chance. She had no doubt as to the identity of Kitty's companion. It was her lover, the married doctor, whose 'position in society' required that their affair be kept secret.

'Sarah! *Mon Dieu*! What are *you* doing here?'

Kitty's voice was not warm. But then why should it be? Sarah had never made friends with her. And now, with Louis gone, any claim she'd had on Kitty's world was gone too.

'Can I come in?'

'You look terrible.'

As Sarah walked down the narrow passage to the room where she'd spent her first evening with Louis, her stomach threatened to betray her. It had been this way every morning for the past seven weeks, but by this time of day the worst was usually over.

'You all right?' Kitty asked, propping the door open with one of Adrian Fawley's bronze animals. It was stiflingly hot in the house. And Kitty's perfume no match for the street's drifting smells.

'Wouldn't say no to a glass of water.'

'Looks to me as if you could do with something stronger.'

'Water'll be fine.'

While Kitty was out of the room, Sarah took several deep breaths, a trick she'd learned to control nausea. When she felt better, she selected a cushion, and sat down. Most of the objects surrounding her were familiar, but there were one or two additions. There was a Chinese silk screen she hadn't seen before, and a lamp made of overlapping petals of coloured glass.

In this room Kitty held her regular *soirées*. Her love of a party, reflected in her canvases, was one of the reasons Sarah was here now. Kitty was a social animal, but she kept her private life a secret from her friends. She understood, what Sarah was learning so painfully, that some things *had* to be secret.

Kitty's paintings had titles like 'Enthralled' and 'Visceral Pleasures'. Her women wore exotic clothes, and smoked cigarettes in long holders. Her men looked as if they'd been drugged. How will you view *me*? Sarah wondered, as Kitty, glass in hand, walked back into the room.

'So . . .' Kitty settled herself on a cushion, and lit a cigarette. 'To what do I owe the honour?'

'I'm sorry,' Sarah murmured, between gulps of water. 'I shouldn't have come. I've no right to ask a favour of you.'

'I think you should let me be the judge of that.'

Sarah steeled herself against the ice in Kitty's voice. 'How have you been?' she enquired politely.

'Now now, *ma chère*, that's not why you've come. Is it about Louis?'

'Have you heard from him?'

'Haven't you?'

'He's all right,' Sarah answered truthfully. 'I think the Appeal Board was the worst part.'

Kitty watched the smoke from her cigarette float towards the open window. Of course Sarah had come to talk about Louis. What other reason could there be? That they were estranged was common knowledge. The reasons, Kitty presumed, were the obvious ones: family; Louis's pacifism; the war . . . Louis *had* written to her as it happened, but not one word had he said on the subject of Sarah. The people he wrote about were either artists, or fellow prisoners. One name in particular had stayed in her mind; a young medical student, Peter Larsen, whose desertion of their cause Louis had deplored. 'He's let himself be man-powered, more fool him,' he'd written. The words had depressed Kitty. Like most of Louis's friends she'd hoped prison would temper his views.

'I'm not interrupting, am I?' Sarah asked.

Kitty's own feelings on the subject of war were contradictory. She hated the very thought of it, but she was not a pacifist. On the other hand she felt a fierce loyalty to Louis. If she'd been in Sarah's shoes . . .

'You're pregnant, aren't you?' she said suddenly. It was a guess, but she was certain she was right. Something about the face . . . 'Have you told Louis?' she went on, when there was no answer.

Sarah shook her head.

'Why not?'

The answer to that was a shrug.

Look,' Kitty said, 'it's none of my business whether you tell him or not, but if you want me to help you . . . That is why you've come, isn't it?'

'Yes.'

Kitty did her best to hide her irritation. 'Why me?' she protested. 'You have other friends.'

Sarah swallowed what was left of her water. How could she tell Kitty it wasn't *her* she wanted, but the man she'd seen her walking with on the beach.

'When did you last hear from him?' Kitty asked. 'You are corresponding, I take it.'

'He writes twice a week.'

'I see.'

Sarah fixed her eyes on the drawing above Kitty's head. Another addition. When she realised the drawing was Louis's – a gift before he went away? – the nausea returned. 'I need to see someone,' she said curtly. 'A doctor. Not anyone my parents know.'

Kitty flicked the ash from the end of her cigarette. Louis had described the various characters in his hut to her. One, a writer, was the father of two-year-old twins. 'Imagine,' he'd written, 'the impact of a child, your own child, on your work . . .' 'I still think you should tell him,' she said.

Sarah took out her handkerchief, and held it to her mouth. Watching her, Kitty felt a mixture of pity and scorn. Everything about Sarah Dutton suggested composure: the well-cut dress, with the fashionable wide collar; the clean white gloves; the leather satchel full of books. Only the handkerchief betrayed her.

'You have a friend,' Sarah persisted. 'A doctor. I saw you with him last week. What I wondered was . . .'

Kitty ground her cigarette into the ash tray. 'He's an eye surgeon, Sarah,' she said coldly. 'Not a gynaecologist.'

'I knew I shouldn't have come.'

'How did you know about him anyway?'

'I'm sorry,' Sarah blurted, jumping to her feet 'I had no right . . .'

'Oh do sit down!' Kitty hadn't meant to speak sharply, but really, the girl was the limit! She'd get what she wanted, wouldn't she? Her sort always did. 'It's not the end of the world, you know,' she grumbled. 'This sort of thing, it's been happening to women for centuries.'

'It's not Louis's fault,' Sarah insisted. 'I wouldn't want you to think . . . He'd marry me if he knew.'

It wasn't what Kitty had expected her to say at all. 'Sit down, please,' she said quietly.

Sarah obeyed.

'What is it you want, Sarah? An abortion?'

There was a gasp, then the words, 'I don't even know for certain that I'm pregnant.'

'Because if it's an abortion . . .'

'No! I couldn't. I mean . . . I haven't thought . . .'

'Haven't you?'

Sarah pressed her hands into her stomach. In the room along the passage she and Louis had first made love. They'd taken a risk that night, but never thereafter. Louis had been very careful about that. 'Just the test,' Sarah muttered. 'Once I know for sure, I can decide . . .'

Kitty was a long time answering. She could have told Sarah she'd had an abortion herself, at about Sarah's age. She could have confided her feelings for Peter Sing, whom Sarah was so anxious to consult. She could have broken her own rule about never interfering, and pleaded Louis's case. The fact that she did none of these things was not because she didn't trust Sarah. On the contrary, she'd begun to do both the moment Sarah spoke in defence of Louis. Most women, in her position, would have laid the blame on the man. It was what Peter's wife would have done. She'd never met Vivienne Sing, and hoped she never would, but she knew her well enough. Miserably homesick for England, unable to bear a child, she was the kind of woman who blamed her husband for everything.

'I'll speak to him,' she agreed. 'Can't guarantee anything though.'

It was the first time Sarah had looked anything but wretched. 'Thank you,' she said.

'If it *is* positive . . .'

Sarah rose to her feet again. 'You won't say anything, will you? To Louis, I mean. I'm not sure yet, you see, if I want, if we can ever . . .'

'You have my word,' Kitty promised, moving past her to the door.

'I'm very grateful . . .'

She led her visitor along the passage, and out on to the street. The air, after a day of fierce nor'westers, was as stifling outside as it was in the house. 'I'll be in touch,' Kitty said. 'Try not to worry.'

8

Peter Sing looked at the young woman sitting opposite him and thought how like his wife she was. Not that the resemblance was physical. It was more to do with *essence*. There was something essentially English about both women. His wife had the peaches and cream Anglo look, which he'd always found, to his cost, so compellingly seductive. Sarah Dutton's looks were darker, stronger, more aristocratic. But her Englishness was as unmistakable as his wife's.

Sarah had first come to see him last Monday. When Kitty asked him if he'd talk to her his first instinct was to say no. He knew the Dutton family by reputation, and was prepared to bet they would treat him exactly as Vivienne's family in England had: with patronising kindness. One of the reasons he'd fallen for Kitty Whyte was that *her* world, and that of the Duttons, were so far apart. It was his way of getting even with his wife, who refused to acknowledge the existence of anyone not part of Christchurch society.

'I don't often ask favours of you,' Kitty had reminded him gently.

'You never do,' he'd answered 'You're altogether too generous.'

That first meeting with Sarah was brief. Having ascertained her problem, he told her what was needed, and arranged to see her again the following morning. The specimen she'd left with him had tested positive. Sarah Dutton was pregnant.

'You realise, of course, there's nothing more I can do.'

The girl nodded.

'You must see a GP. That is, unless . . .'

Their eyes met. Peter felt his own narrow into a frown. How come this girl, this privileged European girl, could have a baby so easily when his own wife . . . 'It's your life,' he said coldly. 'You must do what you think best.'

The girl smiled. It made him feel uncomfortable. 'Men never help women in these circumstances, do they?' she said softly.

'If you're asking me, will I arrange an abortion for you, the answer is no. My reasons are personal. Nothing to do with your situation.'

'Yes, I see.' The girl got to her feet. 'Thank you for your help, Mr Sing.'

'Now look here . . .'

'There's nothing more to talk about.'

'Sit down, Miss Dutton, *please*.'

Sarah, startled by his change of tone, did as he asked. On the wall behind the desk was a framed certificate from The Royal College of Surgeons in London. On the desk itself was a photo of a woman, not Kitty Whyte. At their first meeting, Mr Sing had made it clear he was a busy man. Most of the men Sarah knew were *busy*.

'Is that where you come from?' she asked, pointing to a painting of Shanghai harbour on the far wall.

Peter laughed. 'Good heavens, no. I come from a little town in Central Otago. You've probably never heard of it.'

'I don't want an abortion, Mr Sing. I want to have the baby.' Sarah flattened her hand against her chest. Her heart was racing wildly. Not till that moment had she known what her decision would be.

'In that case,' Peter answered, after a moment's silence, 'I think I can help you.' He picked up his pen, and began to write on his pad. Sarah, craning her neck, saw that he was writing in Chinese. 'Of course you may change your mind,' Peter continued. 'About your young man, I mean. Kitty told me . . .' He cleared his throat. He wasn't used to speaking Kitty's name in public. 'As I understand it, you don't want to marry him,' he said.

Sarah opened her eyes wide. Peter felt the familiar tug in his gut. The girl was a beauty all right. No doubt about that.

'Have you ever loved anyone more than your life, Mr Sing?' she asked.

'I beg your pardon?'

'I mean that quite literally. To love someone so much the thought of him not being there is like death.'

Peter looked down at his pad. The words said what he couldn't speak aloud, that he wanted this young woman's baby for himself. 'I can't say I have, no,' he answered her.

'I've loved like that for most of my life,' Sarah said. 'I don't think I had a life of my own at all. I lived for *him*.'

'Are you telling me . . . ?'

'It's only now,' she went on, 'with what's happened, that I can admit it.' She hunched her shoulders, causing him to wonder if she were feeling ill. 'It's ironic really,' she said.

Peter chewed the end of his pen. He was used to confessions. They came his way most days of his working life. But this one had him stumped. 'You've known your young man all your life? Is that what you're telling me?' he ventured.

'Not him. My brother.'

Peter drew an astonished line across his pad. 'Your brother,' he repeated.

'There's no need to look so shocked. We didn't commit incest or anything.'

Peter gestured his innocence of any such thought.

'It's not how I feel *now*,' Sarah elaborated. 'That's what I've been trying to tell you. The tie's been broken, and not just by me. But the feeling's still there, the memory of it, and that's the problem. Other things, feelings, will always be compared to it. I'm not saying they should be or anything. It's just how it is.'

Peter shook his head. He didn't care for the tenor of her talk. It was too intense; too abdicating of responsibility. 'You can't say that,' he argued. 'No one can. The only thing we know for sure is that things change. You won't feel like this in five years' time.'

'He's my brother,' Sarah reiterated. 'I'll always love him.'

Peter thought of his own brother and sister, of the casual, slightly embarrassed relationship he had with each of them, and wondered if he'd missed out on something. 'What about the child's father?' he asked. 'What are your feelings for him?'

While he waited for her reply Peter went over in his mind what Kitty had told him about Sarah Dutton. Pretty, spoiled, with a brain she would almost certainly waste in later life. He had no quarrel with the first part of Kitty's description. It was the last bit troubled him. Why should her life be wasted? One of the few positive things to come out of this war was the opportunities it gave to women. He'd tried to point this out to Vivienne, but got a flea in his ear for his pains. Vivienne was even further down the road of abdication than Sarah.

'You say you'll always love your brother,' he prompted. 'Is that also true of this other man?'

Sarah jerked her head, as if to deny any such thing. But the answer she gave was ambiguous. 'Probably,' she said.

Peter's mind went back to Kitty. 'Beulah Dowling apart,' she'd asserted, 'Louis de la Tour is the best artist working in this country today.'

'And where does Sarah Dutton fit into it?' he'd enquired.

'Nowhere,' Kitty had replied. 'Not any more. Her choice, not his.' Later she'd told him the relationship could never have lasted, even if there'd been no war. 'You know how it is when you love the thing you're not,' she'd said, causing him more distress than he cared to acknowledge. 'Well that's how it was with those two. *Un amour mortel* from the word go.'

'I still don't quite see,' he said now. 'Your brother's role. I'm not sure I . . .'

The girl's laugh stopped him in his tracks. Kitty hadn't done justice to Sarah Dutton. She was full of surprises.

'Richard doesn't have a role, Mr Sing,' she said. 'He's twelve thousand miles away.'

'He's a soldier?'

'A pilot. He's been in from the beginning. He's with the New Zealand Squadron now.'

Peter drew a border round the edge of his pad. Eighteen months active service in the Air Force. Statistically the man's dead, he thought . . . 'So you've not seen him for a while,' he surmised.

'Not since January, 1937.'

'I see.'

'I don't think you do.' Sarah caught the look on his face, and gestured uncertainly. Then, to his further astonishment, she blushed. 'I don't mean to be rude,' she apologised.

'Go on. Please.'

'When I first met Louis . . . That's his name, did Kitty tell you? Louis de la Tour.'

'Interesting name.'

'You'll hear it again, Mr Sing. Louis's a genius.'

Peter smiled.

'Didn't Kitty tell you?'

'I assumed she was exaggerating.'

Sarah jammed her fist into her chest. She didn't want to talk about Louis. Talking about him made him real, and the only way she could manage her life now was to consign him to his chosen darkness. 'He's in prison,' she said. 'Stop me if you've heard all this. He's a pacifist. A war resister, whatever you like to call it. He won't compromise. If he'd been prepared to do something, *anything*. But he won't. Not even for me.' She cleared her throat. Peter had the feeling she was in need of a cigarette. 'He's not to know about the baby,' she continued. 'I made that clear to Kitty. When the war's over . . .' She paused, and moistened her lips. 'When it's over,' she said firmly, 'he'll have his art. He'll always have that.'

'And what will you have?'

While he waited for her reply, Peter took out his handkerchief and wiped the sweat from his palms. He had no business wanting this woman's baby. Even to think such a thing was unethical.

'I'll have our child,' Sarah said.

Peter plunged his hands into his pockets. Damn you! he wanted to shout. Damn you to hell! 'I take it your family will support you?' he said, in his coldest professional voice.

There was no answer.

'This brother you're so fond of . . .'

Sarah waved an impatient hand. 'I'll tell you something for free, Mr Sing,' she said. 'Love's a delusion. It's not worth the trouble.'

In spite of himself, Peter smiled. 'Are you quoting, or telling?' he inquired.

'Both.'

'You're very young to be so cynical.'

'Almost everyone I know is with the wrong person.'

'Sometimes that can't be helped.'

'I can't turn myself into someone else,' Sarah stated flatly.

Peter glanced at his watch. The action was habitual; not intended to signal preoccupation. But it brought Sarah to her feet.

'I'm sorry,' she said. 'I've taken too much of your time.'

'Not so, not so at all.'

'I'm late for a lecture anyway.'

Sensing she would not be delayed a second time, Peter stood up, and moved out from behind his desk. He would have liked to offer her something: friendship; a shoulder to lean on. But the truth was, there was no room in his life for such quixotic undertakings. Kitty was claim enough on his time. 'If you have any trouble,' he said. 'If your family . . .' He took the hand she offered him, and shook it warmly. 'You know where to find me,' he reminded her.

'Goodbye, Mr Sing,' Sarah said.

'Goodbye, Miss Dutton. Good luck.'

9

Cheyney Grange, in autumn, is a place of spectacular beauty. The deciduous trees, planted near the house by the first, disputed Dutton, blaze their defiant reds and golds at a clear cold sky; or else, on darker days, burn holes in the swirling mountain mists.

Arthur Dutton could never make up his mind whether he was glad of those essentially domestic trees, or whether he would have preferred his view of the mountains unimpeded. But he was glad of them today. Their mood matched his own. He would survive this latest blow as he'd survived all the others that had come his way. People who didn't know him, and even some who did, looked on him with envy. They saw his life as soft, privileged, free. Well, he could accept the middle word, though he'd add a rider to the effect that with privilege came responsibility, and he'd never been one to shirk his duty. But *soft*? *Free*? In what way? Hard work and worry were his daily experience. It was hard work got him through the Depression, saving the family fortune (well, the remnants of it), and as many jobs as he could justify. Now there was a war, and he'd work and worry his way through that too. War was an evil – Arthur never denied that – but in his opinion it was a *necessary* evil. Which only made it the more imperative men like him should struggle to keep alive the values of the civilised life. What else was all the suffering for if there wasn't to be a better world at the end of it? Oh, yes, he would take whatever this war threw at him. There'd never been any question about that. What he hadn't bargained for, and what had brought him outside now to contemplate the mountains, was this wretched business of Sarah's.

He'd been so happy when she'd announced she was coming home for the weekend. He'd hoped, with de la Tour out of the picture, to see far more of her at the Grange. But this weekend was her first visit since the New Year.

'Sarah has something to tell you,' his wife had said to him, as they were dressing for dinner. 'She's already spoken to me.'

'You make it sound ominous.'

Margot had given him a sideways look, the kind that said, I don't want to deal with this now. I have a headache coming on. 'Don't be too hasty, dear, will you?' she implored, when he asked for a clue as to what it was all about. 'Remember, there is a war on.'

Over dinner he'd decided his daughter had made up her mind to chuck university. It would be just like her. She'd have some hare-brained scheme to train as a VAD or join the Women's Auxiliary. He had no quarrel, in principle, with women doing these things. *Single* women, that is. Married women, in his view, were far better occupied working from home. There was more than enough to keep them busy. Every self-respecting town in the country had its Patriotic Committee. Women, with their baking and their sewing, were the principal fundraisers. As for his daughter, if she wanted to do more, she could help her mother with her Red Cross work, or take up knitting for the Air Force Relations Organisation. It would be sheer foolishness for her to give up her studies now. In a few months time she would have her BA.

The one thing of which he'd been reasonably sure, watching his daughter toy with her food, was that she hadn't come home to talk about Richard. Since the day he'd told her she couldn't go to England they'd not discussed Richard again except in general terms, or when reading his letters. It hadn't escaped Arthur's attention that Sarah no longer received individual letters from her brother. He'd imagined this was because of the utterly changed nature of Richard's life. He was flying Lancasters now, bombing the hell out of German shipping. What could he say to his sister that hadn't already been said in his weekly letters home? *Restraint* came high on Arthur Dutton's list of virtues. Especially where women were concerned.

'So, young lady, what's all the mystery?'

They'd gone into the library to talk. There was a fire burning, and the kind of soft light Arthur found most conducive to problem-solving. Sarah, he thought, was looking particularly attractive. A little peaky, but that was to be expected with all the studying she did. She was wearing a silk gown of her mother's. He'd noticed it at dinner and been mildly surprised. She'd given up dressing for dinner a long time ago.

He'd not been able to take in what she was saying at first. The words had come at him like a series of blows.

'You're what?' he'd gasped.

After which, there was no longer any room for doubt. 'I'm pregnant, Daddy,' she'd said, repeating the terrible words. 'I'm going to have a baby.'

He didn't like to remember what he said after that. The rage, the accusations, the disbelief. She took it all, answering him when he gave her the chance, defending that scoundrel, Louis de la Tour. 'I'm sorry, Daddy,' she said, when his fury had abated. 'I didn't expect you to like it. But it's happening to *me*, not you. I hoped you'd be more understanding.'

'Understanding? Of what? The fact that my daughter's a . . . ?' The word, thank God, had not been spoken. But they both knew what he meant.

That would have been the end of the conversation had he not halted her at the door. It was astonishing to him how calm she was. 'If you're worrying about your reputation,' she'd attempted to retaliate.

'That's right! Mock away! It's what your generation do, isn't it? But just let me remind you . . .'

'There's no need, Daddy, really,' she'd said.

He'd had the words all ready for her. He was a public figure. How could he urge others to stay strong, to make sacrifices, when his own daughter had thrown herself away on, of all people, a *pacifist*? Then there was his brother, Adrian. In line, as one of the country's top Judges, for the Privy Council. A scandal like this could wreck his chances.

But he never got to say any of it because what his daughter did next left him speechless. She walked back into the room, and kissed him.

'She's gone,' his wife came in to tell him, a few minutes later.

But he already knew that. He'd heard her car take off down the drive.

Arthur loosened his jacket, and turned back to the house. He must find Margot. Make his peace with her. To get through this thing, salvage what honour they could, a united front was essential.

'Darling? Are you there?'

The house was unusually quiet. Outside, the vast silence of the mountains had been broken by the fretful barking of dogs, and Frank McNichol's whistle calling them to heel. There must have been birds too, but Arthur couldn't recall hearing them. The great migratory swarms had passed now, leaving only the permanent residents, and the occasional, curious kea.

'Margot?'

The door of the kitchen opened, and Betty, housekeeper at the Grange since Arthur's boyhood, popped her head around the door. 'She's outside, sir,' she said. 'In the rose garden.'

'Thank you, Betty.'

How much had the servants heard? he wondered, as he made his way past the stairs to the back of the house. Not that there were many servants left now. The war had snapped up all but Betty, and that pathetic creature, Elsa Klopstock, whom Frank had found wandering on the side of the road, and brought to the Grange for food and shelter.

'She needs a place,' Betty had insisted. 'Somewhere safe. Klopstock's a German name.'

'She's Maori, isn't she? She looks Maori. Have you asked her where she comes from?'

Betty, who'd doubtless guessed he was going to give in, had smiled. 'She's not always easy to understand,' she'd said.

Elsa and Betty; Frank and his half-wit son, Tyrone; Joe Metcalfe, who also boasted Maori blood. Not much of a crew, Arthur thought sourly, as he stepped out into the sunshine again. He could see Joe now, coming out of the stables, heading for the kitchen in search of his morning cuppa. Joe had been one of the first to volunteer, but his lungs had let him down, and they'd sent him back.

'Ah . . . there you are.'

Margot Dutton looked up at her husband. That she had no wish to speak to him was written all over her face. Arthur's smile, in response, was ironic. He'd always wanted mother and daughter to be close. Now, with their world in ruins, it seemed they were.

'Last of the Queen Marys?' he inquired, indicating the blooms in her basket.

'I thought I'd take them back to town.'

'Good idea.'

'I should have gone with Sarah last night.'

'She's at Rosevilla, is she?'

'Thank God, yes. I phoned this morning.'

'Margot . . .'

'This isn't one of your factory problems, Arthur. You can't make it go away.'

Arthur lowered his head, and sniffed one of the blooms. The scent tickled his nostrils.

'You're such a snob!' Margot burst out. 'Where do you think you're living?' She gestured angrily at the house. 'That isn't Windsor Castle, you know.'

Arthur was too taken aback to reply. In all the years they'd been married he'd never once heard his wife talk like that.

'As a matter of fact . . .' Margot hesitated. Then, in a second angry gesture, she took off her gloves and threw them to the ground. 'Oh, never mind,' she said.

'I think you should finish what you were going to say.'

'We're no better than anyone else. We've just got more money, that's all.'

'I don't see what that's got to do with . . .'

'Sarah's going to have a baby, Arthur. Our daughter's going to have a child.'

'I'd like to get my hands on that blackguard!'

'He's no more to blame than Sarah.'

'Can't tell me she wouldn't marry him if he asked her. It's *his* brat she's having.'

'You don't *want* to understand, do you? You never have wanted to.'

Arthur's hand closed over a thorny branch. When he looked down, he saw that he was bleeding. 'Artists,' he fulminated.

'There are different rules for them, is that what you're saying? You tell me, Margot. You're the one with the connections.'

For the first time since Sarah's abrupt departure, Margot smiled. 'Poor Aunt Clara,' she said. 'What a lot she has to answer for.'

'Now wait a moment.' Arthur rubbed his hand against his trouser leg. 'There's absolutely no call . . .' The look in his wife's eyes stopped him. When she reached out for his hand, and calmly cleaned the blood away with her tongue, he was momentarily unmanned. 'Oh my dear,' he stammered.

'Our first grandchild, Arthur,' she said softly. 'Think of it like that.'

'I can't . . .'

'You will. In time. Just don't decide anything now.'

'I rather thought Sarah was the one who'd be making the decisions.'

'Oh, she's made those already.'

'What does that mean?'

'She's your daughter, Arthur. She's doesn't flinch from facts.'

'Are you telling me she's going to keep the baby?'

'Yes.'

The muscles in Arthur's neck tightened like screws. One woman he could cope with, but a conspiracy . . . 'Then she'll *have* to marry,' he said, spitting out the words. 'If not de la Tour, then somebody else.'

'And how do you suggest she goes about doing that?'

Arthur pulled his hand free. He mustn't give into weakness again. Someone had to keep their head around here. 'I know you think I'm out of touch,' he said. 'And I know you despise what I do. No, don't interrupt, please. It pains me to remind you that *what I do* pays the bills. I know there was a time when *you* helped *me*. And I'm sorry, genuinely, that you no longer have that . . .' He hesitated over the word. 'Independence,' he conceded. 'But if we're going to help our daughter . . .'

'You are going to help her then?'

'Well, of course I am. What on earth did you think?'

His wife's arms shot out. The unexpectedness of her embrace knocked him off balance, landing him among a pile of pruned branches, whose thorns, mercifully, lodged in his clothing.

'Oh dear, now look what I've done,' Margot laughed.

She helped him to his feet, and began pulling the thorns from his jacket and trousers. He allowed her to minister to him for a few moments, then he said, 'I want to suggest something to you, Margot. If you agree, we'll put it to Sarah. We can drive back to town this afternoon.'

The look or his wife's face was suspicious. 'You're not thinking of adoption, are you?' she objected. 'Because she won't hear of it, Arthur. I can tell you that now.'

'All I'm thinking about is the next few months,' he hedged. 'I see no reason to parade her condition . . .'

'Go on.'

'My sister would have her. She might even be able to transfer her degree up there.'

'Auckland . . .'

'I know. It's a long way away. But she'd be with family . . .'

'I don't know, Arthur. I don't really know your sister.'

'Nancy's a brick. She'll take the whole thing in her stride.'

'You make it sound . . .'

Arthur grabbed his wife's hand. One thing at a time, he counselled himself. Get Sarah out of Christchurch. Let Nancy talk some sense into her. But right now, get this woman on your side.

'I don't want people pointing the finger,' he said. 'I don't see why Sarah should have to endure that.' (And I don't want her stuck with a bastard child for the rest of her life either, he added privately.)

Margot's teeth nibbled at her lower lip. She was wearing slacks, a fashion she seemed to favour more and more these days. With her hair loose, and her face free from makeup, she looked younger than her years. Arthur felt a momentary pang. He'd not been unfaithful to her for some time now, but it troubled him, as he waited for her reply, that he'd been unfaithful at all.

'Yes, I do see,' Margot said.

He raised her hand to his lips. 'I shouldn't have spoken to her the way I did,' he conceded. 'She's not my little girl any more.' He bent down to pick up the discarded gloves. What he wanted to do now was take his wife to bed. 'I think we should go upstairs,' he proposed, glancing back at the house.

'It's ten o'clock in the morning, Arthur.'

'That never used to worry you.'

'You're talking about twenty years ago.'

He bent down, and nuzzled her neck. 'Then we'll just have to put the clock back, won't we?' he said.

10 ∫

Sarah reached Auckland after an exhausting thirty-hour journey, during which she was sick three times, and had to endure the attentions of an unpleasantly odoriferous soldier, her companion on the train from Wellington, who seemed to think his uniform entitled him to ignore her pleas for privacy. Sarah hadn't seen her Aunt Nancy since childhood, but she had no difficulty picking her out from among the crowd waiting on the platform. Nancy Quayle, née Dutton, half a head taller than her brothers, had long ago decided, since she couldn't disguise her height, she might as well accentuate it. Her hats sported perky feathers; her shoes, chunky heels that hit the ground with force, drawing attention to her stately progress. Seeing her now, peering short-sightedly at the people alighting from the train, Sarah felt, for the first time in weeks, a surge of optimism. Aunt Nancy wouldn't look at her with brimming eyes, as her mother did; or talk to her about 'the long-term future' like her father. She didn't know her Uncle Stanley, but she felt certain, as she pushed through the crowd, that he'd go along with whatever his wife said. Even if he didn't, things could hardly be worse than they were at home. Since her father had opted to accept the situation, and stop reminding her of her sins, she'd begun to feel like a cuckoo in the nest. The old, bantering familiarity between father and daughter had disappeared without trace. These days Arthur Dutton was polite, anxious, apologetic. It was to escape that, and the message in her parents' eyes when they thought she wasn't looking, that she'd agreed to come to Auckland.

'Aunt Nancy?'

The feathered hat turned. A face bearing an uncanny resemblance to the ancestor whose portrait hung in the dining room of Rosevilla, stared down at the travel-weary girl. 'You won't be needing *that* in Auckland,' Aunt Nancy said, fingering the fur coat Sarah's mother had insisted she wear.

'It was cold when I left.'

'Cold place, Christchurch. Cold people too. Don't tell your father I said so.'

Sarah grinned. ('She's a bit of a card, your aunt,' her father had enthused. 'I'm sure you two'll get along like a house on fire.')

'Porter!' Aunt Nancy shouted. 'Jiminy Crickets,' she drawled behind her hand, as a man with a mop of white hair, and a stoop like the hunchback of Notre Dame hobbled towards them. 'I know there's a war on but honestly . . . Can you manage that?' she doubted, as the porter hoisted Sarah's cases off the ground.

'It's my job,' the man wheezed.

'You should be at home enjoying a well-earned retirement.'

'I'll not take Government's money. Never have taken it. Not about to start now.'

'Admirable sentiments,' Aunt Nancy approved. 'Come along then.'

Sarah followed obediently. Till now she'd regarded this visit as merely a means to an end. She'd stay with her aunt a week or two, then find a job and a place of her own. Afterwards, well, she'd just have to manage as best she could. She wouldn't be able to work full-time, but she was confident, once the baby was born, her father would increase her present somewhat meagre allowance. She'd be out of his way in Auckland, which was what he wanted. He surely wouldn't punish her further.

'You've nothing to worry about,' her mother had said as the whistle blew for her departing train. 'Nancy'll take care of you.'

It shamed Sarah now to recall her mother's tears. There was so much suffering about, to most of which Sarah was simply immune. It was as if her pregnancy had innoculated her against the creeping sickness of the times. Her one bad moment came just before she left. Her father called her into his den to tell her Desmond Linwood had been posted missing on Crete. 'His name's not turned up on any of the POW lists,' he told her.

'So God knows what's happened to him. He's not the only one either. Charles Creichton's got a son-in-law in the same boat.' Sarah had run from the room and driven straight round to Daisy's. She was an infrequent guest in the Mountford house, but Daisy had opened her arms to her, and for most of the night they'd cried together as if their friendship had never ended. 'I'm so sorry, Daisy, so dreadfully sorry. This bloody war . . .'

'Right then,' Aunt Nancy sighed, when they were seated in the taxi. 'That's done.' She patted her niece on the knee. 'Hot bath, hot meal, and bed for you, young lady.'

'Sounds heaven.'

'We'll talk in the morning.'

Sarah rested her head against the seat and let the unfamiliar sights roll past her. She'd never seen so much traffic: trams, motor buses, cars, trucks laden with produce, bicycles . . . Had it not been for the sprinkling of uniforms among the crowds in the streets she could have thought the war over, and people energetically going about their business. But then a familiar poster swung into view, urging citizens to save their bottles and ointment jars and toothpaste tubes, and the war was present once again.

Their route took them along the waterfront. The busy wharves, where ships bound for England were tied up alongside smaller, coastal vessels, gave way, after a few minutes, to beaches and palm trees and houses built to take advantage of the harbour view. Here pleasure boats were moored; and children, in defiance of the season, played in the sand. To Sarah's relief, her aunt seemed to feel no need to talk. That, presumably, was being saved for the morning.

'You don't hear from Louis any more?' her mother had asked, hovering over her as she packed her bags.

'He stopped writing a month ago.'

'I always liked Louis.'

It had been a bad moment. She couldn't tell her mother the truth, which was that she missed Louis's letters almost as much as she missed him. Since the day of his arrest he'd written to her twice a week. She couldn't expect him to go on, not when she never replied. But the day she realised his letters had stopped, she felt an unreasoning rage against him. He wasn't the only one suffering for his principles.

'I'm not going to *pretend*, Mother,' Sarah had insisted, when the inevitable question was asked. 'I'm not going to call myself *Mrs* or anything.'

Sarah didn't meet her uncle that night. True to her word her aunt fed her and sent her off to bed. But next morning, at breakfast, she was introduced to a portly gentleman, several inches shorter than his wife, who smelt of lavender water, and talked to her about the war. 'We haven't seen the worst yet,' he asserted cheerfully. 'Not by a long chalk. The Pacific's where we should be looking, not Europe. We're vulnerable in New Zealand. All that coastline.'

'Not scare-mongering, are you, Uncle? I thought that was a crime.'

Her uncle chuckled. 'You never told me the wench was a wit,' he berated his wife.

'Oh, get away with you, Stan,' Aunt Nancy retorted.

'I'm right though, aren't I? Japan's the real enemy.'

After he'd gone Aunt Nancy came back to the table and poured them both a second cup of tea. Sarah wasn't sure she knew what happiness looked like, but she had the feeling she was seeing a woman content with her lot. It was hard to reconcile this with the portrait her mother had painted. 'There's nothing sadder than a childless woman,' she'd said.

'You'll find little Stanley and I make a good team,' her aunt announced, intuiting her niece's train of thought. 'I married beneath me, I'm glad to say.'

Sarah smiled, and sipped her tea. For a moment she was tempted to talk to her aunt about Louis. There'd been times in the past months when the urge just to speak his name had sent her running to her room to gaze at his Madonna. 'You're all I have left of him,' she'd whisper, in a rush of self-pity. But then the baby would move inside her, reminding her of the choices they'd both made, and she'd turn her back on the sorrowing woman, Louis's masterpiece to date, and speak the words of her new-found faith. 'I have you, my son (for it was a boy she was carrying. She was certain of that). I have *you*.'

'Your uncle's a salesman,' Aunt Nancy disclosed, clattering her cup on to her saucer. 'Don't let the family hoodwink you. They'll tell you he's a distributor. Or even a publisher. I've heard that said. But it's all flannel. What he does, is drive round in his trusty motor and sell encyclopedias to people.'

'Mother told me I'd never be short of something to read.'

'You'll go on with your studying, won't you?'

Sarah thought of the books she'd brought with her, and felt a flash of guilt. She'd not confided her decision to abandon her studies to anyone. That would have meant revealing the rest of her plan – to live her own life – and she wasn't ready for that yet. Her mother had assumed the books weighting her suitcase were textbooks, but they weren't, they were the novels that had once been her passion. Currently, inspired by the recent movie, she was re-reading *Wuthering Heights*. She'd even considered calling her baby Laurence, after the actor Laurence Olivier. If Richard could have heard her, telling her unborn child the story of Heathcliff and Cathy, he would have laughed. 'You'll make a horrible mother,' he used to taunt, watching her drag her doll around by its hair. 'Why don't you put some clothes on the poor creature?'

'Did you hear me?' Aunt Nancy prompted.

'Sorry . . . Yes. I mean, no. I've uh . . . I've applied for a postponement. Maybe next year.'

'That's the first silly thing I've heard you say.'

Sarah hunched her shoulders. Don't *you* start, she protested silently. I won't last a week if this is how it's going to be.

'Education for women. Your generation don't realise. Some of us had to go without.'

'I'm going to have a baby, Aunt Nancy,' Sarah reminded.

'Indeed you are,' her aunt agreed, swirling the tea in her cup.

Sarah felt the tension drain from her. After all, she needn't worry. Aunt Nancy's lectures, unlike her parents', came without barbs. She was dressed in a style Margot Dutton, wanting to be kind, would have called eccentric. A smudgy print overall covered her serviceable skirt and jumper, while around her head was wound a bright orange scarf. 'Impossible to get help these days,' she'd complained, over the first cup of tea. 'Not that I mind. I just tie my hair up, put on my pinny, and get down on my hands and knees.'

'I suggest we introduce you as Mrs Dutton,' she said now. 'That is, unless you want to go by some other name?'

'What?'

'Mrs Dutton.'

'Who am I supposed to have married, my father?'

'And you'll wear this.' Aunt Nancy delved into the pocket of her overall, and plucked from it a thin gold band. 'It was your grandmother's so you're perfectly entitled.'

'I don't want to be Mrs anyone,' Sarah objected.

'Of course you don't. It's all a lot of tomfoolery. But we can't always do what we want, Sarah my dear. And in this instance I think your father's right.'

'So it was his idea . . .'

'And your mother's. For your own good.'

'How many times have I heard that in the last two months?'

'And you'll hear it again, I daresay. None of us lives in a vacuum, Sarah. It's the one advantage we middle-aged fogeys have over you young folk. We *know* that.'

'But if I pretend *now* . . .' Sarah began.

'"If ifs an' ands were pots and pans",' her aunt quoted merrily. 'Now, if you've finished that tea, I think we should get on with the day.'

That breakfast set the tone for the next three and a half months. As soon as Stanley was out of the door Nancy would sit her niece down for one of her 'little talks'. The burden of these conversations was always the same. No one was blaming Sarah for the position she was in. Most women, if they were honest, would say, 'There but for the grace of God . . .' But the thing had to be faced, and not just from Sarah's point of view. There was the family. Arthur had asked his sister to stress the pain Sarah would cause if she kept the baby. 'My wife will tell you different,' he'd written. 'But she's got her head stuffed with romance, as you know . . .' Nancy had winced at her brother's tone. So like our father, she thought sourly. And so unnecessary! If Arthur wanted this baby to disappear he had the means in his own hands. She wouldn't say as much, of course. That wouldn't be fair to Sarah. But she'd leave him to draw his own conclusions.

'Have you thought what you'll do if your father stops your allowance?' she'd asked, early on in their conversations.

'Why would he do that?'

'Don't be naive, dear.'

Sarah had nibbled the nail of her thumb. She was wearing a kimono, a fetching garment, her aunt had thought, casting an approving eye over her.

'It's what *I'd* do if I was him,' she'd said.

The look Sarah had given her would not have been out of place in an interrogation room. 'You don't seriously imagine you can bring your child up in the bosom of the family, do you?' Nancy had challenged. 'This is the Dutton family we're talking about, Sarah. I don't have to tell *you*.'

For two weeks after that Sarah didn't appear at breakfast. She wanted to be left to sleep, she told her aunt. When she did get up, later in the morning, she left the house almost immediately. Nancy bided her time. Sooner or later Sarah would come back. It was a hard world out there. And Nancy, who'd made it her business to find out, knew not enough was being paid into Sarah's account to cover rent and board. 'As I explained in my last letter,' she wrote to her brother, 'I don't know where she goes each day, and I don't ask. But I imagine she's looking for a flat . . .'

'If she thinks I'm going to increase her allowance,' Arthur wrote back, 'she's got another think coming.'

In the end it was the doctor who persuaded Sarah to give up her daily wanderings. 'If you want to keep this baby,' he warned, 'you'll learn to eat regularly, and put your feet up.'

'Right then,' Aunt Nancy said, the morning she judged it safe to broach the subject again. 'Breakfast in bed for you from now on, young lady.'

'Aunt Nancy?' The girl's face was a study in Dutton determination. 'Do you think my father'll stop the payments? He writes to you, doesn't he? I've seen the letters.'

'You want my honest opinion?'

'Yes.'

'I'm certain of it.'

'You mean he's told you . . .'

Nancy tucked her long legs underneath her, and settled down

in her chair. This room was nothing like as luxurious as the bedrooms at Cheyney Grange or Rosevilla, but she'd bet her bottom dollar it was a five-star apartment compared to anything Sarah had been shown. She knew what city flats were like. The sort Sarah could afford anyway. Decaying houses smelling of cabbage and disinfectant. 'How many illegitimate children have you known, Sarah?' she asked, coming straight to the point. 'Not the adopted ones. They have the protection of the law. But the ones people call *bastards*.'

'That's not fair . . .'

'Are any of your friends unmarried mothers?'

Sarah picked up her breakfast tray, and rattled it on to the floor. 'My father's put you up to this, hasn't he?' she accused.

'Believe it or not, I'm on your side, Sarah.'

'Doesn't sound like it.'

'Listen.' Nancy uncurled her legs, and leaned towards her niece. 'If you decide to keep the baby I'll help you all I can. But I wouldn't be speaking the truth if I didn't say I think that would be a tragic mistake. Not just for you, for your child.'

'Daddy *promised* . . .'

'Promises can be broken.'

'I can get a job. There's lots I can do.'

'And would you earn enough to educate your child? Because he'll need the very best education money can buy, Sarah. He or she.'

Sarah tugged at her thumb nail with her teeth. 'Perhaps I should go home,' she smouldered. 'I'm an embarrassment to you, aren't I?'

'Oh, don't be so silly. No one's embarrassed. Least of all me.'

'But you think I should give up the baby . . .'

Nancy bent down to retrieve the tray. She lifted the cup of tea and handed it to her niece. It would surprise her brother to know she wasn't doing any of this for his sake. Arthur, his older sister firmly believed, was far too fond of getting his own way. But the fact of the matter was, Sarah's life *would* be ruined if she kept this child. Even if Arthur came round, and acceded to his wife's romantic notions, what could the future possibly hold? No one worth their salt would marry the girl. And a career, under the circumstances, would be impossible.

'All this isn't anything to do with Richard, is it?' Sarah asked.

'Why on earth should it be?'

'I don't know. I don't know what to believe any more. Who to trust.'

'Richard knows, does he?'

Sarah shook her head. 'Daddy asked me not to tell him. He thought it might worry him.'

Nancy nodded, though she wasn't much concerned with Richard at this point. 'You know what I think?' she said. 'I think you should eat up your breakfast.'

Sarah gave her a weary smile. 'Lecture over, is it?' she asked.

'For today,' her aunt replied.

The following week Sarah received an unexpected visitor. Her Uncle Adrian was in Auckland, her aunt had told her, to hear a case in the High Court. Sarah greeted him suspiciously. These days she regarded every family member as a potential enemy. ('Your mother might *say* she'll have you and the baby,' her aunt repeatedly predicted, 'but your father'll never agree.')

Sarah's suspicions proved justified. Uncle Adrian, after initial prevarication, confessed the real reason for his visit. An approach had been made to him by an old friend. 'Well, he's more of an acquaintance actually,' he qualified, 'but everyone agrees he's a man of excellent family and character . . .'

More on this theme followed, at the end of which, prompted by an increasingly impatient Sarah, Adrian got to the point. 'My friend wishes to adopt a child,' he said. 'He didn't specify which sex, so I assume it doesn't matter. He has a son already, two years old I think he said. What he wants is to provide this little boy with a sibling. Complete his family.'

Sarah, too angry to speak, stared at her uncle, whose resemblance to her father merely fuelled her feelings of rage. She hated her family: hated her name. She couldn't imagine this conversation taking place in the rundown villas of Sydenham. Or in a Maori household. Recently she'd read an account of Maori life in which illegitimate babies were described as 'unexpected blessings'.

'Thing is,' Uncle Adrian ploughed on, 'your child would have a far better life with my friend and his family than he could ever hope to have with you. He'd grow up in the best of homes, with no stigma attached to his name. Think about it, Sarah.

Whose happiness is it you're considering? Your own? Or your child's?'

'You say this man approached you.'

'That's right.'

'How did he know?'

'How did he know what?'

'That you had a baby for sale.'

'Sarah!'

'I'll tell you what I'll think about, Uncle Adrian. I'll think about who's telling lies here. Does my mother know about this?'

Adrian Dutton shook his head. He'd agreed to undertake this mission for his brother because he genuinely believed it was right. Now, seeing the look on his niece's face, he was no longer sure. But he'd told the truth about Fergus McLean. He *had* approached him. They'd met at a Masonic Lodge dinner in Dunedin. Fergus had confided his anxiety about raising his son as an only child. Adrian had relayed the conversation to Arthur, and the idea had taken root.

'Not a word to Margot, mind,' Arthur had cautioned. 'It'd only upset her.'

Since then a number of letters had changed hands. The first, from Adrian to Fergus, raised the possibility of Sarah's baby being made available for adoption. The second, from Fergus to Adrian, expressed delight at the idea of a Dutton baby coming into his family. 'I can tell my wife the child's bound to be intelligent,' Fergus enthused. 'What's more, I can appeal to the rescuer in her, since you tell me the war is to blame for the unhappy circumstances . . .'

Adrian's answer, which contained a brief biography of Sarah, informed Fergus the adoption could be arranged privately. 'There would be no delays,' he wrote, 'and no need to go through the authorities.'

'I think you'd better go, Uncle Adrian,' Sarah said.

'Are you all right?'

'I get this pain sometimes, in my chest. It's nothing to do with the pregnancy.'

'I'll call Nancy, shall I?'

'No. I'm fine. Just go. Please.'

Adrian stood up. Everything about this meeting distressed

him, not least his sister's refusal to stay in the room and back him up. Women were the very devil sometimes. At least you knew where you were with the law. 'We all love you, Sarah,' he sighed. 'We're only trying to help.'

That night Sarah took the scrapbook out of her suitcase, and began to re-read the cuttings and letters she'd not looked at for more than a year. The last personal letter she'd received from her brother had been written before the war. But then it was a long time since she'd bared her soul to him too. At first she'd held back out of pique. Later, it was in response to her father's wishes. Richard was not to be distracted by unnecessary anxiety. It had been easy enough to comply. Why should she make an example of herself when her brother, in respect of Daisy Linwood, had got off scot-free?

The letters were neatly arranged, in chronological order. It came as a shock to Sarah to realise how close she and her brother had once been. Louis de la Tour, who'd had to stand comparison with him for so many months, had won in the end. Now it was as if the two men were changing places. The brother she'd consigned to the shadows was being resurrected before her eyes. Why did you stop writing? Why? Why? she kept asking. Only when she reached the end did the answer come. His letters, like hers, had been subject to censorship. What was the point of writing when language had been hijacked for propaganda?

Suddenly she knew what she was going to do. She was going to lift her side of the censorship. She was going to tell her brother the truth.

It was after midnight when she put pen to paper. And past one when she finally sealed the envelope.

'Dear Richard,' she began, 'are you going to mind this letter very much, I wonder? Will you be cross I've kept things from you, or think less of me because of what's happened? Oh Richard, Richard, why are you so far away . . . ?'

12 ∫

The telegram from the Air Ministry lay next to the pile of mail on the hall table at Rosevilla, awaiting the return from the country of Sir Arthur and Lady Dutton. Sir Arthur had a board meeting that afternoon, and Lady Dutton, who hadn't been to town for several weeks, had written to Hazel to tell her she'd be driving down with her husband.

These days, with only Hazel left to run things at Rosevilla, Margot felt less and less inclined to spend time there. The war had reconciled her to Cheyney Grange. There were fewer reminders, among the mountains, of war's horrors and inconveniences.

For the best part of eighteen months, before the war changed everything, Margot had wanted nothing more than to be at Rosevilla with her husband. It was almost like the first year of their marriage all over again. She supposed it had something to do with Richard's absence, and Sarah's preoccupation with Louis de la Tour. She and her husband were on their own, in every sense that mattered. But then the war came, and Arthur got so busy she never saw him, and the anxiety she felt for her son became her daily companion, as feared and familiar as a gaoler.

The first time Margot opted to stay on at the Grange, her husband raised no objection. His work for the Patriotic Fund, and his efforts to raise money to buy Spitfires for the New Zealand Squadron, absorbed what spare time he had. He hardly noticed whether his wife was in the house or not.

'I can as easily pack Red Cross parcels here as in town,' Margot had said, anxious not to be accused of malingering. She needn't have worried. The war had returned Arthur Dutton to the public arena. He was, his wife reflected, as the conflict moved into its second year, probably as happy now, as fulfilled, as when he'd been a member of the Government.

To her surprise, after the initial shock of loneliness, Margot began to enjoy the country life she'd once so despised. She longed for Sarah to visit but knew, while she was absorbed in her university work, there was little chance. Besides, she was married in all but name to Louis de la Tour. Other people may not have noticed the change in her, but no mother could misinterpret that blossoming, or fail to observe that her daughter was now a woman. It would give Sarah a shock to see her mother, in torn slacks and an old pullover of Richard's, heaving thistles out of the garden. But physical work, Margot had discovered, was the best way to dull the persistent fear for her son.

'You'll be making me redundant,' Frank McNichol had joked, the day she extended her weeding to include the borders of the drive.

'No chance of that,' Margot had said, straightening her aching back.

'Mind you don't overdo it now,' Frank had advised.

But overdoing it was exactly what Margot was aiming for. Not even Betty could dissaude her. Betty, Margot sometimes thought, was really her only friend. These days she had difficulty remembering the names of all her former friends in town. As for relatives, there was a cousin somewhere in Auckland, another who'd moved to Australia, but that was it. We Ainsley-Bowers are a dying breed, she'd long ago concluded.

Margot liked being with Betty. She was so much easier a person to be around than the abrasive Hazel. She even liked being with Elsa, whose strange, hybrid language was now quite comprehensible to her. 'I don't know what you'll make of our latest addition,' she'd written to her daughter, 'but Betty swears she's worth her weight in gold.'

One of the first things Margot did the weekend Sarah drove up to tell them about her pregnancy, was introduce her to Elsa.

'Don't you wonder where she's come from?' Sarah had asked, but lost interest before her mother could finish her reply.

Sarah's news had come as a shock, but that had soon passed, leaving in its place a sense of liberation that had transformed

Margot, in a matter of days, from a woman marking time to a woman with a purpose. It had even seemed possible the spark between her husband and herself might reignite. Arthur, when he'd recovered his composure, had exhibited a tenderness towards her every bit as seductive as in the days before the war. But it hadn't lasted. And the more they talked, the wider the gulf between them grew. Margot wanted to offer Sarah and the baby a home. Her husband insisted they 'wait and see'.

'I intend to go up for the birth, Arthur,' Margot announced, as they were packing the car for town. The back seat of the Wolseley, their most recently acquired motor, was filled with produce. With petrol coupons at a premium, there was no way of knowing when they'd be back.

'What's that, my dear?'

'Auckland,' Margot said, knowing he'd heard her perfectly well the first time. 'I want to be there for the birth.'

Arthur climbed into the driver's seat, and waited while his wife said goodbye to Betty and Elsa, who'd come out on to the verandah to wave them off.

'Cheerio,' Betty called, when Margot too was in the car. 'Drive careful.'

'I'm going whether you agree or not,' Margot said, over the noise of the engine.

''Bye, ladies,' Arthur shouted.

The car pulled away from the house, and coasted towards the open gates.

Sarah's baby was late. Not surprising in a first confinement, but Margot was worried. Nancy had been scrupulous in keeping them informed, but Margot had the feeling, stronger of late, that she wasn't being told the whole story.

'What do you think?' she'd asked Betty last night. 'Would you go if you were me?'

'I'd be there now,' Betty had answered.

'You can ring up when we're in town,' Arthur said, as they turned on to the empty road. 'See how she is.'

Margot smiled to herself.

'Much more satisfactory than a party line.'

'Oh, indeed,' Margot agreed. 'We wouldn't want the neighbours hearing.'

Arthur gave his wife an anxious look. Was he going to have trouble with her then? Was there more to this than anxiety for Sarah? 'I'm glad you decided to come with me this time,' he said, patting her knee. 'It'll be nice to have you to come home to.'

If I can get a berth on the ferry tomorrow, Margot was calculating, I'll be in Auckland the following evening . . .

For a time after that neither of them spoke. Margot rested her eyes on the familiar sights: the isolated farmhouses; the rows of pines planted as protection against the wind; the scattered townships, with their war memorials and their clusters of wooden houses; the mountains, framed in the rear-vision mirror . . . On some farms lambing had started. The skittish little creatures, hearing the car approach, scooted about in their paddocks, like leaves tossed in the wind.

'That's all we are, isn't it?' Cynthia Linwood had said, last time she visited the Grange. 'Leaves in the wind . . .'

Cynthia had aged ten years since her son had been posted missing.

'Have you told Cynthia and Harold?' Margot asked.

Arthur's grip on the wheel tightened. 'Don't you think they've got enough on their plates?' he retorted.

'We'll have to tell people sometime.'

'I don't know which is more painful,' Cynthia had confessed. 'The *hope* that he's alive, or the *fear* that he isn't.'

'Piers Rattray,' Arthur said suddenly, honking the horn, and waving his hand out the window.

'Who?'

'You know. You met him at the last point-to point. Harry Rattray's son.'

'Oh. Yes.'

'He'll be off soon. He must be eighteen, near enough.'

'Wasn't there something . . . ?' Margot forced herself to concentrate. She would go to Auckland no matter what Arthur said, but she'd rather go with his blessing. 'Of course,' she said, as the homestead emerged briefly from its shelter of trees, 'Willowbank. Richard was at school with the older boy.'

'That place has been in their family for as long as the Grange has been in ours. The first Rattray was a colonel in the Yeomanry. I'm sure I've told you the story. Great Uncle Steven . . .'

'Oh, for heaven's sake! Is that all you ever think of? I'm sick and tired of hearing about your family.'

Arthur was so startled he took his hand off the wheel. The car veered drunkenly on the loose gravel. 'They're your family too,' he muttered, as he regained control.

'No they aren't,' Margot answered sharply. 'Sarah is my family. Sarah and Richard, and Sarah's child.' She stopped. Her breath was coming in short, angry bursts. The desire to lash out at this man and his power had come on her like a fever. 'I know these letters get read out,' Sarah had written in her last, 'so there's no point my saying anything just to *you*, Mummy . . .' The words had been festering in Margot's mind. Arthur had insisted they write joint letters to their daughter. 'You can add your bit at the end,' he'd instructed. Since it was how they'd been managing things with Richard, she'd thought nothing of it. Now a terrible doubt took hold of her. Were her words censored? Did Sarah know she still wanted her and the child?

Damn you for losing my money, damn you! The shocking thought articulated itself as the last of Willowbank's paddocks disappeared from view. If she wasn't careful, the curse would be spoken.

'You might as well get used to the idea, Arthur,' Margot said, as calmly as she could. 'I'm going up to Auckland, and I'm bringing Sarah and the baby back with me.'

They didn't speak again till they reached Rosevilla.

'What is it?' Margot breathed, coming on her husband leaning against the hall table, a piece of paper, which she'd identified instantly as a telegram, clutched in his hand.

Arthur's arm dropped to his side. For several seconds Margot went on staring, then she let go the bag she was carrying, and snatched the telegram from his fingers.

'He's not dead,' she heard, through the thunder in her ears. 'Burned, the telegram says. He bailed out. Somewhere over Dorset . . .'

When Hazel (who'd heard the car pull up in the drive, and had the tea trolley ready to wheel into the sitting room) popped her head round the kitchen door to see what was happening, the sight that met her eyes drew from her a rare gasp of sympathy. 'They were cryin', the pair of 'em,' she told Pamela, who was in the habit of calling in on her way home from her job in the munitions factory. 'It got to me, I can tell ya. Them two lah-di-dahs sobbin' their eyes out.'

'It's Sarah I feel sorry for,' Pamela said. 'What's she been doing up in Auckland anyway?'

'Just goes to show, don't it?' Hazel concluded. 'War don't spare nobody.'

13

The phone rang as Sarah was sitting in the dark in her aunt's living room. She'd been trying to decide whether the contractions she'd been having for the last hour and a half were strong enough, or close enough together, to warrant phoning Dr Leggat. Aunt Nancy had been very precise. 'I'll be gone two hours at the most,' she'd said. 'But if it starts while I'm away you're to phone the doctor. Now you *promise*, Sarah . . .'

As she was going out of the door, still fussing, she called over her shoulder, 'Stanley should be home any minute. It's not like him to be late.'

But Uncle Stanley hadn't come home, and the contractions had started within minutes of her aunt leaving the house, and now the phone was ringing, and Sarah couldn't decide whether to pick it up, or leave it alone.

'Hullo?' she said.

'One moment, caller.'

'Hullo?'

'Christchurch? Can you hear me, Christchurch?'

'This is Auckland 2327.'

'Trying to connect you.'

'Nancy?'

Through the static, Sarah recognised her father's voice. 'It's me, Daddy,' she answered. 'Aunt Nancy's out.'

'Are you there?'

'It's *me*, Daddy. Sarah.'

'Can't hear a damn' thing.'

'Is something wrong?'

'Ah . . . Nancy. You can hear *me*, can you?'

Sarah bit into the side of her mouth. When her tongue followed her teeth, she tasted blood. 'Yes,' she mouthed into the phone.

'Thing is, we've had some news. Bad, I'm afraid . . . Hullo? Hullo?'

'I'm here,' Sarah said.

'Look, I think we'd better try again. This is difficult enough . . .'

'No!' Sarah shouted.

'Nancy?'

Sarah swallowed quickly. 'I can hear you,' she said, pitching her voice in a passable imitation of her aunt. 'You said you had some news?' she prompted.

'Sarah's asleep, is she?'

'Yes.'

'I was afraid she might have . . .'

Sarah caught her breath. The pains were close together now. There was no longer any doubt. 'Could be any time,' she said, in her aunt's brisk voice.

'Richard's been shot down,' her father said. 'Don't know the details . . .'

'What?'

'. . . badly burned,' Sarah heard.

'Oh God!'

'Margot's taken it pretty hard.'

'It's not true . . .'

'Nancy?'

'Say it's not true. *Please*, Daddy . . .'

'"No immediate danger"' the telegram said. His face and arms took the worst.'

Sarah clamped her hand to her mouth. Pain like she had never known it before tore through her body. She leaned against the wall, and drew in a long, shuddering breath.

'Thing is, what do we do about Sarah? Margot thinks we shouldn't tell her. Not till . . .'

'Yes,' Sarah managed.

'You agree?'

'Yes.'

'Damned awful business. Both my children . . .'

But Sarah couldn't take any more. She dropped the receiver;

then, as her father's lament faded, she fell to the floor.

Which was where her uncle, arriving home a few minutes later, found her.

'No, Mrs Dutton. I don't want you to push. We have to wait for the doctor.'

'I'LL BLOODY PUSH IF I WANT TO.'

Sister Porteous gasped in horror. It was bad enough being sworn at by a patient, but by *this* patient ... Though she'd known from the beginning there was something not quite right. Mrs Dutton had been brought in by her uncle, with labour apparently well-advanced. Anyone could see she was of good family. But then the contractions had stopped, and for the best part of ten hours nothing had happened. That in itself wasn't unusual. What was, was the fact that the mother-to-be didn't seem to have a tongue in her head. 'Husband overseas is he, dear?' Sister Porteous had asked. She was only trying to be kind.

'Perhaps she's deaf,' one of the nurses had suggested.

'Dr Leggat would have told us if that were so,' Sister Porteous had answered primly.

She bent down, and adjusted the mask for gas and air over the patient's face. 'Just breathe quietly,' she ordered.

There was a brief struggle as the patient tried to tear the object from her face. Sister Porteous was used to these reactions. Some women simply didn't know what was good for them.

It was a relief when the door opened, and Dr Leggat walked in. He'd gone home to rest when the contractions faded. Mrs Dutton would be his responsibility now. 'Everything seems satisfactory, Doctor,' she reassured, as he proceeded to scrub up. 'Cervix nicely dilated.'

'Aie..eeee!' Sarah screamed.

Sister Porteous readjusted the mask. 'Now now, Mrs Dutton,' she scolded. 'We don't want to upset Dr Leggat, do we?'

'You're doing fine, Mrs Dutton,' the Doctor congratulated, when he'd completed his own examination. 'Not too tired, are we?'

'How long ... ? How much longer ... ?'

'You're in the home straight now. You'll have your baby very soon.'

'I want . . .'

'What's that?'

'My aunt . . . I want . . .'

'She's waiting outside . . . There there,' Dr Leggat soothed, over the top of another scream.

'I can see the head,' Sister Porteous informed, a few minutes later.

'No need to cut,' Dr Leggat decided.

'A natural child-bearer,' Sister Porteous agreed.

The next scream brought conversation to an end. It was the last but one. The shoulders were out now. The worst was over. 'One more push,' Doctor Leggat encouraged. 'That's it, that's it . . .'

'A girl,' Sister Porteous observed. The slight tremor in her voice was to be regretted. The mucky little creature emerging from between Sarah Dutton's legs was a job well done, that's all. But the word 'miracle' would keep surfacing.

'Congratulations, Mrs Dutton,' Dr Leggat said, when his work was done. 'You've got a beautiful daughter.'

But there was no space in Sarah's head for such words. It was her father's voice she heard. 'Shot down . . . badly burned . . .'

'Please, Aunt Nancy, do as I say.'

'But, darling . . .'

'It's what you wanted, isnt it? It's what you all wanted.'

'Not like this.'

'Like what?'

'You're too upset.'

Sarah pulled herself up in the bed. Her father had paid for her to have a private room. He'd been afraid, even in Auckland, that people might recognise her. Sarah's decision, enforced by Aunt Nancy, to use the family name had infuriated Arthur Dutton. But that was as nothing beside his fear that she'd persist in her folly, and keep the baby.

'Uncle Adrian knows some people,' Sarah said.

'I know. He told me.'

'I want you to ring him up. I want it settled, Aunt Nancy. I want my son . . .'

Seeing her niece in distress, Nancy leaned over the bed, and stroked her arm. Should she tell her the child was female? Would it make any difference? 'I just don't think you should be in such a hurry,' she cautioned. 'You've had a terrible shock . . .'

Sarah indicated the bindings round her breasts. 'What do you think these are?' she rasped. 'I told Dr Leggat I didn't want to see him. I won't change my mind . . .'

'You could bottle feed.'

'I'm going to England, Aunt Nancy. I'm going to look after Richard.'

'Your parents . . .'

'They can't stop me. And if you're going to mention money, please don't. I've thought it all out. I have enough saved. I was keeping it for . . .' She stopped. The muscles in her neck twitched, as if she were trying to force something down her throat. '*Please*, Aunt Nancy,' she begged.

Nancy snapped the clasp of her handbag, and rose to her feet. She couldn't remember when she'd last felt so tired. She'd never minded not having children of her own. But when, at her own request, she'd been shown Sarah's baby, the urge to hold the infant had overwhelmed her. 'Are they always . . . ?' she'd asked the nurse. 'I thought they were usually, you know, red in the face?'

'She's got a touch of jaundice,' the nurse told her. 'Nothing to worry about. Pretty wee thing, isn't she?'

'She's got the Dutton eyes.'

'Beg pardon?'

'Thank you for letting me see her, Nurse.'

'I'm absolutely sure, Aunt Nancy,' Sarah said. 'Richard's the only one who matters now.'

'Yes.'

'You'll do it then?'

Nancy bent down, and kissed her niece on the forehead. 'I'm so very sorry, Sarah,' she whispered. 'It should never have been like this.'

On 26 September, amid news of the war, and the celebrations within New Zealand to mark Dominion Day, the *Christchurch Press* ran a story under the headline, 'PROMINENT CITIZEN AND WIFE KILLED'. The story began with an account of a freak accident on the road near Springfield. After a brief description of the victims the report went on: 'Sir Arthur and Lady Dutton were apparently motoring back to their station home, Cheyney Grange, when their car ran out of petrol. It seems they must have decided to walk to the nearest farmhouse when they were struck by a vehicle heading west on the same road. The driver of the vehicle, who was uninjured in the accident, was travelling with dimmed headlights, in accordance with blackout regulations . . .'

A detailed account of Sir Arthur's political and business career followed.

The report ended with the words, 'Sir Arthur and Lady Dutton are survived by a son, Richard, presently serving with the NZ RAF Squadron in England, and by a daughter, Sarah.'

In the STOP PRESS column of the same paper it was reported that Wing Commander Richard Arthur Cecil Dutton had been injured when his plane crashed over southern England. No details of the flight, or of the Wing Commander's condition, were available at the time of going to press.

Ten days later, in the births column of the *Otago Daily Times*, the following notice was printed: 'To Fergus and Deidre McLean of Iona, a daughter, Frances Isabel, born 25 September'.

The first thing Deidre said, on being shown her daughter was, 'She could do with a hair cut.'

'But she's only ten days old.'

'What sort of colour would you call that?'

Fergus leant over the basinette, and touched the miraculous cheek with its fringe of red-gold hair. 'I'd call it bonny,' he said. 'She's a bonny wee lass, our Frances.'

Part Five

My name is Frances Isabel McLean and Im ten years old. Today is my birthday. This diary was a present from my father. He said, if I got into the habit now, of wrighting things down, I might be glad one day. I asked him what he meant but he just smiled and mufed up my hair. He does that a lot. Smiling I mean. And making me feel good.

The first thing I want to put in the diary is that I love my father very very much. More than anyone else in the world. More than my brother Clarence (though when he isnt being mean to me I love him quite a lot). More than my cat Felix. More than Auntie Dottie. More even than my best friend Gail. I dont love my mother at all, so she doesnt count. Im skared of my mother.

I should have had a party today, but my mother had an acident. She didnt hurt herself, not really, but she said it was my folt. So insted of a party I got a hideing. Thats the sort of thing that happens round here. It wasnt going to be a big party. Just Gail and some of my cosins. But anyway it was canceld.

Well thats all for now. Oh, yes, the date is 25 September, 1951.

In later life Frances was to look back on that date, faithfully recorded in her new diary, and see it as the beginning of her slow expulsion from Eden. But the truth was, her journey had begun much earlier, before memory. What that birthday marked was the beginning of her adult consciousness. Till that day, playing with her brother in the paddocks of Iona, revelling in the intrigues of school and friendship, secure in her father's love, she'd seen the world as a stage for her own, reality-correcting fantasies. Now, subtly, slowly, the balance began to change. Reality refused to buckle to her desires. It insisted on shaping her. It became, without her knowing it, the enemy.

*　　*　　*

It was already late when Fergus decided he must talk to his sister at once, not wait till morning. Brick Munro, the family doctor, had given Deidre a shot which he assured his old friend would knock out an elephant. But there was no way of knowing how she'd be in the morning. The risk of the children waking while he was out was small. The day's events had exhausted them both. But he'd look in on them, just to be sure

He found Clarence buried in his usual tumble of sheets and blankets, among which were scattered pieces of the Meccano set Fergus had given him for his eleventh birthday. That Meccano set had marked a rare breakthrough between father and son. The lad had been so delighted he'd let his father hoist him into his arms. But there was no such reaction on the boy's twelfth birthday. The Arthur Mee Encyclopedias, which Fergus had ordered for him, were received with a polite, 'Gee thanks, Dad. Great.'

'I remember my own twelfth birthday,' Fergus had confided to his wife later. 'Uncle Leonard was about to set off on his adventures. I remember thinking, I'll be old enough to do that soon. I'm almost a man.'

Deidre, busy salvaging wrapping paper from the debris of her son's party, had frowned at him over her glasses. 'He's only a boy, Fergus,' she'd said.

These days Fergus tried not to dwell too much on the extraordinary bond between his wife and son. The boy hadn't grown up a sissy, which was something to be thankful for. But he had taken on his mother's emotional reticence. No, reticence wasn't the word. Fergus was in favour of that kind of thing. 'Paralysis' was more like it. Confronted with anything like an emotional situation Clarence would simply disappear. If he couldn't vanish physically, he'd lapse into a sullen silence. The only indications of his feelings were the rising colour in his cheeks, and the stammer that would afflict him when he could no longer avoid speech.

Fergus brushed his hand across his son's head. 'Sleep tight, old chap,' he whispered. 'God bless.'

A totally different sight met him in his daughter's room. Frances, who was being raised, her mother claimed, like a probationer nurse, was an orderly child. Her clothes for the morning were folded over the chair; her shoes neatly lined up under the bed; her dolls bedded down for the night in the same tidy fashion as herself. It worried Fergus that his daughter was so biddable. Her anxiety to please, a consequence, he felt sure, of her mother's refusal to *be* pleased, had brought her both success at school, and popularity. But Fergus couldn't help feeling anxious about the cost of all this effort in one so young.

He pulled up a chair, and sat as close as he dared to the bed. Fanny was a poor sleeper, prone to nightmares and nocturnal wanderings. Several times lately Fergus had found her in the passage, apparently trying to open a non-existent door. On other occasions she'd woken with a nose bleed. Usually Fergus managed to persuade his wife to stay in bed, let him deal with the problem, but he had to admit, when the nose bleeds were bad, he was glad of Deidre's presence. She may not have been a loving mother to her daughter, but she was always conscientious.

'You'll sleep tonight though, won't you?' he urged softly. 'I won't be gone long.'

One good thing, Frances and Clarence were an affectionate brother and sister. They quarrelled, as all such siblings do, but reconciliation tended to follow swiftly.

'Tell-tale tit, your mother's in a fit, your father's in a washing tub, tell-tale tit!'

Fanny had a habit of running to him whenever her brother got the better of her. It almost always provoked a taunt.

'Sticks and stones,' he'd remind her. 'You're not afraid of a few words, are you?'

When she learned to retaliate he didn't know whether to feel sorry or relieved.

'You're mad, you're barmy, your mother's in the army, she wears black britches with pink and white stitches . . .'

He'd listen to her voice, shrill as a seagull's, and acknowledge, regretfully, that she wasn't his baby any more. She could stand up for herself. Lately she'd been doing rather more than that. She'd taken to running away, a sign of rebellion he deplored since it was he who had to go haring round the paddocks looking for her. She never went far though, thank God. He was a bit too old for that kind of caper.

'I seem to be having trouble with my hearing,' Fergus had

confessed, on his last visit to Brick's surgery. 'I don't hear the children like I used to.'

When the tests were completed Brick suggested a hearing aid.

'First the walking stick, now a deaf aid,' Fergus had joked. 'You'll be ordering my coffin next.'

'I'm sorry about your party,' Fergus whispered, smoothing the hair from his daughter's eyes. He liked to think she'd inherited her cascade of curls from her mother. He'd been told the woman was beautiful. 'What colour would you call it?' Deidre had asked him on that first, miraculous day. Later she'd answered her own question. 'If she were a horse, I'd call it chestnut.'

'You know Fanny's family, don't you?' Dottie had challenged, just the other day. The question had startled him. Since that unfortunate evening, before Clarence came along, neither of them had mentioned the subject of adoption. 'You'll have to tell her who she is sooner or later,' Dottie had persisted.

'Don't see why,' he'd hedged.

'Just because Deidre wants everyone to think Clarence is hers . . .'

The words had stung. It was true, his wife was vehemently opposed to the children being told the facts, a position he'd had no quarrel with himself till that moment. 'I know Fanny's great-uncle, that's all,' he'd conceded.

But that wasn't enough for Dottie. 'Well?' she'd prompted.

'Nothing more to tell.'

It was a bad moment. Dottie knew he was lying, but he wasn't ready yet to tell her, or anyone else for that matter, what he knew. He couldn't explain why, except to say that it was private. At no time had he solicited the information. The opposite, if anything. Over the course of his correspondence with Adrian Dutton, and subsequently, during their occasional meetings at Lodge dinners, he'd gone out of his way to discourage unnecessary confidences. But his reluctance to play the confessor had merely spurred the Judge on. Fanny's mother, Fergus was told, had gone to England soon after her daughter's birth. There was a brother apparently, who needed nursing. 'He's a pitiful sight, poor chap,' the Judge had written, in the card he sent for Christmas, 1943. 'The plastic surgery helped, of course, but they couldn't do anything about his sight . . .'

Fergus had shared none of this with his wife. Where Fanny was concerned Deidre was easily enflamed.

'They're back in New Zealand now,' the card had gone on. 'The parents are dead. You might have read about it. Killed in a motor accident. Dreadful business . . .'

One of the many difficulties Fergus had had over these revelations was the distress he felt for Fanny's mother. Life had dealt her too many unkind blows.

'Has she married?' he'd asked, at his last meeting with the Judge. He was hoping to be told she was settled now, and happy.

'Swears she never will,' he'd been answered. 'Sad really. She's a corker looking girl.'

Fergus's regret that he'd ever raised the subject had been compounded when the Judge, silencing his protests, told him Fanny's mother had gone back to the family farm to take care of the invalid. 'Not that it's anything like it was in my brother's day,' he'd added gloomily. 'It's a guest house now. Matter of necessity. Sarah runs it virtually single-handed.'

'I thought . . . I must have got it wrong . . . Didn't you say she lived in Christchurch?'

'Oh, that place was sold during the war. Got next to nothing for it. Between you and me, McLean, your daughter would have had a hard time of things if her mother had held on to her. My brother's death was only one of a number of shocks the family endured at that time. Arthur was the one with the head for business, you see. We left everything to him.'

Fergus got to his feet. His tongue was working busily in his mouth, searching for the crumb that had lodged under his plate. The distraction was almost welcome. He didn't want to think about Fanny's mother. There were other things to be decided tonight. Though Dottie was right, of course. The children would have to be told the truth, sooner or later.

'Poor wee lass,' he murmured, leaning over the bed, and kissing his daughter's head. This should have been a champion day for her. Ten years old, and pretty as a picture. He should have known it was too much for Deidre. He should have seen what was coming.

'Don't want to put a name to it, old chap,' Brick had said, after this morning's incident. 'It could be something simple. The change of life possibly.'

'She's only forty-three.'

'Happens early in some women.'

It was one of those moments when Fergus had wanted a drink, badly. Brick, of course, knew all about that. 'I'll look in again this evening,' he'd said. 'Chances are you'll want a sedative yourself.'

Fergus picked up his chair, and returned it to its proper place. He'd learned to be careful around Fanny. The slightest lapse could land her in trouble.

He was about to close the door when he discovered his eyes had filled with tears. The sensation momentarily unbalanced him. He steadied himself against the door jamb, and waited for things to return to normal . . .

It had all seemed so possible, once. That day, not so many years ago, when the children invited him and Deidre to tea in their hut. Squatting on the ground, pretending to eat the mud pies made in their honour, he'd felt himself to be the luckiest man alive. Later, walking back to the house, he'd taken his wife's hand, and she'd smiled at him in a way that had made him wonder if, after all, he shouldn't have tried . . . Ridiculous of course. The time for that sort of thing had long passed. 'Not up to much in that department,' he'd told her, on their honeymoon.

He took out his handkerchief, and blew his nose. No point crying over spilt milk. Other things to think about now. Though it troubled him, increasingly of late, that his failures in that 'department' might have something to do with his wife's present difficulties. He should have been more forthcoming with her. Explained how lack of opportunity had metamorphosed, with whisky's help, into lack of interest. She was a nurse. She'd have understood . . .

He pushed his handkerchief back into his pocket. What was he thinking about? The whole business was out of the question, then as now. Language simply not invented for that sort of thing.

'Goodnight, bonny lass,' he whispered into the room. 'Sweet dreams.'

2 ∫

It was cold outside the house. Winter still about in the icy
Antarctic wind. Fergus, testing the ground with his stick, watched
his breath curl in the moonlight.

Despite the late hour he felt sure Dottie would be expecting
him. It was she who'd summoned him from his meeting this
morning. 'Thank God she came to you,' he'd said.

'Fanny always comes to me when there's trouble,' Dottie had
answered tartly.

The path through the orchard dipped in front of him, its twists
and turns as familiar as the knotted trees, spiked with early
blossom, rising to either side. Fergus raised his torch, arching
light over the still bare branches of a crab apple tree. Last autumn
Deidre had got it into her mind that the orchard was being raided.
She claimed to have seen half a dozen neighbourhood children
helping themselves to the harvest of apples and pears. Fergus
had tried to tell her she was mistaken. The only kids who picked
fruit without permission were their own son and daughter.
But she'd gone ahead, and laid a complaint with Taffy Jones,
the local bobby. When Taffy turned up on their doorstep the
following Saturday, with Fanny and Clarence in tow, Fergus saw
for himself the 'irrational behaviour' Dottie had been hammering
on about for years. That he'd seen it before, and ignored it, was
something he was going to have to live with.

'You put him up to this, didn't you?' Deidre had shouted at
her daughter. 'Brazen little hussy!'

'Now now, dear,' Fergus had intervened. 'Thank you, Taffy,'
he'd said, in an aside. 'We'll see to things now.'

'You'll go to your rooms, the pair of you,' Deidre had ordered, when Taffy had ambled off the scene. Fergus, hearing a more reasonable note in his wife's voice, turned to plead his children's innocence. But before he could speak, Fanny opened her mouth.

'We haven't done anything wrong, have we?' she argued.

'You hear that?' Deidre screamed at her husband. 'Stuck-up little madam! I'll teach her to answer back!'

It had taken Fergus the best part of ten minutes to calm his wife. 'Is she often like this?' he'd asked his son later that day. 'When I'm not here, I mean.'

'D . . . nnn . . . Dunnow,' Clarence had stammered.

'What do *you* say, Fanny?'

'She gets a bit ratty sometimes,' his daughter had told him.

'That's cause you're such a nnn . . . such a nark,' Clarence had jeered.

'Am not.'

'That's enough,' Fergus had reprimanded.

'She doesn't get ratty with me,' Clarence had said in a rush.

''Cause you're her pet, that's why.'

It had been an unsettling conversation. Thinking about it, and the incident that lay behind it, had persuaded Fergus he should try, in future, to get home from work earlier. While the children were at school he could relax. But he'd seen enough now to know something was definitely amiss between his wife and daughter. Because he was an optimist he chose to believe the problem would disappear in time. But where his beloved Fanny was concerned he wasn't going to take chances.

Further down the path Fergus's torch, searching for signs of spring, lit on the almost overgrown entrance to the air raid shelter. 'Son-of-a-gun,' he muttered out loud, moving off the path into a tangle of gorse and honeysuckle. 'Robbie better take a look at this.'

Closer to, the bush cleared, revealing the steps cut into the bank, and the heavy wooden door which Deidre had insisted be left padlocked. Fergus poked at the door with his stick. When it swung open, exposing in the torch light the still dry chamber lined with shelves, he smiled. Deidre had cleaned the shelter out within days of the Japanese surrender. Since then, like him, she would have had no call to return. But someone had broken that padlock; the same someone whose stash of treasure – a box of coloured pencils, some old copies of the *London Illustrated*, a drawing book Fergus recognised as one of his own publications, two of Dottie's hand-made cushions, the diary he'd given as a gift only this morning – was arranged neatly on the shelves.

'It's where she goes when she doesn't want to be found. So don't you go spilling the beans.' His sister's voice came back to him in a rush. He'd forgotten all about that conversation.

'Dear good Dottie, whatever would I do without you?' he said out loud.

'Don't talk nonsense!' It wasn't difficult to imagine his sister's reply. 'You don't need me. You've got a wife to take care of you.'

When he'd looked his fill, Fergus squeaked the door shut, and scrambled back up to the path again.

'All that work for nowt,' Robbie had sighed, when Fergus informed him the shelter was now a thing of the past.

'I disagree,' Fergus had argued. 'If it hadn't been for the Americans, New Zealand might be under the Japanese yoke today.'

The prospect, even in retrospect, still terrified. It was one of the reasons Fergus had defied his wife, and joined the Home Guard.

'What will you do if you have to shoot someone?' Deidre had taunted, the day he announced that particular decision. 'You'll never be able to.'

When he assured her she was wrong, she gave him the kind of look usually reserved for her daughter.

'I *am* getting old,' Fergus acknowledged, as he picked his way through the trees. 'The past's starting to seem more real than the present.'

What would Deidre have said, he wondered, if he'd told her his real reason for joining the Home Guard? It wasn't, as she'd imagined, the threat to his country, or the rumours of atrocities, it was something far more personal. Two years before the war he'd had a visitor to stay at Iona, a Japanese engineer named Ahiro Sano. Ahiro was a Rotarian, which should have made them allies. But the young man was more interested in Dunedin's remote beaches than he was in matters Rotarian.

Thinking back on it now, speculating as to what the engineer's function might have been in the war, Fergus still felt pangs of guilt. It was as if he'd failed somehow to make the right, the good connection.

He shivered, and squeezed his hat down on his head. He could see the cottage clearly now. Its lights beckoned him through the trees. Even in winter Dottie seldom bothered to close the shutters.

'Our family was luckier than most,' he acknowledged, as he switched off the now unnecessary torch. All five of his nieces and nephews who'd seen active service had come back. But Philip, Iain's eldest boy, was not the lad he'd been. 'Melancholia' was Brick Munro's word for whatever was ailing him. 'War sickness,' Deidre had corrected, when he told her the diagnosis. 'I've seen it before.'

'There has to be a better way,' Fergus had confided to his brother, Tom. It wasn't as if the war had brought universal peace. Not with fighting in Korea, and half of Europe given over to communism.

'You're beginning to sound like a pacifist,' Tom had teased.

'We were both pacifists once upon a time,' Fergus had reminded him.

As he approached his sister's door Fergus could hear the wireless playing. Dottie still kept up the habit of listening to the evening news bulletin. Though the last few months New Zealand's attention had been focused inwards. A five-month strike on the waterfront had all but paralysed the country. Deidre insisted the strike would never have happened if Labour had still been in power, but Fergus disagreed. He was at one with the Prime Minister, who saw the strike as part of the 'cold war' being waged throughout the world. Declaring a state of emergency (cause of many heated exchanges at Iona) was a responsible decision on the part of the Government, not, as Deidre maintained, an act of Fascism.

'All Sid Holland knows is what he's against,' Deidre had fulminated. 'He hasn't a clue in the world what he's *for*.'

Fergus had tried to keep things calm. 'Perhaps that's all most of us know,' he'd suggested.

'You know what *you're* for.'

'Do I?'

'You're a Christian.'

'So are you.'

His wife had peered at him over the top of her glasses, but said nothing. Later she'd commented, 'It's gone, hasn't it? The good genie Mickey Savage let out of the bottle. It's flown away.'

'What are you talking about?'

'Government exists now to help people make money.'

'Money isn't bad in itself, Deidre.'

To which she'd answered, 'I don't believe in God, Fergus. I believe in revenge.'

It was one of the many things his wife had said recently that played on his mind.

'There you are,' Dottie greeted, as he pushed open the door. 'Thought you might show up. Youngsters asleep, are they?'

Without waiting for his reply, she switched off the wireless, and bustled past him to the kitchen.

Fergus settled himself in his mother's rocking chair. The fire was blazing; the room in its usual colourful muddle. These days Uncle Leonard's Chinese chest was full of things to amuse children. Dottie, under Clarence's expert tuition, had become a champion marble-player. More recently she'd taken up knuckle bones, a game she invariably won because of her large hands. 'I wish you'd married Auntie Dottie,' Fanny once complained to him. 'Why didn't you?'

'Because she's my sister, Miss Nosy-Parker. That's why.'

Listening to Dottie rattling about in the kitchen, Fergus tried to clear his mind of everything but the decision he'd come here to make. He knew what Dottie would tell him to do. Dottie would tell him to have Deidre committed. He'd tried to explain to her how much he owed his wife – his health, for one thing, and the children, most important of all – but Dottie had refused to understand. All she saw was a woman whose moods and convictions deeply threatened hers. She had to think Deidre mad because she couldn't accept that it was Deidre who'd saved her brother from his demons.

It was a relief when Dottie, carrying a tray laden with goodies, came back into the room.

'You realise I won't be able to visit like this again?' he said, helping himself to a generous portion of sultana cake. 'Not while Deidre . . .'

'She's sick, Fergus. You have to admit it now. She should be . . .'

'Locked up? Is that what you were going to say?'

Dottie waved her hands irritably. Fergus could be infuriating at times. Didn't he realise something had to be done, and done now? For heaven's sake, they weren't just talking about this morning's lunacy. Fanny had been telling her things for years, some of which had made her hair stand on end. There was that time driving back from Wanaka, their first holiday after the war. Fanny had described it to her in a child's words, but Dottie had been left in no doubt as to what was going on. 'Dad had to stop the car,' Fanny had said. 'Mum saw something. Clarrie reckons she saw a ghost. She was blubbing, Aunt Dottie. Worse'n me when I fall over.'

Only Fergus, who thought the best of everyone, even that awful little Japanese spy he'd installed at Iona, had refused to see.

'Things can't go on,' Dottie said now. 'I've had a talk with Enid. She agrees with me.'

Fergus brushed the crumbs from his moustache. So it wasn't just Dottie who considered his wife unhinged. 'What do *you* think happened this morning?' he asked.

'You've spoken to Fanny?'

'She's a remarkable girl, Dottie. She was quite cheerful when I tucked her up tonight.'

Dottie's fingers played invisible notes on her cheek. She'd told her brother before what she thought of Fanny's cheerfulness. It was the girl's way of protecting herself. Everyone loves a cheerful child.

'Deidre had some kind of accident with that new wringer you bought her,' she said, making no effort to disguise her impatience. 'I imagine she caught her sleeve or something. You'd have to ask her. Thing is, she wasn't hurt, at least not visibly. You didn't notice any bruising, did you?'

Fergus shook his head.

'Exactly.' Dottie patted the back of her hair, checking for recalcitrant pins. Her hair nets, unlike Deidre's, were almost always full of holes. 'Anyway,' she went on, 'whatever happened, it set her off. It was all Fanny's fault. Fanny pushed her. Fanny was a devil. She'd kill her mother if she could . . . I don't have to spell it out, do I? You've heard it all before.'

Fergus felt in his pocket for his pipe. Fanny, who was so keen to tell tales of her brother, had never once, not even today, confided . . . 'Thank God she talks to you,' he muttered.

'Deidre took the belt to her, Fergus. God knows what might have happened if Clarence hadn't intervened.'

'I saw the marks on her legs.'

'It'll be her face next time.'

The pipe lay cold in Fergus's hand. Dottie didn't keep whisky here, did she? The others did. They hid it from him, but he knew. '*Why*, Dottie?' he pleaded. 'Why does she do it? She's a good mother in so many ways. You remember when the children had measles how she . . .'

'She's a good mother to Clarence, Fergus. She's a *danger* to Fanny.'

Fergus flinched at the word, but made no attempt to deny it. What would be the point? 'I've come to a decision, Dottie,' he said, at last. 'Been thinking about it for some time actually. Today's brought matters to a head, that's all.'

Dottie, looking down at her mottled hands, tried not to let herself feel hopeful. In her mind's eye she was back at Iona, baking for the children, planning their parties, planning Christmas . . .

'I'm going to retire,' Fergus announced. 'As from next week. I can do the final sorting out from home. From now on I'll be around to keep an eye on things.'

Dottie's reaction was not the one Fergus was expecting. Her silence, and the sudden clenching of her fists, distressed him.

'I'm not denying there's something wrong,' he conceded. 'As a matter of fact I spoke to Brick about it this morning.'

Dottie raised her eyes. Fergus couldn't tell whether she was on the verge of laughter or tears. 'So, you're going to retire,' she said.

'That's right.'

'You know, don't you, that your wife behaves herself when you're around? She's clever like that.'

'I'll be there, Dottie. That's what matters.'

'And what about your committees? Are you going to retire from those too?'

'You're thinking of this morning . . .'

'It's Saturday, Fergus. Session meetings are always held on a Saturday. How can you keep an eye on things when you're not there?'

'Then I'll have to resign from Session too.'

'And the orphanage committee? The St. John's Ambulance? Rotary? The School Board? Are you going to say goodbye to all of them?'

'You're worrying unnecessarily, Dottie,' Fergus said, in the voice he knew his sister would recognise as bringing discussion to an end. 'Deidre's always been strict with Frances. She went a bit too far today, that's all.'

It troubled him, as he walked back through the orchard, that his sister had seemed to find this last remark funny.

3

20 October 1951

Today my mother went to hostipal. Its my folt. Auntie Dotties coming
to look after us. That means Ill be able to talk to her in the mornings
as well as after school. I can have my piano lessons here too. And ride
Nugget whenever I want. Thatll be fun. Oh and I bet I'm allowed to
stay up later now as well. We can play canasta and chinese chekers
and rummy. Auntie Dotties really wizard at games. Shell spend hours
playing snakes and ladders and things. Dads been asking Mum for ages
why I have to go to bed so early. Its horible going to bed when the sun's
still shining. None of my friends do. They think its WEIRD. Im not even
supposed to read. Mum says its bad for your eyes to read in bed. But
I've got a torch and when the coast is clear I read under the blankets.
Or draw. Whats really mean is that Clarence is allowed to sit up for
HOURS. He listens to the serials and everything. Sometimes when Dad
turns the volume up I can hear the wireless through the wall. I cant
hear the words but I know the tune for Dad and Dave now. Thats
Dads favorite. I dont know whats wrong with my mother. Dr Munro
told Clarence and me we werent to worry. Shed be right as rain in no
time he said. He asked me why I was wearing a pixie hat inside but
I didnt tell him. Dad said I could have Gail to stay when things have
settled down. Thatll be TREE-MEND-US! If Clarence is in a good mood
we might even have a midnight feast. Auntie Dottie wont mind.
Shell just pretend nothings going on. And Dads so deaf he wont
hear a thing. I wish my mother wasnt sick. I wish she was like
other mothers. Dad says we wont be able to visit her for a wee
while. The worst thing, the thing I dont want to wright about,
is Clarence. When he saw what Mum had done to me he cried.
Ive never seen him cry before.

If I concentrate really hard, Frances thought, as she tucked the

precious diary under her pillow, I'll wake up and everything will
be all right.

'God! Oh my God, what have you *done*?'

Fergus was in the garden with Robbie when he heard his
daughter's screams. It was late afternoon; the children, as he
thought, playing table tennis in the stable. Deidre had taken
the news of his retirement calmly. She'd even kissed him, a
rare occurrence these days. 'We'll manage,' she'd said. 'We'll
get by.'

'We'll do better than that, my dear,' he'd reassured. 'The lean
days are long gone.'

It had been a busy few weeks. Extricating himself from his
business had proved a more arduous task than he'd imagined.
With his brother Iain primed to take over the reins he'd
anticipated a smooth transition. But he'd reckoned without
the sheer volume of information vital to the running of the
company stored in his head. It was three weeks before he could
look up from the paper work.

'Come and see the daffodils,' Robbie had urged, when he
stepped outside for his teatime stroll.

'It's that time of year again,' Fergus had observed. He and
Robbie often stated the obvious to each other. It was tone of
voice that mattered in their conversation, not words.

As he'd walked with his old friend through the gap in
the hedge Fergus had felt the burden of business lift from
his shoulders. He'd even felt grateful to Deidre that she'd
precipitated this decision. He might have gone on for another
ten years, feeling it to be his duty, when all the time Iain
was there, waiting in the wings, eager to have his turn. Iain
was twelve years younger than he was. Let him do the worrying now.

'I see you've planted out the lettuces,' Fergus remarked, as
they made their way through the vegetable garden.

Robbie hoicked the phlegm from his chest, twisted his head,
and spat. As always it brought the two men to a halt. There
was a ritual to be followed at these times. First the coughing,
then the spitting, after which Robbie would take a blackball
from his pocket, pick off the stray flakes of tobacco, and pop

it in his mouth. Later, when he'd finished sucking, he'd light his pipe again.

'You two old rogues,' Deidre used to tease, in the early days of their marriage. 'Listen to you. Coughing and spitting like a couple of monkeys.' But since the children came along she'd not been so tolerant. 'If you'd nursed TB patients, as I have, you'd throw that pipe in the fire . . .'

'Now close your eyes,' Robbie instructed, as they turned on to the path that would take them to the daffodils. The sight that greeted them, seconds later, was one Fergus believed he would see in heaven. 'A host of golden daffodils' didn't remotely do justice.

'Seems to get better every year,' he mused, after the statutory few moments of silence.

'A sight for sore eyes all right,' Robbie agreed.

'Do you remember . . . ?' Fergus began. He was thinking of the day, in the spring of 1942, when a photographer from the *Otago Daily Times* stood on this very spot taking pictures. It was a dark time for the Allies. Optimism in short supply. The editor, a personal friend of Fergus's, had wanted to print something of an uplifting nature. What he'd lighted on was the story of two little English girls, evacuees from Liverpool, who'd come to live with their mother's cousins, Brick and Ada Munro. The photo of those smiling waifs, seven and nine years old, tin helmets on their heads, Union Jacks in their hands, ankle-deep in daffodils, became a national symbol.

''Course I remember,' Robbie answered. They had this conversation every year. 'Don't suppose you've heard any news o' them, have ya?'

'They're at secondary school now. You knew the father was killed?'

'Hmm. Hard on his missus. To go like that, after surviving the war.'

'It's Brick and Ada I feel sorry for. They grew very fond o' those wee lasses.'

'Little wonder, wi' no bairns o' their own.'

Fergus lifted his face to the sky. The southerly wind was reminding him he hadn't worn his hat. But the sight of the fantails, swooping above his head, brought the smile back to his face. Winter was over, for all the chill in the air.

'I've fixed the fence,' Robbie announced, when it seemed they'd done with reminiscing. 'Don't want them dobbins running loose.'

Fergus looked across at the paddock, home to the children's ponies, and nodded approvingly. He and Robbie were of one mind about horses. It had been Deidre's idea to buy one when Clarence was a nipper. First there was Biddy, then, when Fanny came along, there was Nugget. Fergus had indulged his wife because he thought it might encourage her to talk about her past. Her father had been a horse trainer after all. But not one word had he got out of her. Each year, when the profits were announced on Pearse Byrne's little money spinner, he'd raise the subject again, only to be reminded that the past, as far as Deidre was concerned, was a closed book. The only time he'd got close was the day, not long after the war, when they were driving back from Wanaka. He'd drawn her attention to the new bridge over the river, and she'd said something about the water, how treacherous it was. At first he'd thought she was referring to his own little argument with the river. He'd told her all about that early on in the piece. But then he noticed she was shaking. Literally. Her whole body was quivering, as if from a series of electric shocks. He was on the point of asking what the matter was, when she screamed. It scared the living daylights out of him. Out of the kiddies too. He'd had to pull up on the side of the road, and wait for everyone to calm down.

'That nag o'Clarence's has got pretty wild,' Robbie said. 'If it was down to me I'd truck him off to the knacker's yard.'

'Don't think the wife'd appreciate that.'

'The boy hasn't ridden him for years.'

Fergus slid his hand into his pocket and felt for his pipe. Strange how things work out, he thought. Deidre so keen to make her son a rider, and he not giving a toss. Then along comes Fanny, and takes to the whole thing like a duck to water. 'Ever wonder what makes a person tick?' he mused. 'I mean, why is it I can't sing a note when other folk . . .'

'D'ya hear that?' Robbie interrupted.

'What?'

'That noise.'

'Can't hear a thing.'

'Sounds like . . .'

'It's Fanny!' Fergus shouted.

Later, he couldn't remember running back to the house. Just pushing open the door, and flinging away his stick. The first thing he saw, on reaching his daughter's room, was his wife, sitting in the chair he often sat in himself, at night. Her eyes were closed, and she seemed to be singing. There was a box in her lap, one of those boxes which hold photographs. Not till the next morning did he discover what was in it. Tucked between pieces of tissue paper were his son's baby curls.

For the split second it took him to register his wife, the other sound, the one that had brought him here, seemed to stop. Then he heard it again. Fanny wasn't much given to weeping. Being labelled a 'sook' by her brother had dried all but the most recalcitrant tears. He wasn't even sure she was crying now. What he'd heard in the garden, and heard in subdued form now, was the sound of someone fighting for breath.

He stumbled across the room, and sank down on the bed beside his daughter. Her head was face down on the pillow, her knees curled under her chin. Something was different about the back of her head. She seemed to be wearing some kind of cap. Then his eye moved to the floor, and suddenly he was fighting for breath himself. Lying by the bed, in a shimmering bronze heap, was his daughter's hair.

'God! Oh my God, what have you *done*?'

He stooped to gather the precious curls. An image of a woman floating in the water, her long hair tangled with weed, sprang into his mind; art and life for a split second cohering. 'It's all right, sweetheart,' he soothed, straightening his back. 'It'll grow again. It's all right . . .'

His daughter twisted her head. She could hardly open her eyes, so gummed were they with tears. 'Sheer waste to pay a barber,' Deidre had protested, when he'd asked her, all those years ago, to cut Clarence's hair. 'Anyone can use a pair of scissors.'

But it wasn't scissors she'd used today, it was a razor. Fanny's hair was shaved to the scalp.

He pulled the trembling child into his arms, and turned to his wife. Why? he entreated silently. What did she do? What have we both done to make you look at us like that?

4 ∫

'I won't I won't I wont!'

'Won't what, Mrs McLean? What won't you do?'

'Look . . .'

'You won't look.'

Deidre turned her head to the wall. White wall. Man in white coat. White *shape* in the box . . .

'Mrs McLean?'

'Not suitable . . .'

'What's that?'

'Black. You should be wearing black.'

'But you can't see me, Mrs McLean. If you turned round you'd see what I was wearing.'

The patient slowly turned her head. Dr Grossman smiled. Now they were getting somewhere.

'You see,' he encouraged. 'Tweed jacket, brown trousers, white shirt. You don't really want me to wear black, do you?'

'You shouldn't smoke, you know.'

'How do you know I smoke?'

'The skin under your eyes is discoloured.'

Paul Grossman made a fan of his elegant, nicotine-stained fingers, and thought for a moment of his childhood in Vienna, and the piano with the brass candle-holders attached to the front, on which his mother had taught him to play. 'You're an observant woman, Mrs McLean,' he acknowledged. 'No wonder you were such a fine nurse.'

The patient spread her lips in a caricature of a grin.

'She's not insane, I'll stake my reputation on it,' Dr Grossman had insisted when he and his colleagues met to discuss the new admission. 'You've all examined her,' he'd reminded them. 'Do you see any of the signs of mental illness? There's no psychosis, no aphasia, no perceptible delusions. Her general appearance is good; muscle tone likewise. Also, and this is something you've all commented on, she appears to understand the world as well as any of us sitting here in this room. I don't need to remind you, gentlemen, that this is a highly intelligent woman we're dealing with.' He'd paused at that point, sensing he was winning the argument. 'There *is* a certain wilfulness,' he'd conceded. 'I'll grant you that. And, since several of you have made the observation, there does seem to be a tendency to hallucinate. But I maintain what we have on our hands is a woman who can pretend both states, madness and sanity.'

'Why would she do that? Isn't that in itself sick?'

'*Disturbed*, yes, but sick? I'm not sure. It's my opinion, you see, that what Deidre McLean is suffering from is not mental illness but an acute form of neglect. The source is probably in her childhood. What I'd like to do, with your agreement, gentlemen, is pursue a line of therapy, helped by drugs, if necessary, but not ECT, not yet. That could do more harm than good.'

'You don't accept the diagnosis then?'

'Manic depression? Possibly. I don't deny she's depressed. But if I can get to the cause . . .'

It hadn't been easy, but he'd convinced them in the end. For three months Deidre McLean would see no one but him, and the nurses assigned to take care of her. They did things thoroughly at Forest Hospital. It was what people paid for.

'Jab!' The grinning lips spat the word at him. 'Jab! Jab!'

Dr Grossman inched his chair closer to the patient's. The drug he'd administered was by way of being a repressant. What it did, more successfully some days than others, was repress the conscious mind, enabling him to glimpse the buried memories that were the cause, in his view, of her breakdown. 'No one's going to hurt you, Mrs McLean,' he reassured.

'Thinks she's better than everyone else. Thinks she's the cat's pyjamas.'

'Who's that, Mrs McLean?'

'Jab! Jab!'

He waited to see if there'd be more. He'd used this drug before and was convinced of its efficacy. But Deidre McLean was clever. There was no guarantee, even in her present state, that she wouldn't out-fox him. ('You'll find her a challenge,' Brick Munro had said, when the case was first referred to him. 'Husband's an old friend of mine.')

'I'd like to tell you something,' Dr Grossman said, when he judged enough time had passed. (Let's see what she's up to, he was thinking. Use a few wiles of my own.) 'At our first meeting I identified you as a woman of formidable intelligence. I was intrigued, I don't mind admitting. I thought, If I can crack this woman's code, I might begin to understand the rest of her sex. Because you see I've failed, so far, in this country, to do that.' He paused. Deidre McLean's eyes, which had been unfocused, were concentrated on his face. So, he thought, she does know what's going on. 'I've lived here, in your beautiful land, for nearly fifteen years. I've mastered the language. I'm told I even have a Kiwi accent!' He laughed. 'What I don't understand is why there are so many women like you in places like this. My wife tells me it's because of the war, because of all the things women did while the men were away, and now aren't allowed to do any more. But I think it goes deeper than that. I think . . .' His hand went to his jacket pocket in search of his cigarette holder. Normally he didn't smoke in these sessions, but the urge was strong today. 'Do you mind?' he asked, waving the holder in front of her. When she frowned he reluctantly returned it to his pocket. 'Layers,' he said. 'Layers upon layers, like those cakes you all make. I just can't get to the bottom of you.'

'How long have I been here?'

'I beg your pardon?'

'How long have I been in this place?'

Dr Grossman smiled. The woman's eyes were truly remarkable. Now that she'd stopped wearing that ghastly hairnet, and her hair hung loose to her shoulders, she even looked attractive. Not his type, too scrawny, but definitely someone he could take a more than professional interest in. 'You've been here a little over a week, Mrs McLean,' he told her.

'How much over a week?'

'You've been here nine days.'

'You sedated me.'

'What else could we do?' The doctor gestured his helplessness. 'You weren't being very co-operative.'

A smile briefly transformed Deidre McLean's face. She pulled herself up in her chair, and ran her eyes around the room. 'You run a very lax ship, you know, Doctor,' she said, indicating the dishevelled state of her bed. 'What time is it? Gone ten? Heads would have rolled in my day.'

'I see we're feeling better,' Dr Grossman murmured.

'We?' Deidre's eyes flashed. 'Are you a patient here too then?'

'We're all patients in the theatre of life, Mrs McLean.'

Deidre stuck out her lower lip, and strummmed on it with her fingers. It was an extraordinary gesture, at once childlike and impertinent.

'What are you thinking about now?' Dr Grossman asked.

'If you must engage in that filthy habit,' Deidre answered him, 'do it out in the paddock . . .'

'Ah . . . You don't like people to smoke, do you?'

'Don't answer back!'

'Sorry . . .'

'It's you we're talking about, not your father.'

'Yes . . .'

'You're only twelve years old.'

Dr Grossman glanced at his notes. 'One son twelve, one daughter, ten,' he read.

'Did you think I wouldn't find you?'

'I won't do it again.'

'This old shed, dry as tinder . . . I *hate* old places. They stink.'

'The past troubles you, doesn't it?' Dr Grossman said.

'I've told Fergus, I don't have eyes in the back of my head. I can't . . .' The patient's voice rose distressingly.

'Can't what?' Dr Grossman prompted.

'Can't . . . see . . .'

'I'm your friend, Deidre. You can tell me.'

'It's written there. It has to be. I should be able to see . . .'

Dr Grossman's pen flew across the page. 'An accident in the past?' he scrawled. 'Patient feels responsible?'

'I've told him over and over,' Deidre said, her voice slurring as the drug bit deeper. 'There is no vaccination.'

'Vaccination against what?'

The patient breathed on to her open palms, and held them up to her nose. 'There's a strange smell in here,' she accused. 'What is it?'

'Who did you lose, Deidre?' Dr Grossman persisted. 'Who died in the accident?'

'Has someone been making tallow?'

'Tallow?'

'For soap.'

'It was a long time ago, wasn't it? this accident . . .'

Deidre dropped her hands back into her lap. 'I'd like to go home now,' she said.

'Where's home, Deidre? Where is it you want to go?'

'Clarence will be waiting.'

'Clarence is your son . . .'

'He'll be waiting.'

'And your daughter? Will she be waiting too?'

'I don't have any children, Doctor.'

'But you just said . . .'

'Where are you from, Doctor? Are you German?'

'We were talking about Clarence,' Dr Grossman reminded.

Deidre clamped her lips together. The look in her eyes was that of a stubborn child.

'Do you mind telling me what you're doing?' Doctor Grossman enquired. 'It's a game, isn't it?'

Deidre smiled.

'Silence is a powerful weapon when you're a child.'

'I take it you're a Jew,' Deidre said.

'One of the lucky ones.'

'A refugee.'

'Is that what you are, Deidre? Is that how you see yourself?'

'I won't let him fight, Doctor. He won't go with the others. Did you know Bill Cairns?'

'Not a name I recognise, no.'

'He's there. On the stone. They're all there.'

'Stone?'

'Everywhere you go . . .'

'You're talking about war memorials.'

'Phineas O'Reilly. You must have known him.'

'Who is it you won't let fight, Deidre? Your son?'

'Ted Erihana, Charlotte Louise, Lynnea Ann . . .'

'Go on,' Dr Grossman urged, scribbling as he spoke. Any one of these names could be significant.

'What are you seeing now?' he asked, when, with a sudden jerk of her body, the patient lifted her arms, and covered her eyes with her hands.

'No . . .' she moaned.

'You can trust me.'

'Not the baby . . .'

'You're seeing a baby?'

'Not my little bu-bu . . .'

Dr Grossman reached out to take the patient's hands. It was his intention to calm her, but the gesture had the opposite effect. She pulled back, as if hit, and let out a piercing shriek.

'Is someone threatening you?' he persevered. 'Some *thing*?'

'Get out!' she yelled, shoving her fists into his chest. 'Get away from here.'

'Away from where? What am I saving myself from, Deidre?'

'Bad bad bad . . .'

'Yes, I can tell.'

'Bad magic . . .'

'You're doing well, Deidre. You're doing fine.'

'Can't . . . Can't see . . .'

Dr Grossman sat as still as he was able while her hands beat a tattoo on his chest. Always, in these cases, he tried to keep his own feelings separate. But he had to admit he was moved by the woman's raking fingers. She seemed to be trying to anchor herself to his jacket. 'You're all right, Deidre,' he comforted. 'You're safe.'

She looked up at him with panic-filled eyes, then, as suddenly as it had all begun, she slumped back in her chair. Dr Grossman watched till her eyelids had stopped quivering, then he pulled a blanket from the bed and tucked it round her. She'd sleep now. The drug, and her own exhaustion, would see to that.

He took out his ivory holder, positioned a cigarette, and struck a match. It was a relief to contemplate his patient through a haze of smoke. What should he say in his report? If he committed too much to paper his colleagues would begin to think *he* was out of his mind. The woman was hardly *normal*, after all. The hallucinations were there, no doubt about that. But what if they weren't hallucinations, but the product of a vivid imagination? What if, for Deidre McLean, the boundaries between reality and imagination didn't exist? Wasn't that the prerequisite of artistic vision?

For a few distressing seconds he imagined the patient sitting in front of him was Vincent van Gogh. He knew what his colleagues would have prescribed: electroconvulsive therapy, as much as it took to restore the artist to 'normality'. Would it have saved him? And if so, at what price?

But Deidre McLean wasn't an artist, she was a nurse, and the mother of two children. It was his duty, surely, to cure her as quickly as he could, and send her back to her family. If his first thought was right, and the cause of her breakdown lay buried in her past, what was the point in digging? He'd been in this profession long enough to know there were some things best left undiscovered. Not all hurts could be healed. Anyone who said that really was insane.

'Till tomorrow then,' he said, brushing his fingers over Deidre's exposed hand.

'One, two, three, four . . .' she murmured.

'That's right. Sleep.'

'Five, six, seven . . .'

Dr Grossman tiptoed out of the room.

Deidre McLean remained at Forest Hospital for over a year. During that time she had twenty applications of electroconvulsive therapy. There was only one person to whom she could have revealed the terror those treatments induced, and that was the man she had never allowed herself to mourn: Phineas O'Reilly.

For most of that long year Deidre saw only her husband, and the staff and patients of the hospital. It was not thought wise for her children to visit.

Frances's diary kept intermittently but intensely during those months, made no further mention, after the 20 October entry, of the incident that had triggered her mother's breakdown.

'I want to tell a story,' she insisted, when her friends pressed for an explanation of her strangely altered appearance.

'What sort of story?'

'Did you know, if you say something often enough, it comes true?'

'Is your story true then?'

'Once upon a time . . .'

And if I say nothing, Frances resolved, as her story took shape, what *was* true will disappear.

5

Christmas Eve, 1952

I'm so happy I could burst. I've been helping Auntie Dottie all day in the kitchen. I must have shelled a billion peas. Auntie Meg and Uncle George are here. They're sleeping in Mum and Dad's room. Dad's moved into the wee room next to the bathroom. Great-Uncle Angus is here too. He's sharing the blue bedroom with Dad's friend, Mr Reed. It's at the other end of the passage, thank goodness, so I won't hear the snoring. There's something queer about Mr Reed. He keeps calling me his pretty porkupine. I think thats creepy. My hairs grown back really thick now but it looks different from what it used to. Clarence calls me Goldilocks, which is typical. He doesn't mean the Goldilocks in the story, he means the thing Auntie Dottie uses to clean pots. I'm not going to be able to write much tonight because my cousin Grace is going to be sleeping in my room and we'll probably talk all night. She's five years older than me and she's allowed to do all sorts of things I cant like go to the pictures and wear nylons. I bet we don't sleep at all. I bet we catch Dad bringing in the presents, because of course I know its really Dad and not Father Christmas. I've known for ages. Preston, Grace's brother who's a TEENAGER *is sleeping in Clarence's room. Clarence told me they're going to smoke cigaretes.*

Tomorow we're going to see Mum. Dad says we're not to mind if she's changed. She's been very sick he said. She'll be coming home soon. I want her to come home but I dont want Auntie Dottie to go. It's been FANTABULOUS *having Auntie Dottie here. She doesn't make me do things just so all the time like Mum. She doesnt call me by my sirname and go on about things having to be in their right places and jobs having to be done at set times. She lets me ride Nugget whenever I want to and stay up till nine o'clock and read in bed and all sorts. She told me Mum's had something called shock treatment. I've made Mum a hankerchiff holder for Christmas. I made it out of some satin Auntie*

Dottie had in her basket. I've written a poem too. It goes like this.
  Soon it will be Christmas Day,
  And you so very far away.
  I hope this hanky holder pleases,
  And doesn't bring on mucky sneezes.
  And soon I hope you'll come back home,
  And never more be on your own.
  I've done a drawing as well.
That's all for now. I don't want Grace to see what I've written.

Deidre was sitting in her usual place on the verandah when the nurse brought her husband and children to see her. She was wearing a paper hat, and holding one end of a red streamer. When she saw Fergus, she smiled. 'You got away then,' she said.

Fergus planted a kiss on her cheek, and turned to look for his children. They were by the door, huddled together in defiance of the sunlight streaming through the windows. 'Come on, you two,' he encouraged.

Frances reached out for her brother's hand. For once he didn't push her away. They'd been told what to expect. 'Your mother'll look the same, but she won't *be* quite the same,' their father had explained. 'She gets a bit muddled.' What they hadn't been told was that there would be others. That man in the long passage they'd walked down, who was talking to himself; the girl by the window, rocking backwards and forwards in her chair; the old lady in the garden, who called out rude things . . .

'This place gives me the creeps,' Clarence had breathed in his sister's ear.

'Merry Christmas, Mrs Wilkie,' their father had greeted. 'Compliments of the season to you, Miss Hinchcliffe.'

'So these are the kiddies,' the nurse who escorted them had simpered. 'Hullo, you two.'

'How do you do?' Frances had replied politely.

'It's not like an ordinary hospital,' Auntie Dottie had said, fussing around them as they were preparing to leave. Auntie Dottie hadn't wanted them to come. She'd had words with their father about it. 'All that way,' she'd complained. 'You'll never be back in time for the photos.'

'Give your mother a kiss,' Fergus instructed now. 'That's it, Fanny. Good girl.'

'Merry Christmas, Mum,' Frances said. 'We've brought presents.'

Fergus watched as his daughter placed first her own, then her brother's parcel in her mother's lap. Clarence, whose cheeks had turned the colour of ripe plums, shuffled back towards the door. Fergus's eyes darted between his two children. Had he done the right thing bringing them? 'You can't protect them forever,' Dr Grossman had been pointing out for some time now.

'Shall I open them for you?' Frances offered.

Seeing the eager expression on his daughter's face, Fergus sent up a silent prayer. He shouldn't have been so reticent with Dr Grossman. He should have told him how it had been between mother and daughter. But the doctor had a way of asking questions that unnerved him. 'Are you telling me you know nothing of your wife's past?' That sort of thing. He could just imagine what the man would have had to say on the subject of Deidre and Fanny. 'Are you telling me your wife was violent towards your daughter *before* her breakdown? . . . Mmm . . . I see . . . And you did nothing, is that right? . . . Oh, you retired. Of course. How old are you, Mr McLean?'

While Fergus brooded, Deidre's eyes were fixed on the child standing in front of her. She looked familiar, but who was she? Those freckles across her nose and cheeks. Where had they come from? None of the girls in her family had freckles. 'Are you Molly?' she demanded.

Fergus reached for his daughter's hand. 'It's all right, sweetheart,' he reassured. 'Just give her time.' ('Patients who've received shock treatment frequently experience difficulty placing people,' Dr Grossman had warned. 'They'll recognise the face, but they may not be able to say the name.')

'Who's Molly?' Frances hissed.

'No one, dear. Just a name.' Fergus looked round for a chair. He'd been visiting his wife every Sunday for most of a year. The first three months he'd been advised not to visit at all. He was ashamed now of how easily he'd agreed.

'Why don't you show your mother what you've made?' he suggested, smiling at his daughter. It had been a mistake to bring the children. Dr Grossman was wrong. They should be joining in the fun at Iona.

'Shall I show her the drawing first?' Frances asked.

'Drawing?' Deidre rasped.

'Mrs Hercus says she has a real talent,' Fergus told his wife.

Deidre let go of the streamer she'd been clutching since their arrival, and clicked her tongue. Was this the child she'd caught once drawing on her bedroom wall? If so, the wickedness had obviously not been thrashed out of her. What good were drawings? They didn't feed hungry people, or heal wounds. 'What sort of outfit d'ya call that?' she snapped, pointing accusingly at her daughter's dress. It was made of lemon seersucker, and had puff sleeves, and lacey frills at the neck and hem. Frances had been imagining herself a princess in it.

'It was a Christmas present,' Fergus intervened quickly. The family would be out in the garden now. Iain's girl, Ngairie, had been put in charge of games. She was going to teach everyone how to do something called the 'Hoki toki'. 'Got to move with the times, Uncle,' she'd said.

'Never seen the like,' Deidre muttered.

'Auntie Rona gave it to me,' Frances informed her mother.

'That silly cow.'

'Now, now,' Fergus murmured. (Dr Grossman had alerted him to this. 'Your wife may say things that will shock you,' he'd said. 'Things she thinks, but normally wouldn't say.') 'We missed you today, dear,' he said. 'Philip couldn't make it, but the rest of the clan were there. Best turnout since the war, Dottie calculated . . .' He stopped. He'd been about to say what a grand job Dottie had done. Red rag to a bull that would have been.

'If you put cream on it, you could eat it,' Deidre mocked.

When Clarence, hovering by the door, snorted, a look of startled joy came on to Deidre's face.

'Here, let me do it for you,' Frances said, snatching up her present, and pulling at the string.

Deidre shook her head irritably. Fergus wasn't sure if she'd properly registered Clarence yet. Her eyes darted round the room, as if searching for him, coming back to rest, coldly, on her daughter. 'Tilly?' she said.

Frances sunk her teeth into her lower lip. She wouldn't cry.

She *mustn't*. Her mother had her glasses on now, and was staring at her the way grown-ups stared when they thought you weren't telling the truth. Something about her eyes made Frances think of colours that hadn't mixed.

'Can we go now?' Clarence called from the door.

The response from Deidre was instantaneous. She pushed her daughter out of the way, and flung open her arms.

'Come on, son,' Fergus beckoned. 'Your turn.'

There was only one word for the look Clarence gave him. Insolent. But at least the boy did as he was told, sidling across the room to stand beside his sister. 'What's the matter with you, stare-cat?' he growled, out of the side of his mouth.

Fergus sank back in his chair. These days his son was a stranger to him. Such communication as did exist had more to do with the kind of look he'd just been given than with words. At first he'd put the boy's withdrawal down to anxiety about his mother, but lately he'd concluded there were other factors at work: the lad's age; the company he kept; his own failings as a father.

'Merry C . . . Merry Ccc . . .'

'Open your present,' Frances urged. 'Show her what you've made.'

Clarence yanked at the string. There was a crash as the key holder he'd made in his woodwork class fell to the ground. As he bent to pick it up, Deidre grabbed his head and crushed it to her chest. Frances turned an agonised face to her father. Clarence hated being kissed. He hated all physical signs of affection. But her father put his finger to his lips, and shook his head.

'Why don't you show *me* your drawing?' he said quietly. He patted his knee, but was relieved when his daughter ignored his invitation. The chairs in this place were not designed for comfort. 'You'd think they could provide decent furniture,' he'd complained to Dottie. 'With what I shell out each week.'

'It's Felix,' Fanny said, whisking the drawing out from its wrapper, and thrusting it under his nose.

Fergus peered through his bi-focals. 'But it's very good, sweetheart,' he complimented. 'You've got him to the life.'

'Will Mum remember Felix, do you think?'

'I don't know much about art but I'd call this . . .'

'*Will* she?'

Fergus glanced at his watch. Exactly what he'd most feared about this occasion was happening: Deidre oblivious to everyone but Clarence; Fanny looking to him to heal the rift with her mother.

'She liked *Clarrie's* present,' his daughter breathed in his ear.

'And she'll like yours,' he reassured.

'A rare gift,' Mrs Hercus had written in Fanny's last school report. 'In thirty years of teaching I've never encountered such skill with a pencil.' Praise like that was disturbing. It suggested a very particular inheritance. Adrian Dutton had never mentioned artistic talent, so it must come from the father. Which wasn't something Fergus wanted to think about. *He* was Fanny's father.

'Gail says I'm not really Mum's daughter. Is that true?'

The drawing slid to the floor. On the pretext of picking it up, Fergus managed to conceal his agitation. Fanny must have read his mind. How else to explain her asking, now, the question he'd been dreading for years? 'What a thing to say,' he responded hoarsely.

'Not just Gail, Lindsay Whitehead too.'

Fergus glanced at his wife. Still oblivious, thank God. Clarence too, he hoped and prayed. 'We're a family,' he said quietly. 'And don't you let anyone tell you different.' He took out his handkerchief, and pressed it to his mouth. This wretched tickle in his throat was giving him gyp.

'If I'm not hers, then I can't be yours, can I?'

'Don't let's talk about it now, there's a good girl.'

'But Daddy . . .'

'No!' Fergus insisted, at which point (fortunately, he was to think later) he was overcome by a coughing fit.

'Have you got your lozenges?' Fanny shrilled, jumping behind him to rub his back. In the last few months these spasms had become a regular occurrence. Fanny hated them.

Her father nodded. He never went anywhere without Brick's lozenges.

'I'll get some water, shall I?'

'No need,' Fergus answered, as the fit began to subside.

'You should get that cough seen to.'

Deidre's voice came as a relief. Like old times, Fergus thought, as he pocketed his handkerchief. 'All under control,' he assured her.

'Not the way it sounds to me.'

'The wages of sin,' Fergus joked. 'You're always telling me I shouldn't smoke.'

Clarence, by this time, had begun inching his way back towards the door. What *was* that muck the boy put on his hair? Awful-smelling stuff. 'Well done, son,' Fergus acknowledged, as Clarence passed him.

'So, you've done a drawing, have you?' Deidre said, turning her attention to her daughter. 'Show it here then.'

Frances pulled her eyes away from her brother, whose scarlet face was causing her own cheeks to burn.

'Don't expect too much,' her father murmured, as she took the drawing from him.

'Come on, come on,' Deidre snapped.

'She's sketched the horses too,' Fergus informed his wife.

'This isn't a horse.'

'It's Felix. You remember, Mum? Our cat.'

'Can't you find something useful to do?'

Frances snatched back the offending paper. 'I've written a poem as well,' she said defiantly.

Fergus, recognising the tone most calculated to rouse his wife's anger, laid a restraining hand on his daughter's arm.

'What?' Deidre barked.

'It's inside the sachet I made you.'

'Jesus'n Mary!'

Frances's jaw dropped. At school, if anyone said 'Jesus' as a swear word, they got a hundred lines. Or worse. In the silence that followed her mother's outburst she looked round, instinctively, for Clarence. When she located him, hovering by the door, and he grinned and stuck out his tongue, she giggled.

That was Fergus's cue. He must get the children out of here, now. Dr Grossman had told him his wife had made a full recovery. 'In many ways I feel she's more herself now than she was before the breakdown,' he'd said. In which case, God help us, Fergus thought, heaving himself up from his chair.

'You'll come again?' Deidre pleaded. But it wasn't him she was looking at, it was her son.

'Answer your mother, lad,' Fergus instructed.

'Yup,' Clarence said.

'Come closer. She won't hear you.'

The boy took a sullen step forward.

'Closer,' Fergus encouraged.

'Thank you for my present, Clarrie,' Deidre said quietly, when her son was close to her again. 'Let me see now, your woodwork teacher's Mr Drew, if I remember right?'

'Yup.'

'He must be very pleased with you.'

Clarence ran his hand over his chin. There was a shadow now above his lip, where his first whiskers would appear. Fergus observed it with interest, and with sorrow. He and his son would not be close, as men. 'You comin' home soon, Mum?' Clarence asked.

'D'you want me to?'

'Yup.'

Deidre smiled. 'We'll have to see what we can do then, won't we?'

'You're not sick any more, are ya?'

The smile became coquettish. 'I'll tell you a secret,' Deidre said, picking up the streamer she'd abandoned, and draping it round her neck. 'I never was. It was all a silly mistake.'

6 ∫

The day Deidre came home from hospital Frances's diary entry read:

> *Mum came home today. Dr Munro said we were to carry on as normal, no matter what. He said if we found her crying we weren't to feel sorry for her, which just goes to show how little he knows. My mum never cries. She won't be in bed or anything. She's not sick that way. I'm glad Dad doesn't go to work anymore. Since he started High School Clarence spends all his time with his mates, I wouldn't fancy being here on my own with Mum.*
>
> *Mum'll be tickled pink with the house. She didn't notice it when she came in but I think that was because she was so busy talking to Clarence. When she gets up from her rest, and puts her glasses on, she'll see it's shiny as a new pin. Auntie Dottie and I cleaned every single room. We even cleaned the cupboards. Auntie Dottie went back to her house before Mum arrived. She said it was best. I walked with her through the orchard and when I saw she was crying I cried too.*

Deidre McLean was cured. She had a certificate to say so. At the annual conference of the New Zealand College of Psychiatrists, Dr Paul Grossman presented a paper in which Deidre McLean's recovery was cited in support of the growing use of ECT. 'It took a war to reveal to us the benefits of this technique,' he told his audience. 'Let's hope future progress in the field of mental health will not come at such a high cost . . .'

'I was wrong,' he told Fergus McLean. 'I should have prescribed shock treatment from the beginning.'

Within days of Deidre's return to Iona it was obvious to everyone who knew her that she was both different, and the same. Brick Munro had been wrong to predict tears. There were none. Nor were there any changes at the domestic level. The old rules were restored, the old routines re-established, the old preference, for her son over her daughter, re-enacted. But there was one thing new. Whereas in the past Deidre had pursued perfection in the domestic arena, now she sought more distant pastures. As distant, in fact, as China. Deidre McLean had come home from hospital determined to put an end to the starvation in China. Just where this passion came from no one could say. All Fergus could suggest, when asked, was that someone at Forest Hospital must have got hold of her. 'There are all kinds in there, you know,' he'd joke.

'She's decided she's the Good Samaritan,' Dottie wrote in her weekly letter to Meg. 'It'll kill poor Fergus, the way she's carrying on.'

When Meg, who never used the telephone if she could help it, decided to phone her brother, she was informed by an irritated Deidre that he was at a meeting.

'I thought he'd resigned from everything,' Meg said.

'The meeting's being held here. I've set up a local branch of CORSO. Have you any idea, Meg, the suffering that's going on in China right now? The number of children dying? I told Fergus, it's a disgrace the way this family have ignored it. Considering the connection.'

'Uncle Leonard died three years ago, Deidre.'

'Of starvation, shouldn't wonder.'

When Meg wrote back to Dottie she didn't, as in the past, scold her for her attitude to their sister-in-law. It was too late for that. Deidre was twenty-five years younger than her husband. And her illness was not the kind that shortened life.

'So, how's tricks?' Brick Munro asked his old friend.

'Deidre says I have emphysema. Is that what you think?'

'Ah . . .'

'I'd rather know, Brick.'

'It's not fatal, Fergus. Not necessarily.'

'But at my age . . .'

'You should have thrown that pipe away years ago.'

The two men looked at each other across the desk. There were words for what they were feeling, but they couldn't be spoken.

It was difficult enough just thinking them. They'd been friends for forty years.

'Tell ya what,' Brick said, 'I'll prescribe something medicinal for you.'

'That bad then?'

'You've rather an important birthday coming up, haven't you? We always said, if you made it that far . . .'

Fergus traced the line of his moustache. The years of smoking had turned it the colour of rust. 'Three score years and ten,' he acknowledged. 'I've been lucky, Brick.'

'For occasional use only, mind.'

Fergus smiled. 'Naturally.'

There was a pause, during which the two men reflected on the last time they'd talked like this. 30 January, 1938, a date neither of them were likely to forget. Fergus still shaken from his tumble into the river. Brick seeing a doomed man in front of him. 'If you keep drinking you'll be dead in a year,' he'd predicted. But Fergus had stopped, and married Deidre Byrne.

'You've thought about the children, have you?' Brick asked.

Fergus nodded. 'A trust fund. Not as much as I'd have liked, but there you are.'

'Let's hope there'll be no more . . .' Brick ran his fingers through his thinning hair. 'Forest Hospital isn't cheap,' he observed.

'You're telling me,' Fergus agreed.

'It shouldn't be this way. The public asylum . . .'

'No question of that. I've made provision.'

'How is she, by the way?'

Fergus cocked his head to one side. Bald since his mid-twenties, his scalp had taken on the appearance of polished porcelain. His face, by contrast, was tanned and leathery. The mark across his forehead where his hat reached was as familiar to Brick as the grey striped suits he'd been wearing since before the war. Husband and wife have one thing in common, Brick reflected. Neither cares a fig for fashion.

'The house is full of an awful publication called *China Reconstructs*,' Fergus said. 'D'ya know it?'

'Propaganda, from the sound of it.'

'She's got this bee in her bonnet about Uncle Leonard. We're supposed to have neglected him.'

'Not how I remember it. He stopped writing, didn't he?'

Fergus took out his handkerchief, and emptied his mouth of phlegm. Which was the harder, he wondered, to die in battle, or to die in your bed? Neither was what you'd call attractive prospects. 'Deidre and I don't agree on politics,' he admitted. 'We never have.'

Brick pulled on the corners of his waistcoat. His friend's marriage had long been a puzzle to him. Now, presumably, it would be a puzzle he'd never solve. 'Have you ever noticed it's the women who make excuses for these communists?' he reflected. 'My wife does it all the time. Insists they're just people, like you and me.'

'So were the Nazis. That's what I tell Deidre.'

'It's a funny old world.'

'Uncle Leonard wasn't much older than me, you know. He was barely out of his teens when he left New Zealand.'

'I always assumed he meant to come back . . .'

'China was an accident. His ship stopped at Shanghai, and that was it.'

'It got too late, I s'pose, in the end.'

'He *was* a communist, Brick. Whether from force or conviction we'll never know. He used to send things for the family. Jade, silk, that kind of thing. The war put a stop to it, of course.'

'So you don't know how he died?'

Fergus leaned back in his chair. He was tired suddenly. If only it was Dottie he was going home to. Dottie wouldn't interrogate him.

'Matter of fact,' he said, 'we got a full report. From his son. My cousin, come to think of it.' He laughed. 'My Chinese cousin . . . You knew he married over there? A relative of Mao Tse-tung's, no less. Of course we didn't know at the time, when he wrote to tell us, what an important family he was marrying in to. He didn't either, I imagine.' He laughed again. 'Funny when you think about it. My uncle a leader of the New China . . . But to answer your question, Uncle Leonard died in his bed. Lucky, I suppose you'd call it.'

The day Fergus turned seventy he took his daughter aside and said something to her that she was to puzzle over till the day of her own birthday, six years later, when she reached the age of eighteen. At eighteen, you were deemed old enough to die for your country, but not to buy a drink, or marry without permission. At eighteen, facts took over from fairy tales, and reality (the enemy) was declared by omnipotent society to be your friend.

'One day,' father said to daughter, 'when you're older, and able to understand, you'll be glad you're who you are, and not who you think you are.'

'Is this supposed to be a riddle?'

'In a way.'

'I don't like riddles.'

'Think of it as a puzzle then. A crossword puzzle. You like those, don't you?'

'Why can't you tell me the answer now?'

'Because that would be cheating.'

'But, Daddy . . .'

'Not now, sweetheart, everyone's waiting.'

Later, when the guests had gone, Frances cornered her father, and tried to get him to explain the puzzle. But he didn't seem to know what she was talking about.

'I'm sorry, lassie,' he said, in his slurry, evening voice. He'd been talking this way for weeks now. Frances hated it. 'Nothing to be done, you see,' he said.

7

By the end of that year everyone except Frances knew that Fergus McLean was dying. Even Clarence knew. He'd overheard his mother talking to one of her 'Corso cronies' and decided, on the spot, to tell no one, but to watch, and wait. Clarence had never asked himself what he thought about his father. His father just *was*. But he didn't want him to die. The only people he'd ever wished death on were the headmaster of his school, and a girl called Amy Warren.

Clarence, at fourteen years of age, was short and stocky, with thick black hair which he wore plastered against his scalp. He read comics, and clandestine copies of the national newpaper, *Truth* which was banned at Iona. He drove cars, illegally, and played the wag from school. He'd been to see *The Cruel Sea* four times, stealing money from his mother's purse to do so. He had a picture of Marilyn Monroe folded in his jacket pocket. When Amy Warren did the dirty on him he took comfort from the fact that she bore no resemblance whatsoever to Marilyn. He didn't like music much, except for cowboy songs. Gene Autry was his current favourite.

What to do with his life was as unclear to Clarence as the reason why people were born. He lived in the moment because that was all he could trust. There were good moments, and there were bad. He didn't try to make sense of it. All he knew was that most of the bad moments happened at Iona: the good ones in the company of his mates. Recently he and Jock Buchanan, the minister's son, had formed a gang called The Commandoes. Membership was limited to those whose punishment record equalled or excelled a weekly dose of six-of-the-best. So far only

Neill Gresham and Popeye Brown had qualified, but competition was hot, and new recruits were expected daily. It was thanks to Popeye, whose father worked in a garage, that the car was chosen as both symbol of the gang, and its most desired object. Under Popeye's supervision, The Commandoes had become experts in the art of 'borrowing' cars.

'It's a disgrace the way your teachers keep picking on you,' his mother fulminated, after reading his end-of-year report. 'I won't show this to your father. It'll only upset him.'

That Fergus McLean was alive at all Brick Munro considered something of a miracle. He'd talked to Deidre, preparing her, as he thought, for the inevitable, but she'd stopped him with a curt, 'You don't seem to realise, Doctor, *I* can make people better.'

'Oh, his wife looks after him all right, she's always done that,' Dorothy McLean conceded, when Brick stopped to talk to her after church. 'But it's not her keeps him alive, it's his daughter.'

'Do you think I should warn Fanny? It could happen any time.'

'Why spoil it for her? She's got enough to cope with as it is.'

'Things no better then?'

Dorothy pulled her cardigan over her ample breasts, and looked at him as if he'd just announced the world was flat. Brick smiled. For all her comfortable appearance, Dorothy McLean was sharp as a fox.

'In my opinion,' she pronounced, 'my sister-in-law's not cured at all.'

'Really?'

'I'd go further, and say she never will be. Never could be.'

'Strong words.'

'You don't see the half of it.'

Brick glanced over his shoulder. He should have known better than to raise this particular subject. When he spotted his wife chatting to Eileen Hercus, he waved enthusiastically.

'Mad, bad, and dangerous to know,' Dorothy asserted.

'Byron,' Brick said, smiling agreeably.

'You think I'm exaggerating . . .'

'I'll tell you what I think. I think you should do something about that mole. Why don't you come and see me next week?'

The laugh this raised was disconcerting. Brick wasn't aware he'd said anything amusing. 'Better be making tracks,' he muttered.

'There's Fanny now,' Dorothy said.

Turning, Brick saw two girls with arms around each other, crossing the street. 'Who's that with her?' he asked.

'Gail Henty. They're best friends.'

'They seem to be having a high old time.'

'Hasn't anyone ever told you appearances can be deceiving?'

There was no mistaking the rebuke. Brick considered defending himself, reminding her he was a doctor, with some experience in detecting the truth behind the masks people wore. But that was not the kind of conversation men and women had. Not after church anyway.

He touched the brim of his hat. What was it Fergus used to call his sister? Doubting Thomasina? The name suited her. 'Don't ignore that mole now, will you?' he cautioned. 'Cheerio for now.'

'You're just like all the others,' Dorothy's voice pursued him. 'You refuse to call a thing by its name.'

8 ∫

' "The farmer wants a wife, the farmer wants a wife, heigh ho the merry-o, the farmer wants a wife . . ." '

'McLean!'

'Fanny, your mother's calling.'

' "The wife wants a child, the wife wants a child, heigh ho the merry . . ." '

'McLean!'

Frances stopped so suddenly her mouth stayed in the shape of the sound she'd been about to utter. She wasn't usually allowed to bring anyone home after school. Today's reprieve had come like sunshine after a storm.

'Yes, Mum?' she answered.

'Come here when I call you.'

'Coming.'

'Look at you. Covered in mud. Look at those finger-nails. Can't you do anything without getting in a mess?'

'Gail and I have been feeding the horses.'

'Gail?'

'You said she could come.'

Deidre glanced at her daughter's friend and saw, with complete clarity, how she would look in five years' time. She had the same pert little nose as her mother; the same bow-shaped lips. Last Sunday her mother had come to church in high heels, and a ridiculous feathered hat perched on the front of her head. She'd looked like something the cat had dragged in. 'You better get on home,' she told Gail. 'Your mother'll be wondering where you are.'

'It's all right,' Gail retorted cheerfully. 'She knows I'm here.'

'Run along anyway. Frances has chores to do.'

Gail's eyes searched her friend's. She knew how it was between mother and daughter. Everyone knew. 'They should never have been allowed to have children in the first place,' she'd heard her own mother say.

'You'd better go,' Fanny whispered.

The signals from Gail's eyes became frantic. Mrs McLean was an old witch. She wasn't going to leave her friend in her clutches, no matter how scared she was herself. 'Fanny's father said he'd see me at tea,' she revealed boldly. 'He said he was glad I'd come.'

'Fanny's father is resting,' Deidre snapped.

'No, he's not. He's in the glasshouse.'

'Please go,' Fanny pleaded.

Gail looked up at the house, looming, castle-like, above her, and for a moment she believed the tales Arthur Begg had been telling: that Iona was haunted; that the ghost of a Chinaman walked in the orchard at nights; that Frances's mother really *was* a witch . . .

'Call for me in the morning?' Gail hissed, out of the corner of her mouth.

'Cross my heart,' Frances promised. She waved her hand, and her friend was gone.

'You're not to bring that girl here again,' Deidre ordered, as she led her daughter into the kitchen. 'I don't like her. She's a bad influence.'

'But she's my best friend . . .'

'Why can't you choose a nice wholesome girl? Betty Buchanan now. She's in your class, isn't she?'

'All Betty ever thinks about is getting married.'

'Don't be ridiculous.'

'It's true.'

'At twelve years of age . . .'

'She's got it all planned. How many children she'll have. What sort of house. Everything.'

'Is that why you were singing that silly nursery song? Aren't you a bit old for things like that?'

Frances bit the side of her mouth. Her mother was right, wasn't she? The song was *stupid*. No wonder Gail hadn't wanted to join in.

'Marriage,' Deidre muttered, crossing to the bench, which she proceeded to attack with a dishcloth. 'Is that all you girls can think about?'

'Not me,' Frances assured her. 'I think about lots of things.'

'Such as?'

'Well, drawing . . . I think about that a lot.'

Deidre tossed the cloth into the sink, and ran the tap. 'I thought you wanted to be a nurse,' she said, twisting the wet rag in her fists. 'That's what you put on the school form.'

'I didn't know what else to put.'

'You mean, it was a lie?'

'No . . .'

'I've warned you about lying.'

The dishcloth was propelled into the farthest corner of the bench. Frances looked round at the door. These days her father was seldom where she wanted him to be. If he wasn't lying down, he was out in the glasshouse, gazing at his pots. 'I didn't know how to say it, that's all,' she whispered.

'Speak up! How often have I told you?'

'I don't want you to be cross.'

Suddenly Deidre abandoned her task, turned her back to the sink, and stared at the girl on the other side of the room. She had to remind herself every day that this young woman was her daughter, and not a nurse to be trained. Fergus had asked her not to call her by her surname, but probationers were always addressed that way. Why should this one be an exception? 'So, if it's not nursing,' she said, swaying slightly with the effort of concentration, 'what's it to be then?'

Frances swallowed hard. The expression in her mother's eyes was peculiar. Not angry, but not friendly either. Should she tell her the truth? That she wanted to draw things. If she had a pencil in her hand now, and her mother wasn't looking, she'd be sketching her face, trying to capture that look in her eyes. She'd draw the bench too, the way its colour changed in light and shadow, the grains in the wood twisting like veins, as if they were part of the hands that travelled over them so many times a day. Nothing else in the world looked like this kitchen. It was as mysterious as the shelter in the orchard, her hiding place; or the Chinese chest at Auntie Dottie's; or the trunk full of her mother's things in the basement. But if she confided these thoughts she'd be in trouble again, wouldn't she? She'd be accused of *making things up*. Or worse.

'Cat got your tongue?' Deidre prompted.

'I expect I'll get married, like everyone else,' Frances fibbed.

'What sort of ambition is that?'

'I could help *you*. I could work for Corso.'

Her mother threw back her shoulders in a gesture Frances had come to dread. She didn't often get thrashed now, not with her father at home, but no one saw the quick slaps across her cheek.

'That smell,' Deidre challenged. 'What is it? Did you wash your ears this morning?'

Frances braced herself for the tug to her hair which she knew was coming. It never made any difference whether she'd washed her ears or not. They were always found to be dirty.

'Enough to make a person sick,' her mother proclaimed.

'It's 'cause I've been feeding the horses.'

'Into the bath with you this minute. I won't have that stench in the house.'

Frances backed towards the door. Where was her father? He should be here, not mucking about with his stupid begonias.

'Dad told me I . . .'

'Leave your father out of this.'

'But he said . . .'

Deidre, in one swift movement, crossed the room, and cracked her hand down on her daughter's head. 'Spoiled young madam,' she jeered. 'Your father won't always be here to protect you, you know.'

'Don't hit me, Mum. Please don't.'

'What gives you the right . . . ?'

'I'll be good, I promise.'

'Damn' good mind to tan your hide.'

'I'll go and have a bath now. I'll scrub my finger-nails. And behind my ears. Please, Mum. Don't be cross.'

All of a sudden Deidre's body slumped, as if, her daughter thought, peering out at her from under her armpit, someone had punched her in the back.

'Mum?' she tested.

Deidre's face, level with her daughter's, looked as if it had been crushed. Only the eyes, blue as glacial ice, acknowledged the world still. Frances had seen those eyes before, in a painting called *Pieta*. She'd brought it to show her father, but all he'd said was, 'It's Catholic. You don't want to bother with morbid things like that.'

'Mum?' Frances tried again.

'You won't run away, will you?' Deidre muttered. 'You won't leave me?'

If she'd been spoken to in German Frances could hardly have been more surprised! It wasn't just that her mother was no longer angry. It was that she sounded afraid.

'I love you, Mum,' Frances said impulsively.

There was a long, worrying silence. Frances jammed both fists into her cheeks. 'See my finger, see my thumb, see my fist, here it comes.' Her brother had taught her that the day she started school. 'Anyone who hits you,' he'd instructed, 'you hit them right back.'

'I won't run away,' she promised. 'I haven't for ages anyway.'

Slowly, as if waking from sleep, Deidre straightened her back. She was wearing a grey skirt, and a jersey she'd knitted herself. Her hair was pulled back in a bun. Frances, looking up at her, had the sensation she would always be out of reach. She was tall, of course, but it wasn't that. Her mother was the most mysterious person in the world.

'Run along then,' Deidre instructed. 'Cold water only, mind. Your father will want a bath when he comes in.'

9

On 14 September, 1954, the following death notice appeared in the *Otago Daily Times*:

> Fergus Rory McLean, peacefully, in his sleep. Beloved husband of Deidre, and father of Clarence and Frances.
> The funeral will be held at the Presbyterian Church in Stirling Street, at 11 am on 17 September.

Elsewhere in the paper there was a two-column obituary, and a photo, taken at the time of Fergus McLean's award, in the Queen's Birthday Honours, of an OBE. Much was made of the dead man's charitable works, and his achievement in keeping Fergus McLean Publishing afloat during the difficult days of the Depression. 'Of his many successes,' the article declared, 'one in particular stands out – a little book, originally published as a handbook, which has become something of a modern classic: *The Breeding and Training of Horses* by Pearse Byrne . . .'

The day Frances was told her father had died she finally gave up the struggle to match the world of her imagination with the world of reality. 'All artists are liars,' she was to be told, years later, in England. She could smile then, knowing it to be both true, and false. But there were no 'lies' to comfort her on that rainy September morning, when her mother woke her to tell her her father had died in his sleep. There was only the sense, creeping over her flesh, of the coldness of the world.

'It was very peaceful,' her mother said, when she didn't respond.

'But he can't . . .'

'I'm sorry.'

There were tears in her mother's eyes. Frances was to remember that and wonder, later, if it would have made a difference if she'd reached out to her. A grief shared, so many well-meaning voices would have assured her by then, is a grief halved. But how could she have reached out when the woman standing by her bed was, for most of the time, a terrifying stranger? What response could she have hoped for?

'You knew how ill he was,' her mother said.

'He can't die. He wouldn't. I can't live if he's dead.'

'Don't be silly, dear.'

'I want to see him.'

'You can't.'

'Why not?'

'They've taken him away.'

That was the moment when Frances knew reality had won, and would always win, unless she could construct a different world, one from which she could never be expelled. The realisation hit her like a blow to the chest. When her mother tried to take her hand, she pushed her away.

At the funeral, three days later, Frances got the giggles. 'Fergus McLean,' the Reverend Buchanan declared, 'was a man of many parts . . .' It was that set her off. What parts was he referring to? Private parts?

Her brother grabbed her elbow and squeezed it hard, but that only made it worse. In the end she had to pretend a coughing fit. Her mother, in a black suit smelling of mothballs, bent round behind Clarence and hissed, 'You should be ashamed of yourself.'

Which turned the laughter into gulping sobs.

That night Frances was woken by a voice calling her name. It was a few moments before she realised the voice was her mother's.

'I wasn't asleep,' she answered, guiltily. How could she have been? Her father was lying in a box in the ground.

'I'm cold,' the voice said.

Frances couldn't remember when she'd last seen her mother

in pyjamas. Since her return from hospital she was always up and dressed before anyone else. But tonight she didn't even have a dressing gown on. 'Shall I fill you a hotty?' Frances offered.

Her mother moved closer to the bed. In the faint light from the window her face looked like a shell worn smooth by the sea. 'You know, I used to run away too,' she confessed.

'You're shivering.' Frances swung her legs on to the floor. Thank God she hadn't let Felix in yet. Animals on the bed were strictly forbidden. 'I'll get that hotty,' she said.

'Do you believe in God, Frances?'

'What?'

'Pardon. Say, "I beg your pardon". And get back into bed. You'll catch your death.'

Frances did as she was told, pulling the blankets up to her chin. Her mother was staring at her. It was supposed to be rude to stare, but everyone had been doing it today. Each time she turned her head, whether in church, or later, at home, she caught someone at it. They pretended not to be of course, but she could tell. At the tea, after the church service, she and Clarence had eaten their way along the plates of sandwiches and cakes till they felt sick. Then, when the people had gone, they changed out of their best clothes, and Clarence rode off on his bike. He hated being stared at more than anything.

'Move over,' the voice instructed.

'What? I mean, pardon?'

'I want to talk to you.'

Frances squeezed her body into the cool channel at the far edge of the bed. As a child she'd wanted nothing more than to be allowed to cuddle her mother. But the answer had always been the same. 'Go away! I can't stand smoodgy children.'

When she felt the warm body touch hers, Frances's heart began to thump. Her mother had gone to bed without bothering to check the kitchen. That in itself was as strange as anything that had happened all day. Frances had waited for it to grow dark, then she'd gone to bed too. She would have written in her diary, only it was hidden away in the shelter. So she crawled between the cold sheets, and listened for Clarence. She was afraid he'd gone out with his gang. He thought she didn't know about that, but Betty Buchanan had spilled the beans ages ago. Did her mother know Clarence crept out at nights? Nothing had ever been said. Frances had tried to talk to her brother about it, warn him if *she* knew, chances were their mother did too. But he'd just laughed, and told her to keep her hair on. She and Clarence hardly ever talked these days.

'I asked you a question,' her mother prompted.

'Oh . . . yes. Um . . .' Frances willed herself to lie still. 'Stop fidgeting!' her mother would shout, any moment.

'Your father believed in God, of course. But then he was a saint.'

'Yes,' Frances said, though she had no idea what she was assenting to. 'Try not to be too sad,' Betty's father had advised, after the service. 'Your father's with Jesus now.'

'When I was a child I could make people disappear,' the voice on her pillow confided. 'I had the same powers as God. Then the magic began to fail . . .'

Frances dug her teeth into the side of her mouth. At tea today Auntie Dottie had made her promise to tell her everything that happened. But she couldn't tell her about this, could she? She wouldn't be believed.

'Your father was too good for sex,' the voice continued.

'I beg your pardon?'

'Always got your head in a book, haven't you, Tilly? What is it at the moment?'

'*Jane Eyre*,' Frances answered quickly. Her chest was hurting now. Her heart had become a fist, punching at her rib cage.

'And you think they're real, do you? Those stories you read.'

'I don't know.'

'It's a luxury. An indulgence.'

'I'm reading it for school, Mum.'

'And the others? Romances? Fictions? *Sir* Walter Scott.'

'Dad reads his books.'

There was no answer. Frances, edging out of the tunnel she'd made for herself, felt her mother's pyjama bottoms brush against her ankle. A faint smell of Knight's Castile soap reached her nostrils.

'When I was your age,' her mother announced, 'I wanted only one thing. To be a nurse. I had no wish to be married. No wish to have children. All I wanted was to make people better.'

A soft thud outside the window distracted Frances. Was it Clarence returning? Some nights he didn't come back till dawn.

'Have I ever shown you my treasure?' her mother enquired. 'I keep it in the basement.'

Frances's heart did a sickening somersault. The basement had been a favourite place to play when she and her brother were little. The trunk, containing what she must now think of as her mother's *treasure*, had been the magnet that drew them back. Stuffed with medical journals, and photograph albums full of pictures of nurses in neat rows, it had been an endless source of amusement on long, rainy Saturdays. Frances could pluck out of the air now, the black box with the star-shaped medal in it, the silver thermometer case, the starched cap that Clarence had plonked on his head, reducing her to helpless giggles . . .

'You're not Tilly, are you?'

'No.'

'I haven't been a good mother to you.'

'*What?*'

'I never wanted a daughter. I don't like women much.'

'Ya have-been-agood mother,' Frances protested, the words spilling out of her mouth. 'S'my fault that you . . .'

'I want to tell you something,' her mother interrupted.

Frances clamped a hand to her lips. Now she was certain there was no one she could tell this to. She'd be told she'd been dreaming.

'I've never spoken of it to anyone before.'

'Is it to do with your treasure?'

'I suppose you could call it a story, but it's not like the ones *you* read. It doesn't have an ending.'

'Dad told me a story about treasure once. It was about the stuff he used to keep in Auntie Dottie's chest . . .'

'It goes on happening, over and over . . .'

A faint mewing sound alerted Frances to the fact that Felix was on the window-sill, asking to come in. It must have been him she'd heard, earlier. She glanced, petrified, at her mother. 'Chin up,' Mr Buchanan had urged. 'It's what your father would want, you know.'

'Most of the time I forget,' the voice on the pillow said. 'It's a great gift, forgetting.'

'Do you want one of your pills? I could get them for you.'

'Not in a book, you won't find it there. It's a riddle.'

'I don't like riddles.'

'What has a beginning, but no end?'

'I don't know.'

'Think.'

'A book of some kind? I don't know.'

'A river. *That* river. It starts in a lake, and ends God knows where.'

'Rivers flow into the sea, don't they?'

'The sea's not an end. The sea goes on and on.'

'Why don't you ask Dad? He's good at riddles.'

'If it were an end, I'd know.'

Was that *it*? Frances wondered. The answer to the riddle? But then her mother said, 'It's written there. On the water. It has to be,' and everything was confused again.

'Are you all right, Mum?' she asked.

'If only I could read the words . . .'

'Meeow,' Felix squeaked.

'I could have told *him*. Phineas O'Reilly. *He* would have understood.'

Frances put her hands to her ears. 'You're barmy, you're barmy, your mother's in the loony bin,' a voice sang in her head. 'She wears black hair nets and rides a witch's broomstick . . .' Of course no one taunted her with that now. She wasn't a kid any more. These days what people did was talk behind her back.

'"All stories are enlightening." Do you believe that, Frances?'

'I don't know. I s'pose so.'

'*He* believed it.'

'Eee . . . yow . . .' Felix howled.

Go away! Frances urged. Catch a mouse or something.

'You know there's evil in the world when you see that river.'

'You don't like swimming much, do you, Mum?' Frances said, raising her voice above the threat from the window-sill. 'Is it 'cause you're scared of the water?'

'Flashing, like the white of an eye . . .'

I won't listen, Frances resolved. I'll think of something else.

'We held hands along the riverbank. We were dressed in our Sunday best. There was snow on the ground. It crunched under our feet. "Be careful," she said. "Don't slip."'

'Mum?'

'"God put us on this earth to bear children". "Even our most secret thoughts are known to Him". I ask you, Tilly, what sort of God is that?'

Out in the hall the clock whirred, then began to strike. When it stopped at three Frances groaned. Morning was *hours* away.

'She took Molly's hand out of mine,' her mother went on, 'and led her to the water. Molly started to cry. She turned back then and took Sean as well. But she couldn't hold the baby. She didn't have enough hands. So she let the baby go . . .'

There was a taste of blood in Frances's mouth. But it wasn't her nose that was bleeding, it was her gums. She glanced at her mother, judged it safe, and pulled a corner of the sheet up to her lips.

'You don't hear it?' her mother asked.

'Hear what?'

'The baby . . .'

'It's Felix, Mum. He does that at nights. He'll stop soon.'

'Oh, the poor wee scrap . . .'

Frances wound the sheet into the shape of a liquorice strap, and pulled on it with her teeth. She had the weird sensation that the room was full of miniature orchestra players, tuning their instruments. There was her mother, breathing a sort of melody, only it wasn't a melody because Deidre McLean was tone deaf. Then there was the window rattling. Frances had jammed paper down the sides to stop the noise but every few days it worked free, and the rattle started up again. Outside there was the wind, and Felix, of course, bad, bad Felix, growing impatient . . .

'He called her his white poppy. But I can't see her. Can't remember. Just her voice sometimes, singing . . .'

She'll stop soon, won't she? Frances told herself. She won't go on forever.

'I can't see them,' her mother moaned. 'I can't see . . .'

'It's all right, Mum. It's only a dream.'

There was no answer.

'It's not real . . .'

When no answer came to that either, Frances renewed her attack on the sheet. It didn't taste of liquorice, it tasted of Listerine soap, and the strange blue water in which her mother rinsed sheets and shirts and table cloths. 'WHITER THAN WHITE' it said on the packet by the wash tub. But white was the absence of colour. It was nothing, not something, so how could you have more of it?

She was about to peep at her mother, wondering if she'd fallen asleep, when the voice she most dreaded erupted in the darkness, 'What would you know? Spoiled brat like you.'

Frances yanked the sheet from her mouth, and slithered back into her tunnel. Clarence? she pleaded silently. Had he come home, or was she alone in the house with her mother?

'Real is what goes on happening, over and over,' the mocking voice continued. 'Not one of your happy endings.'

'*Wuthering Heights* doesn't have a happy ending.'

'Don't be impertinent!'

'Sorry. I'm sorry.' Frances dug her fists into her cheeks. Answering back was her worst, her very worst fault.

Suddenly her mother threw back the blankets, and clambered out of bed. 'You don't know the first thing,' she sneered, as she beat a path to the door. A crescendo of sound accompanied her footsteps. Everywhere Frances looked she saw ghostly figures tuning their instruments.

'Twisting your father round your little finger.'

Please go, Frances prayed. Please don't say any more.

'Living is horrible, horrible,' her mother said, her voice rising from bass drum to shrill soprano. 'Your father's the lucky one. He's out of it.'

For a long, heart-stopping moment it seemed her mother was going to turn back into the room. But then her shoulders slumped, and she lurched towards the door. Frances counted slowly to a hundred. When she'd finished, she crept out of bed, and let Felix in through the window. 'It's all right,' she comforted the gratefully purring puss. 'You're safe now.'

It was the last time Deidre and Frances talked as mother and daughter. Deidre's breakdown, which took sudden and startling form the following morning, was explained, not surprisingly, as a consequence of the shock of her husband's death. But Frances knew that was not the cause. The cause was the river, and what was written there. And the reason the breakdown came when it did, on that particular morning, was because the previous night Deidre McLean had told her daughter a story, one she'd never told anyone else before. And Frances had failed her. When she tried to read the words, all she saw was the white of an eye . . .

10 ∫

'Clarence, have you seen Mum?'

It was early the next morning. Clarence, slumped at the kitchen table, was wearing the clothes he'd had on the night before. His chin was smudged with stubble.

'*Have* you?'

Clarence looked up from the car manual he was reading. 'Nope,' he answered his sister.

'Aren't you going to school?'

'Nope.'

'You'll get into trouble.'

'So what?'

Frances glanced round the kitchen. Its neglected state alarmed her. Her mother never left dishes in the sink. 'Has Mum been doing the washing?' she asked.

'Search me.'

'I can't find any pants to wear.'

Clarence sniggered.

'I'm gunna be late,' Frances moaned. When there was no response, she went on the attack. 'Where were you last night anyway? You shouldn't leave ... You shouldn't go out like that.'

'Ya'll miss yer bus if ya don't shake a leg,' Clarence muttered.

The agonised look on Frances's face was lost on her brother. Whatever she did now, it seemed to her, she'd get into trouble. If she left the kitchen like it was, it would be her fault. If she missed the bus, she'd be late for school. Normally, at this time, she'd be carrying her father's breakfast tray through to him. They'd greet each other with a kiss, and she'd promise to tell him all her news at the end of the day. It had never been possible to imagine that ritual coming to an end.

'I'd better find Mum,' Frances said.

'She's in the garden.'

'Why didn't you say?'

'Must be. S'not in the house.'

'You're a great help, you are,' Frances fumed.

Her brother's voice stopped her at the door. But the words he was trying to say wouldn't come out. 'I'm sh . . . I'm shorry,' he managed, at last.

'What for?'

His answer was to slump over his book again.

Clarence was right about their mother being in the garden. She was down by the compost, burning rubbish in the incinerator. As Frances approached, she could see her poking at the flames with a spade. 'There you are,' she called.

Her mother glanced over her shoulder, and went on with her task.

Frances forced herself to move closer. Her mother, she noticed, was wearing a pair of man's trousers, and an old jersey, from the top of which poked the collar of her pyjamas. 'Can't Robbie do that?' she suggested.

'Jezebel,' her mother muttered.

'What? I mean, pardon?'

'You heard. Jezebel.'

'Who's she?'

'You read the bible, don't you?'

'Yes, but . . .'

'You're a woman now. You bleed.'

'Mum?'

Deidre, still clutching the spade, twisted her head, and aimed her eyes at her daughter. 'Get away from me,' she hissed. 'I never want to see you again.'

It was an order Frances was only too anxious to obey. But when she tried to move, she found she was paralysed. 'Just carry on as normal,' Dr Munro had advised. But he never said what 'normal' was.

'Are you all right, Mum?' Frances whispered.

'Jezebel! Jessie-bel! You don't fool me. I've known who you are from the beginning.'

'Why don't you come inside? Clarence is home.'

'Blood. Babies. *Disgusting*.'

'Please, Mum,' Frances pleaded. Her eyes searched the garden. No one. There'd never be anyone again, would there? *'Please,'* she repeated. Her mother's usually pale face was pink with heat. Specks of ash had lodged in her hair. But it was her hands Frances was watching; fingers, spreadeagled round the spade, licked by tongues of flame . . .

'Whore!' Deidre howled. 'Slut! Sneaking out at nights. Did you think I wouldn't notice?'

'It's not me,' Frances whimpered.

'Oh, but you're clever, aren't you? With your sweet smile and your innocent look. But I know. I see everything you do.'

'Yes, Mum,' Frances said. Inch by inch the spade was being pulled out of the fire. Frances, staring through waves of stinging smoke, tried to make herself think of *real* things: Felix, the clock in the hall, the horses, Gail, school . . .

'They'll take your baby away from you,' her mother snarled. 'That's what they do to whores.'

'Yes . . .'

'Where are you going?'

'I'll just . . .'

'Come back here!'

'It's all right, Mum . . .'

Suddenly the spade was in the air above her head. Frances had time to register that something was clinging to the blade; something soft and still recognisably white. Then she threw herself against the compost heap, plunging her hands into the fetid soil, and tossing it in her mother's face.

There was a shriek, and a curse, and the spade fell to the ground. Frances looked down, and saw what was clinging to the blade. It was the charred remains of a pair of her own pants.

What happened next was always confused in Frances's memory. She couldn't recall her mother at all at that point. Perhaps she just stood there, staring, while the fire burned out in the incinerator. What she did remember was looking up and seeing Robbie lumbering down the path towards them.

'You all right, wee lass?' he gasped as he reached her.

Then the picture blurred again. She was inside the house, and Auntie Dottie was there, and Robbie was telling her to chew on a blackball, and no one could find Clarence . . . Later Dr Munro came, and then an ambulance, but what was happening to her mother all that time she could only imagine. At the end of the day Auntie Dottie told her there was nothing to be afraid of. But Auntie Dottie didn't know about the river.

This time Deidre McLean stayed in hospital for almost two years. For the first six months she spoke not a single word. When her voice did return it was Clarence she asked for, not her daughter. Whenever Frances's name was mentioned, she looked blank.

By the time Deidre was declared well enough to return to Iona, Frances had become a boarder at a school in the country, and Clarence had left school altogether. His job, at Brown's Garage, was described by everyone but him as temporary.

Deidre McLean was never again a patient at Forest Hospital. The nightmare of shock treatment was over for her. But though she remembered many things, she could never put a name to the young woman who visited her from time to time, claiming, perplexingly, to be her daughter. When, on the eve of this person's eighteenth birthday, she was informed that a letter from her late husband was to be given to her, as per the instructions in his will, she expressed surprise. 'I can't imagine what Fergus could have had to write to her about,' she said. 'But by all means, if that was his wish . . .'

At the end of that year, Frances sailed on the *Queen of Florence* to England.

Part Six

_S_

14 September, 1964.

I'm not sure this is a good idea. It's the tenth anniversary of my father's death, and I woke up this morning with the notion that I should keep a diary banging away in my head. I used to keep one when I was a kid. My father gave me a beautiful, leather-bound journal for my tenth birthday, and that got me started. 'There are good habits and bad,' he told me, I remember. 'Writing things down is a good habit, one you'll be glad you got into when you're older.'

I kept that journal for three years. But when my father died, I stopped. God knows where those juvenile scribblings are now. Burned, I should imagine, along with all my other things.

I don't know why I should have remembered this today, or why it should seem significant. But here I am, pen in hand, taking my father's advice again ...

There's no way I can fill in the last ten years. I've forgotten a lot of it anyway. I'll be twenty-three years old at the end of this month. Ancient. _I suppose you could say some fairly dramatic things have happened to me, but I don't dwell on them. They happened. End of story._

Where I'm living now is in a village in the centre of England. It's called Little Chippingham. I've taken a job here. It's not much of a job but I wanted – needed _actually – to get out of London. One of the more dramatic things that have happened to me recently was that I smashed up my van. It's a long story, too tedious to go into, and I was a fool ever to buy it, but the upshot was, I'm now in debt to the tune of £637. Which is why I'm here, where the money is good (well, better than the pittance I earned in London), and there's no rent to pay._

Before I get going there's something I'd better own up to. You're supposed to tell the truth in a diary, and I don't always do that. Tell the truth, I mean. It's a habit I got into at boarding school. I'm not defending myself or anything. I hated that school, but I can see, looking back, it wasn't *so bad. It's just that it was tempting, with everyone asking questions, to make things up. Of course I got found out. New Zealand is a bit of a goldfish bowl (one of the reasons I live here!), so it was only a matter of time before somebody spilled the beans. But by then inventing my life had become a habit.*

The truth is, I left London because there was nothing there for me anymore.

I've yet to discover what this job entails. 'Secretary-Companion' it said in the advertisement. But I like this place already. Not the Manor so much, it's a bit overpowering, but the village, and the countryside. My employer, Lady Christabel Temple, calls it 'Marlborough Hunt Country'.

Lady Christabel wasn't at all what I expected. I mean, I imagined she'd be old. She's not young, I don't mean that. About forty, I'd say at a guess, though with the make-up she was wearing, it was hard to tell. Auntie Dottie would call her well-preserved.

'But you're even prettier than your photo,' she said, when we met, then went on to make comments about my hair. 'That colour. Pure pre-Raphaelite. Don't ever cut it, will you?'

I wonder what she'd have said if I'd returned the compliment. 'A rinse, is it? Or do you use something more permanent? Peroxide perhaps?'

Actually Auntie Dottie wouldn't call her well-preserved. 'Mutton dressed as lamb,' she'd say.

When Lady Christabel asked me about my parents I told her they were dead.

'I know we're going to get along, Frances,' she said, as she showed me to my room. 'You're just what I've been looking for.'

Architecturally, Chippingham Manor is a mess. Built in the seventeenth century for a rich wool merchant, it fell into disrepair in the eighteenth, only to be revived in the nineteenth by another rich merchant, Septimus Grigg, whose fortune came not from sheep, but from soap. The architect Septimus employed to make the Manor fit for a Victorian gentleman to inhabit demolished walls, and rotting though still magnificent staircases. He ripped out leaded windows and replaced them with ones which gave a proper sense of the acreage owned. He bricked in fireplaces, and lowered exquisitely plastered ceilings, whose only crime was that their beauties had been dimmed by years of smoke from open fires. The result was the mansion you see today, give or take a few coats of paint and the addition of central heating.

The present owner, Sir Oliver Temple, whose purchase of

the Manor in the spring of 1963 caused something of a local furore, has so far shown no interest in making any but cosmetic improvements. Though his wife, whose parties have become as popular a spectator sport as weddings in the village church, is rumoured to have engaged, behind her husband's back, the services of a top London architect.

Sir Oliver's arrival at Chippingham Manor followed hard on the heels of his much publicised dismissal from the chairmanship of *The Vanguard*, England's most famous (some would say, infamous), right-wing newspaper. *The Vanguard* had been in the control of the Temple family since its inception at the height of the Napoleonic Wars. Sir Oliver's forced resignation was almost as shocking, in some circles, as the assassination of President Kennedy six months later. But in 1963 the 'winds of change' were being felt in corners of British life hitherto regarded as sacrosanct. And what the wind tossed from one place, it deposited in another. In Little Chippingham Sir Oliver and Lady Temple became the new 'lords of the manor'. And a young woman from the Old Commonwealth came to live in a house that had seen the rise of Empire, and was watching, now, its inevitable demise.

2 ∫

It was during her third year in England that Frances met Keith. She first saw him striding down Earl's Court Road, looking as if he owned the place. Son of a Taranaki farmer, he was a hunky sort of fellow, with a thatch of startling blond hair. To her subsequent embarrassment, she found herself staring. A few days later he walked into the coffee bar where she was working, and it started.

'I'm off to Europe,' she wrote to Auntie Dottie. 'I'm going to Amsterdam to see the Rembrandts and then to Italy to see *everything*! A friend's coming with me. You'd like her, Auntie Dottie. She's a "good sort"! Her name's Keitha . . .'

Lying about Keith came naturally to Frances. As did lying *to* Keith. When she saw how bored he was in art galleries she pretended her interest was merely that of a tourist. 'Got to have something to tell the folks back home,' she said.

After six months their money ran out, and they came back to London to look for work. Keith landed a job straight away. Frances took a little longer. Their plan was to save enough for the fare home.

The job Frances eventually found was for a firm selling non-mechanised floor polishers. She had to go round London's department stores demonstrating the gadget, which either didn't work, or fell apart after several hours of use. Since she was paid according to how many she sold she made almost no money at all. Most of the women who asked to see the polisher in action looked as if they hadn't spent money on themselves in years. When it came to the point, Frances couldn't let them buy something she knew they'd be throwing away in a week's time.

'You're an idiot!' Keith shouted, the day she got the sack. 'You'll never get home at this rate.'

'It was crap, Keith. A con. I couldn't let people buy the lousy thing. Not the people I saw anyway.'

'It was a job, Fan. Just a job.'

'I'll get another. What's the big deal?'

The quarrel, not their first, took place in their untidy bed-sitting room. Keith's overalls (he was working on a building site) were tossed over the sofa that opened up at night to become their bed. Across the room a screen covered with postcards from their time in Europe hid what passed for a kitchen. The communal bathroom and lavatory were reached through the door that led on to the landing. One of the things about London Frances was glad to leave behind was the smell on that landing. English people, she decided, well, London bed-sit people anyway, lived on a diet of cabbage and mince, and never cleaned their lavatories. Her mother would have approved of her disapproval. And of her efforts with caustic soda and bleach. She might even have approved of Keith. Sitting in the chair with the broken springs, calling her an idiot. The landlord had promised to fix that chair when they first moved in. Funny how you got used to things. The lukewarm baths; the geyser that sounded like cars piling into each other . . .

> 'Dear Mum and Clarence,
>   This is to tell you I'm engaged. His name's Keith Towsey, and he's from Taranaki . . .'

But of course that letter was never written.

'I want to marry you, Fan. There's no need to look so upset.'

That was when the lies had had to stop, from fear of discovery; from a belated sense of owing Keith the truth. Till that time she'd let him believe she came from a normal family: father, mother, brother. A family to whom she would return, in time.

'So what's the big deal?' he'd wanted to know, when her story came to an end. 'You're adopted. Who cares?'

'Don't you?'

'I know plenty of adopted people.'

'Aren't you curious?'

'I don't give a stuff who your family are, Fan. They could be behind bars, for all I care.'

That had made Frances laugh. Somehow Keith could always make her laugh, though really it was no laughing matter, deciding what to say to him.

There were five proposals in all. That first time they were sitting on the deck of the cross-channel ferry. The funnel behind them was belching foul-smelling smoke. Seagulls screamed overhead. Before them lay the white cliffs of England. Behind lay France, and the thousands of miles they'd travelled in Keith's van. Frances would never again be able to look at a Morris van without thinking of the mattress in the back, and the wet metal walls, and Keith's face ardent above hers.

'Being crazy's just as bad as being behind bars,' she answered him, though it wasn't an answer of course, she was just playing for time.

'Your mother's OK now though, isn't she?'

They'd come up on deck for privacy. The wind, razoring into their faces, was their guarantee they wouldn't be disturbed. 'My father once told me I'd be glad when I found out I wasn't who I thought I was,' she said. 'I didn't understand him at the time.'

'You said he wrote you a letter.'

'Yeh . . .'

'D'ya still have it?'

'Of course.'

'Can I see it?'

'Knowing who you're not isn't enough,' Frances answered him. 'I want to know who I am.'

'Marry me,' Keith urged, searching in the folds of her coat for her hand. 'Then you'll know.'

He'd been so certain of her, that was what ruined it. She couldn't escape the feeling he was pleased to be offering her a new identity. 'You think if I marry you I'll stop minding,' she accused, when they were back in London, and he was pressing her, again, for an answer. 'You just want to own me, that's all.'

'Yeh, I wanna own you,' Keith admitted. 'I wanna look after you. I want us to have kids. Does that make me a criminal?'

When he talked like that, all she could say in her defence was, 'Why change things?'

But things did change. Three days after that quarrel in the bed-sit, Keith invited her to buy his van. When she asked him why he was selling it, he told her he was going home without her.

3

21 September 1964

So much for good intentions. A week gone by, and I haven't so much as opened this diary. Lady Christabel keeps me fairly busy, but that's no excuse. The work's hardly arduous: answering correspondence, writing out menus, drawing up guest lists for dinner parties. Not what you'd call back-breaking.

It's too early to say whether I like Lady C or not. She asks a lot of questions, but I suppose that'll stop in time. There's been no mention of her husband.

I'm not sure I agree with Dad about writing things down. It's like talking, it makes things real, and once you know something's real you can't change it. Its shape gets set in bronze.

When I think of the last five years, of the letters I've written to Auntie Dottie and Gail (the ones to Mum and Clarence don't count, since Mum's never replied and Clarence only writes at Christmas), I realise I've lost the habit, if I ever had it, of telling the truth in words. If Auntie Dottie knew what was really going on in my life she'd throw up her hands in horror. As for Gail, well, she's married now, and from the letters she writes I can't say I know who she is anymore, so I guess it can work both ways.

I've started sketching again though, which is a kind of recording I suppose. It'd infuriate Keith if he were here. He hated me 'scribbling'. Most of my sketches are of people, though I've done a few of the interior of the Manor, and a couple of the garden (which I don't like much actually, too formal; though the lake is nice, and the summer house, which I tried to get into, only it was locked, adds a gratifying Italianate dimension). London must have dulled my eyes because now I'm here it's as if I'm seeing England and the English for the first time. And it's not likeness I'm seeing, likeness to us or our landscape, but difference. The land is lovelier. Or do I mean, more loved? That's come as a shock. As for the people, they're another race – shorter, paler, older, sadder . . . It can't be expressed in words.

Of course I don't sketch openly. That would be to give the game away. But I've done several from memory of Mrs Honeybone (she's the housekeeper here), and one I'm rather proud of of her husband, George.

It was George who warned me not to get too pally with Lady C. 'The last girl did that, and came a cropper,' he told me.

The day after that conversation I took my pencils and pad, and followed the path through the village to the river. I wanted to sketch the stone bridge I'd noticed on an earlier walk. I'd seen these bridges before, on expeditions into the country with Keith, but I'd never examined one in detail before.

From whatever angle you look at it, that bridge is beautiful. A perfect rainbow arch over the water. I've no idea how old it is, but it has to have been built in the age of carriages. Now cars and tractors rumble over its cobbled surface, scattering the sheep in the nearby fields, casting a carbon monoxide wake over the tangle of reeds and rushes that clot the edges of the river. When I think of the unlovely, concrete bridges that span our southern waters, I feel a pang of guilt. No amount of gazing could ever transform those utilitarian structures into the mosaic of golden stone and trailing wild flowers which my fingers, all that long, sun-filled afternoon, ached to record. By the time I realised I was going to be late for Lady Christabel, my pad was half full.

I dreamt about that bridge last night. I was on the riverbank, sketching the swans, when my mother suddenly appeared from behind a clump of teazles on the other side. When I saw she was waving, I felt a rush of happiness. The river here's not much more than a stream. No one could possibly be afraid of it. But then I noticed my mother's mouth was moving, and her waving had become frantic. I pointed out the bridge to her. 'I can't hear you,' I yelled. 'Come over here.' But she just went on frantically gesturing. When I woke the voice in my head was George's. 'It's all right, missie,' he said. 'It's only a dream.'

'I know what I wish for you,' my father wrote in his letter, 'happiness with a family of your own . . .'

But if you'd wanted that for me, Dad, you should never have left me money. It's gone now of course, but it was enough to enable me to run away, for real. Now I don't even have the other things you predicted for me.

'Wish I could fathom you,' Keith grumbled, the day I dragged him up a dusty Tuscan hillside to see Piero della Francesca's 'Madonna del Parto.' 'I mean, where does it come from, this hobbyhorse of yours? It's all you ever want to do, look at pictures.'

I don't think Dad meant what he said in his letter, about families and happiness. No one who'd seen the things he'd seen could say something like that and mean it. It's haunted me almost as much as the other things he told me.

If you can see me now, Dad (and you believed you would be able to),
I wonder if you'll understand why I've told so many lies. Pretending to
be an Australian squatter's daughter or the third cousin of the Queen
Mother are not things to be proud of. But from your vantage point you
might be able to make sense of it! Not that I believe in heaven anymore.
Or God. I've let you down about that too.
 'I can see everything you do.' Those were her *words. And the strange*
thing is, they're easier to believe than my father's. Even though she's twelve
thousand miles away, and very much alive. I always knew she could see
right through me.

According to the guide book Little Chippingham is 'as nearly
perfect a specimen of rural tranquillity as any village in England'.
It has one pub, The King's Arms, famed for its pickled eggs; a
church that dates back to the eleventh century; a post office that
looks like a cowshed; a school that looks like a church; and a shop
which, for several weeks after Frances's arrival, displayed in its
window a scattering of six-inch nails, and packets of sanitary
pads, arranged in a pyramid.

Towering over all these, dwarfing the cottages, is Little
Chippingham Manor.

'You'll have to learn to say *pahrty*, not *pardie*,' Christabel
instructed her new secretary. 'Tony Sandford thought you hailed
from South Africa.'

'Sorry.'

'No need to look so crestfallen.'

'Perhaps you should have hired an English girl.'

Christabel looked down at her perfectly manicured nails. She
had high hopes of Frances. The girl was intelligent, attractive,
and seemingly unencumbered. Not a boy friend in sight. And
only a trickle of mail from New Zealand. The only worrying
thing about her was this tendency she had to be smart. 'You
know I'm very pleased with you, Frances, don't you? If you go
on as you have been I'll be wanting to put your wages up.'

'Actually I don't sound South African at all,' Frances said.

'It was only Tony's little joke, dear.'

'Last people on earth I'd want to sound like.'

'You don't like South Africans?'

'How can anyone like people who shoot their own citizens in
cold blood?'

Lady Christabel sighed. 'Such a shame they're not British anymore,' she said. 'It breaks my heart when I think of what's happening. Every day another declaration of independence. Thank God New Zealand's still loyal.'

4 ∫

'Oh, well played!' Lady Christabel clapped her hands in delight.

Tony Sandford turned to her, and bowed. 'Will I do then?' he asked.

'Oh, you'll do, you'll do splendidly.'

'Serve coming up!' Frances shouted. She'd been playing for over an hour, and was fed-up, not with the tennis, which she enjoyed, but with the verbal sparring between Lady C and her guests, that so far seemed to be the main point of the exercise.

'Tony and I against you and Randal,' Lady C had commanded at the start of the game.

Tony Sandford, an actor, was young, well, young*ish*, and had the looks of an English aristocrat. Randal Kane, the architect employed by Lady C to re-design the Manor, was short, fat, and after an hour on the tennis court, covered in sweat.

'Would someone else like to play?' Frances suggested, when the game was over. 'Mrs Kane, how about you?'

'My wife doesn't play tennis,' Randal announced. 'Time to change ends I think.' He pulled a crumpled handkerchief out of his pocket, and mopped the sweat off his face. 'Don't you want to wipe the grins off their faces?' he challenged his partner.

'Not particularly,' Frances snapped.

'Ah,' Randal hissed. 'The filly has a temper.'

Half an hour later it was all over. Frances hadn't consciously given the match away, but when the next three games in a row went to their opponents, she had to admit she was more than partly responsible. The only two good players on the court were herself and Tony Sandford. The honours should have been fairly even. 'Sorry, Mr Kane,' she said, as they walked off the court.

'Mr Kane?' he parroted.

'I'm not very good at revenge.'

'I'll forgive you, but only if you call me Randal.'

'You be nice to Randal now,' Lady Christabel had instructed earlier. 'If he takes a shine to you, and I'm sure he will, I might be able to persuade him to take a nought off his outrageous fees.'

But being nice to Randal was not something Frances could manage. Especially as Lady Christabel seemed determined to be unpleasant to his wife.

'Dear Ginny,' she simpered, over lunch. 'I do like your new hair style. Is that what they call a beehive? I'm afraid we're awfully casual down here. We positively shock the natives.'

'Did you know you have a tiny map of Italy on the side of your neck?' Randal breathed in Frances's ear.

At which point Frances excused herself, and went to help Mrs Honeybone in the kitchen.

When she came back, Tony Sandford was holding the floor.

'Greenbank,' he was saying. 'Commonest name in these parts. Commoner than Smith.'

'Tina and Alice,' Lady Christabel chipped in. 'The two girls who waited on us today. They always help out when I have parties. Tina and Alice *Greenbank*,' she explained.

'Name goes all the way back to the Magna Carta,' Tony went on. 'It's a derivative of Green, the oldest name in England. Matter of fact, in this neck of the woods, if your name doesn't go back at least to the Reformation, you're regarded as an interloper.'

'Not much hope for me then,' Frances quipped.

'Planning on staying, are you?' Tony enquired.

Frances, seeing the look on her employer's face, shrugged. ('Chatterbox,' her mother's voice mocked. 'Spoiled little madam.')

'McLean,' Tony mused. 'Relatives in Scotland, are there?'

'No,' Frances answered.

'One day, if you're still around, I might tell you the history of *my* name.'

Lady Christabel let out a shrill laugh. 'Oh but you must tell us all, Tony dear,' she insisted. 'We don't have secrets in this house.'

By the time the last guest had left it was already dark. Frances, who wanted only to escape to her room, found herself trapped by her employer, who wanted to talk. Had Frances enjoyed herself? What did she think of Tony? Was she happy here? Where did she go on her afternoons off? How would she fancy a trip to London to see Tony's play?

'Actually, *I* used to be an actress,' Frances revealed.

'Oh?'

Damn, Frances cursed silently. Why did I tell her that? Damn and blast!

'It wasn't on your cv.'

'It was only for a while. A season at Brompton Rep. A couple of commercials . . .'

'Still . . . an *actress*.'

'Anyway, I've given up.'

'Was it something you did back home?'

'In New Zealand?'

'That is where you come from, isn't it?'

'Yes.'

'Well?'

'No. I never even thought of it.'

Lady Christabel smiled. 'Amateur theatricals,' she said. 'I understand that's all there is out there.'

When Frances finally made it to her room she was too distracted to draw. 'WHAT AM I DOING HERE?' she scrawled in her diary.

To which Auntie Dottie answered, 'You'll come down to earth eventually, dear.'

Christabel lay back in her bath, and smiled. It had been a highly satisfactory day. Tony had called her his Cleopatra. That could mean only one thing . . .

As for the rest of it, Randal had, as she'd anticipated, fallen for Frances. She knew his tastes. With a little encouragement, and a nice fat salary increase, Frances was sure to come round.

At which thought Christabel wriggled her toes, and watched the scented bubbles play over her small breasts. She'd waited a long time for this girl. Now she'd found her she had no intention of letting her go.

I'll tell her tomorrow, she decided. From now on, she's to be known as Chloe.

'I could live here,' Frances said out loud, as she walked the now-familiar river path.

'I wish you wouldn't do that,' Clarence's voice hissed in her ear. 'Anyone'd think you were cracked.'

Of all the village walks, this was Frances's favourite. The paths that took her across the fields, towards Stonehill in one direction, and Cromlech in the other, provided fine, windy vistas, but it was the river she kept returning to. She'd sketched the bridge from every angle. She'd leaned over its walls to draw the water, snaking through the weeds. She'd studied the movements of the swans and coots and moorhens for whom the river was home. She'd watched small boys cast their fishing lines, and winced when a pike no bigger than her hand was wrenched from the hook and tossed, triumphantly, into a bucket. Occasionally she was joined by a silent figure in a grey overcoat, several sizes too big for him. He'd sit some distance from her, and stare at the water. He neither spoke nor looked at her, and after a while she began to take his presence for granted. He was like the willow on the opposite bank; a breathing sculpture, rooted to the soil. Like everything else, he soon found his way into her drawings.

'If you were here, if you could see, you'd understand,' Frances said, addressing the mirage of her brother. How could she explain it? It was as if her race to get things down on paper was the hook, and she the fish. Already she was beginning to think of the river as her own.

'What has a beginning and no end?'

'You didn't ask that. *She* did.'

'If you don't answer I'll give you a Chinese burn.'

'I hate riddles.'

'That's 'cause you're a stupid *girl* . . .'

'The sea. The human race . . . The river!'

'I'm sh . . . I'm shorry,' Clarence stuttered.

Sometimes her mother appeared, a ghostly companion to the
man in the overcoat. Whenever that happened Frances would
pack up her pencils and head back to the Manor. She'd worked
too long. Her eyes were playing tricks on her.

> *'Dear Auntie Dottie,*
>
> *Nothing much to report. Work as usual. We're off to London
> tomorrow. From where I'm sitting, on the riverbank, I can see
> the railway line, though I'm seldom here at the right time to
> see the trains. Did you get my last letter? I'm a wee bit worried,
> as I didn't hear from you this week. I wish you were still in
> the cottage. It was wrong of Mum to make you leave. Though
> I suppose, if you're not well or anything, it's good that you're
> with Auntie Meg.*
>
> *I love you, Auntie Dottie. I miss you . . .'*

'At least the letters I write in my *head* tell the truth,' Frances
muttered, in her own defence.

> *I want to tell you something, Auntie Dottie, something I don't
> understand. Ever since I got here I've felt I was on familiar
> territory, as familiar as Iona and the cottage and the air-raid
> shelter. I've heard of this happening to people when they first
> see London (it happened to Keith, or so he claimed), but it
> didn't happen to me. Now it has, only it's not foggy streets and
> crenellated buildings and statues of men on horseback that I
> recognise, but the smell of the woods in autumn, the cottages
> gloved into the earth, the closer, friendlier stars . . . This evening
> there's a thread of mist above the river, and I know what
> I'm seeing – those low hills in the distance; the dark stain,
> closer to, that is Manor Wood; the cluster of cottages around
> the green; the oaks, elms, chestnuts, limes – flares of colour in
> the dying light – is what generations of people before me have
> seen. On the other side of the river, smoke from the circle of
> chimneys rises above the mist, and the old spell is cast: what is*

*half seen so much more telling than what is revealed under a
mid-day sun.*

*I've been reading about the past, Auntie Dottie. There's a
museum in the town near here which specialises in local history.
A hundred years ago kettle broth would have been brewing
on those cottage fires. Tonight it's probably sausages, or fish
fingers. But everything else is the same: the larks serenading
the setting sun; the shorn fields; the tangled hedgerows; the
melancholy pigeons in the wood; this river; this bridge; this
person sitting . . .*

*I'm keeping a diary, Auntie Dottie. Did I tell you? I'm
becoming a regular pencil-pusher, what with letters to you, and
my drawings, and the diary I promised Dad I would keep . . .*

'And if you don't get a move on, lassie,' Auntie Dottie's voice
warned, 'you'll get it in the neck from Lady Mutton Dressed As
Lamb.'

'Goodness, child, where have you been? You're covered in
brambles.'
    'Sorry, Lady Christabel. My watch must have stopped.'
    'I thought you were packing.'
    'That won't take long.'
    'You do remember we're taking the morning train?'
    'Yes.'
    'I want to take you to Harvey Nichols. Get you something nice
to wear.'
    'Oh no really. You mean to the play? I can wear my velvet
trousers.'
    'Darling, they're positively *threadbare*.'
    'No one's going to notice.'
    'I will.'
    'You've just given me a rise, Lady Christabel. I can't accept
anything else.'
    Christabel's smile was indulgent. 'Dear Chloe,' she sighed,
'what am I going to do with you?'

6

As the train approached Paddington, and rows of terraced houses with washing flapping in cluttered back yards gave way to railway sheds and fuel towers and defaced advertisement hoardings, Frances observed, with relief, that her heartbeat was only marginally faster than normal. She'd anticipated varying degrees of panic. This was the place, after all, where she and Keith had started, and stopped, being lovers. This was the place where she'd deluded herself she could forget about drawing, and become an actress.

'What the hell did you want to go and do a thing like that for?' Keith had said, when she told him about her adventures at Brompton Rep.

'You'll never be a great actress, duckie,' the ghastly director had pronounced, on opening night. 'But you've got the looks, so you'll probably get on.'

'Guy sounds a real creep,' Keith had comforted.

'Dearest Keith,
'Do you remember the day we walked up the hill to see the "Madonna del Parto"? When I tried to explain why I was crying you got shirty with me. Had you made up your mind by then to ask me to marry you?'

'Dear Keith,
'I wonder if you got my last letter . . .'

'Wake up, Chloe! This is no time to be day-dreaming.'

Three quarters of an hour later Frances and Lady Christabel were installed in a suite at Claridge's.

'Will I meet Sir Oliver in London?' Frances had asked, on the way down. (She'd been told to say *up*, not down. 'You go *up* to London,' Lady C had explained. 'No matter where you start your journey from.' But Frances couldn't get it into her head. London was in the south. *Down*. Like New Zealand.)

'Good heavens, no,' was the answer. 'Oliver's the last person I want to see.'

'Between you'n me an' the gatepost,' Mrs Honeybone had advised, 'I'd forget about Sir Oliver. He's not popular in these parts.'

'You mean with Lady Christabel?'

'Came up 'ere to lick 'is wounds, see. After they sacked 'im from that Nazi rag of 'is.'

When Frances tried to find out more she was treated to a brief political speech. 'What do them city gents know anyways? Shuttin' off paths that 'ave been walked fer centuries. Interlopers, see. They never last long.'

I don't understand, Frances had come away protesting. It wasn't the first time she'd been baffled. A shared language, she'd realised soon after her arrival in England, could be a barrier to understanding.

'But my name's Frances,' she'd insisted, when Lady Christabel began calling her Chloe.

'And mine's Christabel,' her employer had answered. 'We can dispense with formalities now, can't we?'

Frances and Christabel stayed in London ten days. Tony Sandford's play was a success. Christabel went to see it every night. On the Saturday, four days after the play's opening, she didn't return to Claridge's. Next morning an anxious Frances received a phone call. It was Tony. Christabel was on her way back to the hotel now, he told her.

'You're not shocked, are you, Chloe?' Christabel asked, after she'd bathed and changed. 'Oh dear, I do believe you are.'

'It's none of my business.'

'Typical,' Christabel sighed. 'A nation of prudes.'

Sticks and stones, Frances thought darkly.

'Or is it that you'd like him for yourself?'

'Dear Keith,
   'Why haven't you answered my letters . . . ?'

'Dear Clarrie,
   'You're absolutely the most rotten brother anyone could have.
Not a single decent letter in five years!'

'Dear Mum . . .'

On their last day in London Christabel took Chole to the Savoy
for lunch. It wasn't often that she was troubled by conscience,
but she'd hardly seen her young companion all week, and felt
a twinge of guilt that she'd been having such a delicious time
while poor Chloe . . .

'How have you been filling in your days?' she asked, when
the salmon was served. 'Do tell. Of course I knew I didn't have
to worry about you. London is full of such lovely things to do.'

Chole hesitated over her fork, which was packed with just a
little too much food, Christabel observed. 'Oh you know,' she
said. 'Walking. That sort of thing. Sitting in coffee bars.'

'Doesn't sound very exciting.'

'I saw a Polish film at the Academy. *Knife in the Water.* It
was . . .'

'Not tempted to go shopping?'

'I tried on a blouse at Biba.'

'And?'

'The sleeves annoyed me. You couldn't do anything with all
that material ballooning around your wrists.'

Christabel laughed, though what she really felt was annoy-
ance. The girl was fobbing her off, wasn't she? 'You didn't do
anything cultural then?' she enquired, over the cheese. 'Pop into
an art gallery, for instance?'

Chloe, her mouth full, was silent. When she shook her head,
Christabel knew she was lying. 'You're not lonely, are you?' she
demanded peevishly.

'Lonely? No. Not at all.'

'You don't seem to have any friends.'

'Most of the people I know, or rather, knew, are expatriates. Here today, gone tomorrow.'

'Don't you know any English girls?'

'Not in London.'

'Oh come now . . .'

'I'm not lonely, Lady Christabel. Honestly. I'm perfectly happy.'

It wasn't a very satisfactory conversation. Christabel had hoped to ease her conscience, not just about leaving Chloe alone so much, but about the matter of the missing mail. Christabel had never intended to intercept Chloe's mail, but about three weeks ago, just when she was beginning to believe her prayers had been answered, a postcard arrived from New Zealand.

> 'Dear Fan,' it read, 'Well here I am, back in Godzown. Not a lot to report so far. Hanging out with the folks till something better comes along. I miss you. I wish you'd chuck that job of yours and come home. We don't have to get married if you don't want to. Just be together. Hell, I shouldn't be saying all this on a card, but you know me. World's worst letter-writer . . .'

A week later there was another.

> 'Dear Fan, Thanks for yours. I was really chuffed to get it. I've been thinking, Fan, and I reckon I was wrong to sound off about those art galleries you dragged me to. I miss all that now. And another thing, I reckon you're damn good at drawing. I reckon you should come back and go to art school. I've got my act together, you'll be pleased to know. I'll be starting at varsity next March. Doing Law. At Auckland. If you were here we could share a flat . . .'

The writer of these cards was called 'Keith'. He had very untidy hand-writing. No one bothers about postcards, Christabel had reassured herself, as she threw them into the fire.

Nothing else had been destroyed. The ones that arrived each week from 'Miss Dorothy McLean, 27 Paradise Drive, Oamaru', were untouched. As was the occasional envelope from a 'Mrs

Gail Winton, 2 Harbour View Cres., Maori Hill, Dunedin'.

'I'm sorry if I embarassed you about Randal,' Christabel said, as she was paying the bill. 'The last girl, June, she was different from you. She was . . .'

'Don't tell me she and Randal had a fling?'

Christabel laughed. It was going to be all right after all. Chloe would thank her one day. 'As a matter of fact, dear,' she confided, 'young June went too far altogether. That's why I had to get rid of her.'

Christabel and Frances returned to Little Chippingham to find the builders installed, Mrs Honeybone in a sulk, and Randal, deprived of his promised prize, adamant there would be no reduction in his fee.

Late that afternoon, Frances went for a walk. Rain was falling, dulling the sound of all but the pigeons, keening in the woods. The cold easterly wind, which accompanied the rain, had stripped what was left of the leaves on the trees.

It was almost dark as Frances emerged from Mill Lane and stepped on to the empty green. There was comfort to be had from the lights burning in the cottage windows, and the flapping sign outside The King's Arms, but Frances, shivering in her duffle coat, couldn't escape the feeling that she was a long way from home.

That night, drifting in and out of sleep, Frances went back to school.

7 ∫

'*Kaiwaka*,' Mrs Drummond, the headmistress intones. '*Kai* meaning food, *waka* meaning canoe. In other words, girls, a river that eats canoes. Which is why the punishment for anyone found within a hundred yards of its banks is expulsion.'

'If you go too far,' a voice from the back of the hall calls out, 'we'll have to get rid of you.'

'We're all very sorry for your trouble,' Mrs Drummond consoles, pausing in her march across the tennis court to place a hand on Frances's shoulder.

'So what was all that about?' Cindy Baker hisses over the net.

'Would someone else like to play?'

'Braemar College is one of the best schools in the country,' Uncle Iain encourages, on the journey from Dunedin. 'Your Oamaru cousins went there, as you know.'

'I still don't see why *I* have to go.'

'It's your mother's decision, dear.'

'But she's . . .'

'I know, I know.'

The car gathers speed. Tears through Paddington station, past the turn they should have taken, over the river, to Wanaka. *Stop*! the dreaming Frances pleads.

'No one wants you to be unhappy,' her father, disguised as Uncle Iain, murmurs.

'My mother does.'

'Frances McLean, what *are* we going to do with you?'

Where's your husband, Mrs Drummond? Is he that old man you live with?

Comin' up 'ere. Interlopin' . . .

'Look at me when I speak to you, Frances.'

'Sorry, Mrs Drummond.'

'These stories you tell. How many times is it now?'

'Don't know, Mrs Drummond.'

'Lost count, like me.'

'They're not lies. They're fairy tales.'

'So you keep saying.'

'My mother's out of hospital now, Mrs Drummond. I could go home . . .'

'Do you want to?'

Yes, say yes, the dreaming Frances urges. But Mrs Drummond doesn't hear.

'I've been having a talk with your aunt,' Mrs Drummond reveals. 'The one who's been looking after you. I'm sorry if this upsets you, Frances, but she agrees with me. You're much better off here.'

Then I'll get myself expelled!

'We have a name in common, did you know?' the Headmistress goes on chattily. 'My middle name's Isabel too.'

'Tell us a story, Fan,' a voice, not Cindy Baker's, calls through the darkness.

'Yeh, go on, Fan. Tell us the one about your uncle.'

Frances pulls the icy sheet up round her chin. The windows in the dormitory are kept open, even in winter. 'Fresh air never harmed anyone,' Matron's voice booms.

Through the open window, Frances can hear the river . . .

'Uncle Leonard,' she begins. 'My father's brother. He was living in China when the Japanese invaded. He tried to hide but they found him and put him in prison. They tortured him horribly. Filled his stomach up with water, pints and pints of it, then jumped on him.'

'Yuk!'

'I don't believe you!'

'That's sick.'

'He was a Colonel in the British Army. He knew all the secret plans. But he never betrayed anything. No matter what they did to him.'

'Did he die?'

'That's the amazing part. He escaped. It was a miracle. No one had ever got away from the Japanese before. He went on to become a famous war hero.'

'I've never heard of him.'

'That's because he's British, dumbo.'

'How come he's British and you're a New Zealander?'

'If you don't believe me, ask my brother. We used to play with his things when we were kids. Cloaks with dragons on them, and mah-jong sets, and paper kites. He was always sending us things.'

'Where does he live now?'

'Little Chippingham. It's in England. After the war he married a Chinese princess. Wang Ho her name was. But when the Communists came they had to leave. They live in a castle now. I'm going to visit them when I leave school. I'll probably stay there forever, and never come back.'

END OF YEAR REPORT
December 11, 1958.
Frances Isabel McLean.
Headmistress's comments

Frances has been with us four years now. Her academic work is satisfactory, though I have no doubt it could be a great deal better. Particularly disappointing is her performance in Art. That she has talent in this subject is not disputed, but her wayward personality seems to preclude serious attention to the syllabus. It had been hoped she would achieve high marks in the School Certificate examination but sadly this did not eventuate.

As for her other subjects, the reports bear a depressing similarity. 'Could do better.' 'Needs to concentrate.' 'Not working at full capacity.' I would urge those with responsibility for Frances to take very seriously her failure to realise her potential. Braemar College prides itself on the achievement of its pupils. There is still time for Frances to be one of our stars ...

'Don't reckon anyone's read it,' Clarence says to his sister. 'The envelope was still stuck down.'

'God knows what they did to your mother in that place,'

Auntie Dottie grumbles. She picks up the teapot, with its knitted cosy, and holds it high above the cups. 'I mean, what sort of cure is it when she doesn't know her own daughter?'

A cup floats into Frances's hand. A scone follows.

'You're seventeen years old,' Auntie Dottie says fiercely. 'I don't see why you shouldn't be told the truth.'

The tea has been made with water from the river. Specks of a drowned canoe float on its surface.

'She's never been officially certified, you see. Personally I think it's a disgrace, but that's not how others see it.'

> *Academic considerations aside, there is a more serious mattter to be raised. As everyone knows, Braemar College sets great store by its moral education. It is with very great regret I have to report that Frances, in matters of morality, has shown herself to be worryingly deficient . . .*

Frances creeps through the orchard, past the air raid shelter, up to the path that skirts the garden. When she reaches her mother's bedroom, she leans on the sill and peers inside. Everything is in its place. Her mother's bed against the wall closest to the window; her father's, with its matching green quilt, smooth as grass, on the other side of the room; the dressing table with its saucer full of hair pins, and her father's engraved silver hair brush; Great Uncle Leonard's Chinese scroll, hanging above the bricked-up fireplace . . . The one thing that's different is the pile of books on the bedside table. 'Always got your head in a book,' her mother's voice accuses. 1, 2, 3, 4 . . . Each time Frances tries to count them the number changes. She can't see the titles. Just a word here and there. *Regency* . . . something, by Georgette Heyer, and a novel by Sir Walter Scott.

> *But perhaps the most worrying aspect of all is Frances's indifference to the matter of what she is to do with her life. 'Something'll turn up,' she answered, when I questioned her recently on that very subject. A most inadequate response!*

Her mother jumps up from the bed; stares at the face in the window. 'Jezebel!' she shouts 'Jessie-bel!'

8

The crowd filing into the church was the largest Frances had seen in Little Chippingham. More than half the population of the village, she calculated, wrapped in scarves and heavy coats. Some, who'd walked through the snow, scraped their boots on the iron bar placed for that purpose by the church door. Others plonked umbrellas in a curious object, similar to the boot-scraper, but with two rows of neat holes, which the church guide book called an 'arrow-holder'. Frances tried to imagine the kind of congregation that would have brought their arrows to church, but the faces she conjured up looked more like American Indians than Little Chippingham's forebears.

'My regular flock numbers about eleven,' the Reverend Austin Tedcastle, greeting her at the door, admitted. 'But I'm glad to see *you* here.'

'Hey!' Alice Greenbank called, from across the churchyard. 'Wait for us.'

Frances waved enthusiastically. She'd been seeing a lot of Alice and Tina at the Manor lately. Lady Christabel had started entertaining again. Tomorrow, Christmas Day, she'd invited, in addition to Tony, the guest of honour, Farah Nusselbeh, a Lebanese businessman, and the new owner of nearby Withington Hall; Cara Boccolini, an Italian dress designer, whom Frances had mistaken on the phone for a cockney; Ralph Carpenter, an ex-priest, author of a highly-praised confessional novel; Sir Peregrine Cookham, a former Tory Cabinet minister; and Randal and Ginny Kane.

'Will your husband be coming?' Frances had risked asking.

'If he was, I'd have told you.'

The air inside the church, which has no electricity, was only marginally warmer than the sub-zero temperature outside. The furnace in the belfry had been stoked up since midday, but all that had succeeded in doing was melting the ice along the window sills. Candles burned on the altar, and from three hanging candelabra. The effect was to pierce, not dispel, the prevailing gloom.

'I shouldn't be here. I'm not an Anglican,' Frances whispered, as the organ creaked into action.

Alice pulled off her right glove, and blew on her fingers. 'What?' she said.

'I'm a Presbyterian.'

'What's that got to do with anything?'

'Holy Trinity Church, Little Chippingham, is one of the oldest surviving parish churches in England,' the guide book informed. 'It was Catholic, till Henry the Eighth's men came along with their cudgels and their swords . . .'

'My love and blessings to you at Christmas,' Auntie Dottie had written on her card. 'I'm so sorry I haven't got a cake away to you this year, dear. I haven't been well . . .'

'Hope you're OK,' Clarence had scribbled on his. 'Mum sends her love . . .'

Did her mother go to church still? Frances wondered. Did Clarence? What happened at Iona on Christmas Day? Were there celebrations? Iona was no longer owned by the McLean family. Deidre McLean had sold it five years ago. Frances had come home from her last term at school to find her mother and brother installed in the cottage, and Auntie Dottie camped at Uncle Iain's till a more permanent place could be found for her. Things were said about money. Deidre's long stay at Forest Hospital had emptied the coffers. But Frances knew that wasn't it. Iona hadn't been sold for money. It had been all but given away. 'Something has to be done to help refugees,' her mother had explained, hardly pausing for breath between the announcement of the sale, and her description of its cause. 'It's disgraceful how little we're doing to help those poor Hungarians.'

'Who lives at Iona now?' Frances had asked her brother in one of her unanswered letters. It was run as a refugee centre, but who, in 1964, were New Zealand's refugees? The Hungarian exodus had been stemmed years ago.

'Best not to dwell on it,' Auntie Dottie had written. 'What's past is past.'

'Almighty God, who hast given us thy only begotten Son, to take our nature upon him . . .'

The Reverend Tedcastle had the melodious voice of the professional priest. Frances let the words drift over her head. She was tired enough, from running round after Christabel, to assent to anything. The baby born in a stable; the three wise men; the poverty, power, glory . . .

'I'm to give you this apparently,' her mother had said, bringing the subject of Iona and its sale firmly to a close. 'Seems my husband had something to say to you.'

'What is it?'

'What does it look like?'

'It says I'm to open it on my eighteenth birthday.'

Her mother turned away irritably. 'You weren't here on your eighteenth birthday,' she said.

The organ groaned into life again. There was a rustling of pages, then the congregation, coughing and shuffling, rose to its feet.

> '"As with gladness men of old,
> Did the guiding star behold . . ."'

The strength and sweetness of the singing startled Frances. Every evening for the last week carol singers had patrolled the village, warming their voices with wine and mince pies, growing merrier with each stop on the way. Frances had been sent to 'deal with them' when they were heard approaching the Manor. 'Here,' Christabel had instructed, handing her a coin. 'God knows what they're collecting for. Themselves, I should imagine.' Frances had gone to the door and found herself surrounded by familiar faces: George Honeybone; Silas Moss, the publican; Mrs Franklin, who kept the store; Mrs Brady, the post mistress; Alice and Tina . . .

> '"As they offered gifts most rare
> At they cradle rude and bare . . ."'

For most of November Christabel had been in a foul mood. Tony's play was going to run till Christmas. With alterations to be supervised at the Manor that meant Christabel would hardly see him. As if that wasn't enough, an incriminating photo had appeared in *The Times*. 'Actor of the Year Squires Royalty', the caption read.

'She's only minor royalty,' Frances pointed out, when Christabel grew hysterical.

'Are you blind?' Christabel shrieked. 'Look at her! She's young. Barely out of her teens. And the only pretty face that family has ever produced.'

> '"In the heavenly country bright
> Need they no created light . . ."'

But the storm had passed.

'Poor boy,' Christabel cooed, when Tony agreed to come for Christmas. 'She practically threw herself at him. What could he do?'

> '"Thou its light, its joy, its crown,
> Thou its sun which goes not down . . ."'

Alice, beside Frances, was singing heartily. Tina, next to Alice, seemed uncertain of the words. There were other Greenbanks in the church. Frances had no trouble identifying them: stocky of build, with thick, mud-coloured hair, and eyes with a tendency to water. The only Greenbank who didn't fit this pattern was Tina. Her difference from the clan – she was pale and thin, with long, flyaway hair – was a source of continuing speculation in the village.

'"And there were shepherds in the same country abiding in the field, and keeping watch by night over their flock . . ."'

'And you think those stories you read are real, do you?' This time her mother's voice came, not from her memory, but from the back of the church. Frances glanced nervously over her shoulder. Mrs Brady, in the pew behind, frowned at her.

'You know they're real,' Frances answered her mother. 'You read them too.'

'But my story doesn't have an ending. It goes on happening, over and over.'

'"And all that heard it wondered at the things which were spoken unto them by the shepherds."' The vicar closed the bible, and beamed at his congregation. 'Now,' he said, in his commonplace voice. 'Time to light our candles.'

Frances glanced at Alice, who was rummaging in her handbag. She hadn't realised she was supposed to bring a candle. She twisted her head in the other direction. A current of warm air fingered her face. The furnace was doing its job at last.

Suddenly there was a hiss of sound from the back of the church, followed by a tiny explosion of yellow light. Frances, squinting into the darkness, was back in the air raid shelter, lighting her stolen candle. Only this was better. Here a dozen candles burned, no, twenty, fifty! Till all she could see were smiling, silvered faces, and the dance of shadows on bare church walls.

She groped for a handkerchief. She didn't want to cry. Around her were the descendants of the men who'd brought their arrows to this church: Alice and her sister; Silas Moss and his unruly brood; George and Ruby Honeybone; Mrs Brady . . . People she was beginning to think of as friends.

'What the heck's this got to do with you, Fan?' Keith's voice challenged. 'You'll always be an interloper. Singing English Hallelujahs on cold Christmas Eves won't change anything.'

But Keith hadn't always been so mocking. Driving in Greece, rounding a perilous corner, he'd been as moved as she was by the sight that greeted them: a scarred hillside swathed with sunflowers – ripples of gold in the bleached landscape of the south.

'"We do not presume to come to this thy table, O merciful Lord . . ."'

'If you've got any sense,' her mother hissed, from the back of the church, 'you'll forget all about the past.'

9

Christmas dinner at the Manor began at five o'clock. Christabel was seated at the head of the table, with Tony next to her. Frances, despite her protests, had been put next to Randal Kane.

'My advice to you, Nusselbeh,' Randal said, as the goose was being carved, 'is to buy up everything you see round here. Withington Hall was a good move, but if you want to make real money you should get your hands on the lesser pieces of property. Cottages, barns, chapels, schools, they're all coming on the market. The next ten years will see a mass exodus of the middle classes from London, take my word for it. That's when you'll make your killing.'

'I'd prefer it if you'd call me Farah,' Mr Nusselbeh responded coldly. 'The use of the surname is a particular insult in my culture.'

'Beg pardon,' Randal smirked. 'Live and learn.'

But it was Sir Peregrine Cookham who dominated the conversation. 'Personally,' he proclaimed, during the pause between the goose and the pudding, 'I find this mania for independence tragic. With elements of comedy, of course. Those ceremonies we've all seen on television. Down with the old flag, up with the new. As pieces of theatre they come straight out of the tragi-comic tradition. What do you say, Sandford? I've got a point, haven't I?'

Tony stretched his long arms above his head. 'Depends how you look at it,' he said, in the languid voice of one who'd already wined and dined too well. 'I've no doubt, if I was a Zambian, or a Maltese, I'd be deeply moved at the sight of my own flag flying in place of the Union Jack. It wouldn't be tragedy, and it certainly wouldn't be comedy. Celebration is the word I'd choose. Capital C. Ask Frances. She's a colonial.'

'Wonderful. Magical,' Ralph Carpenter declared, when Frances didn't respond. Alice had just put a match to the brandy-soaked pudding. 'I'll have to fast for a week to atone.'

'Welcome to the world,' Randal quipped sourly.

'Your trouble, Sandford,' Sir Peregrine complained, returning to his original theme, 'is that you take the short view. Letting people manage their own affairs, freeing them from the *imperial yoke*, it's the new dogma, mouthed by every Tom, Dick and Jomo Kenyatta, and not worth a twopenny damn. Take my word for it. There won't be any democracy in those countries in five years time.'

'What would you suggest then?' Tony asked. 'The British Empire forever?'

'I told you. You have to take the long view. Now if *we* were still the Government . . .'

'The long view?' Randal interrupted. 'And what, exactly, is that?' His hand, which had been searching for Frances's knee, closed around his empty glass. 'Over here,' he shouted to Alice, whose arms were full of dirty plates.

'You must all come to Beirut,' Farah Nusselbeh said, in the pause which followed. 'We are many peoples there, and many faiths. Yet we live in peace.'

'Beirut,' Cara Boccolini mused. 'Now what 'ave I been 'earing . . .'

'Cyprus,' Randal interjected drunkenly. 'That was the place to go. Before everyone started shooting.'

'To answer your question, Mr Kane,' Sir Peregrine said, projecting his voice over the ruin of the Christmas pudding, the ravaged mounds of brandy butter, and the collapsed castles of whipped cream, 'I foresee the day when the world is broken up like a jigsaw into a thousand tiny nations, each warring with its neighbour for ascendancy. I take it, sir, you're a supporter of Mr Wilson and his companions from the Oxford Union . . .'

Randal made a noise in his throat, but any protest he might have been going to make was cut short.

'No doubt you're a convert to the religion of "Small is

Beautiful",' Sir Peregrine sailed on. 'And everything else that goes with that dangerous little nursery rhyme. You'd have workers take over their bankrupt factories, just as Tony here would have us clap our hands in approval of the spread of tribalism. The British Commonwealth, Mr Kane, is not an organisation committed to ascendancy over anyone. It's a club, if you like, with rules governing membership that are so relaxed they'd never be tolerated in any other organisation. What the Commonwealth enshrines are the principles of free association, mutual respect, and, since we must have the word, *democracy*.'

His speech at an end, Sir Peregrine took a red spotted handkerchief from his pocket, and mopped his brow. Frances took advantage of the hiatus in conversation to move out of the reach of Randal.

'Actually I agree with Sir Peregrine,' Ralph Carpenter said. 'It would be a sad thing if the Commonwealth broke up.'

'Who said anything about a break-up?' Christabel trilled. 'I don't see Canada going out on its own. Or New Zealand. You'll frighten my Chloe if you talk like that.'

10

26 December 1964

This has been my fifth Christmas away from home. There was the one at sea, the two in London (the second spent working all day as a waitress), the fairy tale Christmas in Assisi with Keith, and now this one – the midnight service, the walk after breakfast through the woods, the feast at night. I don't know whether Christabel's guests are enjoying themselves or not. I know Ginny Kane isn't.

Something happened today which has left me in a bad temper. A paddy, my father would call it, though as it's myself I'm furious with, he'd probably say I had the black dog at my back.

I'd managed to escape Christabel for a couple of hours and go down to the river. It was too cold to draw properly – my fingers were sausages – but I wanted to capture the wintry look of the river, with its frosted banks and ice-cold stones. I thought I might see the man in the long overcoat again, but I guess it was too cold for him.

I'd been drawing for about an hour when who should appear on the path but Tony Sandford. My first thought was that Christabel had sent him. She and I had had a row. Our first, though we've had our differences before. The row was about Randal Kane. He's been a sore point between us in the past, but since London the subject has been more or less dropped. Till today that is.

What happened was this. Randal tried to kiss me under one of the sprigs of mistletoe Christabel has festooned about the place. When he didn't succeed, he got angry and grabbed me. I managed to get away, and took refuge with Mrs Honeybone in the kitchen. Actually I thought the whole thing was rather funny. A few minutes later a furious Christabel burst in, and tore strips.

'What do you expect me to do?' I answered her back. 'Go to bed with him?'

I could see Mrs Honeybone's face, half buried in her apron, getting redder by the second.

'*You could do worse!*' *Christabel snapped.*

In the end we sort of made peace, but I wouldn't have put it past her to despatch Tony to deliver a further telling-off. '*Be nice to him, Chloe, that's all she's asking. Flirt a little . . .*'

But Tony hadn't come about Randal at all.

'*Ah ha,*' *he greeted.* '*So this is where you go.*'

I tried to hide my sketchbook, but I didn't move quickly enough. '*Let me see,*' *he commanded.*

'*It's nothing,*' *I hedged.*

'*Come on, Fanny. Show your Uncle Tony.*'

At least he didn't call me Chloe. I was grateful for that.

I don't know why I handed it over to him. It wasn't because he insisted. There must be twenty sketches in that book. Most are of the river and the bridge, but there are a few portraits, and a couple of the view down to the summer house from my bedroom window.

He was a long time looking at them. When, eventually, he spoke, it wasn't, at first, about the drawings.

'*Why do you let her treat you the way she does, Fanny? Don't you realise what she's doing?*'

'*Who? What are you talking about?*'

'*You know perfectly well.*'

'*You seem to like her well enough,*' *I reminded him tartly.*

'*The last girl, June, she was a New Zealander too.*'

'*That's hardly surprising. Since the job was advertised in New Zealand House.*'

'*She was dismissed because she didn't fit into Christabel's scheme of things.*'

'*And I do? Is that what you're saying?*'

'*You're everything she wants. Young, pretty, pliable . . .*'

'*What?*'

'*I've watched you, Fanny. You think you're re-inventing yourself, but you're not. She's inventing you. You're becoming her creature.*'

That made me so wild I actually snatched the sketchbook back from him. At which point he said something like, '*I'm not much of a person, Fanny, a fraud in fact. But occasionally, just occasionally, I get the chance to do a good deed.*' *When I didn't comment, he informed me, illustrating his point I suppose, that Sandford was not his real name.*

'*You mean it's your professional name?*' *I said.*

'*Hmm . . .*'

'*There's nothing wrong with that.*'

The conversation seemed to founder then, but it picked up, at least for me, when he got back to the subject of my drawings.

'They're good,' he said. 'You have talent. I want you to let me borrow them for a while.'

'What for?'

'I want to show them to somebody.'

'But they're only sketches.'

'That doesn't matter.'

Which was when, acting on impulse, I handed the book back to him. I regret it now. Bitterly. Those sketches aren't good at all. They were a record, that's all. A way of fixing things in my mind.

Tony tucked the book inside his coat, and went on talking as if nothing had happened. It was the longest conversation I'd ever had with him.

'Christabel and I . . .' he began, pulling the fur collar of his coat up around his ears.

'It's none of my business,' I said quickly.

'We suit each other,' he went on, ignoring me. 'For the time being anyway. We're both selfish. We couldn't possibly cope with ordinary life. Children. That sort of thing.'

'How do you know? How do you know about anything if you haven't tried?'

'Is that what they teach you Down Under?'

I hate it when people say things like that. I can never think of a reply.

'We're alike, you see. Neither of us can stand living in the real world.'

There were things I could have said about that, but I didn't. I was still smarting from his jibe. When it seemed he too had reached a halt, I decided it was time to go back.

'I'll walk with you,' he volunteered.

I didn't think that was a good idea at all. If Christabel saw us there was no knowing how she'd react. She's as changeable as a weather vane, that woman. But Tony, when I voiced my reservations, just laughed.

'I've been lucky,' he told me, as we crossed the bridge. 'This country's been good to me.'

I half expected him to start singing Rule Britannia. Except that he wasn't that sort of Englishman, the Peregrine Cookham sort. He was better than that.

'Is that how artists succeed then?' I couldn't help asking. 'By luck?'

'You have to have a dollop of talent, I suppose,' he answered. 'Though in my business you can get by without even that.'

I'm glad I resisted the temptation to tell him about my own brief career on the stage.

'All artists are liars,' he announced, as we reached the green. 'And actors are the worst liars of the lot.'

The way he said it, with his jaw clenched, made me smile. There are lies, and lies, I wanted to argue.

'We speak someone else's lines. We wear borrowed robes. We pretend emotions we either don't feel at all, or feel only now and again, in rehearsal.'

'You feel things,' I protested. 'You got pretty worked up at dinner yesterday.'

'Zeitgeist, my dear. Spirit of the times. An expression of the man I'd like to be, not the man I am.'

When we reached the Manor gate he did an entirely unexpected thing. He kissed me. Not lunging, like Randal the Rat, but politely, reverently almost, on my hand first, then on each cheek. He smelt of fur and wood smoke.

'If you don't claim your own story, Fanny,' he said, 'you'll become part of someone else's. Believe me. I know what I'm talking about.'

He couldn't have said anything that would disconcert me more.

'You know why you're so perfect for her, don't you?' he challenged, nodding at the blaze of lights ahead of us. 'It's not your looks, or your figure, or your lovely hair. Those things can be bought in the market place. No, what make you irresistible is your willingness to please.'

The diary dropped to the floor. Frances's hand trailed after it, but the effort required to recover it was too great. As her breathing deepened, a shadowy figure rose from the foot of the bed. 'I'm sorry,' the apparition said, in a voice thick with tears. 'They've taken him away.'

'But you're not my mother,' the dreaming Frances protested. 'My mother never cries.'

11

Frances picks her way gingerly down the path, brushing sticky leaves from her coat, placing her feet carefully to avoid the worst of the mud. *Kai . . . waka*. The river that eats canoes . . .

All artists are liars.

There are lies and LIES.

'What you see around you, girls, is part of our history. Braemar College was not always a school. Nor was the land you see before you the semi-desert it is today. The oldest part of the school, the present boarding house, was erected when this whole valley was a sea of tents and jerry-built shacks. Close your eyes and try to picture it. See the men on horseback, galloping down the muddy main street. See the figures in the distance crouched along the edge of the river. See the gambling den with its pig-tailed owner standing in the doorway. See the lean-to shops with their bundles of boots and shovels, and their over-priced bags of flour. See the little makeshift theatre, with its programme of magic and music hall, and a concert by Sydney's leading soprano. Observe the variety of the population – Scots, Irish, American, Australian, German, Scandinavian, Chinese . . .'

The bush is behind her now. Looking back Frances can see the school, perched on top of the cliff. The path she's just scrambled down is lost in a tangle of fern and manuka. Ahead of her is open land: stony, sandy, tufted with scrub. Her heart beats wildly.

'What happened to the people who were here before the gold diggers came?'

'What people would that be, Frances?'

'The Maoris.'

Mrs Drummond looks unhappy for a moment; then she

smiles. 'Oh there weren't many of them,' she says. 'We're too far south.'

By the time Frances reaches the river she's out of breath. She sinks to her knees, and stares at the swirling white water. Where did that weed come from? she wonders. It wasn't there before.

She lifts her head, and sees a man in a long overcoat climb into a bucket attached to a thick black wire, strung high across the water.

'It's a flying fox,' a voice that could be her father's informs her. 'From the mining days.'

'We held hands along the riverbank . . .'

Frances closes her eyes. When she opens them, both flying fox and man have disappeared.

She pulls a sketchbook from her coat. She'll never be able to draw. Her fingers are swollen like sausages. She sketches two faces, one Maori, one Pakeha. But when she looks at the page again it's George Honeybone and Tony Sandford who stare back at her.

She tears the page out, and tosses it into the river. Her stomach heaves. There's no time. The drawings must be finished by the end of the day.

'Frances McLean, what are you going to do with your life?' Mrs Drummond shouts from the other side of the river.

Frances draws a canoe, laden with greenstone. A figure wrapped in a feather cloak stands at the prow. *Fanciful in the extreme,* a red pen scrawls across the page. Frances looks up into the scornful eyes of Miss McLure, her art teacher. *This man looks as if he's escaped from an asylum!*

'You know there's evil in the world when you see that river.'

A second page follows the first.

Now the pencil has a life of its own. Iona materialises on the page, faces staring from the windows. A paddock bordered by a macrocarpa hedge follows. A horse gallops towards the open gate.

'Flashing like the white of an eye . . .' The voice bounces off the rocks that jut above the surface of the water.

Another horse joins the first, then another, and another. Together, they thunder across the page.

No, the dreaming Frances screams. *Not that way. That's the way to the river.*

'So this is where you go,' Mrs Drummond hisses in her ear. She points an accusing finger at the open sketchbook. 'Show me!' she commands.

'I want to go home.'

'You can't. You have no home to go to.'

'Where's your husband, Mrs Drummond?'

'My husband is no business of yours. Now, show me!'

'But they're not finished . . .'

Mrs Drummond laughs. 'They'll never be finished, will they, Frances?'

12

With the departure, on the second of January, of the last of Christabel's guests, an uneasy silence, punctuated by the cries of pigeons, and the occasional, low-flying military plane, descended on Little Chippingham Manor. The snow, which had fallen over the last days of December, had begun to melt, leaving in its wake, muddy fields and treacherous paths and air pungent with wood-smoke. Frances's diary remained unopened. As did her sketchbook. Like the world around her she was in limbo; waiting for a miracle she was afraid to believe in.

Towards the end of the month Christabel informed Frances they would be going to London again in early February. 'Tony wants to take us to an exhibition,' she said. 'A compatriot of yours apparently.'

Frances tried hard to keep her voice casual. There'd been no word from Tony since he left. For all she knew he could have lost her book of sketches.

'It's at the Vronsky Gallery in Cork Street.'

'Does Tony know about art then?'

'Tony Sandford,' Christabel said, 'is the most civilised man I know.'

'*Dear Keith,* (The letter would never be written of course. All that had stopped when nothing came from him at Christmas.) '*You'll be pleased to know I've paid off my debts. Better than that, I've started saving. Christabel has been very generous. I've had two pay rises since I started working for her . . .*'

4 February 1965

I've decided to try and keep this up again. I can't draw, or rather I don't want to, so this is to stop me going completely bonkers.

I wish Tony would ring. Apart from everything else, I'd like to tell him he was wrong about Christabel. She's been really nice to me since Christmas. When I first got here she was always saying she wanted me to be like one of the family, which didn't feel right at all. I mean, how can you describe one woman and an absent husband as a family?

Lately though she's been treating me more as a friend, which feels a whole lot better. Like the day we went into Oxford. I really enjoyed that. We did a bit of shopping, and I went to the Ashmolean while Christabel was getting her hair cut. Then, over lunch, she told me about her parents. Her father was in the Colonial Service in India. He was killed in the civil war there.

'It was terrible,' she said. 'I've never really recovered from it. We were so close. I was an only child, you see.'

When I asked about her mother she told me she died soon after, of a broken heart. 'Now, when I think of Mummy and Daddy, I think of them as victims of that hideous War of Independence.'

I've been tempted, on a number of occasions since that day, to tell her the truth about myself. Perhaps, if she comes clean about her husband, I'll have to. One good turn deserves another, as Auntie Dottie would say.

The day before her departure for London, Frances overheard a conversation in the post office. It concerned, she realised towards its end, her mysterious companion on the riverbank.

Iris Brady, the post mistress, was party to most things that went on in the village. In the fug of her overheated wooden shed she heard who was born and who had died long before anyone else. Love affairs, quarrels, business transactions, arrivals, departures – these were what kept her in business.

'Reckon 'e were asleep when the brain basket went round,' Iris was complaining to Flo Moss, the publican's wife, as Frances walked in.

Iris and Flo were best friends. People referred to them as Laurel and Hardy. Iris was thin and wore her hair in tight waves. Flo was fat and untidy.

'What can ya expect?' Flo agreed. ''E's German.'

'Ain't natural the way 'e carries on. Down there in all weathers.'

'Silas said 'e were mutterin'. Some foreign curse or other.'

'Ya can hardly blame 'is wife, can ya? She musta been sore pressed to run off like that.'

'Without the boy though. I can't condone that. Not leavin' a child.'

'Yes, well, and look where that ended.' Iris Brady peered over the top of her spectacles. 'Come fer ya stamps, have ya?' she enquired of Frances.

'It's all right,' Frances answered. 'I'm not in a hurry.'

'Shouldn't do nuthin' in a hurry 'cept catchin' fleas,' Flo Moss giggled.

Iris gave her friend a severe look. 'Ya wouldn't 'ave 'ad much to do with the war out your way, I s'pose,' she said, addressing Frances again.

'Well . . .' Frances cleared her throat. Should she tell them about the air raid shelter, and Cousin Philip, who was in the habit of standing on street corners, warning of impending disasters?

'Mind you, we were grateful for the food parcels.'

'What Mrs Brady means,' Flo Moss said, with a quick, corrective glance at her friend, 'is that ya wouldn't 'ave 'ad prisoners-of-war dumped on ya, like us.'

'No, I don't think so.'

'We had 'em 'ere, by the truckload. Workin' in the fields. They were sent back when it was over. All except him. He stayed.'

'Who?'

'Rolf Reichardt. Lives in the caravan up on the common. Ya must 'ave seen 'im.'

'I've noticed a man on the riverbank,' Frances said cautiously.

'That'd be him,' Iris Brady confirmed.

In her diary that night Frances wrote,

> 'What is it about some stories that makes you feel they've happened to you? The story Christabel told me about her parents didn't affect me like that. But the one I heard today, about Mr Reichardt, was familiar in a way I can't account for. As if it had happened to me in another life.
>
> Is that what I'm trying to do in my drawings? Reclaim the lost stories?'

13

'Well now, lassie, what's all this I hear about you running away?'

The man sitting opposite her, calmly pouring tea, is Mrs Drummond's husband.

Frances turns to the window. Cindy Baker's face is pressed to the glass. 'You see,' Frances mouths, 'he does exist.'

'You gave my Dulcie a fine old fright, you know.'

Dulcie. She balances the word on her tongue. It has a nice feel. Dulcie and *Archibald*.

Why are you so old, Mr Drummond?

'Do you want to talk about it?' the old man asks.

'Archibald James Drummond Esquire,' Frances reads on a discarded envelope.

'Because you see, there's a reason why that river's out of bounds. If you knew it I think you might feel a wee bit ashamed. Frightening people's not a very nice thing to do, Frances.'

Her lips are glued together. Her bottom is glued to the chair on which she's sitting. Her feet are glued to the floor.

'Your father,' Mr Drummond says. 'I knew of him, though we never met. A fine man by all accounts. You must miss him.'

Frances presses her hands down on the arms of the chair. Tries, without success, to haul herself up.

'I lived in Dunedin for nearly twenty years. Opoho. I had a wee shop there. Perhaps you know it? 'Nellie's Fruitery'? . . . Och well, it's probably got a different name now. It was a long time ago.'

'If my mother won't have me I can go to my Auntie Dottie,' Frances's unglued lips burble.

But Mr Drummond isn't listening. 'I'm going to tell you a story,' he says. 'It's about the river.'

Frances watches his mouth. His lips make a round O, like those figures at the fair, inviting passers-by to throw ping-pong balls. He's talking about his wife; how they were neighbours once . . . He's talking about drowned babies . . .

I can't condone that. Not drownin' a child.

Now he's a gargoyle, come to life. He's perched above the door of Little Chippingham's church, telling his story.

Frances looks back to the window. When did it get dark? A branch scratches the glass. She can hear pigeons moaning.

'When I married Dulcie,' Mr Drummond says, 'I didn't know whether she knew the story or not. Her mother, Pearse Byrne's second wife, was – is – a formidable woman. All mention of the tragedy was banned. Even my daughter, Nellie, who was by way of being a friend of hers, wasn't allowed to speak of it.'

Laurel and Hardy. Nellie and . . .

Frances's dreaming hand twitches. She stares at Mr Drummond, at his rounded mouth. The mouth closes, and she sees that he's not Mr Drummond at all but a soldier, sleeping in a Tuscan garden. Behind him, looming over him, stands the resurrected Christ. *Piero*, she whispers, shielding her face from Keith's watchful eye, *I love you.*

'But she did know,' the voice that won't be silenced drones on. 'She found their graves, hidden, unmarked, at the back of the church where her mother and father were married.'

'If only I could read the words . . .'

No! Frances's head tosses wildly on the pillow. *Not that voice.*

'People remembered,' Mr Drummond asserts. 'People do, you know.'

'Don't you understand anything?' Deidre McLean accuses. 'The words aren't written on stone. Or on your silly pieces of paper. They're written on the water.'

14

There was a sense of déjà vu, travelling with Lady Christabel to London, settling into the same suite at Claridge's, waiting for Tony to call.

The frustration Frances felt, though its cause was different, was shared by Christabel. 'Tony's being very mysterious,' she complained, as they unpacked. 'What is this Vronsky Gallery anyway?'

'It's very avant-garde,' Frances told her.

'That's what I was afraid of.'

London, in late February, was a dreary place. Frances's arms ached from the constant collisions with other pedestrians, bowed against the slanting rain. When, after two days, Tony still hadn't called her, Frances concluded there was nothing to hope for anyway. The exhibition had been a ploy to get Christabel to London, nothing more.

On the third day Tony phoned to tell her to be at the gallery at five pm the following evening. Frances tried to keep him on the line, but he cut her short with the words, 'Just be there, OK? And don't be late.'

'Who is this artist anyway?' Christabel pouted, when Frances passed on the message. 'Tony refuses to talk about him. Have you heard of him?'

'No.'

'All this fuss over a New Zealander.'

In the taxi on the way to the gallery Christabel suddenly grabbed Frances's hand, and said, 'You must never go back, Chloe. It would be the greatest mistake you could make.'

'Go back where?'

'To New Zealand.'

But Christabel's mood changed when she saw the Vronsky Gallery. Cork Street was a fashionable address and judging by the people emerging from the cars pulling up outside, this particular venue something of a magnet. 'Oh look,' she said, grabbing Frances's hand again. 'Isn't that Senator Wiseman? You know. The one who's supposed to have had an affair with Audrey Hepburn . . . Oh, and there's Farah Nusselbeh . . .'

The gallery was hot and crowded. Frances, pushing her way through the press of people in smart blazers and Mary Quant dresses, made straight for the paintings. She couldn't understand how people could stand about talking and drinking when all around them were images of such startling intensity they pulled at her eyes, dragging her into their web. In the group of oils ahead of her, paint seemed to have been literally thrown at the canvas.

Closer to, the distorted images took on more human shape. There were elements of the grotesque that reminded Frances of Edvard Munch, but there was none of Munch's savagery. An intense meditation on the human face, on one particular human face, was what she concluded she was looking at.

'Like them, do you?' a familiar voice enquired.

Frances turned to smile briefly at Tony. She'd forgotten her disappointment. He'd invited her here, that was all that mattered. 'Why have I never heard of him before?' she said.

'He lives in Cornwall. Keeps himself pretty much to himself. But he's no new boy. This is a retrospective, remember.'

'I used to haunt places like this when I lived in London.'

Tony's smile was teasing. He glanced over his shoulder. Frances, following his gaze, saw that Christabel was deep in conversation with Mr Nusselbeh. Next to her a man with a notebook and pencil was peering at a landscape. Later Frances would identify that painting as part of Louis de la Tour's Cornish series. But for the moment all she noticed was how few people were really looking.

'Who is she?' Frances asked, drawing Tony's attention back to the oils.

'A model, I expect. Doesn't it say?'

Frances was reluctant to look away again. Casting her eye

quickly down the printed Notes she read, 'When you've lost someone and you try to see them again in your imagination, you can only ever capture part of the face. The whole eludes you. What I've tried to do in these paintings is re-create that whole from the pieces, not as this person was, or is, but as the image I carry inside me.'

'Hey, why don't I introduce you?' Tony indicated a knot of people in the centre of the room. 'He should remember me. We met at a dinner party.'

'Which one is he?'

'The untidy one. With the shock of hair. They say it went white when he was in his twenties. Something to do with the war.'

'I wonder what part of New Zealand he's from.'

'Why don't you ask him?'

Frances looked back at the paintings. There was one called 'Quarrel', which she could hardly bear to look at. The mouth had been painted in heavy impasto. She could hear the words it was shouting: 'Jezebel! Jessie . . . bel!'

'Frances McLean, Louis de la Tour.' The introductions were effected so speedily Frances had no time to worry about what to say.

'A fellow countrywoman of yours,' Tony explained.

Louis de la Tour smiled. 'You like my stuff,' he said. 'Thank you. I suspect you're the only person here who's taking them seriously.'

'They're marvellous. Those oils' – she gestured over her shoulder – 'I've never seen anything so . . .' She'd been going to say 'painful', but it wasn't what she meant.

Louis turned to whisper something to the woman at his side. She replied with a quick, intimate smile.

'I mean,' Frances rushed on, 'they're not like anything anyone else is doing. The later Expressionists, a bit, but then others' – she pointed again – 'that one, for instance, what's it called, "Picnic"? It has echoes of Matisse.'

'You're an artist yourself,' Louis said.

'Not really.'

'You see like one.'

The woman leaned forward. 'Darling, we should circulate,' she murmured.

Louis held out his hand. 'Nice meeting you, Frances,' he said.

'Well?' Tony queried, when Louis de la Tour had melted back into the room. 'What did you think?'

'Is that his wife?' Frances asked.

'Good heavens, no. He's never married. Not the type.'

'I forgot to ask him where he was from.'

Christabel, left in the lurch by Farah Nusselbeh, scanned the room for a familiar face. Where *was* Chloe? She paid her to be a companion, didn't she? When she spotted the girl talking to Tony she felt a spurt of rage. Tony was squiring *her*, not Chloe.

'Tony!' she called, as she approached.

'Ah . . . my Cleopatra.'

'Your *neglected* Cleopatra,' she complained.

'What do you think?' Chloe asked eagerly. 'Aren't they marvellous?'

Christabel permitted herself a long sigh. The Arab had been no use at all. Not one invitation to Withington Hall, and his conversation tonight confined to the risk involved in investing in modern art. 'I prefer something I can recognise,' she said sourly.

Tony's laugh was the one she liked to think of as reserved for her. He laughed like that sometimes when they were making love. She flashed him an intimate smile, which he returned.

'Would you excuse us, love?' Tony said, smiling at Frances. 'There's something I want to talk to Christabel about.'

With Chloe out of the way, Christabel's anger evaporated. Tony was the best looking man in the room, and he was *hers*. She'd seen the looks on people's faces. He was starting to be recognised. This television series he was working on would make him a household name. She linked her arm in his and smiled possessively up at him.

'Come outside a minute,' Tony said.

Christabel imagined he wanted to kiss her, but when they stepped through the doors on to the wet pavement, all he did was put a protective arm around her. Christabel, fashionably dressed in mini skirt and high boots, shivered.

'I want to talk to you about Frances,' Tony said.

Christabel's spine stiffened. She'd had arguments with Tony before about Chloe's name. She couldn't understand why he was so against the change.

'Did you know she draws?' he asked.

'What of it?'

'You did know?'

('I reckon you're damn good at drawing . . .') 'A hunch, that's all,' she said. (There'd been another communication at Christmas. She'd recognised the writing. Not a card this time, but a letter.)

'She's good,' Tony said. 'Bloody good. I've been showing her stuff to the people at the Slade.'

'*What*?'

'They agree with me. They want to offer her a place. She'll have to be interviewed of course. Go through the formalities. But they don't anticipate any problems.'

Christabel waited till she could trust herself to speak. Then she said, 'Have you told *her* this?'

'I wanted to talk to you first.'

'I don't understand,' Christabel said icily. She was shivering again, but it wasn't from the cold. 'How did *you* come to be involved?'

Tony grinned. He didn't seem to have the faintest idea how enraged she was. 'It was pure chance,' he said. 'I stumbled across her by the river. Boxing Day I think it was. She was down there sketching.'

'So that's where she goes. Sly little minx.'

'You're cold. We should go back in.'

'I'm not cold. I'm *furious*.'

'I thought you'd be pleased. You're always telling me how much you hope she'll stay in England.'

'That's not the point.'

'Isn't it?'

'You don't know anything about it.'

'I know what I see, Christabel. Forgive me for saying this, but what I see is a woman terrified of being left on her own.'

'How dare you say such a thing! Plotting with Chloe behind my back . . .'

'No one's been plotting.'

'It's June all over again, isn't it? Don't try and deny it. I know she made a play for you.'

Tony's lips tightened, drawing an ugly line across his face. 'I hardly even knew her,' he said coldly. 'I'd only just met *you*, if you remember.'

'I won't let you take her away from me,' Christabel said, in the high, thin voice Tony had come to dislike. 'You can pull all the tricks you like.'

'The Slade is not a trick, Christabel.'

'Chloe is mine, forever and ever.'

That night, in her dreams, Louis de la Tour takes Frances by the hand, and leads her to the door of the Slade. They knock. Mrs Drummond answers. She beckons them to follow her. They walk in single file down a long narrow passage. There's a sound of water running. When Frances turns to ask Louis where the river is, she discovers the man behind her is Tony.

'I'm not who you think I am,' he says, grinning at her.

'Nor am I,' she answers.

15

18 February 1965

I can't believe it, I can't believe it, I can't believe it!!! I've got a place at the Slade. The SLADE! When I think who's studied there. Augustus John, Stanley Spencer . . .

I'm to start next September. It's all happened so quickly I keep expecting to wake up and find it's all a dream. When Tony told me, at Louis de la Tour's exhibition, that the Slade people wanted to see me, I was excited of course, but I was nervous too. Especially as Tony warned me Christabel might try and stop me.

As things turned out, Tony was wrong. About Christabel I mean. She was thrilled when I told her the news. She even wanted to come with me to the interview. If I knew how to get hold of Tony I'd let him know how wrong he was. But he and Christabel have quarrelled, I don't know what about, and I'm afraid, if I ask Christabel for his phone number, she'll hit the roof.

Tony, I owe all this to you. How can I ever repay you?

The interview was not at all the ordeal I'd imagined. Three people, two men and a woman, asked me what I'd done. Had I worked much with oils? Did I have any watercolours to show them? That sort of thing. Then they showed me round, and I met some of the tutors, and we talked a bit about the course. That was it. When I asked how long I'd have to wait for their decision they said they'd already made it. There was a free place available for me in September.

I STILL CAN'T BELIEVE IT!

We go back to the country tomorrow. Christabel has asked me to make it my home while I'm studying. It's amazingly generous of her, but I don't know. It would be odd to be there and not be working.

'We can convert the summer house into a studio,' she said. 'I'll ask Randal to do some designs.'

The thought of the Rat hovering around again temporarily put me off

guard. 'Shouldn't we consult Sir Oliver?' I asked. It was a stupid thing
to say, but for once I didn't get knocked back.

'My husband is not a well man,' Christabel answered. She had a look
on her face I've seen before. As if she thinks someone might be listening
in to our conversation. 'He first became ill a long time ago, when he was
married to someone else.'

I was tempted to interrupt her, but changed my mind when I saw the
look was still there.

'Oliver and I were married during the war,' she went on. 'I hadn't
been in this country very long.'

I did interrupt her then. I'd forgotten about India.

'We were happy at first,' she explained. 'He used to call me his "breath
of fresh air". Then his children started making trouble.'

'He has children?'

'A son and a daughter. I'm afraid they take after their mother.'

'What happened?'

'I refused to have them in the house. A man's first loyalty is to his wife,
after all.' (I'm making this up, but the gist is accurate.) 'Of course they're
grown-up now, thank heavens. Gerald lives in Paris. He's something in the
Foreign Office. And Naomi married some frightful little Texan jeweller.'

When I asked if they saw their father at all she told me he divided his
time between them. 'He does it to punish me,' she complained bitterly.

'Does he never come back here then?'

'Oh yes. He comes home when he's on a drinking binge. That's the most
exquisite punishment of all.'

It was hard to know what to say to her. I felt sorry for her, of course,
but I couldn't help wondering what Sir Oliver's version of the story might
be. I remembered something Tony said to me once. I'd asked him about
Sir Oliver, if he knew where he was, and he'd said the less I knew about
all that the better. Of course that only made me more curious, but I'd had
to be satisfied with his assurance that Sir Oliver hadn't been murdered,
or locked away, as I seemed to be implying. 'He's one of the richest men
in England. That's why Christabel hangs on to him.'

'But what about him? I mean, if they're never together . . .'

'Christabel has ways of keeping a man in line,' he'd said, closing
the subject.

I can't remember how Christabel got the conversation back to the summer
house and Randal, only that, when she did, I had the uneasy feeling she
was taking it for granted I'd accept her offer. 'It's your life that matters
now, Chloe,' she said.

I've been thinking about those words, and wondering what to say to
her. It's a bit like when Keith assumed I'd marry him. I might have been

tempted, but that assumption annoyed me so much I said no. Cussed, *my mother would call it.*

Later

I'd fallen asleep with this in my lap. I really must try and write in it more regularly. When I haven't written for days there's too much to say.

I went back yesterday to have another look at Louis de la Tour's paintings. I didn't have long. Christabel's been fairly demanding since her quarrel with Tony. But there was enough time for me to confirm the impression I'd got that he is *a genius. Even if the critics, well some of them, seem to think he can't paint his way out of a paper bag.*

Don't ask me why, but I came away from the gallery in tears. Just as well Keith wasn't with me! It started when I was looking at those faces again, or rather the one face, painted in just about every mood you can imagine. There was nothing to indicate where the woman came from, but I was certain she wasn't English. The backgrounds, where they existed, were hazy, but there was an unmistakable feel of New Zealand.

'I'm often asked if I consider myself an exile,' de la Tour wrote in his Notes. 'My answer has to be paradoxical. Certainly I'm conscious every day of a sense of loss. Of homelessness. But I reject utterly any suggestion that I'm entitled therefore to pity. It's not just the quiet generosity I have encountered here (and elsewhere in Europe), a generosity of the spirit, a tolerance which only occasionally smacks of indifference. It's the conviction I have that for many creative people a condition of internal exile is inevitable. I left New Zealand because I was a pacifist, and in 1945 there was no place in the national psyche for that aberrant faith. But if that had been the only reason for my departure I would have returned by now. The reasons why I haven't are too complex, and too personal, to discuss here. Let's say I'm obsessed with journeys. They're a condition of modernity after all.'

I'm not sure I understand the last bit, but I've been having this argument with him in my head ever since I read those words. 'Why not *go back,' I want to say, 'since your country is still so much your subject?'*

'In de la Tour's case, country of origin is hardly relevant,' the Guardian *critic wrote. 'His art is his country.'*

Well, maybe so, but something about that statement offends me. Is it the suggestion that good art can only come out of certain select countries? Not that the idea of art *as a country hasn't got a lot going for it. Imagine who your fellow-citizens would be!*

'I like to think of myself as a painter, not an artist,' de la Tour declared at the end of his Notes. 'The word art *bothers me.'*

'So where do you hang your hat, Mr de la Tour? What land do you call home?'

16

Christabel waited till Chloe had gone up to her room, then, pulling on a jacket, she let herself out through the kitchen, and made her way across the dark garden to the summer house. They'd got back from London in the late afternoon. George Honeybone had met them at the station. The alterations were finished. All that was needed to make the Manor perfect was for spring to arrive. But what was the use of spring without Tony?

'You should have forced matters,' she said, addressing the conjured-up figure of Randal Kane. 'You had no scruples about June.'

'But was that what you really wanted?' an inner voice challenged.

'I wanted her to be like me,' Christabel answered.

The summer house was at the far end of the garden, beyond the lake. When Chloe, soon after her arrival, asked why it was locked, Christabel told her about the trouble they'd had in their first year here. Both summer house and chapel (used these days as a tool shed) had been broken into. Nothing had been taken, but a fire had been lit in the summer house. For weeks after the event Christabel had waited for the rumours to start. But no word of scandal reached her. Whoever the trespasser was, he, or she, couldn't have been very observant.

She plunged the key into the lock, and pushed open the door. No one came here but her. That had been the rule from the beginning.

While she felt for the light switch she thought back to the night of that ghastly exhibition, and Tony's cruelty, which she still hadn't forgiven. Perhaps if he knew the truth . . . But no one knew that. Not even Oliver. The truth was here, within these walls.

The summer house was a late addition to the Manor. Mid-nineteenth century, Randal had judged. Probably part of the improvements undertaken by Septimus Grigg. There was just the one room, oddly-shaped to fit the outside walls, which were octagonal. Christabel had furnished it with chairs (into one of which she slumped now), a sofa, and a desk, also locked.

There was a musty smell to the room. Since the start of her affair with Tony Christabel hadn't felt the need of its lonely comfort. The place needed airing.

For several minutes she sat without moving, almost without breathing. She'd come here for a purpose, but her will had deserted her. All around her, on the walls, were pictures: family photographs, framed items from newspapers; every one of them sharply etched on her mind. If she turned her head she'd see her father in his blood-stained butcher's apron. Another turn would reveal her mother and younger sister, sitting on a tartan rug, laughing over the rims of their bakelite cups. Ahead of her, covering an entire wall, were the lovingly hoarded clippings: 'Local Girl Wins Beauty Contest,' 'Miss Doreen Potts of Motueka Models the New Season's Swimwear' . . .

Christabel pulled her jacket tight across her chest. It was cold in here, as well as damp. She'd told Chloe the truth about Oliver. She didn't have *that* on her conscience. And she'd told Oliver the truth about Doreen Potts. As much of it as he needed to know. Now she was going to destroy the evidence. This room would no longer exist. It was going to be Chloe's, forever.

She heaved herself out of the chair. The family photos first. God knows why she'd kept them. To remind herself how far she'd come, possibly. She'd had no contact with anyone back there since her marriage.

'Goodbye Mummy, goodbye Daddy,' she said bitterly, as she ripped the snaps from the wall. 'As if I'd ever have called them that,' she added, under her breath.

The photos that included her sister were less easily disposed of. Janet had at least *tried* to stay a friend. But Janet was married now, with children, no doubt. They would have nothing to say to each other.

When all the evidence was removed, Christabel turned to the newspaper photos. She could still feel the excitement of winning her first beauty contest. The whole world had seemed to beckon. But then she'd met Geoffrey, respectable, *married* Geoffrey, and the world had shrunk to the size of a small New Zealand town.

At last the walls were cleared. Christabel gathered up the torn remants of her life from the floor, and stuffed them in the empty grate. The last person who'd lit a fire here was the mysterious trespasser. Oliver had let it be known that anyone found on his property in future would be severely dealt with.

The fire was brief and comfortless. When the flames had died down, Christabel took another key from her pocket, and opened the desk. Now would come the hardest part.

The first thing she encountered was a box of photographs. She remembered the day she carried them out here. Oliver had left in a rage. He'd called her, among other things, a hard-hearted bitch. Her revenge was to strip the Manor of all evidence of their marriage. She'd not been able to destroy the photos, not then. She'd still felt a residual pride in having married so public, and wealthy, an Englishman. But there was no room for that pride now. The photos of Sir Oliver and Lady Temple on the steps of the Chelsea Registry Office, the bride in a wide hat, carrying a single rose, the groom in morning suit, would exist no more. Nor would the several reports of the occasion: 'This is Sir Oliver's second marriage. His first, to the former Rachel Hallenstein, was dissolved on February 17th of this year. The new Lady Temple, formerly Doreen Potts, is from New Zealand . . .'

As she put a match to the corner of the largest photograph she recalled the glow of satisfaction she'd felt, knowing the news would be trumpeted all round Motueka. She'd wanted her parents to suffer, to regret their hardness of heart. But most of all, she'd wanted to hurt Geoffrey.

There were other photographs in the desk, ephemeral pieces from the voyage over, and her single years in London. Disposing of these caused little pain.

Then there was only the one box remaining. Smaller than a chocolate box, tied with a pink ribbon. Christabel's hand shook as she unknotted the bow and lifted the lid. The last time she'd touched these relics was the night Oliver left for America.

'Chloe,' she whispered. 'My darling . . .'

Her hand reached into the box. A parcel no bigger than her finger fell into her palm. The paper had become damp, but the lock of hair inside it was still as sweet and fresh as the day she'd cut it from her baby's head. She bent down to sniff its secrets. Chloe had had *her* colouring and *her* eyes. But the shape of her face was Geoffrey's.

Careful not to let her tears fall on the hair, she replaced it in the box, and reached for the document she had made up her mind to destroy. 'Chloe Angela', the yellowing paper declared. 'Date of birth, August 22, 1938. Mother's name, Doreen Elizabeth Potts. Occupation, Photographic Model. Father unknown.'

Christabel had to strike several matches to light that particular little fire. When it had burned down, she switched off the light, closed the door behind her, and made her way, stumbling in the dark, to the edge of the lake. A few seconds later a set of keys, and the stories they'd kept hidden, were consigned to a watery oblivion.

17

Frances, waking in her bedroom on the top storey of the Manor, listened to the tap-tap of the branch against her window, and the melancholy crying of pigeons, and marvelled at the sunlight seeping through her curtains. London's skies had been unremittingly grey, but this morning, her first back in Little Chippingham, it was possible to believe in spring.

She glanced at her watch. Almost two clear hours before Christabel would expect her. Should she go for a walk? Spring would be tangible in the woods: aconites peeping through the dead leaves and the first shoots of bluebells. In a few weeks the lawns would be carpeted with crocuses; the lake a mirror for its border of daffodils. It would have been good to see it, but Frances, in the course of a dream-filled sleep, had reached a decision. She was going to hand in her notice. In a month's time, less if Christabel agreed, she would be on her way home.

Throwing back the blankets, Frances pushed her feet into her slippers, and padded to the window. The lawn was silvered with frost, but at its centre, where the sun's rays reached, there were moist patches of green. In this light the garden seemed less formal, as much the work of nature as of generations of gardeners. I'd like to paint it as it looks now, she thought, peering through the lattice at the distant summer house. I'd like to fill the garden with all the people who've ever lived here.

She laughed out loud. She couldn't remember when she'd last felt so happy. The only cloud on her horizon was the approaching interview with Christabel, and the news, waiting for her on her return yesterday, that Auntie Dottie was no better.

'I'm sorry you've been worried, darling,' her letter said. 'The doctors say I have a touch of angina, that's all. Otherwise I'm good as gold.'

Frances had had to go to the dictionary to find out what angina was. 'Severe pain accompanying heart disease,' she'd read. She'd come close to panic then. But later she'd read Louis de la Tour's Note again, and been comforted. 'Everything I do relates to the mystery of death,' he'd written. 'If my work has a purpose it is in this struggle to come to terms with the one thing in life of which we can be totally sure.'

She didn't want Auntie Dottie to die. But it was wrong to hang on to people too. Her father's letter, which she knew by heart, had taught her that.

There was other mail waiting for her. A letter from Gail, asking her to be godmother to her week-old daughter ('We're calling her Francesca, after you.'), and a parcel with a book inside but no indication of who'd sent it. The only clue was the Dunedin postmark. Could it have been Clarence? It would be just like him to send a present without even bothering to include a note. The book was one she'd seen before. In fact she'd read it eagerly, as a child. It was called *The Breeding and Training of Horses* by Pearse Byrne. The fact that it had been on the shelves at Iona suggested it was either Clarence who'd sent it, or – and this was the real mystery – her mother.

Suddenly Frances knew what she would do with her spare two hours. She'd go to the river. It was important she find the right words for Christabel. Her reasons for turning down her offer of a home were nothing to do with the place or the people. On the contrary, she was beginning to feel she belonged in Little Chippingham. But once she'd made the decision to go back to New Zealand, everything else fell into place. She would stay there till September. She'd look after Auntie Dottie, and be a godmother to Francesca, and get to know Clarence again. She might even make her peace with her mother. One miracle had just happened in her life. Why not a second?

It was almost full light by the time she reached the bridge. The cows in the lane behind her were making their obedient way towards the milking shed. And in the field opposite, Matthew Greenbank, father of Alice and Tina, was calling to his dogs. Standing on the bridge, leaning on the parapet, Frances took in deep gulps of frosty air, then watched as the thin vapour of her breath spiralled over the water.

When she got to the river, she took off her coat and spread it on the ground. She'd come here to plan her speech to Christabel, but as always the magic of the place made nonsense of her preconceived ideas.

Was it her imagination, or had the weed grown thicker since she was last here? In one place it appeared to have reached up the bank to the bridge, from where it trailed down to the water again, like unkempt hair. She was still trying to work this out when she spotted Rolf Reichardt standing, not in his usual place, but further upstream, beyond a clump of alder.

She got to her feet. The conversation in the post office came flooding back to her. Would he understand her if she spoke to him?

As she moved along the path she saw what had attracted the German's attention. On the opposite bank, exposed for all the world to see, a white swan was nesting. As Frances moved through the long grass, the swan's feathers slowly rose.

'Excuse me,' she said, when Mr Reichardt turned to investigate the disturbance. 'I know who you are,' she added impulsively.

The German raised an arm, as if to cover his face. It was then Frances noticed he was crying.

'I'm so sorry,' she said, softly.

'You know, ja?'

She nodded.

'My son,' he said. 'Drowned. There.' He pointed to his usual perch on the bank. 'Thomas Gerhard,' he said. 'He had seven years.'

'No . . .' Frances wasn't sure whether she'd spoken or not. He did say, *drowned*?

'You too?' the German asked. 'You lose someone?'

Tears slid from her eyes. Was that what her mother had been trying to tell her when she waved from behind the teazles? How could anyone drown in this slow water?

'Yes,' she said. 'It was a long time ago.'

He seemed to find her reply perfectly natural.

No other words were exchanged. When it was time to go,

Frances put out her hand. Mr Reichardt took it in his calloused palm, held it a moment, then let it fall.

Running back to the Manor, Frances tried to fix in her mind the expression on Mr Reichardt's face. Her earlier sketches were useless. She'd not understood. But try as she might, all she could see were the tears streaming down his cheeks, and the long overcoat, tied with string.

18

'*11 April 1954.*

'*My dearest Fanny,*

'*So, here you are, eighteen years old. Not my wee lassie anymore, but a beautiful young woman. Ah Fanny, how I wish I could see you. How proud I would be. But we all have our destinies, and mine was to have the joy of you for a short time only.*

'*I hope you are well. I hope you are happy and confident. Do you still ride? I would like to think God might have forgiven me my sins by the time you read this, and I will have been allowed to watch you one more time, galloping round the paddock on Nugget. Though perhaps you've outgrown horse-riding by now. You'll be off to University I daresay, with your head full of books and ideas.*

'*As I sit here, by the fire, I try to imagine what life will have in store for you. I know what I wish for you – happiness with a family of your own – but Fanny you will know by now I'm a conventional sort of fellow with only a limited understanding of other forms of fulfilment. It troubles me that I haven't shown more interest in your drawing. It didn't need your teacher to alert me to your talent. I recognised it when you were not much more than a bairn. If art is to be the direction your life takes, you have my blessing, sweetheart. Dunedin already boasts one famous woman artist – Frances Hodgkins. Your namesake, come to think of it. She's spent most of her life in Europe, far from friends and family. I don't imagine it's been easy, but it's what she chose. When I think of you on a lonely path like that I feel a chill in my bones, despite the roaring fire in front of me. I've always imagined the creative life as a kind of addiction, dangerous and devouring. But perhaps I'm wrong. Perhaps it shouldn't be compared to other forms of addiction. Nor should I equate you,*

*my dearest daughter, with the cliché of the tormented artist.
You won't be penniless for one thing! And you have too much
love of life to embrace suffering for its own sake.*

*'Enough of speculation. I've other things to write to you
about, difficult things to put on paper, impossible to talk
about. I'm not a brave man, sweetheart. If I was I'd have told
you sooner.*

*'Fanny, I don't imagine the last few years have been easy for
you. Your mother . . . Where can I begin? Your mother isn't
the woman I married. A lot of the blame for that is mine. I
disappointed her. I suspect she was never a happy woman,
but when I met her she was at least fulfilled. Perhaps you'll
understand that better than I. Perhaps it's what unhappy
people do to make their lives bearable. I don't know. Its
beyond me. What I do know is that she was a splendid nurse.
Calm, brave, compassionate. I lost count of the number of
people who testified, during our courtship, to the miracles
she'd worked. I took her away from all that. I wanted her
strength for myself. And she gave it to me, Fanny, despite her
disappointment. She failed me in nothing, till you came along.*

*'I should be talking to you about all this. You're old enough.
And I know I don't have much time left. But I watched you
playing the piano tonight (your mother was calm, as she is
at these times. Strange in one who has no ear for music), and
the thought that kept going through my head was 'things once
said cannot be unsaid'. I'm not justifying myself, Fanny. I'm
sure I should have talked to you. But that thought was like a
warning.*

*'What I want to say to you, sweetheart, is that I'm convinced
your mother's harshness towards you has almost nothing to do
with you, with the person you are. It comes from some terrible
sadness inside her. I would even go so far as to say she loves
you, deep down, though that may be hard for you to accept
after all her unkindness.*

*'I suppose I'm talking about forgiveness, Fanny. I believe
it's what we must all try to do, forgive each other. At least I
hope you'll forgive me for wanting the world to be the way it
should be.*

'In case you're wondering, dear, I've written to Clarence. A

different letter, obviously, since he hasn't had quite the same difficulties with his mother. But when he reads his letter he will be in possession of the same basic facts as you. I hope, for both your sakes, these facts don't come as too much of a shock. Or if they do shock at first, you'll see them later as a source of comfort. Inheritance is a mysterious business, Fanny. Who you are, what makes you who you are. When you've read your letters, you and Clarence, and thought about them, I hope you will feel your inherited loads have become a little lighter.

'Fanny, you once asked me if your mother was really your mother. Do you remember? I didn't answer for the same reasons I haven't talked to you about the other things in this letter. Your Auntie Dottie's always telling me I'm a typical male, I avoid things. Well she's right, of course. But by the same token I have the male ability to sit things out. Dottie is a wonderful woman, and I owe her a great deal, but there are times, I believe, when it's better to keep what you know to yourself. Knowledge doesn't always liberate. On the contrary, it can impose an intolerable burden. And what I wanted for you and your brother was a burden-free childhood.

'If I've been wrong in this, Fanny, I take comfort from the fact that you and Clarence will have each other to talk to. You were close as youngsters. Watching you play together was one of the sweetest joys of my life. Lately I've seen the gulf between you widen, but that's more to do with your mother's illness than anything else. Clarence is a good lad. I don't always understand him, and I worry that I haven't been the right father for him, but I've never doubted his essential goodness.

'Fanny, the answer to that question you asked me is this. Both you and your brother were born to different parents, not to your mother and me. Clarence we adopted when he was ten months old, but you came to us as a wee thing of barely two weeks. So you see, in all ways that matter, you were ours *from the start.*

'Now before your mind starts to spin with unanswered questions let me calm you a little with the things I do know. First, and I've already touched on this, when you've taken everything in it may comfort you to know you're not the same flesh and blood as your mother. Strange as it may seem I

never met any of her family (she never wanted me to, and I respected her wishes), but I know enough of her background to suspect she wasn't the only one to emerge damaged. Your own background, Fanny, is very different. I was lucky enough to get to know your great-uncle – it was through him you came into our lives – and I can assure you you come from a fine family.

'I really don't want to say much more. The adoption laws in this country are designed to keep children ignorant of their origins. But you have my word on what I've told you about your family. Where they are concerned you can hold your head high.

'Your mother, by the way, doesn't know about my friendship with your great-uncle. All she knows is that the little girl we adopted came from Christchurch. I never met your real mother. But from all accounts she's a woman of distinction. I know nothing at all about your father.

'There. It's done. Are you angry with me? Do you wish I'd told you sooner? All I can say in my defence is that you are my beloved daughter, you are Frances Isabel McLean, and I wish you happiness with all my heart.

'Believe in God, Fanny. He's there, whatever the doubters tell you.

'Thank you for making these last twelve years the richest of my long life.

'God bless you, sweetheart,
Dad.'

Frances folded the letter carefully, and replaced it in the handkerchief sachet Auntie Dottie had embroidered for her. There are lies and *lies*, she reminded herself, as she closed the door behind her.

'W . . . Wh . . . What letter?' Clarence had stuttered, when she tried to talk to him. 'I didn't get any l . . . any . . .'

'You did. You must have.'

'So where is it then?'

'Mum gave it to you. Don't lie, Clarrie. Please. It's too important.'

'Sh . . . Shit!'

'If I can't talk to *you* . . .'

'That's right. C . . . Ca . . . Cry . . .'

'Dad said we *had* to talk.'

Frances reached the bottom of the stairs, and turned towards the morning room. Christabel was waiting.

19

'*What*? You're going to do *what*?'

'Go home. Just till September. It's been five years, Lady Christabel.'

'Oh, I'm *Lady* Christabel now, am I?'

'Please don't be angry.'

Christabel raked her fingers through her hair. Frances couldn't believe the change in her. All she'd done was give in her notice. 'I thought you didn't have a family,' Christabel accused.

Frances looked down at her hands. They were sitting in their usual places in the morning room, letters and menus spread on the coffee table between them. Christabel was wearing a pink woollen housecoat. Her hair, which Frances normally brushed at this time, hung loose to her shoulders.

'Didn't you say your parents were dead?'

'My father died when I was 13. My mother's still alive,' Frances explained.

'So, you're a liar?'

'My mother doesn't recognise me. She thinks I'm someone else. It's the same as if she were dead.'

Christabel threw her head back against the chair. Frances had seen her look old before, but never haggard, like now. 'It's just a job, Fan,' Keith's voice intruded. But if that's all it is, Frances answered him, why do I feel like a murderer?

'And you want to go back to this woman who doesn't know you, and play happy families, is that right?'

'I have a brother too. And an aunt.'

'Oh spare me the family tree, for God's sake.'

'I'm not going for good, Lady Christabel. I'll be back in September. I'll come and visit.'

The sound Christabel made might have been a sob. Frances swallowed hard, forcing saliva past the lump in her throat. 'If you're going you might as well go now, today,' Christabel said huskily. 'I don't want to see you any more.'

'But . . .'

'And you needn't think you're going to be paid either. You've had all you're getting from me.'

Not knowing what else to do, Frances stood up.

'You know what'll happen out there, don't you?' Christabel challenged, looking up at her through reddened eyes. 'You'll meet some crass male, who doesn't care a fig about your painting, and he'll get you pregnant.'

'Oh I don't think . . .'

Christabel laughed. 'Thinking doesn't come into it,' she scoffed.

'Nothing is going to stop me going to the Slade,' Frances insisted quietly.

'Not even Keith?'

'Who?'

'That is his name, isn't it?'

'How do you know about him?'

The smile on Christabel's face reminded Frances of her mother. 'There was a card,' she said casually. 'Ages ago. Didn't I give it to you?'

Frances shook her head.

'Oh well, it was only a card.'

For a few moments all Frances was aware of was the thumping of her heart. Christabel was lying, wasn't she? There'd been more than just a card. 'Was there anything else?' she asked.

'Oh don't be a fool!'

'Was there?'

'Yes! Yes, yes yes. Satisfied?'

'Do you have them still?'

'I burned them. Half a dozen cards, I don't remember exactly. And a letter. At Christmas. I did it for your own good.'

'That was what my mother used to say. She liked burning things too.'

This time the sound Christabel made was unmistakably a sob. 'I was afraid you'd go back to him,' she confessed.

The spark of pity Frances felt was quickly extinguished. This was what Tony had warned her about, wasn't it?

Five minutes later she was back in her room. There was a train at 2.30. If George couldn't drive her to the station she'd ring for a taxi.

She felt strangely calm as she packed. She figured she had enough money, just, for the air fare home. And she knew a cheap place where she could stay in London. 'I'm coming home, Auntie Dottie,' she kept repeating. 'I'm coming home.'

It was as she was packing her sketchbooks that she remembered the parcel from Dunedin. Curious to look at the book again, she picked it up and flicked over the pages. Scattered through the text were a number of amateurish photographs. 'My Daughter Deidre on Eddie' was the first she noticed. 'My Daughter Dulcie Leading Biddy' was the next. She remembered liking those photos as a child, and wondering if Clarence's horse was any relation to the Biddy in the photograph. And she remembered asking her mother if her name before she married was the same as the name on the cover, and her mother's angry answer, 'Byrnes are two a penny in this country!'

Dulcie . . . 'You gave my Dulcie a fine old fright you know.' She hadn't dreamed those words. Mr Drummond had spoken them the day she thought she was going to be expelled. 'There's a reason why that river's out of bounds.' . . . Dulcie. Deidre. Pearse. They were a family, weren't they? The story her mother told, and the story Mr Drummond told, were one and the same.

Frances put the book down, and walked to the window. She couldn't see the river from this angle but she knew it was there. She would always know it was there.

'You know, ja?' Mr Reichardt's voice said, from behind her. She turned, and for a fleeting moment felt him smiling at her.

Living is horrible horrible . . .

'No!' Frances shouted, throwing open the window. Then, more quietly, 'Look,' she said.

'*Dear Mrs Drummond,*
'I'm coming home for a holiday, and wondered if I could see you . . .'

'*Dear Mum,*
'Thank you for the book. When I get home I want to take you to Braemar College. There's someone I want you to meet . . .'

'*Dear Clarrie,*
'Will Mum recognise me, do you think? I'm going to cut my hair short. Don't ask me why. I just have a feeling it might help.'

The last view Frances had of the valley to which she would return again and again in her painting, was from the misted window of the train. There's no precise moment when a river ends and the sea begins, she thought, as her eye traced the water's course through the valley. Meadows, swamps, channels, these are the links.

'What *is* that?' she asked, turning, without thinking, to the man sitting next to her. She was pointing to a field, stretching from the southern end of Manor Wood to the borders of Cromlech. It was part of a patchwork of fields just beginning to show green, only in this one particular meadow there was a scattering of tiny yellow flowers.

The man smiled. He'd recognised the accent. One of our antipodean cousins, he'd deduced. Doing the Grand Tour.

'That's rape,' he told her. 'An early crop. You don't usually see it till April-May. It's a bit of an experiment as a matter of fact. I believe it makes good fertiliser.'

Frances turned back to the window. The spluttering of candles in a darkened church; that golden congregation of sunflowers . . . 'Epiphany,' she said.

'I beg your pardon?'

'Rivers *can't* end. Neither can stories. That's what my mother never understood.' She laughed. 'I'm sorry. I'm not making much sense.'

'Where are you from?'

'Look,' she said. 'You can see the river. It's passing through the field of gold.'

20 ∫

Six months later Frances returned to England. Amongst her luggage were twenty-two filled sketchbooks, and the following rough notes.

IDEA FOR PANEL.
Title: *Missing Persons*? *Journeys*? (see Louis de la Tour's note on this) *The River*?
Not what's seen but what's felt.
Clarence meeting me at the Dunedin railway station. Not recognising me because of my hair. Clarence McLean in a shirt and tie. A partner now in Brown's Garage.
My mother's expression when I walked into the cottage. The way she touched my hair. Anger in her hands when I tried to kiss her.
Auntie Dottie, who's dying . . .
Clarrie taking me through the orchard to Iona. The air raid shelter filled in now. Trees growing where it was. The paddocks full of new houses. Iona not a refugee centre any more, but a Business College. Who shrank the house?
Gail. Her baby. Her weedy husband. Oh God! All of us trying so hard.
Keith, who didn't believe me . . . The look in his eyes as he said, 'You'd never have married me anyway.'
Mrs Drummond's expression when she realised we were related. 'I did wonder when I learned your mother's christian name, but it seemed so . . .' Her hands plucking at the air.
NB THE SERVICE AT THE GRAVESIDE TO BE THE FOCUS

The look on my mother's face as the minister read out the words:

'Here lie the bodies of May, wife of Pearse O'Connell Byrne, and her three children, Sean Patrick (3), Molly Theresa (18 months) and Seamus (12 days), drowned July 13, 1912.'

The new headstones poking out of the undergrowth.

Mr Reichardt, whose face I kept seeing.

My mother struggling to say my name. Managing just once, as the service came to an end.

Mrs Drummond taking me to see her husband's grave. 'All those years in Dunedin,' she said, as she stooped to lay flowers. 'If I'd seen your mother in the street just once, I'd have known her.'

The other cemetery by the Baptist Church. The grave of Clarence Abraham Byrne. My mother motionless beside it, her eyes fixed on Clarrie.

My father, whose face, thanks to Louis de la Tour, I believe I can draw at last.

Visiting Kilkenny Stud, where Mum was brought up. The woman called Jessie Warburton who reminded me of Christabel. Her husband, an American, who flung the word 'potential' about as if it were a baseball bat. My mother's face during all this . . .

My mother asking about her sisters. The photograph album. Mrs Drummond turning the pages: Eliza, Muriel, Beatrice, Winifred, Amy, Tilly . . . my aunts.

The maps Mrs Warburton produced. The one titled *Deadman's Flat* which she let me have.

The Kaiwaka River. Standing on the banks with Clarence. The bridge; the rocks; the current . . . Kilkenny visible through the pine trees. Braemar College out of sight, further upstream. Clarrie pissed off that I'd made him come with me.

Ambrose Warburton Junior booming down on us like a tank. 'Great little property this, don't ya agree? Tons of potential!'

The other river, creeping through my memory . . .

Driving back to Dunedin in the fading light, the river vanishing over my shoulder, Clarence at the wheel, my mother beside him. Mum turning to say, 'Death isn't the end, it's the beginning. Do you believe that, Tilly?' When I answered, I didn't know, I only knew about stories, she said, '*He* did. *He* knew.'

Her face in the rear vision mirror – transfigured.

Epilogue

∫

At Cheyney Grange an extraordinary event is about to take place. The year is 1965, the month September, the day one that will be remembered differently, in other parts of the world, for the arrival, in South Vietnam, of 12,000 American troops. Sarah Dutton has followed the build-up of tension in South East Asia with that sense of hopelessness that comes from distance, and the knowledge, gained through suffering, of the confusion at the heart of so many fateful decisions.

Sarah's life, since her return from England with her brother, has been dedicated to two things: Richard; and the search for answers to the questions Louis de la Tour used to ask. Is war inevitable? How can the cycle of violence in human history be broken? Was the war against Hitler a just war? How can there be *justice* in warfare? The Sarah Dutton who devoured historical novels, and pictured her own life in terms of a grand romantic passion, no longer exists. For the last twenty-four years she has read almost no fiction. History, philosophy, essays, the works of Thoreau and Emerson, Thomas More's Utopia, the poems of Emily Dickinson – these have been her strength and her comfort. And though she hasn't found answers, she has found acceptance, of a sort. She is not alone in history. Her brother's hideous injuries have been inflicted before.

Everything else in Sarah's life has been subsumed within this central quest. When, after her return from England, she discovered the extent of the debt incurred by her now less than revered father, there was only a brief time of shock before she set about calmly salvaging what she could of the family fortune. Rosevilla was sold, with all its contents. The one thing rescued from the auctioneer's hands was the portrait of the New World Madonna. The tenacity with which Sarah has clung to this painting, its pride of place above her bed at Cheyney Grange, is one of a number of anomalies in an otherwise well-ordered life.

Louis de la Tour's name has hardly ever been mentioned. When Richard, in one of his rare, reminiscing moods, asked what had become of him, Sarah produced the perfect, casual answer. 'Oh he's quite famous now,' she told him. 'Last I heard he was living in Cornwall.'

Richard, of course, would never see Louis's painting.

With Rosevilla sold, and Sarah's ancient Ford Standard taking the place of her father's Wolseley, brother and sister turned their backs on Christchurch, and settled permanently at Cheyney Grange. Not that the life that began for them then has resembled, in any but haunting ways, the carefree years of their childhood. Sarah still rides, but almost always alone. And it isn't her beloved Caesar she takes out into the mountains, but a succession of horses, bred by Frank McNichol, none of which has ever quite felt like hers. 'Frank's revenge,' she calls these mounts, remembering how she used to protest at being driven back to school by the man on whom she is now, in so many ways, dependent.

Had it not been for Frank McNichol Cheyney Grange would have been lost entirely. The generous terms on which he offered to buy the farm made it possible for Sarah and her brother to keep the house, stable, and garden. It was Frank's idea too that Sarah should take in paying guests. He's even been prepared to help out when necessary. Yet Sarah has never quite rid herself of a feeling of resentment towards her taciturn saviour. Partly because, unlike herself, her brother has never accepted their loss of independence.

'Jesus Christ!' he exploded, when she first broke Frank's plan to him. 'Is there to be no end to this?'

'It'll be all right, Rich. We'll have our home.'

'Is that what you call it?'

'We won't always have people staying. There'll be times . . .'

'You know what I think,' Richard said, in the voice she most dreaded to hear him use. 'I think we're descended from a line of liars and cheats. Our father was only acting in accordance with his genetic inheritance. We came here pretending to be something we weren't. We plundered the land. We claimed to be acting out of economic necessity, but that wasn't it, oh no, no siree, we were looking after Number One, keeping our noses clean and our feet dry while other people . . .'

'But you and I didn't do that, Rich,' she pointed out. *'We* lost everything.'

'Serves us fucking well right!'

When Richard raged like that there was, till recently, only one person who could calm him, and that was Elsa Klopstock. Lumpy Elsa, who'd stayed on to help when better jobs beckoned. She'd offered, one particularly ugly day, to give Richard a massage. Sarah had been sceptical, but Elsa had insisted.

'It's all right,' Sarah had soothed, when the large brown hands began their work. 'It's only Elsa.'

Over the years Sarah has acknowledged, publically and privately, the enormity of her debt to Elsa. After that day Richard still refused to see people, but he'd open his door to her. He'd even smile, twisting his burned face in a gargoyle grin that never failed to bring tears to Sarah's eyes. When friends came to visit – and there were fewer and fewer of those as the years went by – Richard would lock the door of his room, pull the blinds, and turn up the volume on the radio.

'You're driving people away,' she complained to him once.

'Exactly,' he answered sourly.

Only two people have penetrated his defences. The first was Elsa. The second is the cause of today's celebration.

I'm forty-five years old, Sarah thinks, looking in the mirror at the face she's been taking for granted for so long now she's ceased to notice it. Living at the Grange, seeing only the paying guests, and the familiar faces of the McNichols and Elsa, there's been little incentive to fuss about her appearance. On her rare trips to the city, to shop, or attend a lecture (Was Louis right? she's asked herself, over and over. Is pacifism the answer?), she'll drag out a suit or coat purchased before the war, apply a touch of lipstick, and think no more of how she looks.

'My son will be twenty-four this month,' she says out loud. The words strike, as all such words do, a direct blow at her heart. The pain she feels at such moments has never lessened. On the contrary, it's grown sharper and clearer as the years have slipped by. Her one comfort – there being no one she can talk to – is the hope that New Zealand will never again be called on to fight another nation's wars. That hope was almost dashed the day she read her country was to send troops to Vietnam. But when she read on she learned they were to be a token force only, not much more than a hundred. It was absurd to think her son, her unnamed child, would be among them.

What would he think of me? she asks her reflection in the mirror. What would he see?

She's speculated so many times about *him*. Does he resemble her, or Louis? Has he inherited his father's gifts, or is he a liar and a cheat as Richard has declared all Duttons to be? Whose eyes does he have? Is his hair red, or dark, as hers still is, despite the threat of grey? Sometimes she's come so close to picturing him she feels she can put out a hand and touch him. Her emotions at these times are so intense she almost stops breathing. The pain of loss is at its sharpest, but so too is a perverse pride. 'My son,' she'll whisper. 'My child . . .'

The worst day of the year, the one she dreads with a sick feeling of terror, is his birthday. Not even Richard can call her back from her grief on that day. 'You look after him, Elsa,' she'll instruct, when that black dawn comes round again. 'I'm going for a ride.'

Even if the house is full of guests, and Elsa unfairly burdened, she'll stay out till nightfall, riding her horse till they're both exhausted, keening her sorrow to the mountain tops. It would not have surprised her, on any of these occasions, to see the shade of Paddy O'Connor rise from the snow-swathed peaks of Ghost Ridge. One thing her reading has taught her is that anything, absolutely anything, is possible in this infinitely mysterious world.

Returning to the Grange, ashen-faced and exhausted, is the one time Sarah feels relief that her brother can't see her. Elsa, she suspects, has long ago guessed the cause of her peculiar behaviour. Something in her eyes, and the way her arms reach out, gently removing her coat, placing a mug of hot cocoa in her hands, urging her towards the bath she's already started running, suggest an instinctive knowledge. Sarah knows what she *should* do. She should talk to Elsa. She of all people wouldn't judge. But some atavistic impulse prevents her taking the comfort so sweetly and silently offered. The regret she feels each time this happens, haunts her, like the ghost of the day's darker pain. But when her mind moves on, and presents her with the idea of talking to someone else – her friend, Prue for instance, or a member of her family already in the know – she shrinks from that possibility too. The war did change things. People are no longer so quick to judge. But having, at the outset, forbidden the three people in her family who were involved ever to speak of it, how can she lift that ban now? And Richard, whom she meant to confide in, only her letter telling him of her pregnancy never reached him, has for so long been sunk in miseries of his own, she's not had the heart to burden him.

'Perhaps it'll be different now,' she says aloud, to the mirror. 'I'm to be free, after all . . .'

The thought brings her image into sudden, sharp focus. She leans forward, peering curiously at this woman called Sarah. I'm middle-aged, she thinks. Almost as old as my mother when she died . . .

She shakes her head vigorously. She mustn't cry. Not today. There will be other moments to acknowledge it's her mother she's missed all these years, not her father. Arthur Dutton has almost receded from memory.

It *will* be different now, she pledges. The conviction that that is what her mother would want brings a smile to her face. 'England,' she says, voicing her decision aloud. 'There was a time when Mummy wanted to go as much as I did.' Her smile widens. 'Perhaps I'll be like Aunt Clara, and never come back.'

The mystery of what became of Sarah's runaway aunt has never been solved. 'I should have asked Beulah Dowling while I had the chance,' Sarah regretted once, to Richard. 'All those years in Paris. She might have heard something.'

But Richard has only ever wanted to talk about the artists of the Quattrocento. Such names as Beulah's are too painful a reminder of what he has lost.

The reflection in the mirror blurs. 'Damn!' Sarah curses, dabbing at her eyes. But there's no stopping her thoughts now. It's as if the prospect of freedom has unleashed a torrent of hitherto disallowed questions. It's not the wider world she's traversing, as she prepares herself for the morning's ceremony, but her own inner landscape.

How different would things have been if our parents hadn't been killed? she asks her slowly re-emerging face. Would Mother have coped?

The reply she gets is not an answer, but another challenge. What has driven you all these years? You've worked harder than you need. Was it in order to forget, or to atone?

'You should have lived, Mummy,' Sarah murmurs, answering the questions that have come to her in Margot Dutton's voice. 'I needed you.'

She rubs her handkerchief over the mirror. Standing at her shoulder is her mother, wearing the striped silk evening gown she wore for her son's farewell dinner. 'Remember dear,' she says. 'We stood for something. It wasn't all lies . . .'

'Wait!' Sarah cries, as the lovely face begins to recede. 'Don't go . . .'

'I love you.'

Sarah spins round on her stool. She didn't just imagine it. Someone *is* in the room.

'Sa'ha!' she hears, from outside her door. 'C'n I cumin?'

Sarah's hand flies to her mouth. Elsa. 'She has a home here for the rest of her life,' Richard has promised. Elsa and Richard, Frank and his simpleton son, Tyrone. Family.

'Ya luks boot,' Elsa grins, from the doorway. 'Told ya.'

Elsa's way of talking, so difficult for strangers to follow, poses no problems for Sarah. They've always understood each other.

'Everything OK?' Sarah asks.

She gestures self-consciously. It was Elsa made her go and buy the ridiculously short dress she's wearing. It has a high rounded collar, which has the advantage of hiding the wrinkles on her neck, but at this moment, seeing the simplicty of Elsa's skirt and blouse, and the straw hat resurrected for the occasion, she's inclined to think her purchase ill-advised. The finely woven magenta wool, expertly cut in the shift style, would have delighted her fashion-conscious mother, but Sarah has spent too much of her life in trousers.

Elsa pulls up a chair, and sits down. Everything is in order, she reassures. The guests beginning to take their seats; the vicar, who's just arrived from Ashburton, tucking into tea and scones in the kitchen. Over a quarter of a century has passed since Cheyney Grange last hosted such a party. For these are not paying guests, but friends and family, come to celebrate a wedding no one had seen coming.

'Who's with Richard?' Sarah asks.

'Desda,' Elsa answers.

Sarah's eyes brim. Damn, she thinks, I'll never get through the day at this rate.

Desda is to be best man. Desmond Linwood, whom Sarah at one time hated, then pitied, but now counts a friend. Desmond came back from war so changed it's hard to remember the arrogant young man he once was. His war was spent on Crete, fighting with the partisans. No one knows for sure what he did. He never talks about it. But his wife, when he's out of earshot, tells people proudly about his Military Cross.

'I'm so glad we got the Reverend Hastings,' Sarah says, unnecessarily, since they've been through all this before. It was her decision to ask the Vicar of St John's in Ashburton to conduct the ceremony. She'd wanted an excuse to see the Creation Panel again. 'We're so lucky,' Rev. Hastings had enthused, showing off his church, not knowing her connection. 'De la Tour's work fetches enormous prices these days. Mind you,' he'd added, with a wink, 'not all my parishioners think it's a work of art. I've had some fairly colourful complaints.'

The presence, at Cheyney Grange, of the Reverend Hastings is another of Sarah's anomalies.

Sarah glances at her watch. After eleven. Time to go and attend to the bride.

'Sh'looks luvey,' Elsa says, reading her mind.

'Did she like the flowers?'

'Bootie,' Elsa answers.

Sarah arranges her matching, pill-box hat on her head, and walks to the door. In the room along the passage her childhood friend is preparing to marry the man she claims never to have stopped loving. In the next hour Daisy Mountford, née Linwood, will become Daisy Dutton. When, five years ago, Daisy started visiting the Grange on a regular basis, no one, least of all Sarah, thought her motivated by anything but pity, and the need to give her life purpose in the wake of her separation from her husband. At first Richard refused to see her; then he agreed she could sit with him in the dark. Finally, one bitter, snow-bound day, Daisy asked Elsa if she could take over the by-now routine massage. That was the start of it. Daisy slipped into the darkened room, put her hands on Richard's shoulders, and talked to him, she told Sarah later, of their childhood, and her marriage, and how, though everything seemed changed, some things were still the same. 'I told him straight out I'd always loved him,' she confided. 'There didn't seem any point pretending.'

Sarah still doesn't know at what point Daisy actually saw Richard. Nothing was said. But one day, not so very long after that first massage, Daisy came into the library, where Sarah and Richard habitually spent their evenings, and quietly listened as Sarah read aloud to her brother. After that it was only a matter of time before Daisy took over that job too. Listening to the voice she'd always associated with selfishness and frivolity, Sarah acknowledged, again, that there were indeed more things in heaven and earth than she'd ever dreamed of. To hear the words of Camus and Stendhal – Richard's favourites – from the lips of Daisy Linwood was enough to make anyone believe in miracles. Though Sarah, where her own life is concerned, has never quite been able to give up her scepticism. Some things are too painful to expose to the temptations of hope.

'As soon as we're married I'm going to take Richard to Christchurch,' Daisy announced last week. They were in the kitchen, cooking for the wedding. It was almost as if they were children again, anticipating a party. 'I've been reading about this new treatment . . .'

'Darling, you mustn't. You'll only upset yourself. Don't you think it's all been done?'

'But this doctor, he's Chinese, he's the best in New Zealand. He's goes to America every year to study the new techniques.'

'What does Richard say?'

'I haven't told him yet.'

'This doctor. What's his name?'

'Peter Sing. *Sir* Peter Sing actually, so you see . . .'

But Sarah didn't hear the rest. The rising colour in her cheeks, she quickly explained, was caused by the heat from the stove. She'd forgotten Peter Sing. She'd made herself forget as much of that time as she could. But it was more than just the memory of his part in her story that caused her temperature to rise, it was the thought of Kitty Whyte, whom she'd turned to for help, and hardly thought of since. There would be no room for Kitty in Peter's life now. She would have been the price he'd paid for his knighthood.

'You won't force him, Daisy, will you?' Sarah begged, running her hands under the cold tap, surreptitiously splashing her face. 'If he doesn't want to go . . .'

'I'm not you, Sarah. I don't believe in accepting things. If I did, I'd still be married to James.'

It was the nearest they'd come to a quarrel. Later, brooding on the conversation, Sarah experienced the pain in her chest which she'd always associated with loss. At first she couldn't think what it meant, then she realised. 'My life at Cheyney Grange is over,' she'd whispered, into the darkness of her room. 'I'm no longer needed.' She couldn't even cite the paying guests as an excuse for staying on. Daisy, whose marriage to James Mountford had been childless, had more than enough money to go round.

'Everything all right?' Sarah calls, as she pushes open the door of Daisy's room.

The figure standing in front of the mirror turns, and smiles. Sarah throws out her arms in amazed approval. Daisy looks beautiful. No concession has been made to her bridegroom's sightlessness. The woman in front of her is unmistakably a bride.

'Will I do?' Daisy asks.

'Oh darling . . .'

'He does see, you know. With his hands. He'll see this . . .' She lifts a layer of chiffon and flutters it in front of her face. 'And this . . .' She touches the flowers in her hair. 'I'm wearing his favourite scent too.'

Sarah takes her friend's hand, and holds it up to her cheek. 'Any doubts?' she murmurs. 'It's not too late . . .'

'None at all,' Daisy answers firmly. 'This is the happiest day of my life.'

Fifteen minutes later the ceremony begins. For some of the

guests it's their first sight of the wounded Richard. But there are no expressions of shock, no horrified looks exchanged. Our generation may have been blighted, Sarah thinks, as she looks round the drawing room at the flushed faces, the bright array of hats and flowers, the hopeful smiles, the fluttering hands, but we do know how to behave. Whatever else we lack, it's not courage.

The Reverend Hastings rises magnificently to the occasion. He talks of war and sacrifice, but in such a way even Louis de la Tour would not have been offended. He addresses Richard directly, smiling into his sightless eyes, congratulating him on winning a bride of such poise and beauty. Desmond, Sarah observes, has his arm on Richard's shoulder. The sight affects her deeply. From the back the two men look like any other friends, supporting one another through a timeless ritual.

Daisy never takes her eyes off the man at her side. When her turn comes to speak her vows, she touches his face, a gesture which causes more than one person in the room to fumble for a handkerchief. When the vicar pronounces them man and wife, Richard takes Daisy in his arms, and kisses her lingeringly on the lips.

It's all over very quickly. There's no music, and no speeches. Just the kiss, and the approving laughter, then bride and groom move forward to greet their guests. Sarah, who is experiencing something akin to seasickness, slips past the rows of chairs to the door. Turning back, she sees a man in cream trousers and a black velvet jacket, a cravat covering his scarred neck, his mother's favourite rose in his button hole, holding out his hand in response to the words whispered in his ear by the woman at his side. Almost, she thinks, as if the war hadn't happened.

Suddenly she sees how it could have been for her adored elder brother, whose creed she long ago committed to memory: 'Colour is Light, Light is Love, Love is God'. He left New Zealand vowing to return. 'Laugh if you want,' he'd said to his sister, 'but I intend to transform the way people see this country. The way they see themselves.' Confident, arrogant, ignorant of the hurts he'd inflicted, unable, as were all their peers, Louis excepted, to imagine the retribution that awaited them. Yet if the war hadn't happened, she thinks now, what prizes might have been his?

'So, this is where you've hidden yourself,' Adrian Dutton complains, coming on his niece in the kitchen. 'Anything I can do?'

'Elsa and Betty have managed everything brilliantly,' Sarah answers, moving across the room to kiss her uncle on the cheek. 'You remember Betty?'

'Thought I recognised her.'

'It was marvellous of her to come. She's over eighty now.'

'We're none of us getting any younger,' her uncle sighs.

'Do you want a drink? I've still got some of Daddy's whisky . . .'

'Now there's an idea. Champagne's all very well when you're young . . .'

'I keep it in the library.'

As she leads the stooping, silver-haired man out into the hall, past the displays of daffodils ('Best we've had in years,' Frank McNichol has boasted), Sarah is struck by the thought that this might be the last time the elder members of the Dutton family are gathered under the same roof. She's seen very little of her relatives over the years. Aunt Nancy hasn't been able to afford the trip south, for which Sarah has been grateful. Her aunt has never been one to respect taboos. As for Uncle Adrian, he used to visit when his wife was alive, but since her death he's been reluctant to move far from his Christchurch home. Knighted on his retirement from the Privy Council, he's never quite rid himself of the feeling of shame that came over him when the loss of the family wealth was made public. It's been shame, rather than grief, that has aged him.

'But you're all right, aren't you, Uncle?' Sarah once asked him. 'You've enough to live on?'

'Everyone knows, you see. That's the thing. If only Arthur had been a member of the Lodge we might have been able to contain it.'

'Do you remember Pamela?' Sarah asks, when the whisky's poured, and she and her uncle are seated in the worn leather chairs that never fail to remind her of her father. 'The maid at Rosevilla. I often wonder what happened to her.'

'Same thing happened to all of us,' her uncle answers. 'The war.'

Sarah considers this a moment, then says, 'You know, I'm not sure I wouldn't rather have been born her than me. She had everything to gain, whereas I . . .'

'Not feeling sorry for yourself, are you?'

'I always meant to look her up.'

'You had enough on your plate.'

'Like I always meant to look up the Ormonds . . . Ray Ormond,' she explains, when her uncle looks blank. 'He was with Richard in England. They were in the same squadron.'

'Rings a bell.'

'He didn't come home,' Sarah reminds him. 'He was shot down over the Atlantic.'

'Of course. I remember now. It's the parents you feel sorry for.'

'You know, Uncle,' Sarah confesses, in the pause that follows, 'when I think back to the year before the war, I'm embarrassed by the rubbish I used to spout. I remember insisting, to Prue I think it was, that Munich was the start of my Year of Destiny. Which of course it was. Though not in the way I envisaged.'

Sarah doesn't see the look her uncle gives her. 'You used to get that expression on your face when you were a little girl,' he remarks softly.

'You're right,' Sarah agrees. 'The war *was* what happened to us. There's no point blaming.'

Adrian observes his nieces' hands, clenched round the arms of her chair, and curses his clumsiness with words. His wife would have known exactly what to say to make those fists unclench. 'What are you going to do with yourself?' he asks. 'Richard won't be needing you anymore. Have you thought about the future?'

It's the question Sarah's been dreading. She gets up to search for a cigarette. 'I'll probably travel,' she answers, pouncing on a half-empty packet on one of the bookshelves. 'I always meant to, you know. I've enough money. Daisy's been a fairy godmother to all of us.'

'"You could always move in with me.'

'Live in the city? I don't think so. But thank you, Uncle. I appreciate it.'

'You never finished your degree, did you?'

Sarah drops back into her chair. 'Do you know, I can hardly remember. It's another life. Not one I want to go back to either.

Imagine bumping into Prue's kids in the canteen! I'd have to wear a disguise.'

Adrian looks at the woman seated opposite him, sees that she has aged, but sees too the dark good looks that mark her as a Dutton. What a waste, he thinks. She could have had her pick of husbands.

'Where will you go?' he asks. 'We seem to have lost touch with the family in Dorset.'

'Oh I wouldn't bother with them anyway,' Sarah assures him, through a haze of smoke. 'Italy's the place I've got my eye on. You remember Richard spent all that time there before the war? Well I'd like to go to the places he went. He still talks about it. Sometimes I think his true home is Italy. Italy and the Renaissance.'

'Sensible fellow. You know what you're looking at with the Old Masters. Not like this modern nonsense.'

Sarah takes care her uncle doesn't see her smile. 'His favourite is Piero della Francesca,' she continues. 'I think he must have visited every church and gallery in Tuscany in search of his works.'

'And is that what you're going to do?'

'*My* favourite is Vermeer,' she tells him. 'So I'll have to go to Holland too.'

There's a pause, during which Adrian drums his fingers on the table. A habit of my father's, Sarah thinks, then tries to bury the thought. Observations on the nature of inheritance are dangerous.

'Talking about artists,' her uncle says. 'Do you ever . . ?'

'Never,' Sarah interrupts. 'All that ended years ago.'

'Quite.'

'I might go and see his work though,' she surprises herself by saying. 'He's in the permanent collection at the Tate now.'

'Strange young man. Bit uncouth, I thought. But clever, very clever.'

'Uncle Adrian?' Sarah flicks the ash from her cigarette. Her voice is calm. No one would guess she'd just been winded by a sharp pain in her chest. 'I know I said we were never to speak of it but . . .'

Her uncle manages to look both alarmed and disapproving. He downs his whisky, and stares at the door.

'My son. I need to know if he's all right. Just that. Is he? Is he, Uncle Adrian?'

'Your son . . .'

'It's his birthday on the twenty-fifth. He'll be twenty-four. All I want to know is . . .'

'Sarah! You didn't have a son, you had a daughter.'

'*What?*'

'Surely you knew?'

'A daughter?'

'You signed the papers.'

'I didn't look at them. Didn't read . . .'

Adrian glances at the bottle of whisky. It would be wrong, wouldn't it? to pour another. It occurs to him that this is just like that unfortunate day at Nancy's. He's never forgotten the look Sarah gave him then. It was one he'd seen before, on the faces of men in the dock.

'Don't cry, my dear,' he murmurs. 'What difference does it make, after all?'

'A daughter . . .'

'It's in the past. You said yourself . . .'

'You know where she is, don't you? You know her name.'

'I can't . . .'

'Uncle Adrian!'

'It would be a betrayal of trust.'

'Don't say that! I'm your niece. This isn't a court of law!'

'Sarah . . .'

'I hate men like you sometimes!' she shouts, twisting round in her chair so that she can no longer see the Dutton face. The anger she feels frightens her. She's been down this path before, and knows where it leads.

'You said you didn't blame,' her uncle reminds her gently.

'It's easy for you . . .'

Adrian resists the temptation to contradict. 'No one is without sorrows,' he wants to say.

'I'm sorry, Uncle,' Sarah manages eventually. 'The truth is . . .' The words make a dam at the back of her throat. Would she have signed away a girl child? Is Uncle Adrian right to insist there was no difference? 'The truth is,' she repeats, as the dam slowly breaks, 'if I were to have my time over again, I'd do the same.'

Adrian takes in a long breath; sighs it out between his teeth. He knows, as a lawyer, that the past never loses its power to ambush. But that knowledge singularly failed to prepare him for this. 'So what do you want from me?' he asks warily. 'You know I can't give you a name. It's against the law.'

'What kind of law is it that . . . ?' Again Sarah chokes back her words. They'll only take her down that same, angry path. 'Just to know that my child is all right,' she compromises. She can't say the word *daughter* yet. It's too strange on her tongue.

Adrian's fingers drum a silent SOS. What he knows of Frances McLean's life is not good. Father dead; mother institutionalized; the girl, last he heard, packed off to boarding school. God knows where she is now.

'Your daughter's fine, Sarah,' he says, rising from his chair to put a hand on her shoulder. If she can't see my face, he's reasoned, she won't doubt my words. 'Of course, she's a grown woman now.'

'Have you seen her? Do you know where . . . ?'

'I've never set eyes on her,' he answers truthfully. 'But I'm told she's beautiful. And clever. Like yourself.'

'What has she done with her life? Do you know that? Did she go to university?'

'Sarah . . .'

'Please, Uncle Adrian.'

'I don't know the answers to your questions, my dear, and that's the truth. All I can tell you is that she went to a fine family. She would have had every advantage.'

'I couldn't bear it, you see, if I thought she'd died.'

'Then you can put your mind at rest.' Adrian pats her shoulder wearily. He wants that whisky badly. He's too old for all this excitement. 'Now dry your eyes, there's a good girl,' he urges, 'and let's rejoin your guests.'

'Thank you,' Sarah says, when they emerge again in the hall.

Her hand is on his arm. Surely she isn't going to start up again? He rubs his eyes. She's stopped in front of the gilt mirror, which is the first thing visitors to the Grange see when the front door is opened. Below the mirror is a mahogany table, on which rests, in honour of the wedding, a display of daffodils, fanned like a peacock's tail. The picture she makes – the deep red of her dress against the arc of gold – dazzles him. 'You must let me help you with your fare,' he mutters. 'Be good for you, this trip. Give you a new perspective.'

That night, when the last guest has retired to bed, Sarah returns to the library. She'd been lying awake, listening to the breathing house, struggling to come to terms with the idea of a daughter, when an impulse that seemed to have no connection with her child, propelled her out of bed. Whenever, over the last busy weeks, she'd imagined this night, it had been Richard and Daisy who were uppermost in her mind. How would she feel watching them drive off in Daisy's new American car? The honeymoon would be Richard's first foray into the world since he came back to live at Cheyney Grange. How would he cope? Daisy has rented a house at Lake Wanaka. 'Glendhu Bay,' she'd confided excitedly to Sarah. 'It's very secluded.' They were to be there a month.

But Richard and Daisy have been supplanted in Sarah's mind. Not even Daisy's confession, as she was changing for the journey, that she'd made the appointment with Peter Sing, distracted Sarah from her new preoccupation.

'You've told Richard then,' she'd assumed.

'I'll tell him when we get to Wanaka,' Daisy had answered.

Now, shivering over the last of the embers in the grate, Sarah wrestles with the thoughts that have kept her from sleep. For so many years she's pictured a son, altering his features with the passing of time, conjuring him up in the rooms of this house, hoisting him into the saddle to ride with her into the mountains, how can she banish someone so familiar? Start again, with a stranger? Try as she might no image will form. 'My . . . daughter,' she says slowly.

She pokes at the ash with her foot. Nothing. No face, no name. Was this what she left her warm bed for? To experience emptiness?

She moves to the chair she'd sat in this afternoon, and sinks into it. Her flesh is prickling as if from sunburn, yet when she looks at her skin it's goose pimples she sees. There's nothing here but ashes, she tells herself.

She gets to her feet again, and moves along the shelves of

books, running her fingers along the spines, as she used to as a child. Here are Richard's favourites. Stendhal's *The Red and the Black*. Camus's *The Outsider, The Plague* . . . 'There is no love of life without despair of life,' Camus wrote.

Suddenly her hand reaches out; grasps a book with a slim blue spine. She looks down. *The Breeding and Training of Horses*, by Pearse Byrne. Something jars her memory. A takeover. Last year some time. Fergus McLean Publishing is now MacStones. This little book is out of print.

She returns to the chair; curls her legs up underneath her; opens the book at the first page. 'A horse is like a child,' she reads. 'He must be treated with firmness and kindness. If he is disobedient, it is the fault of the master.' Opposite the text is a small, out of focus photograph. It's of a young girl on horseback. Sarah holds the page up to the light. 'At Kilkenny,' the caption reads. 'My daughter Deidre on Eddie.'

The prickling on Sarah's skin intensifies. She shifts her body; scratches; stares at the little girl who stares straight back at her. It's a joke. A trick of the mind. Why should a book she's not thought of in years bring her, in the middle of the night, to this icy room?

'Sister Byrne,' she says softly. 'Sister Deidre Byrne . . .'

('Her name's Deidre,' Mrs Parmenter leaned over from the next bed to tell her. 'I think of her as Deidre of the Sorrows.')

'It's the eyes that have betrayed you,' Sarah says to the girl.

She looks up from the photo, smiles, and looks back. Caesar was bred at Kilkenny. 'Eddie' could be his grandsire.

At which point she's seized by doubt. Sister Byrne she can recall vividly. Who could forget that stern face? Those penetrating eyes? But how can she be sure she's remembered her words? 'It would be a mistake to imagine your life will go on in the old way.' She's certain of those. And the things that were said about love, about it being dangerous, and a delusion. But was there ever any talk of Kilkenny? Or of horses?

Troubled, Sarah gets up from her chair, and crosses to the window. The day has been bright and cold, the mountains sharp against an azure sky, the trees, with their fragile first leaves, standing as if pinned by the sun's sharp rays. She doesn't need light to see what lies beyond this window, or further, out of sight, where swans nest by the lake, and daffodils multiply year after year. In one flying thought she can see from this window to the mountains. She's never needed to own the land she loves so much. It's a gift; a way of seeing she can take with her wherever she goes.

'You disapproved of me,' she reproaches, addressing the woman in a white uniform who has appeared above Ghost Ridge. 'But I've done the same as you. I've taken care of someone.'

The white shape continues to hover.

'Only now I'm no longer needed,' she confides.

The shape begins to fade. Sarah presses her nose to the glass; wills it to return. She feels as she did all those years ago, in hospital, compelled to explain. 'Sister Byrne,' she calls.

Stars drift across her field of vision. They seem to be dancing. She presses closer. A squashed man-in-the-moon grins down at her. 'No blame,' she hears, or says herself. 'What you did was born of love, not fear.'

She moves back. One step, then another. The white shape is a star now, dancing with the other stars.

'You hear it too, don't you?' she whispers. 'The music of the spheres.'